BUNYAN'S DEVOTIONAL WORKS.

THE

SPIRIT OF PRAYER:

The Saint's Privilege and Profit:

THE DESIRE OF THE RIGHTEOUS GRANTED:

THE

UNSEARCHABLE RICHES OF CHRIST:

AND

PAUL'S DEPARTURE AND CROWN.

BY JOHN BUNYAN,

AUTHOR OF THE PILGRIM'S PROGRESS, AND THE HOLY WAR.

PHILADELPHIA:
AMERICAN BAPTIST PUBLICATION SOCIETY.
118 ARCH STREET.

STEREOTYPED BY GEORGE CHARLES.
PRINTED BY KING & BAIRD.

INTRODUCTION.

THIS volume, composed of Bunyan's DEVOTIONAL WORKS, is designed, in the order originally indicated, to follow his Awakening and Inviting Works. It will meet the wants of all new-born souls. It will instruct them by just degrees in the nature, manner, medium, and encouragements of Prayer. It will begin at the beginning, and lead them on, step by step, in a devout and happy intercourse with God, through Jesus Christ, animated and guided by the Holy Spirit of Adoption, advancing to the highest conceivable elevation of faith, hope, and love; and ending in "joy unspeakable and full of glory."

Devotion is the highest element of our nature. Its corruption into Superstition and Idolatry is the most mournful feature in the History of Mankind. Its renovation by grace is the most glorious result of the work of Jesus Christ. This will be felt yet on earth, when, according to prophecy, "all the ends of the world shall remember and turn unto the Lord; and all the kindreds of the nations shall worship before Him." Psalm xxii. 27. "Thus saith the Lord of hosts, It shall yet come to pass, that there shall come people, and the inhabitants of many cities; and the inhabitants of one city shall go to another, saying, LET US GO SPEEDILY TO PRAY BEFORE THE LORD, AND TO SEEK THE LORD OF HOSTS; I will go also." Zech. viii. 20, 21. In that day, as well as now, we are sure this volume will be welcome.

It consists of five distinct works—The Spirit of Prayer; The Saint's Privilege and Profit; The Desire of the Righteous Granted; The Unsearchable Riches of Christ; and Paul's

Departure and Crown, or the Way to Live, so as to be always Ready to Die. For the first time these are combined in this order, with reference to a common aim. So far as we know, only the first has previously appeared in any American edition. It will be our object in this brief Introduction to throw all the light we have been able to collect from different sources, upon the origin and character of each.

The first, which is styled THE SPIRIT OF PRAYER, was written by Bunyan in 1663, the third year of his cruel imprisonment in Bedford jail. It seems to have been called forth by the "Act of Uniformity" of Charles II., issued on Bartholomew's Day, August 24th, the preceding year—that infamous St. Bartholomew's of England, only less cruel than the bloody St. Bartholomew's of France, a century before, because it shed less innocent blood. (See Note, page 54.) Robert Philip justly remarks on this treatise, "As extempore prayer was then a *State crime*, so no one can wonder, however much he may regret, that the Prayer Book came in for some of that odium, which odious means of enforcing it created." Besides, "wanton and impious prejudices were then rampant, against all avowed dependence upon the Holy Spirit for help in prayer. It is due to Bunyan's catholic spirit, to place his work on Prayer in this light. It is full of wise and warm appeals on the spirit of prayer, and quite as severe against extempore parade, as against heartless formality."

The second, called THE SAINT'S PRIVILEGE AND PROFIT; or, THE THRONE OF GRACE DISCOVERED, was written at a later period, but savors of the same divine unction, and displays even superior insight. It teems with brilliant Thought, fresh from the heart, while Fancy acts as a handmaid in the imperial train of Faith. Its grand characteristics are Evangelical Instruction and Encouragement. Never was the Throne of Grace, before or since, so fully opened by an uninspired hand, to the most guilty, unworthy, and self-condemned. Never was Encouragement made more irresistible, by motives drawn from the very bosom, so to speak, of Divine Mercy, opened in the Cross of Christ.

The third, The Desire of the Righteous Granted, is one of the twelve valuable works left in manuscript at the time of Bunyan's death. It is numbered 51, in Doe's Catalogue; but as it has no preface, nor other note of time, we have no certain means of determining the year of its composition. It is, however, a work of great merit. Its style of thought is rich and massive. It contains a profound philosophy of mind. Its expositions of Scripture, and of the human heart, are singularly clear and just. Its practical discriminations are admirable. Its dialogues, with objecting or inquiring souls, are full of vivacity, tenderness, and wisdom. Almost every page sparkles with spiritual aphorisms, solid, brilliant, and precious as diamonds. The illustrations are uncommonly felicitous. We give a specimen or two from these rare mines. "Some men's desires are narrow upwards, and wide downwards; narrow as to God, but wide for the world. But it is not so with the righteous. The temple that Ezekiel saw in his vision was still widest upwards; it spread itself towards heaven. So is the church, and so is the righteous, and so are their desires." Again, "A full purse and a lean soul, is a sign of a great curse. 'He gave them their desires, but sent leanness into their soul.' Take heed of that. Many, while they were lean in estates, had fat souls: but the fattening of their estates, has made their souls as to good, as lean as a rake."

The fourth, on The Unsearchable Riches of Christ is in a still higher strain. It belongs to the same class as the preceding; and immediately follows it as No. 52, in Doe's Catalogue. It is probable they were written near together. Yet they have little resemblance except in their common tendency to encourage enlarged and holy desires in Prayer. The sources of encouragement are widely different. The former draws it from experience, reason, and the promises of Scripture; the latter from the loftiest views of the Divine Attributes, and especially from the incomprehensible greatness of the Love of Christ. Every conceivable form and degree of discouragement, from without and from within, is met and overwhelmed from this commanding position. The tempter is confronted from a height which he can neither scale nor turn. The tempted soul is taught how to rise, as on the wings of eagles, to this lofty position; there to "triumph in Christ;" and in the confidence inspired by His transcendent and changeless love, to smile at the impotent malice of earth and hell, and to prosecute the work of holiness and usefulness "without fear." Take a single sentence. "Fear and trembling as to misery hereafter, can flow but from what we know, feel, or imagine; but the text speaks of a love that is beyond what we can know, feel, or imagine, even of a 'love that passeth knowledge;' consequently of a love that goes beyond all these."

The last treatise, Paul's Departure and Crown, is little known in this country. The only clue to its date is found in its immediate object, which is to inspire courage under existing persecution; and to urge Christians, by every salutary counsel and stirring motive, to do up their daily work, so as to be at any moment ready for death. As Robert Philip remarks, "Bunyan evidently feared at the time that Martyrdom awaited some of his people, as well as himself." This inclines us to fix its date, in 1660, just before his imprisonment in Bedford jail. It is such a strain as might have well cheered his own "Faithful" at Vanity Fair. It is a fitting, practical close to this glorious volume; which will be found worthy, in all respects, of its predecessors, and of its Author; and, we trust, will soon become 'familiar and endeared as household words,' by the name of Bunyan's Devotional Works.

J. N. B.

Philadelphia, Feb. 22, 1851.

THE SPIRIT OF PRAYER:

OR,

A DISCOURSE TOUCHING PRAYER.

WHEREIN ARE BRIEFLY DISCOURSED,

1. WHAT PRAYER IS; 2. WHAT IT IS TO PRAY WITH THE SPIRIT; 3. WHAT IT IS TO PRAY WITH THE SPIRIT AND WITH THE UNDERSTANDING ALSO.

"For we know not what we should pray for as we ought; only the Spirit helpeth our infirmities." Rom. viii. 26.

THE SPIRIT OF PRAYER.

LIKEWISE THE SPIRIT ALSO HELPETH OUR INFIRMITIES; FOR WE KNOW NOT WHAT WE SHOULD PRAY FOR AS WE OUGHT.—ROM. viii. 26.

CHAPTER I.

WHAT PRAYER IS.

I WILL PRAY WITH THE SPIRIT, AND I WILL PRAY WITH THE UNDERSTANDING ALSO. 1 COR. xiv. 15.

PRAYER is an ordinance of God, and that to be used both in public and private: yea, such an ordinance as brings those that have the spirit of supplication into great familiarity with God. It is also so prevalent an action, that it getteth of God, both for the person that prayeth, and them that are prayed for, great things; it is the opener of the heart of God, and a means by which the soul, though empty, is filled. By prayer the Christian can open his heart to God, as to a friend, and obtain fresh testimony of God's friendship to him.

I might spend many words in distinguishing between public and private prayer; as also between that in the heart, and that with the voice. Something also might be spoken to distinguish between the gifts and graces of prayers; but eschewing this method, my business shall be at this time only to show you the very *heart* of prayer, without which, all your lifting up of hands, and eyes, and voices, will be to no purpose at all. "I will pray with the Spirit."

The method that I shall go on in, at this time, shall be, 1. To show you what true prayer is. 2. To show you what it is to pray with the Spirit. 3. What it is to pray with the Spirit and the understanding also. And so, 4. To make some short use and application of what shall be spoken.

I. WHAT PRAYER IS.

Prayer is a sincere, sensible, affectionate pouring out of the heart or soul to God, through Christ, in the strength and assistance of the Holy Spirit, for such things as God hath promised, or are according to his word, for the good of the church; with submission, in faith, to the will of God.

In this description are these seven things. 1. It is a sincere; 2. A sensible; 3. An affectionate, pouring out of the soul to God, through Christ; 4. By the strength or assistance of the Spirit; 5. For such things as God hath promised, or are according to his word; 6. For the good of the church; 7. With submission, in faith, to the will of God.

1. For the first of these: It is a *sincere* pouring out of the soul to God. Sincerity is such a grace as runs through all the graces of God in us, and through all the acts of a Christian, and hath the sway in them too, or else their acts are not any thing regarded of God; and so of and in prayer, of which particularly David speaks, when he mentions prayer: "I cried unto the Lord with my mouth, and he was extolled with my tongue. If I regard iniquity in my heart, the Lord will not hear me." Ps. lxvi. 18. Part of the exercise of prayer is sincerity, without which God looks not upon it as prayer in a good sense. "Then ye shall seek me, and find me, when ye shall search for me with all your heart." Jer. xxix. 12, 13. The want of this made the Lord reject their prayers, where he saith, in Hosea vii. 14, "They have not cried unto me with their heart," (that is, in sincerity,) "when they howled upon their beds." But for a pretence, for a show in hypocrisy, to be seen of men, and applauded for the same, they pray. Sincerity was that which Christ commended in Nathaniel, when he was under the fig-tree: "Behold an Israelite, indeed, in whom there is no guile."

John i. 47. Probably this good man was pouring out his soul to God in prayer under the fig-tree, and that in a sincere and unfeigned spirit before the Lord. The prayer that hath this in it as one of the principal ingredients, is the prayer that God looks at. Thus, "The prayer of the upright is his delight." Prov. xv. 8.

And why must sincerity be one of the essentials of prayer which is accepted of God, but because sincerity carries the soul in all simplicity to open the heart to God, and to tell him the case plainly, without equivocation; to condemn itself plainly, without dissembling; to cry to God heartily, without compliments. "I have surely heard Ephraim bemoaning himself thus, Thou hast chastised me, and I was chastised, as a bullock unaccustomed to the yoke." Jer. xxxi. 18. Sincerity is the same in a corner alone, as it is before the face of all the world. It knows not how to wear two vizards, one for an appearance before men, and another for a short snatch in a corner; but it must have God, and be with him in the duty of prayer. It is not a lip-labor that it doth regard, for it is the *heart* that God looks at, and that which prayer comes from, if it be that prayer which is accompanied with sincerity.

2. It is a sincere and *sensible* pouring out of the heart or soul. It is not, as many take it to be, even a few babbling, prating, complimentary expressions, but a sensible feeling there is in the heart. Prayer hath in it a sensibleness of diverse things; sometimes the sense of sin, sometimes of mercy received, sometimes of the readiness of God to give mercy, and the like.

Sometimes it is a sense of the *want of mercy*, by reason of the danger of sin. The soul, I say, feels, and from feeling, sighs, groans, and breaks at the heart. For right prayer bubbleth out of the heart when it is overpressed with grief and bitterness, as blood is forced out of the flesh by reason of some heavy burden that lieth upon it. David roars, cries, weeps, faints at heart, fails at the eyes, loseth his moisture, &c.; Hezekiah mourns like a dove; Ephraim bemoans himself; Peter weeps bitterly; Christ hath strong crying and tears; and all this from a sense of the justice of God, the guilt of sin, the pains of hell and destruction. "The sorrows of death compassed me, and the pains of hell gat hold upon me: I found trouble and sorrow. Then cried I unto the Lord." And in another place, "My sore ran in the night." Again, "I am bowed down greatly; I go mourning all the day long." In all these instances, and in hundreds more that might be named, you may see that prayer carrieth in it a sensible, feeling disposition, and that first from a sense of sin.

Sometimes there is a sweet sense of *mercy received;* encouraging, comforting, strengthening, enlivening, enlightening mercy, &c. Thus David pours out his soul, to bless, praise, and admire the great God for his loving-kindness to such poor vile wretches. "Bless the Lord, O my soul; and all that is within me, bless his holy name. Bless the Lord, O my soul, and forget not all his benefits: who forgiveth all thine iniquities: who healeth all thy diseases; who redeemeth thy life from destruction; who crowneth thee with loving-kindness and tender mercies; who satisfieth thy mouth with good things; so that thy youth is renewed like the eagle's." And thus is the prayer of saints sometimes turned into praise and thanksgiving, and yet is prayer still. This is a mystery; God's people pray with their praises; as it is written, "Be careful for nothing; but in every thing by prayer, and supplication with thanksgiving, let your requests be made known unto God." A sensible thanksgiving for mercy received, is a mighty prayer in the sight of God; it prevails with him unspeakably.

In prayer, there is sometimes in the soul a sense of *mercy to be received.* This again sets the soul all on a flame. "Thou, O Lord God," saith David, "hast revealed to thy servant, saying, I will build thee an house; therefore hath thy servant found in his heart to pray this prayer unto thee." This provoked Jacob, David, Daniel, with others, even a sense of mercies to be received; which caused them, not by fits and starts, nor yet in a foolish, frothy way to babble over a few words written in a paper, but mightily, fervently, and continually, to groan out their condition before the Lord, as being sensible, I say, of their wants, their misery, and the willingness of God to show mercy.

A good sense of sin, and of the wrath of God, with some encouragement from God to come unto him, is a better Common Prayer Book than that which is taken out of the Papistical mass book, being the scraps and fragments of the devices of some popes, some friars, and I wot not what.

3. Prayer is a sincere, sensible, and an *affectionate* pouring out of the soul to God. Oh, the heat, strength, life, vigor, affection, that is in right prayer! "As the hart panteth after the water brooks, so panteth my soul after thee, O God. I have longed for thy precepts. I have longed after thy salvation. My soul longeth, yea, fainteth for the courts of the Lord; my heart and my flesh crieth out for the living God. My soul breaketh for the longing that it hath to thy judgments at all times." Mark ye here, "My soul longeth, yea, fainteth," &c. O what affection is here discovered in prayer! The like you have in Daniel: "O Lord, hear; O Lord, forgive; O Lord, hearken and do; defer not, for thine own sake, O my God." Every syllable carrieth a mighty vehemency in it. This is called the fervent, or working prayer, by James. And so, again, Luke xxii. 44, "And being in an agony, he prayed more earnestly," or, had his affections more and more drawn out after God for his helping hand. O! how wide are the most of men with their prayers from this prayer, that is prayer in God's account! Alas! the greatest part of men make no conscience at all of this duty; and as for them that do, it is to be feared that

many of them are very great strangers to a sincere, sensible, and affectionate pouring out of their hearts or souls to God: but even content themselves with a little lip-labor and bodily exercise, mumbling over a few imaginary prayers. When the affections are indeed engaged in prayer, then the whole man is engaged, and that in such sort, that the soul will spend itself to nothing, as it were, rather than it will go without that good desired, even communion and solace with Christ. And hence it is that the saints have spent their strength, and lost their lives, rather than go without the blessing. Psalm lxix. 3; xxxviii. 9, 10; Gen. xxxii. 24—26.

All this is too evident by the ignorance, profaneness, and spirit of envy, that reign in the hearts of those men that are so hot for the forms, and not for the power, of praying. Scarce one of forty among them knows what it is to be born again; to have communion with the Father through the Son; to feel the power of grace sanctifying their hearts; but for all their prayers, they still live drunken, whorish, and abominable lives, full of malice, envy, deceit, persecuting also the dear children of God. O what a dreadful after-clap is coming upon them! which all their hypocritical assembling themselves together, with all their prayers, shall never be able to help them against, or shelter them from.

Again, it is a *pouring out of the heart* or soul. There is in prayer an unbosoming of a man's self; an opening of the heart to God; an affectionate pouring out of the soul in requests, sighs, and groans. "All my desires are before thee," (saith David;) "my groanings are not hid from thee." And again, "My soul thirsteth for God, for the living God: when shall I come and appear before God? When I remember these things, I pour out my soul in me." Psalm xlii. 2, 4. Mark, "I pour out my soul:" it is an expression signifying, that in prayer there goeth the very life and whole strength to God. As in another place, "Trust in him at all times; ye people, pour out your hearts before him." Psalm lxii. 2, 4. This is the prayer to which the promise is made, for the delivering of a poor creature out of captivity and thraldom. "If from thence thou shalt seek the Lord, thou shalt find him, if thou seek him with all thy heart, and with all thy soul." Deut. iv. 29.

Again, it is a pouring out of the heart or soul *to God.* This showeth also the excellency of the spirit of prayer. It is the great God to which it retires. "When shall I come and appear before God." And it argueth, that the soul that thus prayeth indeed, sees an emptiness in all things under heaven; that in God alone there is rest and satisfaction for the soul. As Paul saith, "Now she that is a widow indeed, and desolate, trusteth in God." So saith David, "In thee, O Lord, do I put my trust; let me never be put to confusion. Deliver me in thy righteousness, and cause me to escape: incline thine ear to me, and save me. Be thou my strong habitation, whereunto I may continually resort. For thou art my rock and my fortress: deliver me, O God, out of the hand of the unrighteous and the cruel man. For thou art my hope, O Lord my God, thou art my trust from my youth." Psalm lxxi. 1—5. Many in a wording way speak of God; but right prayer makes God a man's hope, stay, and all. Right prayer sees nothing substantial, and worth the looking after, but God. And that (as I said before) it doth in a sincere, sensible, and affectionate way.

Again, it is a sincere, sensible, affectionate, pouring out of the heart or soul to God, *through Christ.* This, through Christ, must needs be added, or else it is to be questioned, whether it be prayer, though in appearance it be never so eminent and eloquent.

Christ is the *way* through whom the soul hath admittance to God, and without whom it is impossible that so much as one desire should come into the ears of the Lord of Sabaoth. "If you ask any thing in my name—Whatsoever you ask the Father in my name, I will do it." This was Daniel's way in praying for the people of God; he did it in the name of Christ: "Now, therefore, O our God, hear the prayer of thy servant, and his supplications, and cause thy face to shine upon thy sanctuary that is desolate, for the Lord's sake." And so David, "For thy name's sake," (that is, for thy Christ's sake,) "pardon mine iniquity; for it is great." But now, it is not every one that maketh mention of Christ's name in prayer, that doth, indeed, and in truth, effectually pray to God in the name of Christ, or through him. This coming to God through Christ is the hardest part that is found in prayer. A man may more easily be sensible of his evil works, aye, and sincerely too desire mercy, and yet not be able to come to God by Christ. That man that comes to God by Christ, must first have the knowledge of him: for he that comes to God must believe that he is. And so he that comes to God through Christ, must be enabled to know Christ. "Lord," saith Moses, "show me thy *way*, that I may know *thee*.

This Christ, none but the Father can reveal. And to come through Christ, is for the soul to be enabled of God to shroud itself under the shadow of the Lord Jesus, as a man shroudeth himself under a thing for safeguard. Hence it is that David so often terms Christ his shield, buckler, tower, fortress, rock of defence, &c. Not only because by him he overcame his enemies, but because through him he found favor with God the Father. And so Christ saith to Abraham, "Fear not, I am thy shield," &c. The man then that comes to God through Christ, must have faith, by which he puts on Christ, and in him appears before God. Now he that hath faith, is born of God, born again, and so becomes one of the sons of God; by virtue of which, he is joined to Christ, and made a member of him. And therefore, secondly, He, as a member of Christ, comes to God; I say, as a member of him, so that God looks on that man, as part of Christ: part of his body, flesh, and bones;

united to him by election, conversion, illumination; the Spirit being conveyed into the heart of that poor man by God. So that now he comes to God in Christ's merits, in his blood, righteousness, victory, intercession; and so stands before him, being accepted in his beloved. And because this poor creature is thus a member of the Lord Jesus, and under this consideration hath admittance to come to God; therefore, by virtue of this union also, is the Holy Spirit conveyed into him, whereby he is able to pour out himself, that is, his soul, before God, with his acceptance.

And this leads me to the next, or fourth particular.

4. Prayer is a sincere, sensible, affectionate, pouring out of the heart or soul to God through Christ, *by the strength* or *assistance of the Spirit.* For these things do so depend one upon another, that it is impossible that it should be prayer, without there be a joint concurrence of them: for though it be never so famous, yet without these things, it is only such prayer as is rejected of God. For without a sincere, sensible, affectionate, pouring out of the heart to God, it is but lip-labor, and if it be not through Christ, it falleth far short of ever sounding well in the ears of God. So also, if it be not in the strength and assistance of the Spirit, it is but like the sons of Aaron, offering with strange fire. But I shall speak more to this under the second head; and therefore, in the mean time, that which is not petitioned through the teaching and assistance of the Spirit, it is not possible that it should be according to the will of God.

5. Prayer is a sincere, sensible, affectionate pouring out of the heart, or soul, to God, through Christ, in the strength and assistance of the Spirit, *for such things as God hath promised,* &c. Prayer it is, when it is within the compass of God's word; and it is blasphemy, or at best, vain babbling, when the petition is beside the book. David, therefore, in his prayer, still kept his eye on the word of God. "My soul," saith he, "cleaveth to the dust; quicken me according to

thy word." And again, "My soul melteth for heaviness; strengthen me according to thy word." And, "Remember thy word unto thy servant, on which thou hast caused me to hope." And, indeed, the Holy Ghost doth not immediately quicken and stir up the heart of the Christian without, but by, with, and through the word, bringing that to the heart, and by opening that, whereby the man is provoked to go to the Lord, and to tell him how it is with him; and also to argue, and supplicate, according to the word. Thus it was with Daniel, that mighty prophet of the Lord. He understanding by books, that the captivity of the children of Israel was hard at an end; then, according to that word, he maketh his prayer to God. "I Daniel," saith he, "understood by books," (viz., the writings of Jeremiah,) the number of the years whereof the word of the Lord came to Jeremiah, that he would accomplish seventy years in the desolations of Jerusalem. And I set my face unto the Lord God, to seek by prayer and supplications, with fasting, and sackloth, and ashes." So that I say, as the Spirit is the helper and the governor of the soul, when it prayeth according to the will of God; so it guideth by and according to the word of God and his promise. Hence it is that our Lord Jesus Christ himself did make a stop, although his life lay at stake for it:—"I could now pray to my Father, and he should give me more than twelve legions of angels; but how then shall the Scriptures be fulfilled, that thus it must be?" As if he should say, 'Were there but a word for it in Scripture, I should soon be out of the hands of mine enemies; I should be helped by angels. But the scripture will not warrant this kind of praying, for that saith otherwise.' It is a praying, then, according to the word and promise. The Spirit, by the word, must direct, as well in the manner, as in the matter of prayer. "I will pray with the Spirit, and I will pray with the understanding also." But there is no understanding without the word; for if they reject the word of the Lord, what wisdom is in them? Jer. viii. 9.

6. *For the good of the church.* This clause reacheth in whatsoever tendeth either to the honor of God, Christ's advancement, or his people's benefit. For God, and Christ, and his people, are so linked together, that if the good of one be prayed for, namely, the church, the glory of God, and advancement of Christ, must needs be included. For as Christ is in the Father, so the saints are in Christ; and he that toucheth the saints, toucheth the apple of God's eye; and therefore pray for the peace of Jerusalem, and you pray for all that is required of you. For Jerusalem will never be in perfect peace until she be in heaven; and there is nothing that Christ doth more desire than to have her there. That also is the place that God through Christ hath given her. He, then, that prayeth for the peace and good of Sion, or the church, doth ask that in prayer, which Christ hath purchased with his blood; and also that which the Father hath given to him as the price thereof. Now, he that prayeth for this, must pray for abundance of grace for the church; for help against all its temptations; that God would let nothing be too hard for it; that all things may work together for its good; that God would keep them blameless and harmless as the sons of God, to his glory, in the midst of a crooked and perverse nation. And this is the substance of Christ's own prayer in John xvii. And all Paul's prayers did run that way, as one of his prayers does eminently show: "And this I pray, that your love may abound yet more and more in knowledge, and in all judgment; that ye may approve things that are excellent; that ye may be sincere, and without offence, until the day of Christ; being filled with the fruits of righteousness, which are by Jesus Christ, unto the glory and praise of God." But a short prayer, you see, and yet full of good desires for the church, from the beginning to the end; that it may stand, and go on, and that in the most

excellent spirit, even without blame, sincere, and without offence, until the day of Christ, let its temptations or persecutions be what they will.

7. And because, as I said, prayer doth *submit to the will of God*, and say, "Thy will be done," as Christ hath taught; therefore the people of the Lord, in all humility, are to lay themselves and their prayers, and all that they have, at the foot of their God, to be disposed of by him as he in his heavenly wisdom seeth best. Yet not doubting but that God will answer the desire of his people that way that shall be most for their advantage and his glory. When the saints, therefore, do pray with submission to the will of God, it doth not argue, that they are to doubt or question God's love and kindness to them; but it is because they at all times are not so wise, but that sometimes Satan may get advantage of them, so as to tempt them to pray for that which, if they had it, would neither prove to God's glory nor his people's good. Yet "this is the confidence we have in him, that if we ask any thing according to his will he heareth us; and if we know that he heareth us, whatsoever we ask, we know that we have the petition that we ask of him," that is, we asking in the spirit of grace and supplication. For, as I said before, that petition that is not put up in, and through, the Spirit, is not to be answered, because it is beside the will of God; for the Spirit only knoweth that, and so, consequently, knoweth how to pray according to that will of God:—"For what man knoweth the things of a man, save the spirit of man that is in him? even so the things of God knoweth no man, but the Spirit of God." But more of this hereafter.

CHAPTER II.

WHAT IT IS TO PRAY WITH THE SPIRIT.

THUS you see, first, what prayer is. Now, to proceed, we must inquire:

II. WHAT IT IS TO PRAY WITH THE SPIRIT.

"I will pray with the Spirit." Now, to pray with the Spirit, (for that is the way of the praying man, and none else, so as to be accepted of God,) it is for a man, as aforesaid, sincerely, and sensibly, with affection, to come to God through Christ, &c.; which sincere, sensible, and affectionate coming, must be by the working of God's Spirit.

There is no man, nor church, in the world, that can come to God in prayer, but by the assistance of the Holy Spirit. "For through Christ we *all* have access BY ONE SPIRIT unto the Father." Ephes. ii. 18.

Wherefore Paul saith, "We know not what we should pray for as we ought; but the SPIRIT ITSELF maketh intercession for us with groanings which cannot be uttered. And he that searcheth the hearts, knoweth what is the mind of the Spirit, because he maketh intercession for the saints, according to the will of God." And because there is in this Scripture so full a discovery of the spirit of prayer, and of man's inability to pray without it, therefore I shall in a few words comment upon it.

For we consider first the person speaking, even Paul, and in his person all the apostles,—'We extraordinary officers, the wise master-builders, that have some of us been caught up into paradise—"We know not what *we* should pray for."' Surely, there is no man but will confess, that Paul and his companions were as able to have done any work for God, as any pope or proud prelate in the church of Rome, and could as well have made a Common Prayer Book, as those who at first composed this, as being not a whit behind them either in grace or gifts.

"For we know not *what* we should pray for." We know not the *matter* of the things for which we should pray, neither the *object* to whom we pray, nor the *medium* by, or through whom we pray; none of these things know we, but by the help and assistance of the Spirit. Should we pray for communion with God through Christ? should we pray for faith, for justification by grace, and a truly sanctified heart? none of these things know we: for as "no man knoweth the things of a man, save the spirit of a man that is in him; even so the things of God knoweth no man, but the Spirit of God." But here, alas! apostles speak of inward and spiritual things, which the world knows not. John xiv. 17; 1 Cor. ii. 14.

Again, as they know not the matter, &c., of prayer, without the help of the Spirit; so neither know they the *manner* thereof without the same; and therefore he adds, "We know not what we should pray for, *as we ought;* but the Spirit helpeth our infirmities, with groanings which cannot be uttered." Mark here, *they* could not so well and so fully come off in the manner of performing this duty, as these in our days think they can.

The apostles, when they were at the best, yea, when the Holy Ghost assisted them, yet then were fain to come off with sighs and groans, falling short of expressing their mind, but with sighs and groans *which cannot be uttered.*

But here, now, the wise men of our days are so well skilled, as that they have both the manner and matter of their prayers at their finger-ends; setting such a prayer for such a day, and that twenty years before it comes. One for Christmas, another for Easter, and six days after that. They have also bounded how many syllables must be said in every one of them. For each saint's day, also, they have them ready for the generations yet unborn to say. They can tell you, also, when you shall kneel, when you shall stand, when you should abide in your seats, when you should go up into the chancel, and what you should do when you come there. All which the apostles came short of, as not being able to compose in so profound a manner; and that for this reason included in the Scripture, because the fear of God tied them to pray as they ought.

"For we know not what we should pray for as we ought." Mark this, "as we ought;" for the not thinking of this word, or at least the not understanding it, in the spirit and truth of it, hath occasioned these men to devise, as Jeroboam did, another way of worship, both for matter and manner, than is revealed in the word of God. But, saith Paul, we must pray as we ought; and this we cannot do by all the art, skill, cunning, and device of men or angels. "For we know not what we should pray for as we ought, but the Spirit;"—nay, farther, it must be the "Spirit *itself*" "that helpeth our infirmities;" not the Spirit and man's lusts. What man of his own brain may imagine and devise, is one thing; and what they are commanded, and ought to do, is another. Many ask and have not, because they ask amiss, (James iv. 3,) and so are never the nearer enjoying those things they petition for. It is not to pray at random, that will put off God, or cause him to answer. While prayer is making, God is searching the heart, to see from what root and spirit it doth arise. "And he that searcheth the heart knoweth" (that is, approveth only,) "the meaning of the Spirit, because he maketh intercession for the saints according to the will of God." For in that which is according to his will only, he heareth us, and in nothing else. And it is the Spirit only that can teach us so to ask; he only being able to search out all things, even the deep things of God. Without which Spirit, though we had a thousand Common Prayer Books, yet, "We know not what we should pray for as we ought," being accompanied with those infirmities, that make us absolutely incapable of such a work. Which infirmities, although it is a hard thing to name them all, yet some of them are these that follow:

1. Without the Spirit, man is so infirm that he cannot, with all other means whatsoever, be enabled to think one right, saving thought of God, of Christ, or of his blessed things. And therefore he saith, of the wicked, "God is not in all their thoughts," (Psalm x. 4,) unless it be that they imagine him altogether such a one as themselves. Psalm l. 2. "For every imagination of the thoughts of their heart is only evil, and that continually." Gen. vi. 5; viii. 21. They, then, not being able to conceive aright of God, to whom they pray, nor of the things for which they pray, as is before showed; how shall they be able to address themselves to God, without the Spirit help this infirmity? Peradventure you will say, by the help of the Common Prayer Book; but that cannot do it, unless it can open the eyes, and reveal to the soul all these things before touched; which, that it cannot, is evident; because that is the work of the Spirit only. The Spirit itself is the revealer of these things to poor souls, and that which doth give us to understand them; wherefore Christ tells his disciples, when he promised to send the Spirit, the Comforter, "He shall take of mine and show unto you." As if he had said, 'I know you are naturally dark and ignorant as to understanding any of my things; though ye try this course and the other, yet your ignorance will still remain; the veil is spread over your heart, and there is none that can take away the same, nor give you spiritual understanding, but the Spirit.' The Common Prayer Book will not do it; neither can any man expect that it should be instrumental that way; it being none of God's ordinances, but a thing since the Scriptures were written, patched together one piece at one time, and another at that; a mere human invention and institution, which God is so far from owning,

that he expressly forbids it, with any other such like, and that by manifold sayings in his most holy and blessed word. See Mark vii. 7, 8; and Col. ii. 16—23; Deut. xii. 30—32; Prov. xxx. 6; Deut. iv. 2; Rev. xxii. 18.

For right prayer must, as well in the outward part of it, in the outward expression, as in the inward intention, come from what the soul doth apprehend in the light of the Spirit; otherwise it is condemned as vain and an abomination, because the heart and tongue do not go along jointly in the same: neither, indeed, can they, unless the Spirit help our infirmities. And this David knew full well, which made him cry, "Lord, open thou my lips, and my mouth shall show forth thy praise." I suppose there is none can imagine, but that David could speak, and express himself as well as others, nay, as any in our generation, as is clearly manifest by his word and works; nevertheless, when this good man, this prophet, comes into God's worship, then the Lord must help, or he can do nothing. "Lord, open thou my lips, and then my mouth shall show forth thy praise." He could not speak one right word, except the Spirit itself gave utterance. "For we know not what we should pray for, as we ought; but the Spirit itself helpeth our infirmities." But,

2. It must be praying with the Spirit, that is the effectual praying; because, without that, as men are senseless, so hypocritical, cold, and unseemly in their prayers; and so they, with their prayers, are both rendered abominable to God. It is not the excellency of the voice, nor the seeming affection and earnestness of him that prayeth, that is in any thing regarded of God without it. For man, as man, is so full of all manner of wickedness, that as he cannot keep a word or thought, so much less a piece of prayer clean, and acceptable to God through Christ; and for this cause the Pharisees, with their prayers, were rejected. No question but they were excellently able to express themselves in words, and also for length of time, too, they were very notable; but

they had not the Spirit of Jesus Christ to help them, and therefore they did what they did with their infirmities or weaknesses only, and so fell short of a sincere, sensible, affectionate pouring out of their souls to God, through the strength of the Spirit. That is the prayer that goeth to heaven, that is sent thither in the strength of the Spirit. For,

3. Nothing but the Spirit can show a man clearly his misery by nature, and so put a man into a posture of prayer. Talk is but talk, as we use to say, and so it is but mouth worship, if there be not a sense of misery, and that effectually too. O, the cursed hypocrisy that is in most hearts, and that accompanieth many thousands of praying men that would be so looked upon in this day, and all for want of a sense of their misery! But now the Spirit, *that* will sweetly show the soul its misery, where it is, and what is like to become of it; also the intolerableness of that condition: for it is the Spirit that doth effectually convince of sin and misery without the Lord Jesus, and so puts the soul into a sweet, serious, sensible, affectionate way of praying to God according to his word. John xvi. 8.

4. If men did see their sins, yet without the help of the Spirit, they would not pray. For they would run away from God, with Cain and Judas, and utterly despair of mercy, were it not for the Spirit. When a man is, indeed, sensible of his sin, and God's curse, then it is a hard thing to persuade him to pray; for, saith his heart, 'There is no hope; it is in vain to seek God. I am so vile, so wretched, and so cursed a creature, that I shall never be regarded.' Now, here comes the Spirit, and stayeth the soul, helpeth it to hold up its face to God, by letting into the heart some small sense of mercy to encourage it to go to God; and hence it is called the Comforter.

5. It must be in or with the Spirit; for without that no man can know how he should come to God the right way. Men may easily say they come to God in his Son; but it is

the hardest thing of a thousand to come to God aright and in his own way, without the Spirit. It is the Spirit that searcheth all things, yea, the deep things of God. It is the Spirit that must show us the way of coming to God, and also what there is in God that makes him desirable: "I beseech thee," saith Moses, "show me thy *way*, that I may know thee." Exod. xxxiii. 13; and John xvi. 14. "He shall receive of mine, and shall show it unto you."

6. Because, without the Spirit, though a man did see his misery, and also the way to come to God; yet he would never be able to claim a share in either God, Christ, or mercy, without God's approbation. O, how great a task it is, for a poor soul that comes, sensible of sin and the wrath of God, to say in faith but this one word, Father! I tell you, however hypocrites think, yet the Christian, that is so indeed, finds all the difficulty in this very thing. He cannot say, God is his Father. "Oh!" saith he, "I dare not call him Father;" and hence it is that the Spirit must be sent into the hearts of God's people for this very thing, to cry, Father! it being too great a work for any man to do, knowingly and believingly, without it. When I say *knowingly*, I mean, knowing what it is to be a child of God, and to be born again. And when I say *believingly*, I mean, for the soul to believe, and that from good experience, that the work of grace is wrought in him. This is the right calling of God, Father; and not, as many do, to say in a babbling way the Lord's prayer, (so called,) by heart, as it lieth in the words of the book. No; here is the life of prayer, when in, or with, the Spirit, a man being made sensible of sin, and how to come to the Lord for mercy, comes, I say, in the strength of the Spirit, and crieth, Father. That one word, spoken in faith, is better than a thousand prayers, as men call them, written and read in a formal, cold, lukewarm way.

O, how far short are the people of being sensible of this, who count it enough to teach themselves and children to say the Lord's prayer, the creed, with other sayings; when, as God knows, they are senseless of themselves, their misery, or what it is to be brought to God through Christ! Ah, poor soul! study your misery, and cry to God to show you your confused blindness and ignorance before you be too rife in calling God your Father, or learning your children either so to say. And know, that to say God is your Father, in a way of prayer or conference, without an experiment of the work of grace on your souls, it is to say you are Jews and are not, and so to lie. You say, Our Father; God saith, You blaspheme. You say you are Jews, that is, true Christians; God saith, You lie. "Behold, I will make them of the synagogue of Satan, which say they are Jews, and are not, but do lie." And, "I know the blasphemy of them that say they are Jews, and are not, but are the synagogue of Satan." And so much the greater the sin is, by how much the more the sinner boasts it with a pretended sanctity, as the Jews did to Christ, in the 8th of John; which made Christ, even in plain terms, to tell them their doom, for all their hypocritical pretences. And yet, forsooth, every whoremaster, thief, and drunkard, swearer and perjured person; they that have not only been such in times past, but are even so still; these, I say, by some must be counted the only honest men, and all because, with their blasphemous throats, and hypocritical hearts, they will come to church, and say, Our Father. Nay, further, these men, though every time they say to God, Our Father, they do most abominably blaspheme, yet must be compelled thus to do. And because others that are of more sober principles, scruple the truth of such vain traditions, therefore, they must be looked upon to be the only enemies of God and the nation: whereas it is their own cursed superstition, that doth set the great God against them, and cause him to count them for his enemies. And yet just like to Bonner, that blood-red persecutor, they commend, I say, these wretches, although never so vile, (if they close in with their traditions,) to be good churchmen, the honest subjects; while God's people are, as it hath always been, looked upon to be a turbulent, seditious, and factious people.*

Therefore give me leave a little to reason with thee, thou poor, blind, ignorant sot. It may be, thy great prayer is to say, "Our Father which art in heaven," &c. Dost thou know the meaning of the very first words of this prayer? Canst thou indeed, with the rest of the saints, cry, "Our Father?" Art thou truly born again? hast thou received the Spirit of adoption? dost thou see thyself in Christ, and canst thou come to God as a member of him? Or art thou ignorant of these things; and yet darest thou say, "Our Father?" Is not the devil thy father? and dost thou not do the deeds of the flesh? and yet darest thou say to God, "Our Father?" Nay, art thou not a desperate persecutor of the children of God? hast thou not cursed them in thine heart many a time? and yet dost thou out of thy blasphemous throat suffer these words to come, even, "Our Father?" He is the Father of them whom thou hatest and persecutest. But as the devil presented himself amongst the sons of God, (Job i.) when they were to present themselves before the Father, even our Father; so it is now; because the saints are commanded to say "Our Father," therefore all the blind, ignorant rabble in the world must also use the same words, "Our Father."

And dost thou indeed say, "Hallowed be thy name," with thy heart? Dost thou study, by all honest and lawful ways, to advance the name, holiness, and majesty of God? Doth thy heart and conversation agree with this passage? Dost thou strive to imitate Christ in all the works of righteousness which God doth command of thee, and prompt thee forward to? It is so, if thou be one that can truly with God's allow-

* This treatise was written in 1663, while Bunyan was a prisoner in Bedford jail. He here explains the cause of his long imprisonment, and that of thousands more in those unhappy times. It is well to remember that *Bunyan was the first sufferer for conscience' sake under Charles II.* J. N. B.

ance cry, "Our Father." Or is it not the least of thy thoughts all the day? and dost thou not clearly make it appear, that thou art a cursed hypocrite, by condemning that with thy daily practice, which thou pretendest in thy praying with thy dissembling tongue?

Wouldst thou have the kingdom of God come indeed, and also his will to be done on earth as it is in heaven?—Nay, notwithstanding thou, according to the form, sayest, Thy kingdom come;* yet would it not make thee ready to run mad, to hear the trumpet sound, to see the dead rise, and thyself just now to go and appear before God, to reckon for all the deeds thou hast done in the body? Nay, are not the very thoughts of it altogether displeasing to thee? And if God's will should be done on earth as it is in heaven, must it not be thy ruin? There is never a rebel in heaven against God; and if he should so deal on earth, must it not whirl thee down to hell? And so of the rest of the petitions. Ah! how sadly would even those men look, and with what terror would they walk up and down the world, if they did but know the lying and blaspheming that proceedeth out of their mouth, even in their most pretended sanctity? The Lord awaken you, and learn you, poor souls, in all humility, to take heed that you be not rash and unadvised with your heart, and much more with your mouth! When you appear before God, (as the wise man saith,) be not rash with thy mouth, and let not thine heart be hasty to utter any thing, especially to call God, Father, without some blessed experience when thou comest before God. But I pass this.

7. It must be a prayer with the Spirit if it be accepted, because there is nothing but the Spirit that can lift up the soul or heart to God in prayer. "The preparation of the

---

* There are few petitions more comprehensive and important than this, *Thy kingdom come.* It embraces the progress and effectual power of the gospel in all the world—the fulfilment of a thousand prophecies—the consummation of all the holy hopes awakened in human bosoms in all ages, by the word of God. J. N. B.

heart in man, and the answer of the tongue, is from the Lord." Prov. xvi. 1. That is, in every work for God, (and especially in prayer,) if the heart run with the tongue, it must be prepared by the Spirit of God. Indeed the tongue is very apt, of itself, to run without either fear or wisdom: but when it is the answer of the heart, and that such an heart as is prepared by the Spirit of God, then it speaks so as God commands and doth desire.

They are mighty words of David, where he saith, that he lifteth up his heart and his soul to God. Psalm xxv. 1. It is a great work for any man without the strength of the Spirit; and therefore I conceive that this is one of the great reasons why the Spirit of God is called a Spirit of supplication, because it is that which helpeth the heart when it supplicates indeed, to do it; and therefore saith Paul, "Praying with all prayer and supplication in the Spirit!" and so in my text, "I will pray with the Spirit." 1 Cor. xiv. 15.

Prayer, without the heart be in it, is like a sound without life; and an heart, without it be lifted up of the Spirit, will never pray to God.

8. As the heart must be lifted up by the Spirit, if it pray aright; so also it must be held by the Spirit, when it is up, if it continue to pray aright. I do not know what, or how it is with others' hearts, whether they be lifted up by the Spirit of God, and so continued, or no; but this I am sure of,

First, That it is impossible that all the prayer-books that men have made in the world, should lift up or prepare the heart. That is the work of the great God himself.

And, in the second place, I am sure, that they are as far from keeping it up, when it is up. And indeed here is the life of prayer, to have the heart kept up with God in the duty. It was a great matter for Moses to keep his hands lifted up to God in prayer; but how much more then to keep the heart in it.

The want of this is that which God complains of, that they

draw nigh to him with their mouth, and honor him with their lips, but their hearts are far from him; but chiefly, they that walk after the commandments and tradition of men, as the scope of Matt. xv. 8, 9, doth testify. And verily, may I but speak my own experience, and from that tell you the difficulty of praying to God as I ought, it is enough to make you poor, blind, carnal men, to entertain strange thoughts of me. For, as for my heart, when I go to pray, I find it loath to go to God, and when it is with him, so loath to stay with him, that many times I am forced in my prayers, first to beg God that he would take mine heart, and set it on himself in Christ; and when it is there, that he would keep it there. Nay, many times I know not what to pray for, I am so blind; nor how to pray, I am so ignorant; only blessed be grace, the Spirit helps our infirmities.

Oh! the starting-holes that the heart hath in the time of prayer! None knows how many by-ways the heart hath, and back-lanes, to slip away from the presence of God. How much pride also, if enabled with expressions! How much hypocrisy, if before others! And how little conscience is there made of prayer between God and the soul in secret, unless the Spirit of supplication be there to help!

When the Spirit gets into the heart, then there is prayer indeed, and not till then.

9. The soul that doth rightly pray, it must be in and with the help and strength of the Spirit; because it is impossible that a man should express himself in prayer without it. When I say it is impossible for a man to express himself in prayer without it, I mean, that it is impossible that the heart, in a sincere, and sensible, affectionate way, should pour out itself before God, with those groans and sighs that come from a truly praying heart, without the assistance of the Spirit. It is not the mouth that is the main thing to be looked at in prayer, but whether the heart is so full of affection and earnestness, in prayer with God, that it is impossible to express

their sense and desire: for then a man desires indeed, when his desires are so strong, many, and mighty, that all the words, tears, and groans, that can come from the heart, cannot utter them. The Spirit helps our infirmities, and makes intercession for us with sighs and groans that cannot be uttered.

That is but poor prayer, which is only discovered in so many words.

A man that truly prays one prayer, shall after that never be able to express with his mouth or pen the unutterable desires, sense, affection, and longing, that went to God in that prayer.

The best prayers have often more groans than words; and those words that it hath are but a lean and shallow representation of the heart, life, and spirit of that prayer. You do not find any words of prayer, that we read of, come out of the mouth of Moses, when he was gone out of Egypt, and was followed by Pharaoh; and yet he made heaven ring again with his cry. But it was the inexpressible and unsearchable groans and cryings of his soul in and with the Spirit. God is the God of spirits, and his eyes look further than at the outside of any duty whatsoever. I doubt this is but little thought on by the most of them that would be looked upon as a praying people.

The nearer a man comes, in any work that God commands him, to the doing of it according to his will, so much the more hard and difficult it is; and the reason is, because man, as man, is not able to do it. But prayer (as afore said) is not only a duty, but one of the most eminent duties, and therefore so much the more difficult. Therefore Paul knew what he said, when he said, "I will pray with the Spirit." He knew well it was not what others writ or said, that could make him a praying person; nothing less than the Spirit, could do it.

10. It must be with the Spirit, or else, as there will be a

failing in the act itself, so there will be a failing, yea, a fainting, in the prosecution of the work. Prayer is an ordinance of God that must continue with a soul, so long as it is on this side glory. But, as I said before, it is not possible for a man to get up his heart to God in prayer; so it is as difficult to keep it there, without the assistance of the Spirit. And if so, then for a man to continue from time to time in prayer with God, it must of necessity be with the Spirit.

Christ tells us, that men ought always to pray, and not to faint, Luke xviii. 1, 2; and again tells us, that this is one definition of an hypocrite,—that either he will not continue in prayer, (Job xxvii. 10,) or else if he do it, it will not be in the power, that is, in the spirit of prayer, but in the form, for a pretence only. Matt. xxiii. 14. It is the easiest thing of an hundred to fall from the power to the form, but it is the hardest thing of many to keep in the life, spirit, and power of any one duty, especially prayer: that is such a work, that a man without the help of the Spirit cannot so much as pray once, much less continue, without it, in a sweet praying frame, and in praying, so to pray, as to have his prayers ascend into the ears of the Lord of Sabaoth.

Jacob did not only begin, but held it: "I will not let thee go, unless thou bless me." Gen. xxxii. So did the rest of the godly. Hos. xii. 4. But this could not be without the Spirit of prayer. It is through the Spirit that we have access to the Father. Eph. ii. 18.

The same is a remarkable place in Jude, when he stirreth up the saints by the judgment of God upon the wicked, to stand fast, and continue to hold out in the faith of the gospel. As one excellent means thereto, without which he knew they would never be able to do it, saith he, "Build up yourselves in your most holy faith, praying in the Holy Ghost. Jude 20. As if he had said, Brethren, as eternal life is laid up for the persons that hold out only, so you cannot hold out unless you continue praying in the Spirit. The great cheat that the devil and Antichrist delude the world withal, is to make them continue in the mere form of any duty,—the form of preaching, of hearing, of praying, &c. These are they that have "a form of godliness, but deny the power thereof: from such turn away." 2 Tim. iii. 5.

CHAPTER III.

WHAT IT IS TO PRAY WITH THE UNDERSTANDING.

HERE followeth the third thing; namely,

III. WHAT IT IS TO PRAY WITH THE SPIRIT, AND WITH THE UNDERSTANDING.

The apostle puts a clear distinction between praying with the Spirit, and praying with the Spirit and understanding. Therefore, when he saith he will pray with the Spirit, he adds, "And I will pray with the understanding also." This distinction was occasioned through the Corinthians not observing, that it was their duty to do what they did to edification of themselves and others too; whereas they did it for their own commendations. So I judge; for many of them having extraordinary gifts, such as to speak with divers tongues, &c., therefore they were more for those mighty gifts, than they were for the edifying of their brethren; which was the cause that Paul wrote this chapter to them, to let them understand, that though extraordinary gifts were excellent, yet, to do what they did for the edification of the church was more excellent. "For if I pray in an unknown tongue, my spirit prayeth, but my understanding (and also the understanding of others) is unfruitful. Therefore, I will pray with the Spirit, and I will pray with the understanding also."

It is expedient, then, that the understanding should be occupied in prayer, as well as the heart and mouth: "I will pray with the Spirit, and I will pray with the understanding also." That which is done with understanding, is done more effectually, sensibly, and heartily, as I shall show farther anon, than that which is done without it. Which made the apostle pray for the Colossians, that God would fill them with the knowledge of his will, in all wisdom and spiritual understanding. Col. i. 9. And for the Ephesians, that God would give unto them the spirit of wisdom and revelation, in the knowledge of him. Eph. i. 17. And so for the Philippians, that God would make them abound in knowledge, and in all judgment. Phil. i. 9. A suitable understanding is good in every thing a man undertakes, either civil or spiritual; and therefore it must be desired by all them that would be a praying people. In my speaking to this, I shall show you what it is to pray with understanding.

Understanding is here to be taken both for speaking in our mother tongue, and also experimentally. I pass the first, and treat only on the second.

For the making of right prayers, it is required that there should be a good or *spiritual understanding* in all them who pray to God.

To pray with understanding, is to pray as being instructed by the Spirit, in the understanding of the *want* of those things which the soul is to pray for. Though a man be in never so much need of pardon of sin, and deliverance from wrath to come, yet if he understand not this, he will either not desire them at all, or else be so cold and lukewarm in his desires after them, that God will even loath the frame of spirit in asking for them. Thus it was with the church of the Laodiceans, they wanted knowledge of spiritual understanding: they knew not that they were poor, wretched, blind, and naked. The cause whereof made them, and all their services, so loathsome to Christ, that he threatens to spue them out of his mouth. Rev. iii. 17. Men without understanding may say the same words in prayer as others do; but if there be an understanding in the one, and none in the other, there is—O there is a mighty difference in speaking the very same words! The one speaking from a spiritual understanding of those things that he in words desires, and the other words it only, and there is all.

Spiritual understanding espieth in the heart of God a readiness and *willingness to give* those things to the soul that it stands in need of. David by this could guess at the very thoughts of God towards him. Psalm xl. 5. And thus it was with the woman of Canaan. Matt. xv. 22–28. She did by faith and a right understanding discern, beyond all the rough carriage of Christ, tenderness and willingness in his heart to save, which caused her to be vehement and earnest, yea, restless, until she did enjoy the mercy she stood in need of.

An understanding of the willingness that is in the heart of God to save sinners,—there is nothing will press the soul more to seek after God, and to cry for pardon, than it. If a man should see a pearl worth an hundred pounds lie in a ditch, yet if he understood not the value of it, he would lightly pass it by; but if he once get the knowledge of it, he would venture up to the neck for it. So it is with souls concerning the things of God. If a man once get an understanding of the worth of them, then his heart, nay, the very strength of his soul runs after them, and he will never leave crying till he have them. The two blind men in the gospel, because they did certainly know that Jesus, who was going by them, was both able and willing to heal such infirmities as they were afflicted with, therefore cried, and the more they were rebuked, the more they cried. Matt. xx. 29, 30, 31.

The understanding being spiritually enlightened, hereby there is *the way* (as afore said) discovered, through which the soul should come unto God; which gives great encouragement unto it. It is else with a poor soul, as with one who hath a work to do, and if it be not done, the danger is great, and if it be done, so great is the advantage. But he knows not how to begin, nor how to proceed; and so through discouragement, lets all alone, and runs the hazard.

The enlightened understanding sees largeness enough in the *promises* to encourage it to pray; which still adds to it strength to strength. As when men promise such and such things to all that will come for them, it is great encouragement to those that know what promises are made, to come and ask for them.

The understanding being enlightened, way is made for the soul to come to God with *suitable arguments;* sometimes in a way of expostulation, as Jacob, Gen. xxxii. 9; sometimes in a way of supplication; yet not in a verbal way only, but even from the heart there is forced by the Spirit, through the understanding, such effectual argument, as moveth the heart of God. When Ephraim gets a right understanding of his own unseemly carriages towards the Lord, then he begins to bemoan himself. Jer. xxxi. 18, 19, 20. And in bemoaning himself, he uses such argument with the Lord that it affects his heart, draws out forgiveness, and makes Ephraim pleasant in his eyes through Jesus Christ our Lord. "I have surely heard Ephraim bemoaning himself thus," saith God. "Thou hast chastised me, and I was chastised, as a bullock unaccustomed to the yoke: turn thou me, and I shall be turned; for thou art the Lord my God. Surely after that I was turned, I repented, and after I was instructed," (or had a right understanding of myself,) "I smote upon my thigh: I was ashamed, yea, even confounded, because I did bear the reproach of my youth." These be Ephraim's complaints and bemoanings of himself; at which the Lord breaks forth into these heart-melting expressions; saying, "Is Ephraim my dear son? Is he a pleasant child? for since I spake against him, I do earnestly remember him still; therefore my bowels are troubled for him: I will surely have mercy upon him, saith the Lord."

Thus you see, that as it is required to pray with the Spirit, so it is to pray with the understanding also. And, to illustrate by a similitude what hath been spoken, set the case, there should come two men a-begging to your door. The one is poor, lame, wounded, and almost a starving creature; the other is a healthful, lusty person. These two use the same words in their begging. The one saith, he is almost starved, so doth the other; but yet the man that is indeed the poor, lame, or maimed person, speaks with more sense, feeling, and understanding of the misery that is mentioned in their begging, than the other can do; and it is discovered more by his affectionate speaking, his bemoaning himself. His pain and poverty make him speak more in a spirit of lamentation than the other; and he shall be pitied sooner than the other, by all those that have the least drachm of natural affection or pity. Just thus it is with God. There are some who out of custom and formality go and pray; there are others who go in the bitterness of their spirits. The one prays out of bare notion, and naked knowledge; the other hath his words forced from him by the anguish of his soul. Surely that man is the man that God will look at, even him that is of an humble and contrite spirit, and that trembleth at his word. Isa. lxvi. 2.

An understanding well enlightened is of admirable use also, both as to the *matter* and *manner* of prayer. He that hath his understanding well exercised, to discern between good and evil, and in it placed a sense either of the misery of man, or the mercy of God; that soul hath no need of the writings of other men, to teach him by forms of prayer. For as he that feels the pain needs not to be learned to cry, Oh! even so he that hath his understanding opened by the Spirit needs not so to be taught of other men's prayers, as that he cannot pray without them; the present sense, feeling, and pressure that lieth upon his spirit, provokes him to groan out his request unto the Lord. When David had the pains of hell catching hold on him, and the sorrows of hell compassing him about, he needs not a bishop in a surplice to learn him to say, "O Lord, I beseech thee, deliver my soul; (Psalm cxvi. 3, 4;) or to look into a book, to teach him in a form to pour out his heart before God. It is the nature of the heart of sick men, in their pain and sickness, to vent itself for ease, by dolorous groans and complainings to them that stand by. Thus it was with David, in Psalm xxxviii. 1–12. And thus, blessed be the Lord, it is with them that are endued with the grace of God.

It is necessary that there be an enlightened understanding, to the end that the soul be kept in a *continuation* of the duty of prayer.

The people of God are not ignorant how many wiles, tricks, and temptations the devil hath, to make a poor soul who is truly willing to have the Lord Jesus Christ, and that upon Christ's terms too; I say, to tempt that soul to be weary of seeking the face of God, and to think that God is not willing to have mercy on such a one as him. 'Ay,' saith Satan, 'thou mayest pray indeed, but thou shalt not prevail. Thou seest thine heart is hard, cold, dull, and dead; thou dost not pray with the Spirit, thou dost not pray in good earnest, thy thoughts are running after other things, when thou pretendest to pray to God. Away, hypocrite; go no further; it is but in vain to strive any longer.' Here now, if the soul be not well informed in its understanding, it will presently cry out, 'The Lord hath forsaken me, and my God hath forgotten me!' Whereas the soul rightly informed and enlightened saith, 'Well, I will seek the Lord, and wait; I will not leave off, though the Lord keep silence, and speak not one word of comfort. He loved Jacob dearly, and yet he made him wrestle before he had the blessing. Seeming delays in God are no tokens of his displeasure; he may hide his face from his dearest saints. He loves to keep his people praying, and to find them ever knocking at the gate of heaven. It may be,' says the soul, 'the Lord tries me, or he loves to hear me groan out my condition before him.'

The woman of Canaan would not take seeming denials for real ones; she knew the Lord was gracious, and the Lord will avenge his people, though he bear long with them. 'The Lord hath waited longer upon me than I have waited upon him. And thus it was with David. "I waited patiently," saith he; that is, 'It was long before the Lord answered me, though at the last he inclined his ear unto me, and heard my cry.' Psalm xl. 1. And the most excellent remedy for this is, an understanding well informed and enlightened. Alas! how many poor souls are there in the world, that truly fear the Lord, who, because they are not well informed in their understanding, are oft ready to give up all for lost, upon almost every trick and temptation of Satan! The Lord pity them, and help them to pray with the Spirit, and with the understanding also! Much of mine own experience could I here discover. When I have been in my fits of agonies of spirit, I have been strongly persuaded to leave off, and to seek the Lord no longer; but being made to understand what great sinners the Lord hath had mercy upon, and how large his promises were still to sinners; and that it was not the whole, but the sick; not the righteous, but the sinner; not the full, but the empty, that he extended his grace and mercy unto; this made me, through the assistance of his Holy Spirit, to cleave to him, to hang upon him, and yet to cry, though for the present he made no answer. And the Lord help all his poor, tempted, and afflicted people to do the like, and to continue, though it be long, according to the saying of the prophet; and to help them, to that end, to pray, not by the inventions of men, and their stinted forms, but with the Spirit, and with understanding also.

And now to answer a query or two, and so to pass on to the next thing.

Query 1. 'But what would you have us poor creatures to do, that cannot tell how to pray? The Lord knows I know not either how to pray, or what to pray for.'

Answer. Poor heart! thou complainest that thou canst not pray. Canst thou see thy misery? Hath God showed thee that thou art by nature under the curse of his law? If so, do not mistake; I know thou dost groan, and that most bitterly. I am persuaded, thou canst scarcely be found doing any thing in thy calling, but prayer breaketh from thy heart. Have not thy groans gone up to heaven from every corner of thy house? I know it is thus; and so also doth thine own sorrowful heart witness, thy tears, thy forgetfulness of thy calling, &c. Is not thy heart so full of desires after the things of another world, that many times thou dost even forget the things of this world? Prithee read this Scripture, Job xxiii. 3–12.

Query 2. 'Yea, but when I go into secret, and intend to pour out my soul before God, I can scarce say any thing at all.'

Answer. Ah, sweet soul! it is not thy *words* that God so much regards, as that he will not mind thee except thou comest before him with some eloquent oration. His eye is on the brokenness of thine heart; and that it is that makes the tender pity of the Lord run over. "A broken and a contrite heart, O God, thou wilt not despise." Psalm li. 17.

The *stopping* of thy words may arise from over-much trouble in thy heart. David was so troubled sometimes, that he could not speak. Psalm lxxvii. 3, 4. But this may comfort all such sorrowful hearts as thou art, that though thou canst not, through the anguish of thy spirit, speak much, yet the Holy Spirit stirs up in thine heart groans and sighs, so much the more vehement. When the mouth is hindered, yet the spirit is not.

Moses, as afore said, made heaven ring again with his prayers, although, that we read of, not one word came out of his mouth. But,

If thou wouldst more fully express thyself before the Lord; study, first, Thy sinful state; secondly, God's promises; thirdly, The heart of Christ: which thou mayst know or discern, 1. By his condescension and bloodshed. 2. By the mercy he hath extended to great sinners formerly. And plead thine own vileness, by way of bemoaning; Christ's blood, by way of expostulation; and in thy prayers, let the mercy that he hath extended to other great sinners, together with his rich promises of grace, be much upon thy heart. Yet, let me counsel thee, 1. Take heed that thou content not thyself with words. 2. That thou do not think that God looks only at them neither. But, 3. However, whether thy words be few or many, let thine heart go with them; and then shalt thou seek him, and find him, when thou shalt seek him with thy whole heart. Jer. xxix. 13.

Objection 1. 'But though you have seemed to speak against any other way of praying, but by the Spirit, yet here you yourself can give directions how to pray.'

Answer. We ought to prompt one another forward to prayer, though we ought not to make for each other forms of prayer.

To exhort to pray with Christian direction, is one thing; and to make stinted forms for the tying up the Spirit of God to them, is another thing.

The apostle gives no form to pray withal, yet directs to prayer. Eph. vi. 18; Rom. xv. 30–32.

Let no man therefore conclude, that because we may with allowance give instructions and directions to pray, that therefore it is lawful to make for each other, forms of prayer.

Objection 2. 'But if we do not use forms of prayer, how shall we teach our children to pray?'

Answer. My judgment is, that men go the wrong way to learn their children to pray, in going about so soon to learn them any set company of words, as is the common use of poor creatures to do.

For to me it seems to be a better way for people betimes to tell their children what fallen creatures they are, and how they are under the wrath of God, by reason of original and actual sin; also to tell them the nature of God's wrath, and the duration of the misery; which if they conscientiously do, they would sooner learn their children to pray than they do.

The way that men learn to pray, is by conviction for sin; and this is the way to make our sweet babes do so too. But the other way, namely, to be busy in learning children forms of prayer, before they know any thing else, is the next way to make them hypocrites, and to puff them up with pride. Learn therefore your children to know their wretched state and condition. Tell them of hell fire, and their sins; of damnation and salvation; the way to escape the one, and to enjoy the other; (if you know yourselves;) and this will make tears run down your sweet babes' eyes, and hearty groans flow from their hearts; and then also you may tell them to whom they should pray, and through whom they should pray: you may tell them also of God's promises, and his former grace extended to sinners, according to the word.

Ah! poor sweet babes; the Lord open their eyes, and make them holy Christians. Saith David, "Come, ye children, hearken unto me; I will teach you the fear of the Lord." Psalm xxxiv. 11. He doth not say, I will muzzle you up in a form of prayer; but, "I will teach you the fear of the Lord:" which is, to see their sad state by nature, and to be instructed in the truth of the gospel, which doth through the Spirit beget prayer in every one that in truth learns it. And the more you learn them this, the more will their hearts run out to God in prayer.

God never did account Paul a praying man, until he was a convinced and converted man; no more will it be with any else. Acts ix. 11.

Objection 3. 'But we find that the disciples desired that Christ would teach them to pray, as John also taught his disciples; and that thereupon he taught them that form called, "The Lord's Prayer."'

Answer. To be taught by Christ, is that which not only they, but we desire; and seeing he is not here in his person to teach us, the Lord teach us by his word and Spirit! For the Spirit it is which he hath said he would send to supply his room when he went away, as it is, John xiv. 16; and xvi. 17.

As to that called a form, I cannot think that Christ intended it as a stinted *form* of prayer. 1. Because he himself layeth it down diversely, as is to be seen, if you compare Matt. vi.; Luke xi. Whereas, if he intended it as a set form, it must not have been so laid down; for a set form is so many words and no more. 2. We do not find that the apostles did ever observe it as such; neither did they admonish others so to do. Search all their epistles; yet surely they, both for knowledge to discern, and faithfulness to practise, were as eminent as any be ever since in the world which would impose it.

But, in a word, Christ by those words, "Our Father," &c., doth instruct his people what rules they should observe in their prayers to God. 1. That they should pray in faith. 2. To God in the heavens. 3. For such things as are according to his will, &c. Pray thus, or after this manner.

Objection 4. 'But Christ bids us pray for the Spirit; this implieth, that men without the Spirit may, notwithstanding, pray and be heard.' See Luke xi. 9–13.

Answer. The speech of Christ there is directed to his own disciples., ver. 1. Christ, in telling them that God would give his Holy Spirit to them that ask him, is to be understood of giving *more* of the Holy Spirit: for still they are the disciples spoken to, who had a measure of the Spirit already; for he saith, "When ye pray, say, Our Father," ver 2. "I say unto you," ver. 8. "And I say unto you," ver. 9. "If ye then, being evil, know how to give good gifts unto your children; how much more shall your heavenly Father give the Holy Spirit to them that ask him?" Christians ought to pray for the Spirit, that is, more of it, though God hath endued them with it already.

Question 3. 'Then would you have none pray, but those that know they are disciples of Christ?'

Answer. Let *every soul that would be saved,* pour out itself to God, though it cannot through temptation conclude itself a child of God. And I know if the grace of God be in thee, it will be as natural to thee to groan out thy condition, as it is for a sucking child to cry for the breast.

Prayer is one of the first things that discovers a man to be a Christian. Acts ix. 11. But yet if it be right, it is such a prayer as followeth: 1. To desire God in Christ, for himself, for his holiness, love, wisdom, and glory. For right prayer, as it runs on to God through Christ, so it centres in him, and in him alone. "Whom have I in heaven but thee? and there is none upon earth that I desire" (long for, or seek after) "besides thee." Psalm lxxiii. 25. 2. That the soul might enjoy continually communion with him, both here and hereafter. "I shall be satisfied, when I awake with thine image, or in thy likeness." Psalm xvii. 15. "For in this we groan, earnestly," &c. 2 Cor. v. 2. 3. Right prayer is accompanied with a continual labor after that which is prayed for. "My soul waiteth for the Lord, more than they that watch for the morning." Psalm cxxx. 6. "I will arise now, and seek him whom my soul loveth." Cant. iii. 2. For mark, I beseech you, there are two things that provoke to prayer: the one is a detestation of sin and the vain things of this life; the other is a longing desire after communion with God, in a holy and undefiled state and inheritance. Compare but this one thing with most of the prayers that are made by men, and you shall find them but mock prayers, and the breathings of an abominable spirit; for even the most of men either do not pray at all, or else only endeavor to mock God and the world by so doing. Do but compare their prayer and the course of their lives together, and you may easily see that the thing included in their prayer is the least looked after in their lives. O sad hypocrites!

CHAPTER IV.

APPLICATION OF THE SUBJECT.

THUS have I briefly showed you, 1. What prayer is; 2 What it is to pray with the Spirit; 3. What it is to pray with the Spirit and with the understanding also.

IV. I shall now speak a word or two of application; and so conclude with, 1. A word of information; 2. A word of encouragement; 3. A word of rebuke.

1. A word of INFORMATION.

For the first, to inform you; as prayer is the duty of every one of the children of God, and carried on by the Spirit of Christ in the soul; so every one that doth but offer to take upon him to pray to the Lord, had need to be very wary, and go about that work especially with the dread of God, as well as with hopes of the mercy of God through Jesus Christ.

Prayer is an ordinance of God, in which a man draws very near to God; and therefore it calleth for so much the more of the assistance of the grace of God, to help a soul to pray as becomes one that is in the presence of Him. It is a shame for a man to behave himself irreverently before a king, but a sin to do so before God. And as a king, if wise, is not pleased with an oration made up with unseemly words and gesture; so God takes no pleasure in the sacrifice of fools. Eccl. v. 1, 4. It is not long discourses, nor eloquent tongues, that are the things which are pleasing in the ears of the Lord; but it is a humble, broken, and contrite heart, that is sweet in the ears of the heavenly Majesty.

Therefore, for information, know that there are these five things that are obstructions to prayer, and even make void the requests of the creature:

1. When men regard iniquity in their hearts, at the time of their prayers before God. "If I regard iniquity in my heart, the Lord will not hear my prayer." Psalm lxvi. 18. When there is a secret love to that very thing which thou with thy dissembling lips dost ask for strength against. For this is the wickedness of man's heart, that it will even love, and hold fast, that which with the mouth it prays against: and of this sort are they that honor God with their mouth, but their heart is far from him." Ezek. xxxiii. 31. O how ugly would it be in our eyes, if we should see a beggar ask an alms, with an intention to throw it to the dogs! or, that should say with one breath, 'Pray, bestow that upon me;' and with the next, 'I beseech you give it me not!' And yet thus it is with this kind of persons: with their mouth they say, 'Thy will be done;' and with their heart nothing less. With their mouth they say, 'Hallowed be thy name;' and with their hearts and lives they delight to dishonor him all the day long. These be the prayers that become sin; (Psalm cix. 7;) and though they put them often, yet the Lord will never answer them. 2 Sam. xxii. 42.

2. When men pray for show, to be heard, and thought somebody in religion, and the like.

These prayers also fall short of God's approbation, and are never like to be answered, in reference to eternal life.

There are two sorts of men that pray to this end. 1. Your trencher-chaplains, that thrust themselves into great men's families, pretending the worship of God, when in truth the great business is their own bellies; and were notably painted out by Ahab's prophets, and also Nebuchadnezzar's, who, though they pretended great devotion, yet their lusts and their bellies were the great things aimed at by them, in all their pieces of devotion. 2. Them also that seek repute and applause for their eloquent terms, and seek more to tickle the ears and heads of their hearers, than any thing else. These be they that pray to be heard of men, and have all their reward already. Matt. vi. 5.

These persons are discovered thus: 1. They eye only their auditory in their expressions. 2. They look for commendation when they have done. 3. Their hearts either rise or fall according to their praise or enlargement. 4. The length of their prayer pleaseth them; and that it might be long, they will vainly repeat things over and over; they study for enlargements, but look not from what heart they come; they look for returns, but it is the windy applause of men. And therefore they love not to be in their chamber, but among company; and if at any time conscience thrusts them into their closet, yet hypocrisy will cause them to be heard in the streets; and when their mouths have done going, their prayers are ended; for they wait not to hearken what the Lord will say. Psalm lxxxv. 8.

3. A third sort of prayer that will not be accepted of God, is, when either they pray for wrong things; or if for right things, yet that the things prayed for might be spent upon their lusts, and laid out to wrong ends. Some have not, because they ask not, saith James; and others ask and have not, because they ask amiss, that they may consume it on their lusts. James iv. 2, 3. Ends contrary to God's will, is a great argument with God to frustrate the petitions presented before him. Hence it is that so many pray for this, and that, and yet receive it not. God answers them only with silence. They have their words for their labor; that is all.

Objection 1. 'But God hears some persons, though their hearts be not right with him, as he did Israel, in giving quails, though they spent them on their lusts.'

Answer. If he doth, it is in judgment, not in mercy. He gave them their desire indeed, but they had better have been without it; for he sent leanness into their souls. Woe be to that man that God answereth thus.

4. Another sort of prayers there are that are not answered; and those are such as are made by men, and presented to God in their own persons only, without their appearing in the Lord Jesus. For though God hath appointed prayer, and promised to hear the prayer of the creature, yet not the prayer of any creature that comes not in Christ. "If you ask any thing in my name," says Christ. "And whatsoever ye do in word or deed, do all in the name of the Lord Jesus." Col. iii. 17. Though you be ever so devout, zealous, earnest, and constant in prayer, yet it is in Christ only that you must be heard and accepted. But, alas! the most of men know not what it is to come to him in the name of our Lord Jesus, which is the reason they either live wicked, or pray wicked, and also die wicked. Or else, they seek to attain to nothing else but what a mere natural man may attain unto, as to be exact in word and deed betwixt man and man, and only with the righteousness of the law to appear before God.

5. The last thing that hindereth prayer, is, the form of it without the power. It is an easy thing for men to be very hot for such things as forms of prayer, as they are written in a book; but yet many are altogether forgetful to inquire with themselves, whether they have the spirit and power of prayer. These men are like a painted man, and their prayers like a false voice: they in person appear as hypocrites, and their prayers are an abomination. When they say they have been pouring out their souls to God, he saith, they have been howling like dogs. Hos. vii. 14.

When therefore thou intendest, or art minded to pray to the Lord of heaven and earth, consider these following particulars.

(1.) Consider seriously what thou wantest. Do not as many, who in their words only beat the air, and ask for such things as indeed they do not desire, nor see that they stand in need thereof.

(2.) When thou seest what thou wantest, keep to that, and take thou heed thou pray sensibly.

Objection. 'But I have a sense of nothing; then, by your argument, I must not pray at all.'

Answer. If thou findest thyself senseless in some sad measure, yet thou canst not complain of that senselessness, but by being sensible. There is a sense of senselessness. According to thy sense, then, that thou hast of the need of any thing, so pray, (Luke viii. 9;) and if thou art sensible of thy senselessness, pray the Lord to make thee sensible of whatever thou findest thy heart senseless of. This was the usual practice of the holy men of God. "Lord, make me to know my end." Psalm xxxix. 4. "Lord, open to us this parable," said the disciples. Luke viii. 9.

And to this is annexed the promise, "Call unto me, and I will answer thee, and show thee great and mighty things that thou knowest not," (Jer. xxxiii. 3,) that thou art not sensible of. But,

Take heed that thy heart go to God, as well as thy mouth: let not thy mouth go any further than thou strivest to draw thine heart along with it. David would lift his heart and soul to the Lord; and good reason; for so far as a man's mouth goeth not along with his heart, so far it is but lip labor, only; and though God calls for, and accepteth the calves of the lips, yet the lips without the heart argueth not only senselessness, but our being without sense of our senselessness; and therefore, if thou hast a mind to enlarge in prayer before God, see that it be with thy heart.

Take heed of *affecting* expressions, and so to please thyself with the use of them, that thou forget the life of prayer.

I shall conclude this use with a caution or two.

And the first is, Take heed you do not throw off prayer, through sudden persuasions that thou hast not the Spirit, neither prayest thereby. It is the great work of the devil, to do his best, or rather worst, against the best prayers. He will flatter your false dissembling hypocrites, and feed them with a thousand fancies of well-doing, when their very duties of prayer, and all others, stink in the nostrils of God; while he stands at a poor Joshua's hand to resist him, that is, to persuade him, that neither his person nor performances are accepted of God. Take heed, therefore, of such false conclusions and groundless discouragements; and though such persuasions do come in upon thy spirit, be so far from being discouraged by them, that thou use them to put thee upon further sincerity and restlessness of spirit, in thy approaching to God.

Secondly, As such sudden temptations should not stop thee from prayer, and pouring out thy soul to God; so neither should thine own heart's corruptions hinder thee. It may be thou mayest find in thee all those evil things before mentioned, and that they will be endeavoring to put forth themselves in thy praying to him. Thy business then is, to judge them, to pray against them, and lay thyself so much the more at the foot of God, in a sense of thy own vileness, and rather make an argument from thy vileness and corruption of heart, to plead with God for justifying and sanctifying grace, than an argument of discouragement and despair. David went this way: "O Lord," saith he, "for thy name's sake, pardon mine iniquity; for it is great." Psalm xxv.

2. A word of ENCOURAGEMENT.

And therefore, I proceed to speak a word by way of encouragement, to the poor tempted and cast down soul, to pray to God through Christ. Though all prayer that is accepted of God in reference to eternal life must be in the Spirit, for that only maketh intercession for us according to the will of God; yet because many a poor soul may have the Holy Spirit working on them, and stirring them to groan to the Lord for mercy, though through unbelief they do not, and for the present cannot believe that they are the people of God, such as he delights in; yet forasmuch as the truth of grace may be in them, therefore, I shall, to encourage them, lay down further a few particulars.

That Scripture in Luke xi. 8, is very encouraging to any poor soul that doth hunger after Christ Jesus. In the 5th, 6th, and 7th verses, he speaketh a parable of a man that went to his friend to borrow three loaves, who, because he was in bed, denied him; yet for his importunity's sake, he did arise and give him; clearly signifying, that though poor souls, through the weakness of their faith, cannot see that they are the friends of God, yet they should never leave asking, and knocking at God's door for mercy. Mark, saith Christ, "I say unto you, though he will not arise and give him because he is his friend, yet because of his importunity," or restless desires, "he will arise and give him as many as he needeth." Poor heart! thou criest out that God will not regard thee—thou dost not find that thou art a friend to him, but rather an enemy in thine heart and by wicked works; and thou art as though thou didst hear the Lord saying to thee, 'Trouble me not, I cannot give unto thee;' as he in the parable: yet I say, continue knocking, crying, moaning, and bewailing thyself. I tell thee, though he will not arise and give thee, because thou art his friend; yet because of thy importunity, he will arise and give thee as many as thou needest. The same in effect you have discovered (Luke xviii.) in the parable of the unjust judge and the poor widow. Her importunity prevailed with him. And verily mine own experience tells me, that there is nothing that doth more prevail with God than importunity. Is it not so with you, in respect of your beggars that come to your door? Though you have no heart to give them any thing at their first asking, yet if they follow you, bemoaning themselves, and will take no nay without an alms, you will give them; for their continual begging overcometh you. Is there pity in you that are wicked, and will it be wrought upon by an importuning beggar? Go thou and do the like. It is a prevailing motive, and that by experience. He will arise and give thee as many as thou needest.

Another encouragement for a poor, trembling, convinced soul is, to consider the place, throne, or seat, on which the great God hath placed himself to hear the petitions and prayers of poor creatures; and that is a throne of grace, Heb. iv. 16,—the mercy-seat, Exod. xxv. 22; which signifieth, that in the days of the gospel God hath taken up his seat, his abiding place, in mercy and forgiveness; and from thence he doth intend to hear the sinner, and to commune with him, as he saith, Exod. xxv. 22, (speaking before of the mercy-seat,) "And there will I meet with thee." Mark, it is upon the mercy-seat: "There I will meet with thee, and I will commune with thee from above the mercy-seat." Poor souls! they are very apt to entertain strange thoughts of God, and his carriage towards them, and suddenly conclude, that God will have no regard unto them, when yet he is upon the mercy-seat, and hath taken up his place on purpose there, to the end he may hear and regard the prayers of poor creatures. If he had said, 'I will commune with thee from my throne of judgment,' then indeed, you might have trembled and fled from the face of the great and glorious Majesty; but when he saith he will hear and commune with souls upon the throne of grace, or from the mercy-seat, this should encourage thee, and cause thee to hope, nay, to come boldly unto the throne of grace, that thou mayest obtain mercy, and find grace to help in time of need. Heb. iv. 16.

There is yet another encouragement to continue in prayer with God; and that is this: As there is a mercy-seat, from whence God is willing to commune with poor sinners; so there is also by this mercy-seat, Jesus Christ, who continually besprinkleth it with his blood. Hence it is called "the blood of sprinkling." Heb. xii. 24. When the high priest under the law was to go into the holiest, where the mercy-seat was, he might not go in without blood. Heb. ix. 7.

Why so? Because, though God was upon the mercy-seat, yet he was perfectly just, as well as merciful. Now, the blood was to stop justice from running out upon the persons concerned in the intercession of the high priest, as in Lev. xvi. 13–16; to signify, that all thine unworthiness that thou fearest, should not hinder thee from coming to God in Christ for mercy. Thou criest out that thou art vile, and therefore, God will not regard thy prayer. It is true, if thou delight in thy vileness, and come to God out of a mere pretence. But if from a sense of thy vileness thou do pour out thy heart to God, desiring to be saved from the guilt, and cleansed from the filth, with all thy heart; fear not, thy vileness will not cause the Lord to stop his ear from hearing thee. The value of the blood of Christ, which is sprinkled upon the mercy-seat, stops the course of justice, and opens a floodgate for the mercy of the Lord to be extended unto thee. Thou hast therefore, as aforesaid, boldness to enter into the holiest by the blood of Jesus, that hath made a new and living way for thee: thou shalt not die. Heb. x. 19, 20.

Besides, Jesus is there, not only to sprinkle the mercy-seat with his blood, but he speaks, and his blood speaks; he hath audience, and his blood hath audience; insomuch that God saith, when he doth but see the blood, he will pass over you, and the plague shall not be upon you.

I shall not detain you any longer. Be sober and humble; go to the Father in the name of the Son, and tell him your case, by the assistance of the Spirit, and you will then feel the benefit of praying with the Spirit and the understanding also.

3. A word of REPROOF.

This speaks sadly to you who never pray at all.

"I will pray," saith the Apostle; and so saith the heart of them that are Christians. Thou then art not a Christian that art not a praying person. The promise is, that every one that is righteous shall pray. Psalm xxxii. 6. Thou then art a wicked wretch that prayest not. Jacob got the name of Israel by wrestling with God, Gen. xxxii.; and all his children bear that name with him. Gal. vi. 16. But the people that forget prayer, that call not on the name of the Lord, they have prayer made for them, but it is such as this, "Pour out thy fury upon the heathen, O Lord, and upon the people that call not upon thy name." Jer. x. 25. How likest thou this, O thou that art so far off from pouring out thine heart before God, that thou goest to bed like a dog, and risest like a hog, or a sot, and forgettest to call upon him? What wilt thou do when thou shalt be damned in hell, because thou couldst not find in thine heart to ask for heaven? Who will grieve for thy sorrow, that didst not count mercy worth asking for? I tell thee, the ravens, the dogs, &c. shall rise up in judgment against thee; for they will, according to their kind, make signs and a noise, for something to refresh them when they want it; but thou hast not the heart to ask for heaven, though thou must eternally perish in hell, if thou hast it not.

This rebukes you that make it your business to slight, mock at, and undervalue the Spirit, and praying by that. What will you do, when God shall come to reckon for these things? You count it high treason to speak but a word against the king, nay, you tremble at the thoughts of it; and yet in the meantime you will blaspheme the Spirit of the Lord. Is God, indeed, to be dallied with, and will the end be pleasant unto you? Did God send his Holy Spirit into the hearts of his people, to that end that you should taunt at it? Is this to serve God? and doth this demonstrate the reformation of your church? nay, is it not the mark of implacable reprobates? O fearful! Can you not be content to be damned for your sins against the law, but must you sin against the Holy Ghost?

Must the holy, harmless, and undefiled Spirit of grace, the nature of God, the promise of Christ, the Comforter of his children, that without which no man can do any service acceptable to the Father; must this, I say, be the burden of your song, to taunt, deride, and mock at? If God sent Korah and his company headlong to hell, for speaking against Moses and Aaron (Numb. xvi.); do you that mock at the Spirit of Christ, think to escape unpunished? Heb. x. 29. Did you never read what God did to Ananias and Sapphira, for telling but one lie against it? (Acts v. 1—9;) also to Simon Magus for but undervaluing it? Acts viii. 18, 22. And will thy sin be a virtue, or go unrewarded with vengeance, that makest it thy business to rage against, and oppose its office, service, and help, that it giveth to the children of God? It is a fearful thing to do despite unto the Spirit of grace. Compare Matt. xii. 31, with Mark iii. 29.

As this is the doom of those who do openly blaspheme the Holy Ghost, in a way of disdain and reproach to its office and service; so also it is sad for you, who resist this Spirit of prayer, by a form of man's inventing. A very juggle of the devil, that the traditions of men should be of better esteem, and more to be owned than the Spirit of prayer. What is this less than that accursed abomination of Jeroboam, which kept many from going to Jerusalem, the place and way of God's appointment to worship; and by that means brought such displeasure from God upon them, as to this day is not appeased? One would think that God's judgments of old upon the hypocrites of that day, should make them that have heard of such things, take heed and fear to do so. Yet the doctors of our day are so far from taking warning by the punishment of others, that they do most desperately rush into the same transgression, viz., to set up an institution of man, neither commanded nor commended of God; and whosoever will not obey herein, they must be driven either out of the land or the world.

Hath God required these things at your hands? If he hath, show us where? If not, (as I am sure he hath not,) then what presumption is it in any pope, bishop, or other, to command that in the worship of God which he hath not required? Nay, further, it is not that part only of the form, which is in several texts of Scripture, that we are commanded to say; but even all must be confessed as the divine worship of God, notwithstanding those absurdities contained therein; which because they are at large discovered by others, I omit the rehearsal of them. Again, though a man be willing to live ever so peaceably; yet because he cannot, for conscience sake, own that for one of the most eminent parts of God's worship, which he never commanded; therefore, must that man be looked upon as factious, seditious, erroneous, heretical, a disparagement to the church, a seducer of the people, and what not.

Lord, what will be the fruit of these things, when for the doctrine of God there is *imposed* (that is more than *taught*) the traditions of men! Thus is the Spirit of prayer disowned, and the form imposed; the Spirit debased, and the form extolled; they that pray with the Spirit, though ever so humble and holy, counted fanatics; and they that pray with the form, though with that only, counted the virtuous! And how will the favorers of such a practice answer that Scripture which commandeth that the church should turn away from such as have a form of godliness, and deny the power thereof? 2 Tim. iii. 5.

And if I should say, that men that do these things aforesaid, do advance a form of prayer of other men's making, above the Spirit of prayer, it would not take a long time to prove it; for he that advanceth the book of Common Prayer above the Spirit of prayer, doth advance a form of men's making above it. But this do all those who banish, or desire to banish, them that pray with the Spirit of prayer; while they hug and embrace them that pray by that form only, and that because they do it. Therefore, they love and advance the form of their own, or others inventing, before the Spirit of prayer, which is God's special and gracious appointment.

If you desire the clearing of the minor proposition, look into the jails in England, and into the alehouses; and, I trow, you will find those that plead for the Spirit of prayer in the jail, and them that look after the form of men's inventions only in the alehouse. It is evident also by the silencing of God's dear ministers, though ever so powerfully enabled by the Spirit of prayer, if they in conscience cannot admit of that form of Common Prayer. If this be not an exalting the Common Prayer Book above either praying by the Spirit, or preaching the word, I have taken my mark amiss.*

It is not pleasant for me to dwell on this. The Lord in mercy turn the hearts of the people to seek more after the Spirit of prayer; and in the strength of that to pour out their souls before the Lord. Only let me say, it is a sad sign that that which is one of the most eminent parts of the pretended worship of God is antichristian, when it hath nothing but the tradition of men, and the strength of persecution, to uphold or plead for it.

---

* Only the year before this was written, in consequence of the Act of Uniformity (1662), nearly two thousand of the best ministers in England had been silenced. Their only crime was a conscientious refusal to subscribe (*ex animo*) their "assent and consent to all and every thing contained in the Book of Common-Prayer." Now, be it remembered, that this Book contains not only Forms of Prayer, but the Offices of Baptism, Confirmation, Burial, and Ordination, which involve doctrines obnoxious to the consciences of a great part of Protestant Christendom to this day, even of those who have no objection to a liturgy. So objectionable were they then, that according to the careful computation of Jeremiah White, no less than sixty thousand persons in England alone, (not to mention Scotland,) chose to suffer all the penalties of the law rather than comply with them. No wonder that the soul of Bunyan was stirred within him at an imposition of human authority, which not only silenced a godly ministry, but crowded the common jails of England with myriads of her worthiest citizens, whose only crime "had this extent, no more." His remonstrance is the appeal of outraged humanity, the solemn cry of martyrdom!

"I am sorry to say," says Defoe, in speaking of the death of the celebrated Baptist, Thomas Delaune, author of the "Plea for Non-Conformists," "he is one of near eight thousand Protestant Dissenters, that *perished in prison* in the days of that *merciful* prince, King Charles II."—J. N. B.

I shall conclude this discourse with this word of advice to all God's people.

1. Believe that, as sure as you are in the way of God, you must meet with temptations.

2. The first day, therefore, that thou dost enter Christ's congregation, look for them.

3. When they do come, beg of God to carry thee through them.

4. Be jealous of thine own heart, that it deceive thee not in thy evidences for heaven, nor in thy walking with God in this world.

5. Take heed of the flatteries of false brethren.

6. Keep in the life and power of truth.

7. Look most at the things which are not seen.

8. Take heed of little sins.

9. Keep the promise warm upon thy heart.

10. Renew thy acts of faith in the blood of Christ.

11. Consider the work of thy regeneration.

12. Count to run with the foremost therein.

Grace be with you.

THE

SAINTS' PRIVILEGE AND PROFIT:

OR,

THE THRONE OF GRACE DISCOVERED.

THE

SAINT'S PRIVILEGE AND PROFIT.

CHAPTER I.

THE TEXT OPENED.

LET US, THEREFORE, COME BOLDLY UNTO THE THRONE OF GRACE, THAT WE MAY OBTAIN MERCY, AND FIND GRACE TO HELP IN TIME OF NEED.—Hebrews iv. 16.

THIS epistle is indited and left to the church by the Holy Ghost, to show particularly, and more distinctly, the high priesthood of Jesus Christ, and the excellent benefits that his people have thereby; in which both the excellency of his Person, and transcendent glory of his Office, beyond either priest or priesthood of the law, are largely set forth before us.

Wherefore, in order to our beneficial reading of this epistle, the Spirit of God calls upon us, first more seriously to consider what an one this excellent Person is. "Wherefore, holy brethren," saith he, "you that are partakers of the heavenly calling;" consequently you that are related to, and that are concerned in, the undertaking of this Holy One, "consider the Apostle and High Priest of our profession, Christ Jesus." chap. iii. 1. Consider how great, and how fit this man is, for so holy and glorious a calling. He being so high, as to be far above all heavens; so great, as to be the Son of God, and equal with the Father. Consider him also as to his humanity, how that he is really flesh of our flesh; sinlessly so; sympathizingly so; so in all the compassions of a man. He compassioneth, pitieth, loveth, succoureth us, is touched with, and feeleth our infirmities, and maketh our case his own. Nay, he again, from the consideration of his greatness and love, puts us upon a confident reliance on his undertaking, and also presseth us to a bold approach to that throne of grace, where he continually abideth in the execution of his office. "Seeing then," saith he, "that we have a great high priest that is passed into the heavens, Jesus the Son of God, let us hold fast our profession. For we have not an high priest which cannot be touched with a feeling of our infirmities; but was in all points tempted like as we are, yet without sin. Let us therefore, come boldly unto the throne of grace.

In the words we have, 1. An exhortation. 2. An implication that we shall reap a worthy benefit if we truly put the exhortation into practice.

The exhortation is, that we shall come boldly to the throne of grace: "Let us therefore, come boldly unto the throne of grace." In all, we have an intimation of five things.

I. That God hath more thrones than one. Else the throne of grace need not be specified by name. "Let us come unto the throne of grace."

II. That the godly can distinguish one throne from another. For the throne here is not set forth by where, or what signs it should be known; it is only propounded to us by its name, and so left for saints to make their approach unto it. "Let us come unto the throne of grace."

III. The third thing is, the persons intended by this exhortation. "Let *us* therefore come." "Us;" what "us?" or who are they that by this exhortation are called upon to come?

IV. The manner of coming of these persons to this throne of grace. And that is through the vail, "boldly," confidently. "Let us come boldly unto the throne of grace."

V. The motive to this exhortation; and that is two-fold, namely: 1. Because we have so great an high priest, that cannot but be touched with the feeling of our infirmities: "Let us therefore, come boldly unto the throne of grace." 2. And because we are sure to speed: "That we may obtain mercy, and find grace to help in time of need."

I shall, as God shall help me, handle these things in order.

I. For the first, GOD HATH MORE THRONES THAN ONE. He hath a throne in heaven, and a throne on earth. "The Lord's throne is in heaven," and "they shall call Jerusalem the throne of the Lord." He ruleth over the angels; he ruleth in his church. He sitteth in Jacob, and ruleth to the ends of the earth; yea, he has a throne and seat of majesty among the princes and great ones of the world. He ruleth, or judgeth among the gods. There is a throne for him as a Father, and a throne for Christ, as a giver of reward to all faithful and overcoming Christians. "To him that overcometh, I will grant to sit with me on my throne even as I also overcame, and am set down with my Father in his throne."

There is also to be a throne of judgment, on which God by Christ at the great and notable day shall sit, to give to the whole world their last, or final sentence; from which (no, not by any means) they shall never be released. This throne is made mention of in the New Testament; and is called by Christ the throne of his glory, and, a great white throne. And his presence, when he sits upon this throne, will be so terrible, that nothing shall be able to abide it, that is not reconciled to God by him before.

Wherefore, it is not amiss that I give you this hint, because it may tend to inform unwary Christians, when they go to God, that they address not themselves to him at rovers, or at random, but that when they come to him for benefits, they direct their prayer to the throne of grace, or to God as considered on a throne of grace. For he is not to be found a God merciful and gracious, but as he is on the throne of grace. This is his holy place, out of which he is terrible to the sons of men, and cannot be gracious unto them. For, as when he shall sit at the last day upon his throne of judgment, he will neither be moved with the tears or misery of the world to do any thing for them, that in the least will have a tendency to a relaxation of the least part of their sorrow, so now, let men take him where they will, or consider him as they list, he gives no grace, no special grace, but as considered on the throne of grace. Wherefore, they that will pray and speed, they must come to a throne of grace, to a God that sitteth on a throne of grace. "Let us therefore, come boldly unto the throne of grace, that we may obtain," &c.

The unbeliever, the erroneous, and superstitious consider not this: wherefore they speak to God, as their fancies lead them, not as the word directs them, and therefore, obtain nothing. Ask the carnal man, to whom he prays; he will say, To God. Ask him where this God is; he will say, In heaven. But ask him how, or under what notion he is to be considered there; and he will give a few generals, but cannot direct his soul unto him as he is upon a throne of grace, as the Apostle here biddeth, saying, "Let us come boldly unto the throne of grace." Wherefore, they come and go, or rather go and come to no advantage at all. They find nothing but their labor or words for their pains. For the right considering of God when I go unto him, and how or where I may find him gracious and merciful, is all in all; and mercy and grace are then obtained when we come to him as sitting upon a throne of grace.

CHAPTER II.

THE THRONE OF GRACE DISTINGUISHED.

II. WE will therefore come to the second thing, namely: That THE GODLY CAN DISTINGUISH ONE THRONE FROM ANOTHER. And the reason why I so conclude, is, as I said, because the throne here, is not set forth unto us here, by where, or what signs it should be known; it is only propounded to us by its name—a throne of grace—and so left for saints to make their approach thereto; "Let us, therefore, come boldly unto the throne of grace."

We will therefore take this conclusion into two parts, and consider it under this double position. 1. That there is a throne of grace. 2. That it is the privilege of the godly to distinguish from all other thrones whatever, this throne of grace.

1. There is a throne of GRACE. This must be true, because the text saith so. It is that of which the mercy-seat so often made mention of in the Old Testament was a type, shadow, or figure; nor are the terms of seat and throne, of any strength, to make this supposition void. For it is common for the antitype to be put forth in words unto us, more glorious than is the figure or shadow of that thing. And the reason is, that the heavenly things themselves are far more excellent than the shadow by which they are represented. What is a sheep, a bull, an ox, or calf, to Christ? or their blood to the blood of Christ? What is Jerusalem that stood in Canaan, to that New Jerusalem that shall come down from heaven? or the tabernacle made with corruptible things, to the body of Christ, or heaven itself? No marvel then if they be set forth unto us by words of an infe-

rior rank; the most full and aptest being reserved to set out the highest things withal.

Before I proceed to give you a more particular description of this throne of grace, as also how it may be known; I will a little touch upon the terms themselves, and show briefly what must be implied by them.

By this word, *grace,* we are to understand God's free, sovereign, good pleasure, whereby he acteth in Christ towards his people. Grace and mercy therefore, are terms that have their distinct significations. Mercy signifies pitifulness, or a running over of infinite love to objects in a miserable and helpless condition. But grace signifies that God still acts in this as a free agent; not being wrought upon by the misery of the creature, as a procuring cause, but of his own princely mind.

Were there no objects of pity among those that in the old world perished by the flood, or that in Sodom were burned with fire from heaven? Doubtless, according to our apprehension there were many. But Noah, and he only, found grace in God's eyes, not because that of himself he was better than the rest; but God acted as a gracious prince toward him, and let him share in mercy of his own sovereign will and pleasure. But this, at first, was not so fully made manifest as it was afterwards. Wherefore, the Propitiatory was not called as here, a throne of grace, but a mercy-seat, albeit there was great glory in those terms also; for, by mercy-seat, was showed, not only that God had compassion for men, but that also to be good, was as his continual resting-place, whither he would at length retire, and where he would sit down and abide, whatever terrible or troublesome work for his church was on the wheel at present. For a *seat* is a place of rest, yea, is prepared for that end; and in that here *mercy* is called that seat, it is to show, as I said, that whatever work is on the wheel in the world, let it be ever so dreadful and amazing, yet to God's church it shall end in mercy, for that is God's resting-place. Wherefore, after God had so severely threatened and punished his church under the name of a whorish woman, as you may read in the prophet Ezekiel, he saith, "So I will make my fury toward thee to rest, and my jealousy shall depart from thee, and I will be quiet, and will be no more angry." And again, speaking of the same people, and of the same punishments, he saith, "Nevertheless I will remember my covenant with thee in the days of thy youth, and I will establish unto thee an everlasting covenant." And again, "I will establish my covenant with thee; and thou shalt know that I am the Lord: that thou mayst remember, and be confounded, and never open thy mouth any more because of thy shame, when I am pacified towards thee for all that thou hast done, saith the Lord God." These with many more places show that mercy is God's place of rest, and thither he will retire at last, and from thence will bless his church, his people.

But yet these terms, "a throne," "the throne of grace," do more exceed in glory; not only because the word grace shows that God by all that he doth towards us in saving and forgiving, acts freely as the highest Lord, and of his own good will and pleasure; but also because he now saith, that his grace is become a King. A "throne of grace." A throne is not only a seat for rest, but a place of dignity and authority. This is known to all. Wherefore, by this word, a throne, or "the throne of grace," is intimated that God ruleth, and governeth by his grace. And this he can justly do. "Grace reigns, 'through righteousness,' unto eternal life, by Jesus Christ our Lord." So then, in that here is mention made of a "throne of grace," it showeth, that sin, and Satan, and death, and hell must needs be subdued. For these last mentioned are but weakness and destruction; but grace is life, and the absolute sovereign over all these, to the ruling of them utterly down: "a throne of grace."

By this, then, God plainly declareth that he is resolved this way to rule, and that he pointeth at sin as his deadly foe; and if so, then, where sin abounded, grace must much more abound. For it is the wisdom and discretion of all that rule, to fortify themselves against them that rebel against them, what they can. Wherefore, he saith again, "Sin shall not have dominion over you, for ye are not under the law, but under grace." Sin seeks for the dominion, and grace seeks for the dominion; but sin shall not rule, because it has no throne in the church among the godly. Grace is king, grace has the throne; and the people of God are not under the dominion of sin, but of the grace of God; the which they are implicitly bid to acknowledge, in that they are bid to come boldly to it for help: "That we may obtain mercy, and find grace to help;" to help, "in time of need." For as from the hand and power of the king come help and succor to the subject, when assaulted by an enemy; so from the throne of grace, or from grace as it reigns, come the help and health of God's people. Hence it is said again, "A glorious high throne from the beginning is the place of our sanctuary." Here, then, the saints take shelter from the roaring of the devil, from the raging of their lusts, and from the fury of the wicked. That also is a very notable place, "He will subdue our iniquities, and thou wilt cast all our sins into the depth of the sea." He speaks here as of God solacing himself in mercy, and as delighting himself in the salvation of his people, and that without comparison. "Who is a God like unto thee, that pardoneth iniquity, and passeth by the transgression of the remnant of his heritage. He retaineth not his anger for ever, because he delighteth in mercy." Thus are mercy and grace got into the throne—reign, and will assuredly conquer all; yea, will conquer, and that with a shout. Mercy rejoiceth against judgment; yea, glorieth when it getteth the victory of sin, and subdueth the sinner unto God and his own salvation; as is yet more fully showed in the parable of the prodigal son. But this briefly, to show you something of the nature of the terms, and what must necessarily be implied thereby.

We will in the next place show what is to be inferred from hence. And,

1. To be sure this is inferred, that converted men are not every way, or in every sense, free from the being of sin. For, were they, they need not betake themselves to a throne of grace for help. When it saith, there is grace in God, it inferreth, that there is sin in the godly; and when it saith, grace reigns, as upon a throne, it implies, that else sin would ascend the throne, would reign, and would have the dominion over the children of God. This also is manifest, when he saith, "Let not sin, therefore, reign in your mortal body, that ye should obey it in the lusts thereof." And the only way to prevent it is, to apply ourselves, as by the text we are directed, to the throne of grace for help against it.

2. The text implies, that at certain times the most godly man in the world may be hard put to it, by the sin that dwelleth in him; yea, so hard put to it, as that there can be no way to save himself from a fall, but by imploring heaven, and the throne of grace, for help. This is called the needy time, the time when the wayfaring man that knocked at David's door shall knock at ours; or when we are got into the sieve into which Satan did get Peter; or when those fists are about our ears which were about Paul's; and when that thorn pricks us that Paul said was in his flesh. But why, or how comes it to pass, that the godly are so hard put to it at these times, but because there is in them, that is, in their flesh, no good thing, but consequently all aptness to close in with the devil and his suggestions, to the overthrow of the soul?

But now here we are presented with a throne of grace, unto which, as David says, we must continually resort; and that is the way to obtain relief, and to find help in time of need.

3. As Christians are sometimes in imminent danger of falling, so sometimes it is so, that they are fallen, are down,—down dreadfully, and can by no means lift up themselves. And this happeneth unto them because they have been remiss, as to the conscientious performance of what by this exhortation they are enjoined to. They have not been constant supplicants at this throne, for preserving grace; for had they, they should, as the text suggests, most certainly have been kept from such a fall; help should have been granted them in their needful time. But that is it of which such are guilty, which is written in the prophet Isaiah: "But thou hast not called upon me, O Jacob; but thou hast been weary of me, O Israel. Therefore, thou art profaned; therefore, thou art given to reproaches."

Now, as they which are falling are kept from coming down, by coming to this throne of grace; so those that are fallen must rise by the sceptre of love extended to them from thence. Men may fall by sin, but cannot raise up themselves without the help of grace.

Wherefore, it is worthy of our inquiry after a more thorough knowledge of this throne of grace, whence, as we may well perceive, our help comes, and by what comes from thence we are made to stand.

I therefore, come now to a more particular description of this throne of grace; and to show how the godly know, or may know it, from other thrones of God.

First, then, This throne of grace is the humanity, or heart and soul of Jesus Christ, in which God sits and resteth for ever, in love towards them that believe in him; forasmuch as Christ did by the body of his flesh, when here, reconcile them unto the Father. "The key of David," saith God, "will I lay upon his shoulder: so he shall open and none shall shut; and he shall shut and none shall open. And I will fasten him as a nail in a sure place; and he shall be for a glorious throne to his Father's house." "For a glorious throne to his Father's house;" that is, for his Father's family, to come to their Father by; for they shall always find him thereon; or, as another Scripture saith, "in him, reconciling them unto himself, not imputing to them their trespasses."

Nor is it possible, if we lay aside the human nature of Christ, for us to find any such thing as a throne of grace, either in earth or heaven; for then nothing can be found to be the rest of God. "This is my well beloved Son in whom I am well pleased," is God's own language; but there is none other of whom he hath so said. Wherefore he resteth in him towards us, and in him only. Besides, grace cannot be extended towards us but in a way of justice; for the law and our sin obstruct another way. Lay the human nature of Christ aside, and where will you find that which shall become such a sacrifice to justice for the sin of men, as that God, for the sake of that, shall both forgive and cause that grace for ever should reign towards us in such a way? It reigns through righteousness, or justice, by Jesus Chrst, and no way else. Christ Jesus, therefore, is this throne of grace, or him, or that, by which grace reigns towards the children of God.

That Scripture also gives us a little light herein: "And I beheld, and lo! in the midst of the throne, stood a Lamb, as it had been slain." This is to show the cause why grace is so freely let out to us, even that there stands there in the midst of the throne, and in the midst of the elders, a Lamb, as it had been slain, or, as it was made a sacrifice for our sin; for, as a Lamb slain once, he now lives in the midst of the throne, and is the meritorious cause of all the grace that we enjoy. And though it seems by this text, that the throne is one thing, and the Lamb another, yet the

Lamb of God is the throne, though not as a lamb or sacrifice, but as one that by his sacrifice has made way for grace to run like a river into the world. The Son of God, Jesus Christ, is all. He is the throne, the altar, the priest, the sacrifice, and all. But he is the throne, the priest, the altar, and the sacrifice, under diverse considerations. He is not the throne as he is the priest; he is not the priest as he is the sacrifice; he is not the sacrifice as he is the altar; yet is truly all these. Yea, there is no throne of grace, no high priest, no propitiatory sacrifice, but he. Of all which we may yet speak further, before we conclude this treatise.

I conclude, then, that Christ Jesus, in his human nature is this throne of grace. In his human nature, I say; he has by that completely accomplished all things necessary for the making way for grace to be extended to men; and that which is not only God's place of rest, but that by, and from which, as upon a glorious throne, his grace shall reign over devil, death, sin, hell, and the grave, for ever.

This human nature of Christ is also called the tabernacle of God; for the fulness of the Godhead dwells in it bodily. It is God's habitation, and his dwelling place, his chair and throne of state. He doth all in, and by it, and without it he doth not any thing. But to pass this, let us come to the next thing.

Secondly, We will now discourse of the placing of this throne of grace, that we may discover where it is erected. And for this we must repair to the type, which, as was said before, is called the mercy-seat; the which we find, not in the outward court, nor yet within the first vail; which signifies, not in the world, nor in the church on earth, but in the holy of holies, or after the second vail, signifying the flesh of Christ. There, then, is this throne of God, this throne of grace, and no where here below. And forasmuch as it is called the throne of God, of grace, and is there; it signifieth that it is the highest and most honorable. Hence

Christ is said to be "far above all heavens, and to have a name above every name."

Wherefore, he that will come to this throne of grace, must know what manner of coming it is by which he must approach it; and that is, not personally, but by runnings out of heart; not by himself, but by his priest, his high priest; for so it was in the type. Into the holiest, where the mercy-seat was, went the high priest alone, that is, personally, and the people by him, had intercession made for them.

This, then, must be done by those that will approach to this throne of grace: they must go to God, as he is enthroned in Christ; by Christ, as he is the high priest of his church; and they must go to him in the holiest, by him.

But again, as this throne of grace is in the holiest, not in the world, not in the church on earth; so it is in this holiest set up above the ark of the testimony: for so was the mercy-seat. It was set up in the most holy place, above the ark of the testimony. The ark of the testimony! What was that? Why, it was the place of the law; the ark in which it was kept. The testimony was the law; the ark was prepared to put that in. This ark in which was put this law, was set up in the holiest, and the mercy-seat was set above it; for so was Moses commanded to place them. "Thou shalt make an ark," saith God, "and thou shalt make a mercy-seat: the ark shall be called the ark of the testimony, and there thou shalt put the testimony, which I give thee;" (that is, the law;) "and thou shalt put the mercy-seat above upon the ark, and there will I meet with thee, from above the mercy-seat, between the two cherubims which are upon," that is, above, "the ark of the testimony, shadowing the mercy-seat."

Thus, then, were things of old ordained in the type, by which we gather what is now to be minded in our worshipping of God. There was an ark made; and the two tables of stone, on which the law was writ, were put therein. This ark, with these two tables, were put into the holiest; and this mercy-seat was set above it. The Holy Ghost, in my mind, thus signifying that grace sits upon a throne; that is, higher than the law, above the law; and that grace, therefore, is to rule before the law, and notwithstanding all the sentence of the law; for it sitteth, I say, upon a throne, but the law sits on none; a throne, I say, which the law, instead of accusing, justifieth and approveth. For although it condemneth all men, yet it excepteth Christ, who in his manhood is this throne of grace. Him, I say, it condemneth not, but approveth, and liketh well his doings; yea, it granteth him, as here we see, as a throne of grace, to be exalted above itself; yea, it cannot but do so; because by wisdom and holiness itself, which is also the Lord of the law, it is appointed so to do. Here, then, is the throne of God, the throne of grace, namely, above the ark of the testimony. On this, God in his grace sits, reigns, and gives sinners leave to approach his presence for grace and mercy. He gives leave, I say, for those sinners so to do, that have washed before in the brazen laver that is prepared to wash in first; of which we may speak more anon.

Now, behold the wisdom of God in his thus ordaining things, in his placing, in the first place the law and Christ; the ark of the testimony, and the mercy-seat or throne of grace, so nigh together; for doubtless, it was wisdom that thus ordained them; and it might so ordain for these reasons: 1. That we that approach the throne of grace, might, when we come there, be made still to *remember that we are sinners;* (for by the law is the knowledge of sin;) and behold just before us is this ark, in which are the two tables that condemn all flesh: yea, we must look that way, if we look at all; for just above it is the mercy-seat or throne of grace. So, then, here is a memento for them that come to God, and to his throne of grace, for mercy, namely, the law, by which they are afresh put in remembrance of themselves, their sins, and what need they have of fresh supplies of grace. I read that the laver of brass and the foot of it, were made of the looking-glasses of the women that were assembled at the door of the tabernacle; methinks to signify, that all might see their own soilures when they came to wash: so here you see the law is placed with the mercy-seat, (only that stood above,) whereby those that come to the throne of grace for mercy, might also yet more be put in mind that they are sinners. 2. This also tendeth to *set an edge upon prayer*, and to make us the more fervent in spirit when we come to the throne of grace. Should a king ordain that the axe and halter should be before all those that supplicate him for mercy, it would put yet an edge upon all their petitions for his grace, and make them yet the more humbly and fervently implore his majesty for favour.

But, behold, the mercy-seat stands above! is set above the ark and testimony that is in it. Here, therefore, we have encouragement to look for good. For observe, though here is the law, and that too in the holiest of all, whither we go; yet above it is the mercy-seat or throne of grace triumphant, unto which we should look, and to which we should direct our prayers. Let us, therefore, come boldly to the throne of grace, notwithstanding the ark of testimony is by; for the law cannot hurt us when grace is so nigh; besides, God is now not in the law, but upon the throne of grace that is above it, to give forth pardons, and grace, and helps at a time of need.

This, then, may serve to inform some whereabout they are, when they are in their closets and at prayer. Art thou most dejected when thou art at prayer? Hear me: thou art not far from the throne of grace; for thy dejection proceedeth from thy looking into the ark, into which God hath ordained, that whosoever looks shall die. Now, if thou, indeed, art so near as to see thy sins, by thy reading of thyself by the tables in the ark, cast but up thine eyes a little higher, and behold, there is the mercy-seat and throne of grace, to which thou wouldst come, and by which thou must be saved. When David came to pray to God, he said he would direct his prayer to God, and would look up. As if he should say, When I pray, I will say to my prayers, 'O my prayers, mount up, stay not at the ark of the testimony, for there is the law and the condemnation; but soar aloft to the throne that stands above; for there is God, and there is grace displayed, and there thou mayst obtain what is necessary to help in time of need.'

Some, indeed, there be that know not what these things mean. They never read their sin nor condemnation for it, when they are upon their knees at their devotion; and so are neither dejected at the sight of what they are, nor driven with this sense of things to look higher for help at need; for need, indeed, they see none. Of such I shall say, they are not concerned in our text, nor can they come hither, before they have been prepared so to do, as may appear before we come to an end.

CHAPTER III.

HOW TO FIND THE THRONE OF GRACE.

AND thus have I showed you what this throne of grace is, and where it stands. And now I shall come to show you how you shall find it, and know when you are come to it, by several other things.

1. First, then, About the throne of grace, there is a rainbow in sight like unto an emerald. This was the first sight that John saw, after he had received his epistles for the seven churches. Before he received them, he had the great vision of his Lord, and heard him say to him, "I am he that was dead and am alive, or that liveth and was dead, and behold I am alive for evermore, and have the keys of hell and of death." And a good preparation it was for a work of that nature that now he was called unto; namely, that he might the more warmly, and affectionately, and confidently attest the truth, which his Lord had now for him to testify to them.

So here, before he entereth upon his prophecy of things to come, he hears a first voice, and sees a first sight. The first voice that he heard was, "Come up hither," and the first sight that he saw, was a throne with a rainbow round about it. "And immediately," saith he, "I was in the spirit: and, behold, a throne was set in heaven, and one sat upon the throne. And he that sat was to look upon like a jasper, and a sardine stone: and there was a rainbow round about the throne."

The first time that we find in God's word mention made of a rainbow, we read also of its spiritual signification, namely, that it was a token of the firmness of the covenant that God made with Noah, as touching his not drowning the earth any more with the waters of a flood. "I do set," saith he, "my bow in the cloud, and it shall be for a token of a covenant between me and the earth. And it shall come to pass, when I bring a cloud over the earth, that the bow shall be seen in the cloud: and I will remember my covenant which is between me and you and every living creature of all flesh; and the waters shall no more become a flood to destroy all flesh."

The first use, therefore, of the rainbow was to be a token of a covenant of mercy and kindness to the world; but that was not the utmost end thereof. For that covenant was but a shadow of the covenant of grace which God had made with his elect in Christ, and that bow but a shadow of the token of the permanency and lastingness of that covenant. Wherefore, the next time we read of the rainbow, is in the first of Ezekiel; and there we read of it only with reference to the excellencies of its color, for it is there said to be exactly like the color of the glory of the man that the prophet there saw as sitting upon a throne. The glory, that is, the priestly robes; for he is a Priest upon the throne, and his robes become his glory and beauty. His robes, what are they, but his blessed righteousness, with the skirts of which he covereth the sinful nakedness of his people, and with the perfection of which he decketh and adorneth them as a bride adorneth herself with jewels?

Now, here again, in the third place, we find a rainbow, a rainbow round about the throne—round about the throne of grace. A rainbow; that is, a token of the covenant, a token of the covenant of grace in its lastingness; and that token is the appearance of the man Christ. The appearance, that is of his robes, his righteousness, "from the appearance of his loins even upwards, and from the appearance of his loins even downwards," even "down to the foot," as you have it in the book of the Revelation. "As the appearance of the bow that is in the cloud in the day of rain, so was the appearance of the brightness round about. This was the appearance of the likeness of the glory of the Lord," &c.

The sum, then, is, that by the rainbow round about the throne of grace upon which God sitteth to hear and answer the petitions of his people, we are to understand the obediential righteousness of Jesus Christ, which in the days of his flesh he wrought out and accomplished for his people; by which God's justice is satisfied, and their persons justified, and they so made acceptable to him. This righteousness, that shines in God's eyes more glorious than the rainbow in the cloud doth in ours, saith John, is round about the throne. But for what purpose? Why, to be looked upon. But who must look upon it? Why, God and his people: the people when they come to pray, and God when he is about to hear and give. "And the bow shall be in the cloud," says God; and I will look upon it, that I may remember the everlasting covenant between God and every living creature of all flesh that is upon the earth."

And I say, as the bow is for God to look on, so it is also for our sight to behold. "A rainbow round about the throne, in sight"—In whose sight? In John's and his companion's,—"like unto an emerald."

We read of Solomon's great throne of ivory, that though there was not its like in any kingdom; yet he was not willing that the bow of it should stand before him. It was round behind. Oh! but God's throne has the bow before, even round about, to view, look upon—in sight. Solomon's was but a shadow, and therefore, fit to be put behind; but this is the sum and substance, and therefore, fit to be before, in view, in sight—for God and his people to behold.

Thus you see that a rainbow is round about the throne of grace, and what this rainbow is. Look, then, when thou goest to prayer, for the throne; and that thou mayst not be deceived with a fancy, look for the rainbow too. The rainbow; that is, as I have said, the personal performances of Christ thy Saviour for thee. Look, I say, for that; it is his righteousness; the token of the everlastingness of the covenant of grace; the object of God's delight, and must be the matter of the justification of thy person and performances before God. God looks at it; look thou at it, and at it only. For in heaven or earth, if that be cast away, there is nothing to be found that can please God, or justify thee. If it be said, Faith pleases God; I answer, Faith is a relative grace. Take, then, the relative away, which, as to justification, is this spangling robe, this rainbow, this righteousness of Christ; and faith dies, and becomes as to what we now treat of, extinct and quenched as tow.

And a very fit emblem the rainbow is of the righteousness of Christ; and that in these particulars:

The rainbow is an effect of the sun that shines in the firmament; and the righteousness by which this throne of grace is encompassed, is the work of the Son of God.

The rainbow was a token that the wrath of God, in sending the flood, was appeased: this righteousness of Christ is that, for the sake of which God forgiveth us all trespasses.

The rainbow was set in the cloud, that sinful man might look thereon, and wax confident in common mercy: this righteousness is showed us in the word, that we may by it believe unto special mercy.

The bow is seen but now and then in the cloud: Christ's righteousness is but here and there revealed in the word.

The bow is seen commonly upon, or after rain: Christ's righteousness is apprehended by faith, upon, or soon after, the apprehensions of wrath.

The bow is seen sometimes more, sometimes less; and so is this righteousness, even according to the degree of clearness of the sight of faith.

The bow is of that nature, as to make whatever you shall

look upon through it, to be of the same color as itself, whether that thing be bush, or beast, or man; and the righteousness of Christ is that which makes sinners, when God looks upon them through it, to look beautiful, and acceptable in his sight; for we are made comely through his comeliness, and made accepted in the beloved.

One word more of the rainbow, and then to some other things. As here you read that the rainbow is round about the throne; so if you read on even in the same place, you shall find the glorious effects thereof to be far more than all that I have said. But,

2. As the throne of grace is known by the rainbow that is round about it; so also thou shalt know it by this: The High Priest is continually ministering before it; the High Priest, or Christ as Priest, is there before God in his high priest's robes, making continual intercession for thy acceptance there.

Now, as I said before, Christ is priest, and throne, and all: throne in one sense, priest in another; even as he was priest, and sacrifice, and altar too, when he became our reconciler to God.

As a priest here, he is put under the notion of an angel that came and stood at the altar to offer incense for the church, all the time that the seven angels were to sound out with trumpets the alarum of God's wrath against the antichristian world; lest that wrath should swallow them up also.

"And," said John, "another angel came and stood at the altar having a golden censer; and there was given unto him much incense, that he should offer it with the prayers of all saints upon the golden altar which was before the throne And the smoke of the incense, which came with the prayers of the saints, ascended up before God out of the angel's hand."

Here, then, you have before the throne, that is the throne

or mercy-seat, the High Priest; for there it was that God appointed that the altar of incense, or that to burn incense on, should be placed. This incense-altar in the type, was to be overlaid with gold; but here the Holy Ghost implies, that it is all of gold. This throne, then, is the mercy-seat, or throne of grace, to which we are bid to come; and, as you see, here is the angel, the high priest with his golden censer, and his incense, ready to wait upon us: for so the text implies, for he is there to offer his incense with the prayers of all saints, that are waiting without, at his time of offering incense within. So, then, at the throne of grace, or before it, stands the High Priest of our propitiation, Christ Jesus, with his golden censer in his hand, full of incense, therewith to perfume the prayers of saints, that come thither for grace and mercy to help in time of need. And he stands there, as you see, under the name of an angel; for he is the angel of God's presence, and messenger of his covenant.

But now it is worth our considering, to take notice how, or in what method, the high priest under the law was to approach the incense-altar. When he came to make intercession for the saints before the throne, he was to go in thither to do this work in his robes and ornaments; not without them, lest he died. The principal of these ornaments were, a breast-plate, an ephod, a robe, an embroidered coat, a mitre, and a girdle. These are briefly called "his garments," (in Rev. i.) and in the general they show us, that he is clothed with righteousness, girded with truth and faithfulness, (for that is the girdle of his reins to strengthen him,) and that he beareth upon his heart the names of the children of Israel that are Israelites indeed: for as on Aaron's breast-plate was fixed the names of the twelve tribes of Israel, and he was to bear the weight of them by the strength of his shoulders, so are we on the heart of Christ.

Thus, therefore, is our High Priest within the holiest to

offer incense upon the golden altar of incense, that is before the throne. Wherefore, when thou goest thither, even to the throne of grace, look for him, and be not content, though thou should find God there, if thou findest not him, (I suppose now an impossibility, for edification's sake,) for without him nothing can be done; I say, without him as a priest. He is the throne, and without him as a throne, God has no resting place as to us; he is a priest, and without him as such, we can make no acceptable approach to God; for by him as priest, our spiritual sacrifices are accepted." "By him, therefore, let us offer the sacrifice of praise to God continually, (confessing to, and) giving thanks, in his name."

And for our further edification herein, let us consider, that as God has chosen and made him his throne of grace; so he has sworn, that he shall be accepted as a priest for ever there. For his natural qualifications, we may speak something of them afterwards: in the meantime know, that there is no coming to God, upon pain of death, without him.

Nor will it out of my mind, but that his wearing the rainbow upon his head, doth somewhat belong to him as priest; his priestly vestments, as afore was said, being for glory and beauty, compared to the color of it. But why doth he wear the rainbow upon his head, but to show that the sign of the everlastingness of the covenant of grace is only to be found in him; that he wears it as a mitre and frontlet of gold, and can always plead it with acceptance to God, for the subduing of the world and the good of his people. But,

3. The throne of grace is to be known by the sacrifice that is presented there. The high priest was not to go into the holiest, nor come near the mercy-seat—which, as I have showed you, was a type of our throne of grace—without blood. "But into the second went the high priest alone once every year, not without blood, which he offered for himself, and for the errors of the people." Yea, the priest

was to take of the blood of his sacrifice, and sprinkle it seven times before the Lord, that is, before the mercy-seat, or throne of grace; and was to put some of the blood upon the horns of the altar of incense before the Lord. So then the throne of grace is known by the blood that is sprinkled thereon, and by the atonement that by it is made there. I have told you, that before the throne of grace there is our high priest; and now I tell you, there is his sacrifice too; his sacrifice which he there presenteth as amends for the sins of all such as have a right to come with boldness to the throne of grace. Hence, as I mentioned before, there is said to be in the midst of the throne (the same throne of which we have spoken before,) a Lamb as it had been slain. The words are to the purpose, and signify that in the midst of the throne is our Sacrifice, with the very marks of his death upon him; showing to God that sitteth upon the throne, the holes of the thorns, of the nails, of the spear, and how he was disfigured with blows and blood, when at his command he gave himself a ransom for his people; for it cannot be imagined that either the exaltation or glorification of the body of Jesus Christ, should make him forget the day in which he died the death for our sins; especially since that which puts worth into his whole intercession is the death he died, and blood he shed upon the cross for our trespasses.

Besides, there is no sight more taketh the heart of God, than to see of the travail of the soul, and the bruisings of the body of his Son for our transgressions. Hence it is said he is in the midst of the throne as he died, or as he had been slain. It is said again, "The Lamb that is in the midst of the throne shall feed them." The Lamb, that is, the Son of God, as a sacrifice, shall be always in the midst of the throne to feed and comfort his people. He is the throne, he is the priest, he is the sacrifice. But, then, how as a Lamb is he in the midst of the throne? Why, the meaning in my opinion is, that Christ, as a dying and bleeding sacrifice, shall be the chief in the reconciling of us to God; or that his being offered for our sins shall be of great virtue when pleaded by him as a priest, to the obtaining of grace, mercy, and glory for us. By his blood he entereth into the holy place; by his blood he hath made an atonement for us before the mercy-seat; his blood it is that speaketh better for us than the blood of Abel did for Cain; also, it is by his blood that we have bold admittance into the holiest; wherefore, no marvel if you find him here a Lamb as it had been slain, and that in the midst of the throne of grace.

Whilst thou art, therefore, thinking on him, as he is in the throne of grace, forget him not as he is priest and sacrifice; for as a priest he makes atonement; but there is no atonement made for sin without a sacrifice. Now, as Christ is a sacrifice, so he is to be considered as passive, or a sufferer; as he is priest, so he is active, or one that hath offered up himself; as he is an altar, so he is to be considered as God: for in and upon the power of his Godhead he offered up himself. The altar, then, was not the cross, as some have foolishly imagined. But as a throne, a throne of grace; so he is to be considered as distinct from these three things, as I have hinted before.

Wouldst thou, then, know this throne of grace, where God sits to hear prayers and give grace? then cast the eyes of thy soul about, and look until thou findest the Lamb there; a Lamb there, as it had been slain: for by this thou shalt know that thou art right. A slain Lamb, or a Lamb as it had been slain, when it is seen by a supplicant in the midst of the throne, whither he is come for grace, is a blessed sight!—a blessed sight, indeed! And it informs him he is where he should be.

And thou must look for this the rather, because without blood is no remission. He that thinks to find grace at God's hand, and yet enters not into the holiest by the blood of Jesus, will find himself mistaken, and will find a dead instead of a living way. For if not any thing below, or besides blood, can yield remission on God's part; how should remission be received by us without our exercising faith therein? We are justified by his blood—through faith in his blood. Wherefore, I say, look when thou approachest the throne of grace, that thou give diligence to seek for the Lamb that is as it had been slain, in the midst of the throne of grace; and then thou wilt have not only a sign that thou presentest thy supplications to God, where, and as thou shouldst, but there also wilt thou meet with matter to break, to soften, to bend, to bow, and to make thy heart as thou wouldst have it. For if the blood of a goat will, as some say, dissolve an adamant, a stone that is harder than flint; shall not a sight of the Lamb as it had been slain, much more dissolve and melt down the spirit of that man that is upon his knees before the throne of grace for mercy; especially when he shall see, that not his prayers, nor his tears, nor his wants, but the blood of the Lamb, has prevailed with a God of grace, to give mercy and grace to an undeserving man. This, then, is the third sign by which thou shalt know when thou art at the throne of grace: that throne is sprinkled with blood; yea, in the midst of that throne there is to be seen to this day, a Lamb as it had been slain; and he is in the midst of it, to feed those that come to that throne, and to lead them by, and to, living fountains of water. Wherefore,

4. The throne of grace is to be known by the streams of grace that continually proceed therefrom, and that like a river run themselves out into the world. "And," saith John, "he showed me a pure river of water of life, clear as crystal, proceeding out of the throne of God and of the Lamb." Mark you, here is again a throne, the throne of God, which, as we have showed, is the human nature of his Son; out of which, as you read, proceeds a river, a river of

water of life, clear as crystal. And the joining of the Lamb also here with God, is to show that it comes, I say, from God, by the Lamb; by Christ, who as a lamb, or sacrifice for sin, is the procuring cause of the running of this river: it proceedeth out of the throne of God and of the Lamb. Behold, therefore, how carefully here the Lamb is brought in, as one from, or through, whom proceeds the water of life to us. God is the spring-head; Christ the golden pipe of conveyance; the elect, the receivers of this water of life. He saith not here, the throne of the Lamb, but, "and of the Lamb," to show, I say, that he it is, out of, or through whom, this river of grace should come. But if it should be understood that it proceedeth from the throne of the Lamb, it may be to show that Christ also has power as a mediator, to send grace like a river into the church; and then it amounts to this, that God, for Christ's sake, gives this river of grace, and that Christ for his merit's sake, has power to do so too. And hence is that good wish, so often mentioned in the epistles, "Grace to you, and peace from God the Father, and the Lord Jesus Christ." And again, "Grace be to you from God the Father, and from the Lord Jesus Christ." For Christ has power with the Father to give grace and forgiveness of sins to men. But let us come to the terms in this text. Here we have a throne, a throne of grace; and to show that this throne is it, indeed, therefore, there proceeds therefrom a river of this grace, put here under the term of "water of life;" a term fit to express both the nature of grace and the condition of him that comes for it to the throne of grace.

It is called by the name of "water of life," to show what a reviving cordial the grace of God in Christ is, shall be, and will be found to be, of all those that by him shall drink thereof. It shall be in him, even in him that drinks it, a well of water springing up unto everlasting life. It will therefore, beget life, and maintain it; yea, will itself be a spring of life, in the very heart of him that drinks it. Ah! it will be such a preservative also to spiritual health, as that by its virtue the soul shall for ever be kept—I say, the soul that drinks it—from total and final decay. It shall be in them a well of living water, springing up unto eternal life.

But there is also by this phrase, or term, briefly touched the present state of them that shall come hither to drink: they are not the healthful, but the sick. It is with the throne of grace as it is with the bath, and other places of sovereign and healing waters; they are most coveted of them that are diseased, and do also show their virtues on those that have their health and limbs: so, I say, is the throne of grace. Its waters are for healing, for soul-healing: that is their virtue. Wherefore, as at those waters above mentioned the lame leave their crutches, and the sick such signs of their recovery as may be a sign of their receiving health and cure there; so at the throne of grace it is where true penitents, and those that are sick for mercy, do leave their sighs and tears. "And the Lamb, which is in the midst of the throne, shall feed them, and shall lead them unto living fountains of waters; and God shall" (there) "wipe away all tears from their eyes." Wherefore, as Joseph washed his face, and dried his tears away, when he saw his brother Benjamin; so all God's saints shall here, even at the throne of grace, where God's Benjamin, or the Son of his right hand is, wash their souls from sorrow, and have their tears wiped from their eyes. Wherefore, O thou that art diseased, afflicted, and that wouldst live, come by Jesus to God as merciful and gracious; yea, look for this river when thou art upon thy knees before him, for by that thou shalt find whereabout is the throne of grace, and so where thou mayst find mercy.

But again. As that which proceeds out of this throne of grace is called water of life, so it is said to be a river, a "river of water of life." This, in the first place, shows, that with God is plenty of grace, even as in a river there is plenty of water. A pond, a pool, a cistern, will hold much, but a river will hold more. From this throne come rivers and streams of water of life, to satisfy those that come for life to the throne of God.

Further. As by a river is showed what abundance of grace proceeds from God through Christ; so it shows the unsatiable thirst and desire of one that comes indeed aright to the throne of grace for mercy. Nothing but rivers will satisfy such a soul. Ponds, pools, and cisterns, will do nothing. Such an one is like him of whom it is said, "Behold he drinketh up a river, and hasteth not: he trusteth that he can draw up Jordan into his mouth." This David testifies, when he saith: "As the hart panteth after the water brooks, so panteth my soul after thee, O God." Hence the invitation is proportionable: "Drink abundantly." Hence they that are saved, are said to receive abundance of grace: "They which receive abundance of grace, and of the gift of righteousness, shall reign in life by one, Jesus Christ." And hence it is said again, "When the poor and needy seek water, and there is none, and their tongue faileth for thirst, I the Lord will hear them, I the God of Israel will not forsake them." But, Lord, how wilt thou quench their boundless thirst? "I will open rivers in high places, and fountains in the midst of the valleys: I will make the wilderness a pool of water, and the dry land springs of water." Behold here is a pool of water as big as a wilderness; enough one would think to satisfy any thirsty soul. Oh, but that will not do; wherefore, he will open rivers, fountains, and springs; and all this to quench the drought of them that thirst for the grace of God, that they may have enough! "They shall be abundantly satisfied with the fatness of thy house, and thou shalt make them drink of the river of thy pleasures. For with thee is the fountain of life," &c.

This abundance the throne of grace yieldeth for the help and health of such as would have the water of life to drink, and to cure their diseases withal. It yields a river of water of life.

Moreover, since grace is said here to proceed as a river from the throne of God and of the Lamb, it is to show the commonness of it. Rivers you know are common in the stream, however they are at the head. And to show the commonness of it, the Apostle calls it "the common salvation;" and it is said in Ezekiel and Zechariah, to go forth to the desert, and into the sea, the world, to heal the beasts and fish of all kinds that are there. This, therefore, is a text that shows us what it is to come to a throne, where the token of the covenant of grace is, where the High Priest ministereth, and in the midst of which there is a Lamb as it had been slain: for from thence there come, not drops, nor showers, but rivers of the grace of God, a river of water of life!

Again, as the grace that we here read of, is said, as it comes from this throne, to come as a river of water of life; so it is said to be "pure," and "clear as crystal." Pure is set in opposition to muddy and dirty waters, and clear is set in opposition to those waters that are black, by reason of the cold and icyish nature of them. Therefore, there is conjoined to this phrase, the word crystal, which all know is clear and shining stone. Indeed, the life and spirit that is in this water, will keep it from looking black and dull; and the throne from whence it comes, will keep it from being muddy, so much as in the streams thereof. "The blessing of the Lord, it maketh rich, and he addeth no sorrow with it." Indeed, all the sorrow that is mixed with our Christianity, proceedeth as the procuring cause, from ourselves, not from the throne of grace; for that is the place where our tears, as was showed you, are wiped away; and also where we hang up our crutches. The streams thereof are pure and clear; not muddy nor frozen, but warm and delightful, and that make glad the city of God.

These words "pure" and "clear" also show us, that this water of itself can do, without a mixture of any thing of ours. What comes from this throne of grace is pure grace, and nothing else; clear grace, free grace; grace that is not mixed, nor need be mixed with works of righteousness that we have done. It is of itself sufficient to answer all our wants, to heal all our diseases, and to help us at a time of need.

It is grace that chooses, it is grace that calleth, it is grace that preserveth, and it is grace that brings to glory; even the grace that like a river of water of life proceedeth from this throne. And hence it is, that from first to last, we must cry, 'Grace, grace unto it!'

Thus you see what a throne the Christian is invited to. It is a throne of grace, whereon doth sit the God of all grace; it is a throne of grace before which the Lord Jesus ministereth continually for us; it is a throne of grace sprinkled with blood, and in the midst of which is a Lamb as it had been slain; it is a throne with a rainbow round about it, which is the token of the everlasting covenant; and out of which proceeds, as here you read, a river, a pure river of water of life, clear as crystal.

Look, then, for these signs of the throne of grace, all you that would come to it; and rest not, until by some of them you know that you are even come to it. They are all to be seen, have you but eyes; and the sight of them is very delectable, and has a natural tendency in them when seen, to revive and quicken the soul. But,

5. As the throne of grace is known and distinguished by the things above named, so it is by the effects which these things have wrought. There are about that throne four and twenty seats, and upon the seats four and twenty elders sit-

ting, clothed in white raiment; and they have on their heads crowns of gold.

There is no throne that has these signs and effects belonging to it but this; wherefore, as by these signs, so by the effects of them also, one may know which is, and so when he is indeed come to, the throne of grace.

And as we commented upon what went before, we will also a little, touch upon this.

By seats, I understand here places of rest and dignity; places of rest, for they that sit on them do rest from their labors; and places of dignity, for they are about the throne. "And the four and twenty elders, which sat before God on their seats, fell upon their faces, and worshipped God." And forasmuch as the seats are mentioned, before they are mentioned that sat thereon, it is to show, that the places were prepared before they were converted.

The elders, I take to be the twelve patriarchs and the twelve apostles, or the first fathers of the churches; for they are the elders of both the churches, that is, both the Jewish and Gentile church of God. They are the ancients, as also they are called in the prophet Isaiah, which are in some sense the fathers of both these churches. These elders are well set forth by that four and twenty that you read of in the book of Chronicles, who had every one of them for sons twelve in number. There, therefore, the four and twenty are.

Their sitting denoteth also their abiding in the presence of God. "Sit thou at my right hand," was the Father's words to his Son, and this signifieth the same.

It is then the throne of grace, where the four and twenty seats are, and before which the four and twenty elders sit.

Their white robes are Christ's righteousness, their own good works and glory. Not that their works brought them thither; for they were of themselves polluted, and were washed white in the blood of the Lamb: but yet God will have all that his people have done in love to him be rewarded; yea, and they shall wear their own labors, (being washed, as afore was hinted,) as a badge of their honor before the throne of grace, and this is grace, indeed. "They have washed their robes and made them white in the blood of the Lamb. Therefore, are they before the throne of God." They have washed as others did before them.

"And they had on their heads crowns of gold." This denotes their victory, and also that they are kings, and as kings shall reign with him for ever and ever.

But what! were they silent? Did they say, did they do nothing while they sat before the throne? Yes, they were appointed to be singers there. This was signified by the four and twenty that we made mention of before, who with their sons were instructed in the songs of the Lord; and all that were cunning to do so then, were two hundred fourscore and eight. These were the figure of that hundred forty and four thousand redeemed from the earth. For as the first four and twenty and their sons, are said to sing and to play upon cymbals, psalters, and harps; and as they are there said to be instructed and cunning in the songs of the Lord; so these that sit before the throne, are said also to sing with harps in their hands, their song before the throne; and such song it was, and so cunningly did they sing it, that no man could learn it, but that hundred forty and four thousand which were redeemed from the earth.

Now, as I said, as he at first began with four and twenty in David, and ended with four and twenty times twelve: so here in John, he begins with the same number, but ends with such a company that no man could number. For, he saith, "After this I beheld, and, lo, a great multitude which no man could number, of all nations, and kindreds, and people, and tongues, stood before the throne, and before the Lamb, clothed with white robes, and palms in their hands; and cried with a loud voice, saying, Salvation to our God, which sitteth upon the throne, and unto the Lamb. And all the angels stood round about the throne, and about the elders and the four beasts, and fell before the throne on their faces, and worshipped God."

This numberless number seem to have got the song by the end; for they cry aloud, "Salvation, salvation to our God and to the Lamb;" which to be sure is such a song that none can learn but them that are redeemed from the earth.

But I say, what a brave encouragement it is for one that is come for grace to the throne of grace, to see so great a number already there, on their seats, and in their robes, with their palms in their hands, and their crowns upon their heads, singing salvation to God, and to the Lamb!

And I say again, and speak now to the dejected, methinks it would be strange, O thou that art so afraid that the greatness of thy sins will be a bar unto thee, if amongst all this great number of pipers and harpers that are got to glory, thou canst not espy one that when here was as vile a sinner as thyself. Look, man! they are there for thee to view them, and for thee to take encouragement to hope, when thou shalt consider what grace and mercy have done for them. Look again, I say, now thou art upon thy knees, and see if some that are among them, have not done worse than thou hast done. And yet behold, *they* are set down; and yet behold they have their crowns on their heads, their harps in their hands, and sing aloud of salvation to their God, and to the Lamb!

This, then, is a fifth note or sign that doth distinguish the throne of grace from other thrones: There are before that to be seen, for our encouragement, a numberless number of people sitting, and singing round about it; singing, I say, to God for his grace, and the Lamb for his blood, by which they are secured from the wrath to come. "And the four and twenty elders fell down before the Lamb, having every one of them harps, and golden vials full of odors, which are the prayers of saints. And they sung a new song, saying, Thou art worthy to take the book, and to open the seals thereof: for thou wast slain, and hast redeemed us to God by thy blood, out of every kindred, and tongue, and people, and nation; and hast made us unto our God kings and priests: and we shall reign on the earth."

Behold, tempted soul, dost thou not yet see what a throne of grace here is, and what multitudes are already arrived thither, to give thanks unto his name that sits thereon, and to the Lamb for ever and ever? And wilt thou hang thy harp upon the willows, and go drooping up and down the world, as if there was no God, no grace, no throne of grace, to apply thyself unto, for mercy and grace to help in time of need? Hark! dost thou not hear them what they say? "Worthy," say they, "is the Lamb that was slain, to receive power, and riches, and wisdom, and strength, and honor, and glory, and blessing. And every creature which is in heaven," (where they are) "and on the earth," (where thou art) "and under the earth, and such as are in the sea, and all that are in them, heard I saying, Blessing, honor, glory, and power, be unto him that sitteth upon the throne, and unto the Lamb for ever and ever."

All this is written for our learning, that we through patience and comfort of the Scriptures might have hope; and that the drooping ones might come boldly to the throne of grace, to obtain mercy and grace to help in time of need.

They bless, they all bless; they thank, they all thank; and wilt thou hold thy tongue? They have all received of his fulness, and grace for grace; and will he shut thee out? Or is his grace so far gone, and so near spent, that now he has not enough to pardon, and secure, and save one sinner more? For shame! leave off this unbelief. Wherefore, (dost thou think,) art thou told all this, but to encourage thee to come to the throne of grace? and wilt thou hang back or be sullen, because thou art none of the first, since he hath said, "The first shall be last, and the last first?" Behold the legions, the thousands, the untold and numberless number that stand before the throne, and be bold to hope in his mercy.

6. As the throne of grace is distinguished from other thrones by these, so out of this throne proceed lightnings, and thunderings, and voices. Also, before this throne are seven lamps of fire burning, which are the seven spirits of God. This then is another thing by which the throne of grace may be known, as an effect of what is before. So again it is said, that from the altar of incense that stood before the throne, there were voices, and thunderings, and lightnings, and an earthquake. All these then come out of the holiest, where the throne is, and are inflamed by this throne, and by Him that sits thereon.

Lightnings here are to be taken for the illuminations of the Spirit in the gospel; as it is said in the book of Psalms, "They looked unto him," (on the throne,) "and were lightened." Or, as it is said in other places, "The voice of thy thunder was in the heavens: the lightnings lightened the world." And again, "His lightnings lightened the world: the earth saw it and trembled."

This lightning, therefore, communicates light to them that sit in darkness. "God," saith the apostle, "who commanded light to shine out of darkness, hath shined in our hearts, to give the light of the knowledge of the glory of God in the face of Jesus Christ." It was from this throne that the light came that struck Paul off his horse, when he went to destroy it, and the people that professed it. These are those lightnings by which sinners are made to see their sad condition, and by which they are made to see their way out of it. Art thou, then, made to see thy condition, how bad it is, and that the way out of it is by Jesus Christ? (for, as I said, he is the throne of grace.) Why then, come orderly in the light of these convictions to the throne from whence the light did come, and cry there, as Samuel did to Eli, "Here I am, for thou hast called me." Thus did Saul by the light that made him see; by it he came to Christ, and cried, "Who art thou, Lord?" and, "What wouldst thou have me to do?" And is it not an encouragement to thee to come to him, when he lights thy candle that thou mightest see the way; yea, when he doth it on purpose that thou mightest come to him? "He gives light to them that sit in darkness, and in the shadow of death." What to do? "To guide our feet in the way of peace."

This interpretation of this place seems to me most to cohere with what went before. For first you have here a throne, and one sitting on it; then you have the elders, and in them presented to you the whole church, sitting round about the throne; then you have, in the words last read unto you, a discourse how they came thither, and that is, by the lightnings, thunderings, and voices that proceed out of the throne.

As you have here lightnings, so thereto are adjoined thunders. There proceeded out of this throne lightnings and thunders. By thunders, I understand that powerful discovery of the majesty of God by the word of truth, which seizeth the heart with a reverential dread and awe of him: hence it is said, "The voice of the Lord is full of majesty. The voice of the Lord breaketh the cedars." The voice, that is, his thundering voice. "Canst thou thunder with a voice like him?" and, "The thunder of his power who can understand?" It was upon this account that Peter, and James, and John, were called the sons of thunder, because, in the word which they were to preach, there were to be not only lightnings but thunders; not only illuminations, but a great seizing of the heart with the dread and majesty of God, to the effectual turning of the sinner to him.

Lightnings without thunder are in this case dangerous, because they that receive the one without the other, are subject to miscarry. They were once enlightened, but you read of no thunder they had; and they were subject to fall into an irrecoverable state. Saul (of Tarsus) had thunder with his lightnings, to the shaking of his soul; so had the three thousand; so had the jailer. They that receive light without thunder are subject to turn the grace of God into wantonness; but they that know the terror of God will persuade men. So, then, when he decrees to give the rain of his grace to a man, he makes a way for the lightning and thunder; not the one without the other, but the one following the other. Lightning with thunder is made a cause of rain, but lightning alone is not. "Who hath divided a water-course for the overflowing of waters? or a way for the lightning of thunder? to cause it to rain on the earth, where no man is; on the wilderness wherein there is no man."

Thus, therefore, you may see how in the darkest sayings of the Holy Ghost there is as great a harmony with truth, as in the most plain and easy; there must be thunder with light, if thy heart be well poised and balanced with the fear of God. We have had great lightnings in this land of late years, but little thunder; and that is one reason why so little grace is found where light is, and why so many professors run on their heads in such a day as this is, notwithstanding all that they have seen.

Well, then, this also should be a help to a soul to come to the throne of grace. The God of glory has thundered, has thundered to awaken thee, as well as sent lightnings to give thee light; to awaken thee to a coming to him, as well as to the enabling of thee to see his things; this, then, has come from the throne of grace to make thee come hither: wherefore observe where it is, by these signs made mention of before, and by these effects, and go and come to the throne of grace.

As there proceed from this throne lightnings and thunders, so from hence it is said voices proceed also. Now these voices may be taken for such as are sent with this lightning and thunder to instruct, or for such as this lightning and thunder beget in our hearts.

It may be taken in the first sense; for light and dread, when it falleth from God into the soul, is attended with a voice or voices of instruction to the soul, to know what to do. Thus it was in Paul's case: he had light, and dread, and voices for his instruction; he had lightnings, and thunderings, and voices. "Good and upright is the Lord; therefore will he teach sinners in the way. The meek will he guide in judgment; and the meek will he teach his way."

Or, by voices you may understand such as the lightning and thunder beget in our hearts; for though man is mute as a fish to Godward, before this thunder and lightning come to him, yet after that he is full of voices. And how much more numerous are the voices, that in the whole church on earth are begot by these lightnings and thunders that proceed from the throne of grace. Their faith has a voice, their repentance has a voice, their subjection to God's word has a voice in it; yea, there is a voice in their prayers, a voice in their cry, a voice in their tears, a voice in their groans, in their roarings, in their bemoaning of themselves, and in their triumphs.

This, then, is an effect of the throne of grace; hence it is said, that they proceed from it, even the lightning, and the thunder, and the voices; that is, effectual conversion to God.

CHAPTER IV.

THE DISTINCTIVE PRIVILEGE OF THE GODLY.

THE next thing that I am to handle is, To show you, that it is the privilege of the godly to distinguish from all thrones whatsoever this throne of grace.

This, as I told you, I gathered from the Apostle in the text, for he only maketh mention of it, but gives no sign here to distinguish it by; no sign, I say, though he knew that there were more thrones than this. "Let us come boldly," saith he, "to the throne of grace;" and so leaves it, knowing full well that they had a good understanding of his meaning, being Hebrews—they being now also enlightened from what they were taught by the placing of the ark of the testimony and the mercy-seat in the most holy place; of which particulars the Apostle did then count it not of absolute necessity distinctly to discourse. Indeed, the Gentiles, as I have showed, have this throne of grace described and set forth before them, by those tokens which I have touched upon in the sheets that go before; for with the book of Revelations the Gentiles are particularly concerned, for it was writ to the churches of the Gentiles; also the great things prophesied of there, relate unto Gentile believers, and to the downfall of Antichrist, as he standeth among them.

But yet, I think that John's discourse of the things attending the throne of grace, was not by him so much propounded because the Gentiles were incapable of finding it without such description, as to show the answerableness of the antitype with the type; and also to strengthen their faith, and illustrate the thing; for they that know, may know more and better of what they know; yea, may be greatly comforted with another's dilating on what they know.

Besides, the Holy Ghost by the word, doth always give the most perfect description of things; wherefore to that we should have recourse for the completing of our knowledge. I mean not, by what I say, in the least to intimate as if this throne of grace was to be known without the text, for it is that that giveth revelation of Jesus Christ; but my meaning is, that a saint, as such, has such a working of things upon his heart, as makes him able by the word to find out this throne of grace, and to distinguish it to himself from others. For,

1. The saint has strong guilt of sin upon his conscience, especially at first; and this makes him better judge what grace, in its nature is, than others can that are not sensible of what guilt is. What it was to be saved, was better relished by the jailer when he was afraid of and trembled at the apprehensions of the wrath of God, than ever it was with him all his life before. Peter then also saw what saving was, when he began to sink into the sea: "Lord, save me," said he, "I perish." Sin is that, without a sense of which, a man is not apprehensive what grace is. Sin and grace, favor and wrath, death and life, hell and heaven, are opposites, and are set off or out, in their evil or good, shame or glory, one by another. What makes grace so good to us, as the sense of sin in its guilt and filth? What makes sin so horrible and damnable a thing in our eye, as when we see there is nothing can save us from it but the infinite grace of God?

Further, there seems, if I may so term it, to be a kind of natural instinct in the new creature to seek after the grace of God; for so saith the word, "They that are after the flesh, do mind the things of the flesh; and they that are after the Spirit, the things of the Spirit." The child by nature nuzzles in its mother's bosom for the breast; the child by grace does by grace seek to live by the grace of God. All creatures—the calf, the lamb, &c., so soon as they are born, will by nature look for, and turn themselves towards the teat. And the new creature doth so too. For guilt makes it hunger and thirst, as the hunted hart does pant after the water brooks. Hunger directs to bread, thirst to water; yea, it calls bread and water to mind. Let a man be doing other business, hunger will put him in mind of his cupboard, and thirst of his cruse of water; yea, it will call him, make him, force him, command him, to bethink what nourishing victuals is, and will also drive him to a search out after where he may find it, to the satisfying of himself. All right talk also to such an one sets the stomach and appetite a craving, yea, into a kind of running out of the body after this bread and water, that it might be fed, nourished, and filled therewith. Thus it is by nature, and thus it is by grace; thus it is for the bread that perisheth, and for that which endureth to everlasting life. But,

2. As nature, the new nature, teacheth this by a kind of heavenly natural instinct; so experience also herein helpeth the godly much: for they have found all other places, the throne of grace excepted, empty, and places or things that hold no water. They have been at Mount Sinai for help, but could find nothing there but fire and darkness, but thunder and lightning, but earthquake, and trembling, and a voice of killing words; which words, they that heard them once, could never endure to hear them again. And as for the sight of vengeance there revealed against sin, it was so terrible that Moses, even Moses, said, "I exceedingly fear and quake."

They have sought for grace by their own performances; but, alas! they have yielded them nothing but wind and confusion. Not a performance, not a duty, not an act in any part of religious worship, but they looking upon it in the glass of the Lord, do find it specked and defective.

They have sought for grace by their resolutions, their vows, their purposes, and the like; but, alas! they all do as the other, discover that they have been very imperfectly managed, and so such as can by no means help them to grace.

They have gone to their tears, their sorrow, and repentance, if perhaps, they might have found some help there; but all has either fled away like the early dew, or if they have stood, they have stunk even in the nostrils of those whose they were: how much more, then, in the nostrils of a holy God!

They have gone to God as the great Creator, and have beheld how wonderful his works have been; they have looked to the heavens above, to the earth beneath, and to all their ornaments; but neither have these, nor what is of them, yielded grace to those that had sensible want thereof.

Thus they have gone, as I said, with these pitchers to their fountains, and have returned empty and ashamed. They found no water, no river of water of life; they have been as the woman with her bloody issue, spending, and spending till they have spent all, and been nothing better, but rather grew worse.

Had they searched into nothing but the law, it had been sufficient to convince them that there was no grace, nor throne of grace, in the world. For since the law, being the most excellent of all the things of the earth, is found to be such as yieldeth no grace, (for grace and truth come by Jesus Christ, not by Moses,) how can it be imagined that it should be found in any thing inferior?

Paul, therefore, not finding it in the law, despairs to find it in any thing else below, but presently betakes himself to look for it there where he had not yet sought it, (for he some time sought it not by faith, but, as it were, by the works of the law;) he looked for it, I say, by Jesus Christ, who is the throne of grace, where he found it, and rejoiced in hope of the glory of God. But,

3. Saints come to know and distinguish the throne of grace from other thrones, by the very direction of God himself. As it is said of the well that the nobles digged in the wilderness, they digged it by the direction of the lawgiver; so saints find out the throne of grace by the direction of the grace-giver. Hence Paul prays that the Lord would direct the hearts of the people into the love of God. Man, as man, cannot aim directly at this throne, but will drop his prayers short, beside, or the like, if he be not helped by the Spirit. Hence the Son saith of himself, "No man can come to me, except the Father, which hath sent me, draw him;" which text doth not only justify what is now said, but insinuates that there is an unwillingness in man of himself to come to this throne of grace: he must be drawn there. "He setteth us in the way of his steps," that is, in that way to the throne, by which grace and mercy are conveyed unto us.

4. We know the throne of grace from other thrones, by the glory that it always appears in, when revealed to us of God. Its glory outbids all. There is no such glory to be seen any where else, either in heaven or earth. But I say, this comes by the sight that God gives, not by any excellency that there is in my natural understanding as such: my understanding and apprehension, simply as natural, is blind and foolish; wherefore, when I set to work in mine own spirit, and in the power of mine own abilities, to reach this throne of grace, and to perceive somewhat of the glory thereof, then am I dark, rude, foolish, I see nothing; and my heart

grows flat, dull, savorless, and lifeless, and has no warmth in the duty; but it mounts up with wings like an eagle when the throne is truly apprehended.

Therefore, that is another thing by which the Christian knows the throne of grace from all others: he meets with that good there that he can meet with no where else. But at present let these things suffice for this.

CHAPTER V.

THE GODLY SPECIALLY CALLED.

It follows, then, that if all these things are with thy soul, the operations of the throne of grace have been upon thee, to bring thee to the throne of grace; first in thy prayers, and then in thy person. And this leads me to the next thing propounded to be spoken to, which is to show who are the persons invited here to come to the throne of grace. "Let *us* therefore come."

III. Now THE PERSONS HERE CALLED UPON to come to the throne of grace, are not all or every sort of men, but the men that may properly be comprehended under these words "us" and "we;" "Let us, therefore, come boldly, that we may obtain." And they that are here put under these particular terms, are expressed both before and after, by those that have an explanation in them.

They are called in this epistle to the Hebrews, 1. Such as give the most earnest heed to the word which they have heard. 2. They are such as see Jesus crowned with glory and honor. 3. They are called the children. 4. They are called the seed of Abraham. 5. They are called Christ's brethren.

So, chap. iii. they are called holy brethren, and said to be partakers of the heavenly calling, and the people of whom it is said, that Christ Jesus is the Apostle and High Priest of their profession. They are called Christ's own house, and are said to be partakers of Christ. They are said to be the believers; those that do enter into the rest; those that have Christ for an high priest, and with the feeling of whose infirmities he is touched and sympathizeth. So, in chap. vi.

they are called beloved, and the heirs of promise—they that have fled for refuge to lay hold on the hope set before them; they are called those that have hope as an anchor, and those for whom Christ as a forerunner hath entered and taken possession of heaven. So, chap. vii. they are said to be such as draw nigh unto God. And, chap. viii. they are said to be such with whom the new covenant is made in Christ. Chap. ix. they are such for whom Christ has obtained eternal redemption, and such for whom he has entered the holy place. Chap. x. they are such as are said to be sanctified by the will of God; such as have boldness to enter into the holiest, by the blood of Jesus; such as draw near with a true heart, in full assurance of faith, (or that have liberty to do so,) having their hearts sprinkled from an evil conscience, and their bodies washed with pure water; they were those that had suffered much for Christ in the world, and that became companions of them that so were used. Yea, he tells them in the 11th chapter, that they and their patriarchs must be made perfect together. He also tells them, in the 12th chapter, that already they "are come to Mount Zion, to the city of the living God, the heavenly Jerusalem, and to an innumerable company of angels, to the general assembly and church of the first-born which are written in heaven, and to God the Judge of all, and to the spirits of just men made perfect, and to Jesus the Mediator of the New Testament, and to the blood of sprinkling, that speaketh better things than that of Abel."

Thus you see what terms, characters, titles and privileges they are invested with, that are here exhorted to come to the throne of grace. From whence we may conclude, that every one is not capable of coming thither; no, not every one that is under convictions, and that has a sense of the need of, and a desire after the mercy of God in Christ.

Wherefore we will come, in the next place, to show the orderly coming of a soul to the throne of grace for mercy;

and for this we must first apply ourselves to the Old Testament, where we have the shadow of what we now are about to enter upon the discourse of, and then we will come to the antitype, where yet the thing is far more explained.

1. First then, the mercy-seat was for the church, not for the world. For a Gentile could not go immediately from his natural state to the mercy-seat, by the high priest, but must first orderly join himself, or be joined to the church, which then consisted of the body of the Jews.

The stranger then must first be circumcised, and consequently profess faith in the Messiah to come; which was signified by his going from his circumcision directly to the passover, and so orderly to other privileges, specially to this of the mercy-seat, which the high priest was to go in to but once a year.

2. The church is again set forth unto us by Aaron and his sons. Aaron as the head, his sons as the members: but the sons of Aaron were not to meddle with any of the things of the holiest, until they had washed in a laver. "And the Lord spake unto Moses, saying, Thou shalt also make a laver of brass, and his foot also of brass, to wash withal: and thou shalt put it between the tabernacle of the congregation and the altar, and thou shalt put water therein. For Aaron and his sons shall wash their hands and their feet thereat. When they go into the tabernacle of the congregation, they shall wash with water, that they die not; or when they come near to the altar to minister, to burn offering made by fire unto the Lord. So they shall wash their hands and their feet, that they die not: and it shall be a statute forever to them, even to him and to his seed throughout their generations."

3. Nay, so strict was this law, that if any of Israel, as well as the stranger, were defiled by any dead thing, they were to wash before they partook of the holy things, or else still to abstain; but if they did not, their sin should remain upon them. So, again, "The soul that hath touched any

such uncleanness, shall be unclean till even, and shall not eat of the holy things, (much less come within the inner vail,) unless he wash his flesh in water."

Now, I would ask, what all this should signify, if a sinner, as a sinner, before he washes, or is washed, may immediately go unto the throne of grace?

Yea, I ask again, why the apostle supposes washing as a preparation to the Hebrews entering into the holiest, if men may go immediately from under convictions to a throne of grace? For thus he says, "Let us draw near the holiest," (ver. 19,) "with a true heart, in full assurance of faith, having our hearts sprinkled from an evil conscience, and our bodies washed with pure water." Let us draw near, he saith, not that we may have, but having first been washed and sprinkled.

The laver, then, must first be washed in; and he that washes not first there, has not right to come to the throne of grace. Wherefore, you have here also a sea of glass standing before the throne of grace, to signify this thing. It stands before the throne, for them to wash in that would indeed approach the throne of grace. For this sea of glass is the same that is shadowed forth by the laver made mention of before, and with the brazen sea that stood in Solomon's temple, whereat they were to wash before they went into the holiest. But you may ask me what the laver or molten sea should signify to us in the New Testament? I answer, It signifieth the word of the New Testament, which containeth the cleansing doctrine of remission of sins by the precious blood of Jesus Christ. Wherefore we are said to be clean through the word, through the washing of water by the word. The meaning then is, a man must first come to Christ, as set forth in the word, which is this sea of glass, before he can come to Christ in heaven, as he is the throne of grace. For the word, I say, is this sea of glass that stands before the throne, for the sinner to wash in first. Know, therefore, whoever thou art that art minded to be saved, thou must first begin with Christ crucified, and with the promise of remission of sins through his blood; which crucified Christ thou shalt not find in heaven as such, for there he is alive; but thou shalt find him in the word, for there he is to this day set forth in all the circumstances of his death, as crucified before our eyes. There thou shalt find that he died, when he died, what death he died, why he died, and the word open to thee to come and wash in his blood. The word, therefore, of Christ's Testament is the laver of all New Testament priests, (and every Christian is a priest to God,) to wash in.

Here, therefore, thou must receive thy justification, and that before thou goest one step further. For if thou art not justified by his blood, thou wilt not be saved by his life. And the justifying efficacy of his blood is left behind, and is here contained in the molten sea, or laver, or word of grace, for thee to wash in.

Indeed there is an interceding voice in his blood for us before the throne of grace, or mercy-seat; but that is still to bring us to wash, or for them that have washed therein, as it was shed upon the cross. We have boldness, therefore, to enter into the holiest by the blood of Jesus, that is, by faith in his blood, as shed without the gate; for as his blood was shed without the gate, so it sanctifies the believer, and makes him able to approach the holy of holies. Wherefore, after he had said, "That he might sanctify the people with his own blood, he suffered without the gate,"—"Let us by him therefore," that is, because we are first sanctified by faith in his blood, "offer to God the sacrifice of praise continually, that is, the fruit of our lips, giving thanks in his name." Wherefore the laver of regeneration, or Christ set forth by the word as crucified, is for all coming sinners to wash in, unto justification; and the throne of grace is to be approached by saints, or as sinners justified by faith in a crucified Christ, and so as washed from sin in the sea of his blood, to come to the mercy-seat.

And it is yet far more evident, that those that approach this throne of grace, must do it through believing; for, saith the apostle, How shall they call on him in whom they have not believed, of whom they have not heard?—for to that purpose runs the text. "How then shall they call on him in whom they have not believed?" (antecedent to their calling on him,) "and how shall they believe in him of whom they have not heard?" (first.) So then hearing goes before believing, and believing before calling upon God, as he sits upon the throne of grace. Now, believing is to be according to the sound of the beginning of the gospel, which presenteth us, not first with Christ as ascended; but as Christ dying, buried, and risen. "For I delivered unto you first of all that which I also received, how that Christ died for our sins according to the Scriptures; and that he was buried, and that he rose again the third day according to the Scriptures."

I conclude then, as to this, that the order of heaven is, that men wash in the laver of regeneration, namely, in the blood of Christ, as held forth in the word of the truth of the gospel, which is the ordinance of God: for there sinners, as sinners, or men as unclean, may wash in order to their approach to God as he sits upon the throne of grace.

And besides, is it possible that a man that passeth by the doctrine of Christ as dead, should be admitted with acceptance to a just and holy God for life? or he that slighteth and trampleth under foot the blood of Christ, as shed upon the cross, should be admitted to an interest in Christ, as he is the throne of grace? It cannot be. He must then wash there first, or die, let his profession or pretended faith, or holiness, be what it will. For God sees iniquity in all men; nor can all the nitre or soap in the world cause that our iniquity should not be marked before God; for without shedding of blood is no remission of sin.

Nothing that polluteth, that defileth, or that is unclean, must enter into God's sanctuary, much less into the most holy part thereof, but by their sacrifice by which they are purged, and for the sake of the perfection thereof they believing are accepted. We have, therefore, brethren, boldness to enter into the holiest by the blood of Jesus, and no way else.

CHAPTER VI.

THE MANNER OF APPROACHING THE THRONE.

IV. BUT this will yet be further manifest by what we have yet to say of THE MANNER OF OUR APPROACH unto the throne of grace.

1. First, then, we must approach the throne of grace by the second vail; for the throne of grace is after the second vail. So, then, though a man cometh into the tabernacle or temple, which was a figure of the church, yet if he entered but within the first vail, he only came where there was no mercy-seat or throne of grace.

And what is this second vail, in, at, or through which, as the phrase is, we must by blood enter into the holiest? Why, as to the law, the second vail did hang up between the holy and the most holy place, and it did hide what was within the holiest from the eyes or sight of those that went no further than into the first tabernacle. Now this second vail in the tabernacle or temple was a figure of the second vail that all those must go through that will approach the throne of grace. And that vail is the flesh of Christ.

This is that which the holy Apostle testifies in his exhortation, where he saith we have boldness to enter into the holiest by the blood of Jesus, by a new and living way which he hath consecrated for us through the vail, that is to say, his flesh. The second vail, then, is the flesh of Christ, the which until a man can enter or go through by his faith, it is impossible that he should come to the holiest, where the throne of grace is, that is, to the heart and soul of Jesus, which is the throne.

The body of Christ is the tabernacle of God, and so that

in which God dwells; for the fulness of the Godhead dwells in him bodily. Therefore, as also has been hinted before, Christ Jesus is the throne of grace. Now, since his flesh is called the vail, it is evident that the glory that dwells within him, namely, God resting in him, cannot be understood but by them that by faith can look through, or enter through his flesh to that glory. For the glory is within the vail; there is the mercy-seat, or the throne of grace: there sitteth God as delighted, as at rest in, and with sinners that come to him by and through that flesh, and the offering of it for sin without the gate. "I am the way," saith Christ. But to what? and how? Why, to the Father, through my flesh. "And having made peace through the blood of his cross, by him to reconcile all things to himself; by him, I say, whether they be things on earth, or things in heaven. And you, that were sometime alienated, and enemies in your minds by wicked works, yet now hath he reconciled." But how? "In the body of his flesh." That, then, must be first. To what? "To present you holy and unblamable, and unreprovable in his sight;" that is, when you enter into his presence, or approach by his flesh, the mercy-seat, or the throne of grace.

This, therefore, is the manner of your coming—if we come aright to the throne of grace for mercy. We must come by blood, through his flesh, as through the vail, by which, until you have entered through it, the glory of God, and that he is resolved that grace shall reign, will be utterly hid from your eyes.

I will not say but, by the notion of these things, men may have their whirling fancies, and may create to themselves wild notions and flattering imaginations of Christ, the throne of grace, and of glory; but the gospel knowledge of this is of absolute necessity to my right coming to the throne of grace for mercy. I must come by his blood, through his flesh, or I cannot come at all: for here is no back door

This, then, is the sum: Christ's body is the tabernacle, the holiest: "Thy law," saith he, "is within my heart." In this tabernacle, then, God sitteth, namely, on the heart of Christ, for that is the throne of grace. Through this tabernacle men must enter, that is, by a godly understanding of what by this tabernacle, or flesh of Christ, has been done to reconcile us to God that dwells in him. This is the way, all the way; for there is no way but this to come to the throne of grace. This is the *new* way into the heavenly paradise, (for the old way is hedged and ditched up by the flaming sword of cherubims,) the new and *living* way, (for to go the other, is present death;) so, then, this new and living way which he has consecrated for us through the vail, that is to say, his flesh, is the only way into the holiest, where the throne of grace is.

2. We must approach this throne of grace, as having our hearts first sprinkled from an evil conscience. The priest that was the representator of Israel, when he went into the holiest, was not to go in, but as sprinkled with blood, first. Thus it is written in the law: "Not without blood;" thus it is written in the gospel; and now since by the gospel we have all admittance to enter in through the vail, by faith, we must take heed that we enter not in without blood; for if the blood, (virtually,) be not seen upon us, we die, instead of obtaining mercy, and finding the help of grace.

This I press the oftener, because there is nothing to which we are more naturally inclined, than to forget this. Who, that understands himself, is not sensible how apt he is to forget to act faith in the blood of Jesus, and to get his conscience sprinkled with the virtue of that, when he attempteth to approach the throne of grace? Yet the Scripture calls upon us to take heed that we neglect not thus to prepare ourselves. "Let us draw near with a true heart, in full assurance of faith, having our heart sprinkled from an evil conscience," that is, with the blood of Christ, lest we die.

In the law all the people were to be sprinkled with blood, and it was necessary that the pattern of things in the heavens should be purified with these, (that is, with the blood of bulls,) but the heavenly things themselves with better sacrifices than these, that is, with the offering of the body and shedding of the blood of Christ. By this, then, must thou be purified and sprinkled, who by Christ wouldst approach the throne of grace.

3. Therefore, it is added, "and our bodies washed with pure water." This allusion the Apostle taketh also out of the law; where it was appointed, as was showed before. Christ also, just before he went to the Father, gave his disciples a signification of this, saying to Peter, and by him to all the rest. "If I wash thee not, thou hast no part with me." This pure water is nothing but the wholesome doctrine of the word mixed with Spirit, by which, as the conscience was before sprinkled with blood, the body and outward conversation is now sanctified and made clean. "Now ye are clean through the word," saith Christ, "which I have spoken unto you." Hence, washing, and sanctifying, and justifying, are put together, and are said to come by the name of our Lord Jesus Christ, and by the Spirit of our God. Thou must then be washed with water, and sprinkled with blood, if thou wouldst orderly approach the throne of grace: if thou wouldst orderly approach it with a true heart, in full assurance of faith; or if thou wouldst, as the text biddeth thee here, namely, "come boldly to the throne of grace, to obtain mercy, and find grace to help in time of need."

To tell you what it is to come boldly, is one thing; and to tell you *how* you should come boldly, is another. Here you are bid to come boldly, and are also showed how that may be done. It may be done through the blood of sprinkling, and through the sanctifying operations of the Spirit, which are here by faith to be received. And when what can be said shall be said to the utmost, there is no boldness, godly boldness, but by blood. The more the conscience is a stranger to the sprinkling of blood, the further off it is of being rightly bold with God, at the throne of grace; for it is the blood that makes the atonement, and that gives boldness to the soul. It is the blood, the power of it by faith upon the conscience, that drives away guilt, and so fear, and consequently that begetteth boldness. Wherefore, he that will be bold with God at the throne of grace, must first be well acquainted with the doctrine of the blood of Christ; namely, that it was shed, and why; and that it has made peace with God, and for whom. Yea, thou must be able by faith to bring thyself within the number of those that are made partakers of this reconciliation, before thou canst come boldly to the throne of grace.

There is a coming to the throne of grace *before*, or without, this boldness; but that is not the coming to which by these texts we are exhorted. Yet that coming, be it ever so deficient, if it is right, is through some measure of an inlet into the death and blood of Christ—and through some management, though but very little, or perhaps, scarce at all, discerned of the soul,—to hope for grace from the throne: I say, it must arise, the encouragement must, from the cross, and from Christ as dying there. Christ himself went that way to God, and it is not possible but we must go the same way too. So, then, the encouragement, be it little, be it much, (and it is little or much, even as the faith is in strength or weakness, which apprehendeth Christ,) it is according to the proportion of faith. Strong faith gives great boldness; weak faith doth not so, nor can it.

There is a *sincere* coming to the throne of grace without this boldness, even a coming in the uprightness of one's heart without it. Hence a true heart and full assurance are distinguished: "Let us draw near with a true heart, in full assurance of faith." Sincerity may be attended with a great deal of weakness, even as boldness may be attended with pride. But be it what kind of coming to the throne of grace it will, either a coming with boldness, or with that doubting which is incident to saints; still the cause of that coming, or ground thereof, is some knowledge of redemption by blood, redemption which the soul seeth it has faith in, or would see it has faith in: for Christ is precious, sometimes in the sight of the worth, sometimes in the sight of the want, and sometimes in the sight of the enjoyment of him.

There is an *earnest* coming to the throne of grace, even with all the desire of one's soul. When David had guilt and trouble, and that so heavy that he knew not what to do, yet he could say, "Lord, all my desire is before thee, and my groaning is not hid from thee." He could come earnestly to the throne of grace; he could come thither with all the desire of his soul: but still this must be from that knowledge that he had of the way of remission of sins by the blood of the Son of God.

There is also a *constant* coming to the throne of grace: "Lord," said Heman, "I have cried day and night before thee. Let my prayer come before thee: incline thine ear unto my cry; for my soul is full of troubles, and my life draweth nigh unto the grave"

Here you see his constant crying before the throne of grace—crying night and day; and yet the man that cries seems to be in a very black cloud, and to find hard work to bear up in his soul; yet this he had, namely, the knowledge of how God was the God of salvation; yea, he called him his God as such, though with pretty much difficulty of spirit, to be sure.

Wherefore, it must not be concluded that they come not at all to the throne of grace, that come not with a full assurance; or that men must forbear to come, till they come with assurance: but this I say, they come not at all aright, that take not the ground of their coming from the death and blood of Christ; and that they who come to the throne of grace, with but little knowledge of redemption by blood, will come with but little hope of obtaining grace and mercy to help in time of need.

I conclude, then, that it is the privilege, the duty, and glory of a man, to appproach the throne of grace as a prince, as Job said, could he but find it, he would be sure to do. "O that I knew where I might find him!" saith he, that I might come even to his seat! I would order my cause before him, and fill my mouth with arguments. I would know the words which he would answer me, and understand what he would say unto me. Will he plead against me with his great power? No; but he would put strength in me. There the righteous might dispute with him; so should I be delivered forever from my judge."

Indeed God sometimes tries us. He holdeth back sometimes the face of his throne and spreadeth a cloud upon it. And this seems to be Job's case here, which made him to confess he was at a loss, and to cry out, "O that I knew where I might find him!" And this God doth for trial, and to prove our honesty and constancy; for the hypocrite will not pray always. "Will he always call upon God?" No, verily, especially not when thou bindest them, afflictest them, and makest praying hard work to them.

But difficulty as to finding God's presence, and the sweet shining of the face of his throne, doth not always lie in the weakness of faith: strong faith may be in this perplexity, and may be hard put to it to stand at times. It is said here, that God did hold back the face of his throne, and did spread a cloud upon it; not to weaken Job's faith, but to try Job's strength, and to show to men of after ages how valiant a man Job was. Faith, if it be strong, will play the man in the dark, will, like a mettled horse, flounce in a bad way; will not be discouraged at trials—at many or strong trials.

"Though he slay me, yet will I trust in him," is the language of that invincible grace of God.

There is also an aptness in those that come to the throne of grace, to cast every degree of faith away that carries not in its bowels self-evidence of its own being and nature; thinking that if it be faith, it must be known to the soul; yea, if it be faith, it will do so and so, even so as the highest degrees of faith will do; when, alas! faith is sometimes in a calm, sometimes up, and sometimes down, and sometimes at it with sin, death, and the devil, as we say, blood up to the ears. Faith now has but little time to speak peace to the conscience; it is now struggling for life, it is now fighting with angels, with infernals! all it can do now, is to cry, groan, sweat, fear, fight, and gasp for life.

Indeed the soul should now run to the cross; for there is the water, or rather, the blood and water that is provided for faith, as to the maintaining of the comfort of justification. But the soul whose faith is thus attacked, will find hard work to do this, though much of the well-managing of faith, in the good fight of faith, will lie in the soul's hearty and constant adhering to the death and blood of Christ: but a man must do as he can.

Thus now have I showed you the manner of right coming to the throne of grace, for mercy and grace to help in time of need.

CHAPTER VII.

THE FIRST GREAT MOTIVE UNFOLDED.

V. I COME now to THE MOTIVES by which the apostle stirreth up the Hebrews, and encourageth them to come boldly to the throne of grace. 1. The first is, because we have there such an High Priest, or an high priest so and so qualified. 2. Because we that come thither for grace, are sure there to speed, or find grace and obtain it.

For the first of these, we have an encouragement to move us to come with boldness to the throne of grace, because we have a High Priest there; because we have such a high priest there. "For we have not a high priest who cannot be touched with the feeling of our infirmities, but was in all points tempted like as we are, yet without sin. Let us therefore, come boldly unto the throne of grace."

Of this High Priest I have already made mention before, that is, so far as to show you that Christ Jesus is he, as well as he is the altar, and sacrifice, and throne of grace before which he also himself makes intercession. But forasmuch as by the Apostle here, he is not only presented unto us as a throne of grace, but as high priest ministering before it, it will not be amiss, if I somewhat particularly treat of his priesthood also. But the main, or chief of my discourse will be to treat of his qualifications to his office, which I find to be in general of two sorts. First, Legal. Secondly, Natural.

When I say legal, I mean, as the apostle's expression is, not by the law of a carnal commandment, but by an eternal covenant, and the power of an endless life thereby; of which the priesthood of old was but a type, and the law of their priesthood but a shadow. But because their law and their entrance into their priesthood thereby was, as I said, a shadow of good things to come; therefore, where it will help to illustrate, we will make use thereof so to do; and where not, there we will let it pass.

The thing to be now spoken to is, That the consideration of Jesus Christ, as being an high priest before the throne of grace, is a motive and encouragement to us, to come boldly thither for grace. "Seeing then that we have a great high priest that is passed into the heavens, Jesus the Son of God, let us hold fast our profession," and "come boldly to the throne of grace."

Now, he was *made an high priest;* for so is the expression, "Made an high priest forever, after the order of Melchisedec."

First, He took not this honor upon himself, without *a lawful call* thereto. Thus the priests under the law were put into office; and thus the Son of God. "No man taketh this honor unto himself, but he that is called of God, as was Aaron. So also Christ glorified not himself to be made an high priest; but he that said unto him, Thou art my Son, to-day have I begotten thee." Wherefore he was called of God to be an high priest after the order of Melçhisedec. Thus far, therefore, the law of his priesthood answereth to the law of the priesthood of old: they both were made priests by a legal call to their work or office.

But yet the law by which this Son was made high priest excelleth, and that in these particulars:—

1. He was made a priest after the similitude of Melchisedec; for he testifieth, "Thou art a priest forever after the order of Melchisedec." Thus they under the law were not made priests, but after the order of Aaron; that is, by a carnal commandment, not by an everlasting covenant of God.

2. And, inasmuch as not without an oath he was made priest. "For those priests were made without an oath; but this with an oath, by him that said unto him, The Lord sware,

and will not repent, thou art a priest forever after the order of Melchisedec."

3. The priesthood under the law, with their law and sacrifices, were fading, and were not suffered to continue, by reason of the death of the priest, and ineffectualness of his offering. "But this man, because he continueth ever, hath an unchangeable priesthood. For the law maketh men high priests which have infirmity; but the word of the oath, which was since the law, maketh the Son (a priest,) who is consecrated for evermore."

From what hath already been said, we gather, 1. What kind of person it is that is our high priest. 2. The manner of his being called to, and stated in, that office.

1. What manner of person he is. He is the Son, the Son of God, Jesus the Son of God. Hence the apostle saith, "We have a great high priest," "Such an high priest" that is "passed into the heavens." Such an high priest as is "made higher than the heavens." And why doth he thus dilate upon the dignity of his person, but because thereby is insinuated the excellency of his sacrifice, and the prevalency of his intercession, by that, to God for us? Therefore, he saith again, "Every (Aaronic) priest standeth daily ministering, and offering oftentimes the same sacrifices which can never take away sin: but this man, (this great man, this Jesus, this Son of God,) after he had offered one (one only, one once, but one,) sacrifice for sins, sat down on the right hand of God; from henceforth expecting till his enemies be made his footstool. For by one offering he hath perfected forever them that are sanctified." Thus, I say, the apostle toucheth upon the greatness of his person, thereby to set forth the excellency of his sacrifice, and the prevalency of his intercession. "Wherefore, holy brethren, partakers of the heavenly calling, consider the Apostle and High Priest of our profession, Christ Jesus." Or, as he saith again, making mention of Melchisedec, "Consider how great this man was:"

we have "such an high priest," so great an high priest; one that is entered into the heavens—Jesus the Son of God.

2. The manner also of his being called to, and instated in his office, is not to be overlooked. He is made a priest *after the power of an endless life*, or is to be such an one as long as he lives, and as long as we need his mediation. "Now, Christ being raised from the dead, dieth no more; death hath no more dominion over him." He is himself the Prince of life. Wherefore it follows, he hath an unchangeable priesthood. And what then? Why, then "He is able to save them to the uttermost that come unto God by him, seeing he ever liveth to make intercession for them."

But again, he is made a priest *with an oath*. "The Lord sware, and will not repent, Thou art a priest forever." Hence I gather, 1. That before God there is no high priest but Jesus, nor ever shall be. 2. That God is to the full pleased with his high priesthood; and so with all those for whom he maketh intercession. For this priest, though he is not accepted for the sake of another, yet he is upon the account of another. "For every high priest, taken from among men, is ordained for men, in things pertaining to God, to make reconciliation for the sins of the people." And again, "He is entered into heaven itself, now to appear in the presence of God for us."

God, therefore, in that he hath made him a priest with an oath, and also determined that he will never repent of his so doing, declareth, that he is, and forever will be, satisfied with his offering. And this is a great encouragement to those that come to God by him; they have by this oath a firm ground to go upon, and the oath is, "Thou art a priest forever"—'shalt be accepted forever, for every one for whom thou makest intercession; nor will I ever reject any body that comes to me by thee.' Therefore, here is ground for faith, for hope, and rejoicing: for on this consideration, a man has ground to come boldly to the throne of grace.

Secondly. But again, as Christ is made a priest by call, and with an oath, and so, so far legally; so he, being thus called, has *other preparatory legal qualifications.* The high priest under the law was not by law to come into the holiest but in those robes that were ordained for him to minister in before God; which robes were not to be made according to the fancy of the people, but according to the commandment of Moses. Christ, our high priest in heaven, has also his holy garments, with which he covereth the nakedness of them that are his, which robe was not made of corruptible things, as silver and gold, &c., but by a patient continuance in a holy life, according to the law of Moses, both moral and ceremonial. Not that either of these was that eternal testament by which he was made a priest; but the moral law was to be satisfied, and the types of the ceremonial law to be, as on this, eminently fulfilled; and he was bound by that eternal covenant, by which he is made a mediator, to do so. Wherefore, before he could enter the holiest of all, he must have these holy garments made. Neither did he trust others, as in the case of Aaron, to make these garments for him, but he wrought them all himself, according to all that Moses commanded.

This garment, Christ was a great while a making. What time, you may ask, was required? And I answer, All the days of his life; for all things that were written concerning him, as to this, were not completed till the day that he hanged upon the cross. For then it was that he said, "It is finished;" and he bowed his head, and gave up the ghost.

This robe is "for glory and for beauty." This is it that afore I said was of the color of the rainbow, and that compasseth even round about this throne of grace, unto which we are bid to come. This is that garment that reaches down to his feet, and that is girt to him with a golden girdle. This is that garment that covereth all his body mystical, and that hideth the blemishes of such members from the eye of God, and of the law. And it is made up of his obedience to the law, by his complete perfect obedience thereto; this Christ wears always, he never puts it off, as the high priest put off his by a ceremonial command. He ever lives to make intercession; consequently he ever wears this priestly robe. He might not go into the holy place without it, upon danger of death, or at least of being sent back again. Yet *he* died not, but lives ever; is not sent back, but is set down at God's right hand; and there shall sit "till his foes are made his footstool."

This is that, for the sake of which all are made welcome, and embraced and kissed, forgiven and saved, that come unto God by him. This is that righteousness—that mantle spotless, that Paul so much desired to be found wrapt in; for he knew that being found in that, he must be presented thereby to God a glorious man, not having spot, or wrinkle, or any such thing. This, therefore, is another of tbe Lord Jesus' legal qualifications, as preparatory to the executing of his high priest's office in heaven. But of this something has been spoken before; and therefore I shall not enlarge upon it here.

Thirdly. When the high priest under the law was thus accomplished, by a legal call, and a garment suitable to his office, then again there was another thing that must be done, in order to his regular execution of his office; and that was, *he must be consecrated*, and solemnly ushered thereinto by certain offerings, first presented to God for himself.

This you have mention made of in the Levitical law. You have there first commanded, that, in order to the high priest's approaching the holiest for the people, there must first be an offering of consecration for himself, and this is to succeed his call, and the finishing of his holy garments. For this one ceremony was not to be observed until his garments were made and put upon him; also the blood of the ram of consecration was to be sprinkled upon him, his garments, &c., that he might be hallowed, and rightly set apart for the high priest's office. The Holy Ghost, I think, thus signifying that Jesus the Son of God, our great High Priest, was not only to sanctify the people with his blood; but first, by blood must to that work be sanctified himself. "For their sakes," saith he, "I sanctify myself, that they also may be sanctified through the truth."

But it may be asked, when was this done to Christ, or what sacrifice of consecration had he precedent to the offering up of himself for our sins?

I answer, it was done in the garden when he was washed in his own blood, when his sweat was as great drops of blood falling down to the ground. For there it was he was sprinkled with his blood, not only the tip of his ear, his thumb, and toe, but there he was washed all over; there, therefore, was his most solemn consecration to his office; at least, so I think. And this, as Aaron's was, was done by Moses: it was Moses that sprinkled Aaron, it was Moses that sprinkled Aaron's garments. It was by virtue of an agony, also, that Christ's bloody sweat was produced; and what was the cause of that agony, but the apprehension of the justice and curse of Moses' law, which now he was to undergo for the sins of the people.

With this sacrifice he then subjoined another, which was also preparatory to the great acts of his high priest's office, which he was afterwards to perform for us; and that was his drink-offering, his tears, which were offered to God with strong cries. For this was the place and time, that in a special manner he caused his strong wine to be poured out, and that he drank his tears as water. This is called his offering, his offering for his own acceptance with God. After he had offered up prayers and supplications, with strong crying and tears, unto him that was able to save him, he was heard for his piety, for his acceptance as to this office; for he merited his office as well as his people. Wherefore, it follows, "And being made perfect," that is, by a complete performance of all that was necessary for the orderly attaining of his office as high priest, "he became the author of eternal salvation unto all that obey him."

For your better understanding of me as to this, mind that I speak of a two-fold perfection in Christ; one as to his person, the other as to his performances. In the perfection of his person, two things are to be considered: First, the perfection of his humanity, as to the nature of it. It was at first appearing wholly without pollution of sin, and so completely perfect. But yet this humanity was to have joined to this another perfection; and that was a perfection of stature and age. Hence it is said that, as to his humanity, "he increased," that is, grew more perfect For this his increasing was, in order to a perfection, not of nature, simply as nature, but of stature. "Jesus increased in wisdom and stature." The Paschal Lamb was a lamb the first day it was yeaned; but it was not to be sacrificed until it attained such a perfection of age, as by the law of God was appointed to it. It was necessary, therefore, that Christ as to his person should be perfect in both these senses: and indeed "*in due time* Christ died for the ungodly."

Again, as there was a perfection of person, or of nature and personage in Christ, so there was to be a perfection of performances in him also. Hence it is said, that Jesus "increased in favor with God;" that is, by perfecting his obedience to him for us. Now, his performances were such as had a respect to his bringing in of righteousness for us in the general; or, such as respected preparations for his sacrifice as an high priest. But let them be applied to both, or to this and that in particular, it cannot be, that while the most part of his performances were wanting, he should be as perfect, as when he said, "The things concerning me have an end."

Not but that every act of his obedience was perfect, and carried in it a length and breadth proportionable to that law by which it was demanded; nor was there at any time in his obedience that which made one commandment to interfere with another. He did all things well, and so stood in the favor of God. But yet one act was not actually all, though virtually any one of his actions might carry in it a merit sufficient to satisfy and quiet the law. Hence, as I said, it is told us, not only that he is the Son of God's love, but that he increased in favor with God; that is, by a going on and doing, by a continuing to do, that always pleased the God of heaven.

A man that pays money at the day appointed, beginning first at one shilling, or one pound, and so ceaseth not until he hath in current coin told over the whole sum to the creditor, does well at the beginning; but the first shilling, or first pound not being the full debt, cannot be counted or reckoned the whole, but a part; yet is not an imperfect part, nor doth the creditor find fault at all, because there is but so much now told, but concludes that all is at hand, and accepteth of this first, as a first fruits. So Christ, when he came into the world, began to pay, and so continued to do, even until he had paid the whole debt, and so increased in favor with God.

There was, then, a gradual performance of duties, as to the number of them, by our Lord when he was in the world, and consequently a time wherein it might be said that Christ had not, as to act, done all that was appointed him to do—to do as preparatory to that great thing which he was to do for us. Wherefore, in conclusion, he is said to be made perfect: "And being made perfect, he became the author of eternal salvation unto all them that obey him."

Objection. It will be objected, then, that at some time it might be said of Christ, that he was imperfect in his obedience.

Answer. There was a time wherein it might have been said, Christ had not done all that he was to do for us on earth. But it doth not follow thereupon, that he therefore was imperfect in his obedience; for all his acts of obedience were done in their proper time, and when they should, according to the will of God. The timing of performances adds or diminishes as to the perfection of obedience, or the imperfection of it. Had the Jews killed the passover three days sooner than the time appointed, they had transgressed. Had the Jews done that on the fourth day to Jericho which was to have been done on the seventh day, they had sinned. Duty is beautiful in its time; and the Son of God observed the time. "I must," saith he, "work the works of him that sent me while it is day;" that is, in their seasons. You must keep in mind that we speak all this while of that part of Christ's perfection as to duties, which stood in the number of performances, and not in the nature or quality of acts. And I say as to the thing in hand, Christ had duties to do, (with respect to his office as High Priest, for us,) which immediately concerned himself; such duties as gave him a legal admittance unto the execution thereof; such duties, the which, had they not orderly been done, the want of them would have made him an undue approacher of the presence of God, as to that. Wherefore, as I said afore, by what he did thereabout, he consecrated, or sanctified himself for that work, according to God, and was accepted for his piety, or in that he feared, and did orderly do what he should do.

Fourthly. The next thing preparatory to the execution of this office of High Priest was *the sacrifice* itself. The sacrifice you know must, as to the being of it, needs precede the offering of it: it must be, before it can be offered. Nor could Christ have been a High Priest, had he not had a sacrifice to offer. "For every high priest is ordained to offer gifts and sacrifices: wherefore, it is of necessity that this man have also something to offer."

And I bring in the sacrifice as the last thing preparatory, not that it was last, as to being, for it was before he could be capable of doing any of the aforenamed duties, being his body, in and by which he did them; but it was the last as to fitness. It was not to be a sacrifice before the time, the time appointed of the Father; for since he had prepared it to that end, it was fit as to the time of its being offered, that that should be when God thought best also.

Behold, then, here is the High Priest with his sacrifice; and behold again, how he comes to offer it. He comes to offer his burnt-offering at the call of God. He comes to do it in his priestly garments, consecrated and sanctified in his own blood. He comes with blood and tears, or by water and blood, and offereth his sacrifice, himself a sacrifice to God for the sin of the world; and that too at a time when God began to grow weary of the service and sacrifice of the world. Wherefore, when he cometh into the world, he saith, "Sacrifice and offering thou wouldst not, but a body hast thou prepared me, (thou hast fitted me.) In burnt-offerings and sacrifices for sin thou hast had no pleasure: then said I, Lo, I come, (in the volume of thy book it is written of me,) to do thy will, O God."

Thus you see our High Priest proceeded to the execution of his priestly office. And now we are come to his sacrifice, we will consider a little the parts thereof, and how he offered, and pleads the same.

The burnt-offering for sin had two parts, the flesh and the fat, which fat is called the fat of the inwards, of the kidneys, and the like. Answerable to this, the sacrifice of Christ had two parts, the body and the soul. The body is the flesh, and his soul the fat; that inward part that must not by any means be kept from the fire. For without the burning of the fat, the burnt-offering, and sin-offering, both which were a figure of the sacrifice of our High Priest, were counted imperfect, and so not acceptable.

And it is observable, that in this kind of offerings when they were to be burned, the fat and the head must be laid, and be burned together. "And the priest shall cut it into pieces, with his head and fat; and the priest shall lay them in order on the wood, that is, on the fire which is upon the altar;" to signify, methinks, the feeling sense that this sacrifice of his body and soul should have of the curse of God due to sin, all the while that it suffered for sin. And therefore, it is from this that this sacrifice has the name of burnt-offering: "It is the burnt-offering, for the burning, because of the burning upon the altar all night until the morning, and the fire of the altar shall be burning in it."

The fat made the flame to increase and to ascend; wherefore God speaks of the fat, saying, "The fat of mine offerings." And again, of Christ, "He shall see of the travail of his soul, and be satisfied." The soul-groans, the soul-cries, the soul-conflicts that the Son of God had, together with his soul-submission to his Father's will, when he was made a sacrifice for sin, did doubtless flame bright, ascend high, and cast out a sweet savor unto the nostrils of God, whose justice was now appeasing for the sins of men.

His flesh also was a part of this sacrifice, and was made to feel that judgment of God for sin that it was capable of. And it was capable of feeling much, so long as natural life, and so bodily sense, remained. It also began to feel with the soul, by reason of the union that was betwixt them both. The soul felt, the body bled; the soul was in an agony, and the body sweat blood; the soul wrestled with the judgment and the curse of the law, and the body, to show its sympathy, sent out dolorous cries, and poured out rivers of tears before God. We will not here at large speak of the lashes, of the crown of thorns, or how his face was bluft with blows and blood; also how he was wounded, pierced, and what pains he felt while life lasted, as he suffered for our sins; though these things are also prefigured in the old law, by the nipping or wringing off the head, the cutting of the sacrifice in pieces, and burning it in the fire.

Now you must know, that as the high priest was to offer his sacrifice, so he was to bring the blood thereof to the mercy-seat or throne of grace, (where now our Jesus is); he was to offer it at the door of the tabernacle, and to carry the blood within the veil: of both which a little. 1. He was to offer it, and how? Not grudgingly, nor as by compulsion, but of a voluntary will and cheerful mind. "If his offering be a burnt sacrifice of the herd, let him offer a male without blemish; he shall offer it of his own voluntary will." Thus did Christ, when he offered up himself, as is manifest by that which follows. He offered himself, a male, without blemish. He gave himself a ransom; he gave his life a ransom. He laid down his life of himself. He longed for the day of his death, that he might die to redeem his people. Nor was he ever so joyful in all his life, that we read of, as when his sufferings drew near. Then he takes the sacrament of his body and blood into his own hands, and with thanksgiving bestows it among his disciples; then he sings a hymn, then he rejoices, then he comes with a "Lo, I come." Oh the heart, the great heart, that Jesus Christ had for us to do us good! He did it with all the desire of his soul.

2. He did it, not only voluntarily and of a free will, but of love and affection to the life of his enemies. Had he done thus for the life of his friends, it had been much; but since he did it out of love to the life of his enemies, that is much more. "Scarcely for a righteous man will one die; yet peradventure for a good man some would even dare to die. But God commended his love toward us, in that, while we were yet sinners, Christ died for us."

3. He did it without relinquishment of mind, when he was in. No discouragement disheartened him. Cry and bleed he did, yea, roar by reason of the troubles of his soul, but his mind was fixed. His Father sware and did not repent, that he should be his priest; and he vowed and said, he would

not repent, that he had threatened to be the plague and death of death.

4. He did it effectually and to purpose. He hath stopped the mouth of the law with blood; he hath so pacified justice, that it now can forgive; he hath carried sin away from before the face of God, and set us quit in his sight; he hath destroyed the devil, abolished death, and brought life and immortality to light through the gospel; he hath wrought such a change in the world by what he has done, for them that believe, that all things work together for their good, from thenceforward and forever.

I should now come to the second part of the office of this high priest, and speak to that; as also to those things that were preparatory to his executing it; but first, I think convenient to treat a little of the altar also, upon which this sacrifice was offered to God.

Some, I conceive, have thought the altar to be the cross on which the body of Christ was crucified, when he gave himself an offering for sin; but they are greatly deceived; for he also himself was the altar, through which he offered himself; and this is one of the treasures of wisdom which are hid in him, and of which the world and Antichrist are utterly ignorant. I touched this in one hint before, but now a little more express.

The altar is always greater than the gift; and since the gift was the body and soul of Christ—for so saith the Scripture, "He gave *himself* for our sins"—the altar must be something else than a sorry bit of wood, or than a cursed tree.

Wherefore, I will say to such, as one wiser than Solomon said to the Jews, when they superstitiated the gift, in counting it more honorable than the altar, "Ye fools, and blind! for whether is greater, the gift, or the altar that sanctifieth the gift?"

If the altar be greater than the gift, and yet the gift so great a thing as the very humanity of Christ; can it, (I will now direct my speech to the greatest fool,) can that greater thing be the cross? Is, or was the cross, the wooden cross, the cursed tree, that some worship, greater than the gift, that is, than the sacrifice which Christ offered, when he gave himself for our sins? O idolatry! O blasphemy!

Question. But what then was the altar?

Answer. The divine nature of Christ, that eternal Spirit, by and in the assistance of which, he offered himself without spot unto God. "He through the ETERNAL SPIRIT offered himself."

And it must be THAT, because, as was said, the altar is greater than the gift; but there is nothing but Christ's divine nature greater than his human;—to be sure a very sorry bit of wood, a tree, the stock of a tree, is not.

It must be this, because the Scripture says plainly, the altar sanctifies the gift; that is, puts worth and virtue in it. But was it the tree, or the Godhead of Christ, that put virtue and efficacy into this sacrifice that he offered to God for us? If thou canst but tell thy fingers, judge.

The altar was it of old that was to bear up the sacrifice until it was consumed; and with reference to the sacrifice under consideration, the tree could not bear up that; for our sacrifice being a man consisting of soul and body, that which could bear him up in his suffering condition, must be that which could apply itself to his reasonable and sensible part for relief and succor, and that was of power to keep him even in his spirit, and in a complete submissiveness to God, in the present condition in which he was; and could the tree do this, think you? Had the tree that command and government of the soul and sense of Christ, of the reason and feeling of the Lord Jesus, as to keep him in this bitter suffering—in that evenness and spotlessness in his torment, as to cause that he should come off this great work, without the least smell or tang of imperfection? No, no. It was through the ETERNAL SPIRIT that "he offered himself without spot unto God."

Question. Wherefore then served the cross?

Answer. I ask, and wherefore then served the wood by which the sacrifices were burned? The sacrifices were burned with wood upon the altar. The wood then was not the altar —the wood was that instrument by which the sacrifice was consumed; and the cross that by which Christ suffered his torment and affliction. The altar then was it that did bear the wood and sacrifice; that did uphold the wood to burn, and the sacrifice to abide the burning; and with reference to the matter in hand, the tree on which Christ was hanged, and the sacrifice of his body, were both upheld by his divine power. Yet the tree was no more a sacrifice, nor an altar, than was the wood upon the altar; nor was the wood, but the fire holy, by which the sacrifice was consumed. Let the tree then be the tree, the sacrifice the sacrifice, and the altar the altar; and let men have a care how, in their worship, they make altars upon which, as they pretend, they offer the body of Christ; and let them leave off foolishly to dote upon wood, and the works of their hands: the altar is greater than the gift or sacrifice, that was, or is upon it.

CHAPTER VIII.

THE FIRST GREAT MOTIVE CONTINUED.

We come now to the second part of the office of this High Priest, and to show how he performeth that. In order to which, I must, as I did with reference to the first, show you what things, as preparatory, were to precede the execution of it.

We have here, as you see, our Passover sacrificed for us, for our encouragement to come to the throne of grace; and now let us look to it, *as it is presented in the holiest of all*, and to the order of its being so presented.

First, then, before there was any thing further done, I mean, by this High Priest, as to a further application of his offering, the judgment of God was waited for by him, with respect to his estimation of what was already done, that is, how that was regarded by him; the which he declared to the full by raising him from the dead. For in that he was raised from the dead, when yet he died for our sins, it is evident that his offering was accepted, or esteemed of value sufficient to effect that for the which it was made a sacrifice, which was for our sins: this, therefore, was in order to his being admitted into heaven. God, by raising him from the dead, justified his death, and counted it sufficient for the saving of the world. And this Christ knew would be the effect of his death, long before he gave himself a ransom, where he saith, "This also shall please the Lord better than an ox or bullock, that has horns and hoofs." And again, "For the Lord God will help me; therefore I shall not be confounded: therefore I have set my face like a flint, and I know that I shall not be ashamed. He is near that justifieth me; who will contend with me? Let us stand together: who is mine adversary? let him come near me. Behold, the Lord God will help me, who is he that shall condemn me? Lo, they all shall wax old as a garment; the moth shall eat them up." All this is the work of the Lord God, his Father, and he had faith therein, as I said before. And since it was God who was to be appeased, it was requisite that he should be heard in the matter, namely, whether he was pacified or no; the which he has declared, I say, in raising him from the dead.

And this the Apostles, both Paul and Peter, insinuate, when they ascribe his resurrection to the power of another, rather than to his raising of himself, saying, "This Jesus hath God raised up;" "God hath raised him up from the dead;" "But God raised him up from the dead," and the like. I say, therefore, that God, by raising up Christ from the dead, hath said, that thus far his offering pleased him, and that he was content.

But lest the world, being besotted by sin, should not rightly interpret actions; therefore God added to his raising him up from the dead, a solemn exposing him to view, not to all men, but to such as were faithful, and that might be trusted with the communicating of it to others. "Him," saith Peter, "God raised from the dead, and showed him openly; not to all the people, but unto witnesses chosen before of God, even to us, who did eat and drink with him after he rose from the dead."

And this was requisite, not that it added any thing to the value and worth of his sacrifice; but for the help of the faith of them that were to have eternal salvation by him. And it is for this cause that Paul so enlargeth upon this very thing, that there were them that could testify, that God had raised him up from the dead, namely, that men might see that God was well pleased, and that they had encouragement to come boldly by him to the throne of grace for mercy. And this exposing him to view, was not for the length of a surprising or dazzling moment, but days and nights, to the number of no less than forty; and that to the self-same persons, namely, the Apostles whom he had chosen; "To whom also," says the text, "he showed himself alive after his passion by many infallible proofs, being seen of them forty days, and speaking of the things pertaining to the kingdom of God."

Thus God, therefore, being willing more abundantly to show him unto the world, ordered this great season betwixt his resurrection and ascension, that the world might see that they had ground to believe an atonement was made for sin.

But again, a third thing that was to precede the execution of the second part of his priestly office, was the manner and order of his going into the holiest; I say, the manner and order of his going. He was to go thither in that *robe*, of which mention was made before, that is, in the virtue of his obedience, for it was that which was to make his way for him, as now sprinkled with his blood. He was to go thither with a noise, which the Holy Ghost calls a shout, saying, "God is gone up with a shout, the Lord with the sound of a trumpet." This was prefigured by the bells, as I said, which did hang on the borders of Aaron's garments. This shout seems to signify the voice of men and angels, and this trumpet the voice and joy of God; for so it says, he shall descend. "For the Lord himself shall descend from heaven with a shout, with the voice of the archangel, and with the trump of God;" even as he ascended and went up; for Aaron's bells were to be heard when he went into, and when he came out of the holy place. But what men were to ascend with him, but, as was said before, the men that came out of their graves after his resurrection? and what angels, but those that ministered to him there in the day of his humiliation? As for the evil ones, he then rode in triumph over their heads, and crushed them as captives with his chariot wheels. "He is ascended on high, he has led captivity captive, he has received gifts for men."

Thus, then, he ascended unto, into, the holy paradise, where he was waited for of a multitude of the heavenly host, and of thousands of millions of the spirits of just men made perfect. So approaching the highest heavens, the place of the special presence of God, he was bid sit down at his right hand, in token that, for his sufferings' sake, God had made him the highest of every creature, and given him a name above every name, and commanded that at the name of Jesus now all things in heaven should bow, and promised that at the day of judgment all on earth, and under it, should bow too, to the glory of God the Father.

Thus he presented himself on our behalf unto God, a sacrifice of a sweet-smelling savor, in which God resteth forever; for the blood of this sacrifice has always with him a pleasing and prevailing voice. It cannot be denied; it cannot be outweighed by the heaviness, circumstances, or aggravations of any sin whatsoever, of them that come unto God by him. He is always, as I said before, in the midst of the throne, and before the throne, a Lamb as it had been slain, now appearing in the presence of God for us. Of the manner of his intercession, whether it is vocal or virtual, whether by voice of mouth, or merit of deed, or both, I will not determine. We know but little here, how things are done in heaven, and we may soon be too carnal, or fantastical in our apprehensions. Intercession he makes; that is, he manages the efficacy and worth of his suffering with God for us, and is always prevalent in his thus managing his merits on our behalf. And as to the manner, though it be in itself infinitely beyond what we can conceive while here; yet God hath stooped to our weakness, and so expressed himself in this matter, that we might somewhat, though but childishly, apprehend him. And we do not amiss, if we conceive as the word of God hath revealed; for the Scriptures are the green poplar, hazel, and the chesnut rods that lie in the gutters where we should come to drink; all the difficulty is, in seeing the white streaks, the very mind of God there, that we may conceive by it.

But the text says he prayeth in heaven, he makes intercession there. Again, it saith, his blood speaks; and consequently, why may not his groans, his tears, his sighs, and strong cries, which he uttered here in the days of his flesh? I believe they do, and have a strong voice with God for the salvation of his people. He may then intercede both vocally and virtually; virtually to be sure he does, and we are allowed so to apprehend, because the text suggesteth such a manner of intercession to us: and because our weakness will not admit us to understand fully the thing as it is, our belief that he makes intercession for us, has also the advantage of being purged from its filthiness by his intercession, and we shall be saved thereby, because we have relied upon his blood shed, and the prevalency of the worthiness of it with God for us; though as to this circumstance, the manner of his interceding, we should be something at a loss.

The word says, that we have yet but the image of heavenly things, or of things in the heavens. I do not at all doubt, but that many of those that were saved before Christ came in the flesh, though they were as to the main right, and relied upon him to the saving of their souls, yet came far short of the knowledge of many of the circumstances of his suffering for them. Did they all know that he was to be betrayed of Judas? that he was to be scourged of the soldiers? that he was to be crowned with thorns? that he was to be crucified between two thieves, and to be pierced till blood and water came out of his side? or that he was to be buried in Joseph's sepulchre? I say, did all that were saved by faith that he was to come and die for them, understand these, with many more circumstances that were attendants of him to death? It would be rude to think so; because for it we have neither Scripture nor reason.

Even so, we now that believe that he ever liveth to make intercession for us, are also very short of understanding the manner or mode of his so interceding. Yet we believe that he died, and that his merits have a voice with God for us; yea, that he manages his own merits before God in a way of intercession for us, far beyond what we, while here, are able to conceive.

The Scripture saith that all the fulness of the Godhead dwells in him bodily. It also saith that he is the mercy-seat, that is, the throne of God; and yet again, that he sits on the right hand of the throne.

These things are so far from being comprehended by the weakest, that they strain the wits and parts of the strongest; yet there is a heavenly truth in all. Heavenly things are not easily believed, no not of believers themselves, while here on earth; and when they are, they are so but weakly and infirmly.

I believe that the very appearing of Christ before God, is an intercession as a priest, as well as a plea of an advocate; and I believe again, that his very life there is an intercession there, a continual intercession.

But there is yet something further to be said Christ— the humanity of Christ, if in it dwells all the fulness of the Godhead bodily; how then appears he before him to make intercession? Or if Christ is the throne of grace, and mercy-seat, how doth he appear before God as sitting there, to sprinkle that now with his blood? Again, if Christ be the altar of incense, how stands he as a priest by that altar to offer the prayers of all saints thereon, before the throne?

That all this is written, is true; and that it is all truth, is as true: but that it is all understood by every one that is saved, I do not believe is true. I mean, so understood, as that they could all reconcile the seeming contradictions that are in the Scripture.

There are, therefore, three lessons that God has set us, to

the perfecting of our understanding in the mysteries of God 1. Letters. 2. Words. 3. Meanings.

1. Letters. I call the ceremonial law so; for there all is set forth distinctly, every thing by itself, as letters are to children. There you have a priest, a sacrifice, an altar, a holy place, a mercy-seat; and all distinctly.

2. Now in the gospel, these letters are put all in a word, and Christ is that Word, that Word of God's mind; and therefore the gospel makes Christ that priest, Christ that sacrifice, Christ that altar, Christ that holy place, Christ that throne of grace, and all; for Christ is all. All these meet in him, as several letters meet in one word.

3. Next to the word, you have the meaning; and the meaning is more difficult to be learned than either the letters or the word; and therefore the perfect understanding of that is reserved till we arrive to a higher form, till we arrive to a perfect man. "And when that which is perfect is come, that knowledge which is in part shall be done away." Meantime our business is to learn to bring the letters into a word—to bring the ceremonies to Christ, and to make them terminate in him; I mean, to find the priesthood in Christ, the sacrifice in Christ, the altar in Christ, the throne of grace in Christ, and also God in Christ reconciling the world unto himself by him. And if we can learn this well, while here, we shall not at all be blamed; for this is the utmost lesson set us, namely, to learn Christ, as we find him revealed in the gospel. "I determined," saith Paul, "not to know any thing among you, save Jesus Christ, and him crucified." And Christians, after some time, I mean those that pray, and pry into the word well, do attain to some good measure of knowledge of him. It is life eternal to know him, as he is to be known here, as he is to be known by the holy Scriptures. Keep then close to the Scriptures, and let thy faith obey the authority of them, and thou wilt be sure to increase in faith.

"For therein is the righteousness of God revealed from faith to faith: as it is written, The just shall live by faith."

Believe then that Christ died, was buried, rose again, ascended, and ever liveth to make intercession for thee; and take heed of prying too far, for in mysteries men soon lose their way. It is good, therefore, that thou rest in this, namely, that he doth so, though thou canst not tell how he doth it. A man at court gets by his intercession a pardon for a man in the country; and the party concerned, after he hath intelligence of it, knows that such a one hath obtained his pardon, and that by his interceding; but for all that, he may be ignorant of his methods of intercession; and so are we, at least in part, of Christ.

The meaning then is, that I should believe, that for Christ's sake God will save me, since he has justified me with his blood. "Being justified by his blood, we shall be saved from wrath through him;" through his intercession, or through his coming between the God whom I have offended, and me a poor sinner; through his coming between with the voice of his blood and merits, which speak on my behalf to God, because that blood was shed for me, and because those merits, in the benefit of them, are made over to me by an act of the grace of God, according to his eternal covenant made with Christ. This is what I know of his intercession; I mean with reference to the act itself, that is, *how* he makes intercession. And since *all* the fulness of the Godhead dwells in him bodily, and since he also is the holiest of all, and the rest of God forever; it has been some scruple to me, whether it be not too carnal to imagine as if Christ stood distinct in his humanity—distinct, I say, as to space, from the Father, as sitting upon a throne, and as so presenting his merits, and making vocal prayers for the life and salvation of his people. The more true meaning in my apprehension is, that the presence and worth of the human nature, being with the divine, yea, taken into union with God forever, for the service that was done for God by it in the world, in reconciling his elect unto him, is still, and ever will be, so deserving in his sight, as to prevail (I know not how to express it) with the divine nature, (in whom alone is a power to subdue all impossibilities to itself,) to preserve those so reconciled to eternal life.

When I speak of the human nature, I mean the man Christ, not bereft of sense and reason, nor of the power of willing and acting; but thus I mean, that the human nature so terminates in the will of the divine; and again, the will of the divine so terminates, as to saving sinners, in the merit and will of the human, that what the Father would, the Son wills; and what the Son wills, the Father acquiesces in forever. And this the Son wills, and his will is backed with infinite merit, in which also the Father rests—that those, all those whom the Father hath given him, be with him where he is, that they may behold his glory. And now I am come to the will and affections of our High Priest.

This leads me to the second head of this topic, namely, to his natural qualifications. And,

1. This is one thing that I would urge, He is not of a nature foreign to that of man. The angels love us well, but they are not so capable of sympathizing with us in our distresses, because they are not partakers of our nature.

Nature hath a peculiar sympathy in it: now he is naturally one with us, sin only excepted; and that is our advantage too. He is man as we are; flesh and blood as we are; born of a woman, and in all points made like unto us, that excepted which the Holy Ghost excepteth. "Forasmuch then as the children are partakers of flesh and blood, he also himself likewise took part of the same." "For verily he took not on him the nature of angels, but he took on him the seed of Abraham." This doth qualify him much; for as I said before, there is a sympathy in nature. A man will not be so affected with the hurt that comes to a beast, as he naturally will with the hurt that comes to a man: a beast will be more affected with those attempts that are made upon its own kind to hurt it, than it will be with those that are made upon man: wherefore? why, there is a sympathy in nature. Now that Christ the High Priest of the house of God, is naturally one with us, you see the Scriptures plainly affirm "God sent forth his Son, made of a woman:" he was "made of the seed of David, according to the flesh;" the fathers, "of whom, as concerning the flesh, Christ came," &c.; and this must needs tend to make him a well qualified high priest. We will not now speak of the necessity of his taking upon him the human nature, namely, that he might destroy him that had the power of death, that is the devil, and deliver his people; for that would be here too much beside our matter, and be a diversion to the reader: we are now upon his high priest's office, and of those natural qualifications that attend him, as to that; and I say, nature is a great qualification, because in nature there is sympathy; and where there is sympathy, there will be a provocation to help, a provocation to help, with jealousy and indignation against those that afflict.

A bear robbed of her whelps is not more provoked, than is the Lord Jesus, when there are means used to make them miss of life eternal, for whom he hath died, and for whom he ever lives to make intercession. But,

2. As there is natural sympathy in Christ to those for whom he is an High Priest, so there is relative sympathy. He has not only taken to, or upon, him our nature, but he is become one brotherhood with us. Now you know brotherhood will carry a man further than nature; so then, when nature and relation meet, there is a double obligation. "Now, both he that sanctifieth," which is Christ, "and they who are sanctified," his saints, "are all of one;" which is God; they are all of God, as children of a Father: "for which

cause he is not ashamed to call them brethren, saying, I will declare thy name unto my brethren; in the midst of the church will I sing praise unto thee." Now a relation is much, and a natural relation most of all. Why, here is a natural relation betwixt Christ the High Priest, and those for whom he ever liveth to make intercession; a natural relation, I say, and that with respect to the humanity, which is the nature subject to affliction and distress. "Forasmuch then as the children are partakers of flesh and blood, he also himself likewise took part of the same." So then it is for a brother that he is engaged, for a brother that he doth make intercession.

When Gideon knew by the confession of Zeba and Zalmunna, that the men whom they slew at Tabor were his brethren, his fury came into his face, and he sware they should therefore die. Relation is a great matter. And therefore it is said again, "In all things it behoved him to be made like unto his brethren, that he might be a merciful high priest." A brother is born for adversity; and a brother will go far.

This therefore is a second thing, or another qualification, with which Christ Jesus is furnished to be an High Priest: He is a brother; there is a brotherly relation betwixt him and us; therefore by virtue of this relation be maketh intercession for us more affectionately.

3. There is another thing in Christ Jesus that makes him naturally of an excellent qualification with reference to his priesthood for us, and that is, the temptations and infirmities wherewith he was exercised in the days of his humiliation. It is true, temptations and infirmities strictly considered, are none of our nature; no more are they of his; but yet, if it be proper to say temptations and afflictions have a nature, his and ours, were naturally the same; and that in all points too; for so says the Scripture: "He was in all points tempted like as we are, yet without sin." Are we tempted to distrust God? so was he. Are we tempted

to murder ourselves? so was he. Are we tempted, with the bewitching vanities of this world? so was he. Are we tempted to commit idolatry, and to worship the devil? so was he. So that herein we also were alike; yea from his cradle to his cross he was a man of sorrows and acquainted with griefs, a man of afflictions through the whole course of his life.

And observe it, he was made so, or subjected thereto by the ordinance of God; nay, farther, it behoved him to be made so, that is, to be made like unto us in all things, the better to capacitate him to the work of his priesthood, with the more bowels and compassion. We will read to you the text, "Wherefore in all things it behoved him to be made like unto his brethren, that he might be (qualified to be) a merciful and faithful high priest in things pertaining to God, to make reconciliation for the sins of the people. For in that he himself hath suffered, being tempted, he is able to succor them that are tempted."

See here how he is qualified, and to what end. He was tempted as we are, suffered by temptations as we do, "in all points like as we are;" that he might be sympathizing, "that he might be a merciful and faithful high priest, in things pertaining to God," to make up the difference that is made by sin, between God and his people; "to make reconcilation for the sins of the people."

Yea, he, by being tempted, and by suffering as he did, is prepared and enabled so to do; "for in that he himself hath suffered, being tempted, he is able to succor them that are tempted."

Wherefore, I also call this qualification both natural and necessary Natural, because in kind the same with ours; that is, his temptations were the same with ours; the same in nature, the same in design, the same as to their own natural tendency; for their natural tendency was to have ruined both him and us, but God prevented. They also were necessary, though not of themselves, yet made so by him that can bring good out of evil, and light out of darkness; made so, I say, to us, for whose sakes they were suffered to assault and afflict him, namely, that he might be able to be merciful, faithful, and succoring to us.

4. Another qualification with which our High Priest is furnished, for the better fitting him to make intercession for us, is, that he is our Head, and that we are his members. To be a member is more than to be of the same nature, or the nearest of relations, that excepted. So then now he makes intercession for his own self, for his own body, and for the several members of his body. The high priest under the law did use to offer up sacrifice for himself; first for himself, for his own sins, and then for the errors of the people. I will not say that Christ had any sin that was personally, or by his act, his own; for that would be to blaspheme the name of that Holy One; but yet I will say, he made the sins of the people his own; yea, God the Father made them his; those also for whom he ever liveth to make intercession, are united to him, made members of his body, of his flesh, and of his bones; and so are part of himself.

But we are now about his natural qualifications, and this is one; that they for whom he ever liveth to make intercession are his members, the members of his body. "We are members of his body, of his flesh, and of his bones:" so saith the word. Wherefore here is a near concern, for that his church is part of himself; it is his own concern, it is for his own flesh :"never man yet hated his own flesh, but nourisheth and cherisheth it." Things are thus spoken, because of the infirmity of our flesh. So that had Christ no love to us as we are sinners, yet because we are part of himself, he cannot but care for us,—nature puts him upon it; yea, and the more infirm and weak we are, the more he is touched with the feeling of our infirmities, the more he is afflicted for us. "For we have not an high priest which cannot be touched with the feeling of our infirmities." He at no time loseth this his fellow feeling; because he always is our Head, and we the members of his body. I will add, the infirm member is most cared for, most pitied, most watched over to be kept from harms, and most consulted for.

I love to play the child with little children, and have learned something by so doing. I have met with a child that has had a sore finger, yea, so sore as to be altogether useless; and not only so, but by reason of its infirmity, has been a hinderance to the use of all the fingers that have been upon that hand. Then have I begun to bemoan the child, and said, "Alas! my poor boy, or girl, has got a sore finger?" "Ah!" quoth the child, with water in its eyes, who hath come to me to be bemoaned. Then I have begun to offer to touch the sore finger. "Oh!" saith the child, "pray do not hurt me." I then have replied, "Canst thou do nothing with this finger?" "No," saith the child, "nor with this hand either." Then have I said, "Shall we cut off this finger, and buy my child a better, a brave golden finger?" At this the child has started, stared in my face, gone back from me, and entertained a kind of indignation against me, and has no more cared to be intimate with me.

Then have I begun to make some use of that good sermon which this little child has preached unto me; and thus have I gone on: "If membership be so dear, if this child has such tenderness to the most infirm, and the most useless of its members: if it counts me its friend no longer than while I have a mouth to bemoan, and carriages that show tenderness to this useless finger; what an interest doth *membership* give one in the body, and what compassion hath the soul for such a useless thing, because it is a member?" And turning all this over to Jesus Christ, then instead of matter and corruption, there presently comes honey to me out of the child's sore finger. I take leave to tell you now how I use to play. And though I have told this tale upon so grave a truth as is the membership of Christians with their Head, yet bear with me. No child can be so tender of its sore finger, as is the Son of God of his afflicted members; he cannot but be touched with the feeling of our infirmities.

Ah! who would not make many supplications, prayers, and intercessions, for a leg, for an eye, for a foot, for a hand, for a finger, rather than they will lose it! And can it be imagined, that Christ alone shall be like the foolish ostrich, hardened against its young, yea, against his members? It cannot be.

Should he lose a member, he would be disfigured, maimed, dismembered, imperfect, next to monstrous; for his body is called his fulness, yea, "the fulness of him that filleth all in all." This therefore shows you that Christ as high priest has naturally a respect for those for whom he ever liveth to make intercession; yea an unfathomable respect for them, because they are his members.

5. But again, when nature, relation, and membership are urged to show the fit qualifications wherewith Christ is endued, I intend not to intimate as if the bottom of all lay here; for then it might be urged, that one imperfect has all these; for who knows not that sinful man has all these qualifications in him, towards his nature, relations, and members? I have therefore, as I said, thus discoursed, only for demonstration's sake, and to suit myself to the infirmity of your flesh. I might come, in the next place, to tell you, that Jesus Christ our High Priest is thus, with reference to other designs. We are his purchase, and he counts us so; his jewels, and he counts us so; his estate real, and he counts us so. And you know, a man will do much, speak much, intercede much, and long for that which he is interested in.

But we will come to speak more particularly of the exceeding excellency of his natural qualifications, and show you, that he hath *such as are peculiar to himself alone*, and that we are concerned in them.

1. First, then, He is Holy, and so a suitable High Priest. There is a holiness that sets further from, and a holiness that brings one nearer to, and to be concerned the more with, the condition of those in affliction; and that holiness is that which is entailed to office. When a man is put into an office, the more unholy he is, the worse he performs his office; and the more holy, the better he performs his office. For his holiness obliges him to be faithful unto men, wherein he is concerned by his office. Hence you read, that he is a "faithful High Priest," because he is a holy one, and "such an High Priest became us, who is holy," &c. "Good and upright is the Lord, (Jehovah, Jesus Christ,) therefore he will teach sinners in the way." "He that ruleth over men must be just, ruling in the fear of God." I mention these texts to show you, that holiness, when entailed to office, makes a man do that office the better. Now then, Christ is holy, and he is called, and made of God a High Priest, after the order of Melchisedec, and is to manage that his office for thee with God; that is to say, to continue to make reconciliation for iniquity; for that iniquity that cleaveth unto thee, and that breaketh out, or issueth from thy flesh, after thou art called and converted. For we are now upon the second part, of the execution of the priesthood of Christ: that which he executeth, I say—and by executing takes away the iniquity of our holy things and of our life—after our turning to God by him. Now he that is to do this, is holy, and so one that will make conscience of performing that office for us, with which he is entrusted of God. Hence, he is set in opposition to those high priests that had infirmities, that were not holy—and upon this very account preferred above them. "For the law maketh men high priests which have infirmity; but the word of the oath, which was since the law, maketh the Son, (High Priest,) who is consecrated, (perfected, or holy,) for evermore."

This, therefore, is a great thing, namely, that we have an High Priest that is holy, and so one that will not fail to perform to the utmost the trust committed to him on our behalf, that is, to offer both gifts and sacrifices for sin: this is one thing.

2. There is added to this of his holiness another; and that is, Harmlessness. "For such an High Priest became us, who is holy, harmless." A harmful man, when he is in office, oh, how much mischief he may do! Such a one is partial in doing his office; such a one will put the poor by his right; such a one will buy and sell a cause, a man, an interest—will do or not do, as his harmfulness prompts him to it. So is an evil ruler among the poorer people. But now our Jesus, our High Priest, is holy, harmless; he will wrong no man, he will deprive no man, he will contemn no man, he will deny no man that comes to God by him, the benefit and advantage of his blessed intercession; he respecteth not persons, nor taketh reward. A harmful man will stomach, and hate, and prejudice a man, will wait for an opportunity to do him mischief, will take the advantage, if he can, to deny him his right, and keep from him his due, when yet it is in the power of his hand to help him. Oh! but Christ is harmless, harmless as a dove! He thinks no ill, doth no ill; but graciously, innocently, harmlessly, makes intercession for thee; nor will he be prevailed with to prejudice thy person, or to forbear to take up thy name into his lips, be thy infirmities, and weaknesses, and provocations ever so many, if thou indeed comest to God by him. He is holy, and harmless, and so the more fit to become our High Priest, and to make intercession for us.

3. But again, this is not all; he is also Undefiled. "For such an High Priest became us, who is holy, harmless, undefiled." This term is put in to show that he neither is, nor can be found, neither now, nor at any time, faulty in his office. A man that is holy may yet be defiled; a man that is harmless may yet be defiled. We are bid to be holy and harmless; and in a gospel sense so every Christian is. Oh! but Christ is so in a legal sense; in the eye of the law, per-

fectly so. This is a great matter; for it shows, that as nothing done by us can tempt him to be hurtful to us, so there is nothing in himself that can tempt him to be so. A man that is defiled, has that within him that will put him upon using his office unfaithfully, though he should have no provocation from those for whose good he is to execute his office; but he that is undefiled—undefiled in a law sense, as our Lord Jesus is—is such a one as doth not only not do hurt, and not act falsely in his office, but one that cannot, one that knoweth not how to be unfaithful in his trust. He is holy, harmless, undefiled: this, therefore, is a great thing. He has not the original of hurtfulness in him; there is no such root in him. There is a root of bitterness springing up in us, by which, not only ourselves, but oft-times others are defiled. Oh! but our High Priest is undefiled; he is not corrupt, nor corrupteth; he doth his office fairly, faithfully, holily, justly—according to, or answering our necessities, and the trust reposed in him and committed to him. But,

4. This is not all. As he is holy, harmless, and undefiled; so he is "separate from sinners," both in his conception, in his composition, and the place ordained for him to execute this part of his high priest's office in. He was not conceived in the womb by carnal generation; he was not made up of polluted and defiled nature; he officiateth not with those materials that are corrupt, stained or imperfect, but with those that are unspotted; even with the spotless sacrifice of his own unblemished offering. He, nor his offering, has any such taint as had the priests and their sacrifices under the law, namely, sin and imperfection; he is separate from them in this respect, further than is an angel from a beast. He has none of the qualities, actions, or inclinations of sinners: his ways are only his own; he never saw them, nor learned them but of the Father. There is none upright among men; wherefore, he is separated from them to be a priest.

5. As he is thus, so again, he is said to be higher than the

heavens. "For such an High Priest became us, who is holy, harmless, undefiled, separate from sinners, and made higher than the heavens." The text saith, that neither saint, nor heavens, are clean in God's sight. "Behold, he put no trust in his servants, and his angels he charged with folly:" and again, "Behold, he putteth no trust in his saints; yea, the heavens are not clean in his sight." Wherefore, by this expression, he shows us, that our High Priest is more noble than either heaven or angel; yea, more clean and perfect than any.—It shows us also, that all the heavenly host are at his command, to do as his intercession shall prevail with the Father for us. All angels worship him, and at his word they become, they all become, ministering spirits for them who shall be heirs of salvation.

Besides, by this word he shows that it is impossible that our High Priest should degenerate or decay; for he is made higher than the heavens. The spirits, in the heavens, sometimes, have degenerated; the heavens themselves decay and wax old; and that is the farthest that, by the word, we are admitted to go. But as for him that is above the heavens, that is made higher than the heavens, that is ascended up far above all heavens; he is the same, and his years fail not; "the same yesterday, to-day, and forever."

This, therefore, is added, to show that Christ is neither as the angels nor heavens, subject to decay or degenerate, or to flag and grow cold in the execution of his office; but that he will be found, even at the last, when he is come to the end of his work, and is about to come out of the holy place, as affectionate, as full of love, as willing, and desirous after our salvation, as he was the first moment that he was made High Priest, and took upon him to execute that blessed office for us.

Wherefore, our High Priest is no such one as you read of in the law. He is no dwarf, hath no blemish, nor any imperfection; therefore is not subject to flag or fail in the due execution of his office, but is "able to save to the uttermost them that come unto God by him, seeing he ever liveth to make intercession for them."

And it is well worth our consideration, that it is said he is "*made*" thus; that is, appointed, instituted, called, and qualified thus of God. This shows the Father's heart as well as the Son's, to us-ward, that this priesthood was of him, and the glorious effects thereof by him. "Let us, therefore, come boldly unto the throne of grace, that we may obtain mercy, and find grace to help in time of need."

CHAPTER IX.

THE SECOND GREAT MOTIVE UNFOLDED.

I COME now to the second motive, namely, that we may find mercy and grace to help in time of need; or, we shall find mercy and grace to help, if we come as we should, to the throne of grace.

In this motive we have these three things:

1. That saints are likely to meet with needy times while they are in this world.

2. That nothing can carry us through our needy times but more, or a continual supply of, mercy and grace.

3. That mercy and grace are to be had at the throne of grace, and we must fetch them from thence by prayer, if we would, as we should, go through these needy times.

For the first of these, That saints are likely to meet with needy times, or, with such times as will show them, that they need a continual assistance of the grace of God, that they may go rightly through this world. This is, therefore, a motive that weareth a spur in the heel of it, a spur to prick us forward to supplicate at the throne of grace. This needy time is in other places called the perilous time, the evil day, the hour and power of darkness, the day of temptation, the cloudy and dark day.

And, indeed, in the general, all the days of our pilgrimage here are evil, yea, every day has a sufficiency of evil in it to destroy the best saint that breatheth, were it not for the grace of God. But there are also, as I have hinted, particular specious times, times more eminently dangerous and hazardous unto saints: as,

1. There are their *young* days; the days of their youth and

childhood in grace. This day is usually attended with much evil towards him or them that are asking the way to Zion, with their faces thitherward. Now the devil has lost a sinner; there is a captive has broke prison, and one run away from his master: now hell seems to be awakened from sleep, the devils are come out—they roar, and roaring they seek to recover their runaway. Now tempt him, threaten him, flatter him, stigmatize him, throw dust into his eyes, poison him with errors, spoil him while he is upon the potter's wheel; any thing to keep him from coming to Jesus Christ. And is this not a needy time? Doth not such a one need abundance of grace? Is it not of absolute necessity that thou, if thou art the man thus beset, shouldst ply it at the throne of grace, for mercy and grace to help thee in such a time of need as this is?

To want a spirit of prayer now, is as much as thy life is worth. O, therefore, you that know what I say, you that are broke loose from hell, that are fled for refuge to lay hold on the hope set before you, and that do hear the lion roar after you, and that are kept awake with the continual voice of his chinking chain, cry as you fly! yea, the promise is, that they that come to God with weeping, with supplication, he will lead them.

Well, this is one needy time: now thy hedge is low, now the branch is tender, now thou art but in the bud. Pray that thou be'est not marred in the potter's hand.

2. The time of *prosperity* is also a time of need; I mean, of thy spiritual prosperity. For, as Satan can tell how to suit temptations for thee in the day of thy want, so he has those that can entangle thee in the day of thy fulness. He has his spiritual wickednesses in the high and heavenly places. He can tell how to lay a snare for thee in the land of Canaan, as well as in the wilderness; in thy time of receiving good things, as well as in thy hungry and empty hours. Nay, such times seem to be the most dangerous, not in themselves, but

through the deceits of our heart. Hence Moses gives this caution to the children of Israel, that when God had given them the promised land, and vineyards, and wells, and olive trees; and when they had eaten and were full, "Then," says he, "beware, lest thou forget the Lord, which brought thee forth of the land of Egypt, from the house of bondage." And again, he doubleth this caution, saying, "When thou hast eaten and art full, then thou shalt bless the Lord thy God for the good land which he has given thee. Beware that thou forget not the Lord thy God, in not keeping his commandments, and his judgments, and his statutes, which I command thee this day: lest when thou hast eaten and art full, (and thou in all good things art increased,) then thy heart be lifted up, and thou forget the Lord thy God, which brought thee forth out of the land of Egypt, from the house of bondage." All this may be applied spiritually. For there are, as I said, snares laid for us in our best things; and he that has great enjoyments, and forgets to pray for grace to keep him humble then, shall quickly be where Peter was, after his knowledge of the Lord Jesus by the revelation of the Father.

3. Another needy time, is a time when men are *low and empty as to worldly good.* This time is full of temptations and snares. At this time, men will, if they look not well to their doings and goings, be tempted to strain courtesies, both with conscience and with God's word, and adventure to do things that are dangerous, and that have a tendency to make all their religion and profession vain. This holy Agur was aware of; so he prayed, "Let me not be rich and full, lest I deny thee: let me not be poor, lest I steal, and take the name of God in vain." There are many inconveniences that attend him that is fallen into decay in this world. It is an evil day with him, and the devils will be as busy with him as the flies are with a lean and scabbed sheep. It shall go hard but such a man shall be full of maggots; full of silly, foolish,

idle inventions, to get up, and to abound with fulness again. It is not a time now, Satan will say, to retain a tender conscience, to regard thy word or promise, to pay for what thou buyest, or to stick at pilfering, and filch from thy neighbor. This Agur was afraid of; therefore he prayed that God would keep him from that which would be to him a temptation to do it. How many in our day have, on these very accounts, brought religion to a very ill savor, and themselves unto the snare of the devil, and all because they have not addicted themselves to pray to God for grace to help in this time of need, but rather have left off the thing that is good, and given up themselves to the temptations of the devil, and the subtile and ensnaring motions of the flesh.

4. Another needy time is the day of *persecution*. This is called, as was hinted before, "the hour of darkness," "the cloudy and dark day." This day, therefore, is full of snares, and of evils of every kind. Here is the fear of man, the terrors of a prison, of loss of goods and life. Now all things look black; now the fiery trial is come. He that cannot now pray; he that now applieth not himself to God on the throne of grace, by the priesthood of Jesus Christ, is like to take a fall before all men upon the stage; a foul fall—a fall that will not only break his own bones, but also the hearts of those that fear God and behold it. Come therefore, boldly to the throne of grace, that ye may obtain mercy, and find grace to help in time of need.

5. Another time of need is, that time wherein thou *changest thy condition* and enterest into a new relation. For here also the snares and traps lie waiting for thee. There is a hopeful child goes to service, or to be an apprentice; there is a young man and a young maid entered into a married condition, and though they pray before, yet they leave off to pray then. Why, these people are oftentimes ruined and undone. The reason is, this change is attended with new snares, with new cares, and with new temptations; of

the which, because through unwatchfulness they are not aware, they are taken, drawn to perdition and destruction by them.

Many in my short day have gone, I doubt, down to the pit, this way, that have sometime been to appearance the very foremost and hopefulest in the place where they have lived. O how soon has their fire gone out—have their lamps forbore to burn! How quickly have they lost their love to their ministers, by whom they were illuminated, and to the warmest Christians, through communion with whom they used to be kept awake and savory! How quickly have they found them out new friends, new companions, new ways and methods of life, and new delights to feed their foolish minds withal! Wherefore, O, thou that art in this fifth head concerned, come boldly to the throne of grace, that you may obtain mercy, and find grace to help in time of need.

6. Another time of need is, when the generality of *professors are decayed;* when the custom of fancies and fooleries have taken away all gravity and modesty from among the children of men. Now pray, or thou diest; yea, pray against those decays, those vain customs, those foolish fancies, those light and vain carriages that have overtaken others, else they will assuredly knock at thy door, and obtain favor at thy hand; the which if they do, they will quickly bring thee down into the dirt with others, and put thee in peril of damnation as well as they.

7. Another time of need is, the time of *guilt contracted,* and of the hiding of God's face. This is a dangerous time. If thou now shalt forbear to pray, thou art undone; for the natural tendency of guilt is to drive a man from God. So it served our first father; and ofttimes when God hides his face, men run into desperation, and so throw up all duties, and say, as he of old, Why should I wait upon the Lord any longer? Now thy great help against this is prayer—continuing in prayer. Prayer wrestleth with the devil, and will

overthrow him; prayer wrestleth with God, and will overcome him; prayer wrestleth with all temptations and makes them fly. Great things have been done by prayer, even by the prayer of those that have contracted guilt, and that have by their sins lost the smiles and sense of the favor of God.

Wherefore, when this needy, this evil time has overtaken thee, pray; come boldly to the throne of grace, that you may obtain mercy, and find grace to help in time of need.

8. The day of *reproach and slander* is another time of need, or a day in which thou wilt want supplies of grace. Sometimes we meet with such days wherein we are loaden with reproaches, slanders, scandals, and lies. Christ found the day of reproach a burdensome day unto him; and there is many a professor driven quite away from all conscience towards God, and open profession of his name, by such things as these. Reproach is, when cast at a man, as if he was stoning to death with stones. Now ply it hard at the throne of grace to bear thee up, or thou wilt either miscarry, or sink under ground by the weight of reproach that may fall upon thee.

9. Another time of need is that wherein a man's *friends desert* and forsake him, because of his gospel principles or of those temptations that attend his profession. This is a time that often happeneth to those that are good. Thus it was with Christ, with Paul, with Job, with Heman, and so has been with many other of God's servants in the day of their temptations in this world; and a sore time it is. Job complained under it; so did Heman, Paul and Christ. Now a man is as forlorn as a pelican in the wilderness, as an owl in the desert, or as a sparrow upon the house top. If a man cannot now go to the throne of grace by prayer, through Christ, and so fetch grace for his support from thence, what can he do? He cannot live of himself. Wherefore this is a sore evil.

10. Another time of need is the day of *death*—when I

am to pack up all to be gone from hence, the way of all the earth. Now the greatest trial is come, excepting that of the day of judgment. Now a man is to be stripped of all but that which cannot be shaken. Now a man grows near the borders of eternity; now he begins to see into the skirts of the next world; now death is death, and the grave the grave, indeed. Now he begins to see what it is for body and soul to part, and what it is to go and appear before God. Now the dark entry, and the thoughts of what is in the way from a death bed to the gate of the holy heaven, come nearer the heart than when health and prosperity do compass a man about. Wherefore this is like to be a trying time, a time of need, indeed. A prudent man will make it one of the great concerns of his whole life, to get, and lay up, a stock of grace for this day, (though the fool will rage and be confident,) for he knows all will be little enough to keep him warm in his soul, while cold death strokes his hand over his face, and over his heart, and is turning his blood into jelly: while strong death is loosing his silver cord, and breaking his golden bowl. Wherefore, I say, this motive weareth a spur on his heel, a spur to prick us on to the throne of grace for mercy, and grace to help in the time of need.

But, secondly, I come now to the next thing, which is, To show, that nothing can carry us through our needy times, but more, or a continual supply of, mercy and grace. This the text fully implies, because it directeth us to the throne of grace, for mercy and grace for that very end. And had there been any thing else that could have done it, the apostle would have made mention of it, and would also have directed the saints unto it. But forasmuch as he here makes mention of the needy time, and directs them to the throne of grace for mercy and grace to help, it followeth that mercy and grace, and these only, can help us in the evil time.

Now this mercy and grace are to be distinctly considered. 1. Mercy; for by it we have through Christ the continuation and multiplication of forgivenesses, without which there is no salvation. 2. Grace, for by it we are upheld, supported, and enabled to go through our needy times, as Christians; without which there is no salvation neither. The first, all will grant; the second is clear. "If any man draw back, my soul shall have no pleasure in him. But we are not of them who draw back unto perdition; but of them that believe to the saving of the soul."

1. *Mercy* is that by which we are pardoned, even all the falls, faults, failings, and weaknesses that attend us, and that we are incident to, in this our day of temptation. And for this mercy we should pray, and say, "Our Father, forgive us our trespasses." For though mercy is free in the exercise of it to us-ward, yet God will have us ask, that we may have; as he also saith in this scripture, "Let us come boldly unto the throne of grace, that we may obtain mercy." Here, then, we have one help, and that is, the mercy of God is to be extended to us from his throne through Jesus Christ, for our pardon and forgiveness in all those weaknesses that we are attended with in the needy or evil times; and we should come to God for this very thing. This is that which David means when he says, "Surely goodness and mercy shall follow me all the days of my life; and I will dwell in the house of the Lord forever." And again, "When I said, My foot slippeth; thy mercy, O Lord, help me up"—set me clear and free from guilt, and from the imputation of sin unto death, by Christ.

Nor can any thing help where this is wanting; for our parts, our knowledge, our attainments, or our graces, cannot so carry us through this world, but that we shall be guilty of that that will sink us down to hell, without God's pardoning mercy. It is not the grace that we have received can do it, nor the grace that is to be received that can do it: nothing can do it but the pardoning mercy of God; for because all our graces are here imperfect, they cannot produce a spotless obedience. But where there is not a spotless obedience, there must of necessity follow a continuation of pardon and forgiveness by mercy, or I know what will .become of the soul.

Here, therefore, the apostle lays an obligation upon thee to the throne of grace, namely, that thou mayst obtain mercy, a continuation of mercy; mercy as long as thou art like to live this vain life on the earth; mercy that will reach through all thy days: for there is not a day, nor a duty—not a day that thou livest, nor a duty that thou dost—but will need that mercy should come after to take away thy iniquity. Nay, thou canst not recieve mercy so clearly,as not to stand in need of another act of mercy to pardon weakness in thy no better receiving the last. We receive not our mercies so humbly, so readily, so gladly, and with such thankfulness as we should; and therefore, for the want of these, have the need of another and another act of God's sin-pardoning mercy, and need shall have thereof, as long as evil time shall last with us.

But is not this great grace, that we should thus be called upon to come to God for mercy? Yea, is not God unspeakably good, in providing such a throne of grace, such a sacrifice, such an High Priest, and so much mercy for us, and then to invite us to come with boldness to him for it? Nay, doth not his kindness yet further appear by giving us items and intimations of needy times, and evil days, on purpose to provoke us to come to him for mercy?

This, then, shows us, as also we have hinted before, that the throne of grace, and Christ Jesus our High Priest, are both provided upon the account of our imperfections, namely, that we who are called might not be, by remaining weaknesses, hindered of, but obtain, eternal inheritance. Weaknesses, such weaknesses remain in the justified, and such slips and failings are found in and upon them, as called for a course of mercy and forgiveness to attend them.

Farther, this also intimates, that God's people should not

be dejected at the apprehensions of their imperfections; I say, not so dejected, as therefore to cast off faith and hope, and prayer. For a throne of grace is provided for them, to the which they may, they must, they ought continually to resort for mercy, sin-pardoning mercy.

2. As we are here to obtain mercy, so we are here to find *grace.* They that obtain mercy, shall find grace; therefore they are put together. "That they may obtain mercy, and find grace;" only they must find mercy first; for as forgiveness at first goes before sanctification in the general, so forgiveness afterwards goes before particular acts of grace for further sanctification. God giveth not the Spirit of grace to those that he has not first forgiven by mercy, for the sake of Christ. Also, so long as he as a Father forbears to forgive us his adopted, so long we go without those further additions of grace that are suggested in the text. But when we have obtained mercy to forgive, then we also find grace to our renewing. Therefore he saith first, "obtain mercy," and then, "find grace."

Grace, here, I take to be that grace which God has appointed for us, to dwell in us, and that by and through the continual supply of which we are to be enabled to do and suffer, and to manage ourselves in doing and suffering according to the will of God. "Let us have grace, whereby we may serve God acceptably, with reverence and godly fear." So again, "He giveth more grace: wherefore he saith, God resisteth the proud, but giveth grace unto the humble." The grace therefore that is meant, is grace given, or to be given; grace received, or to be received; grace, a root, a principle of grace, with its continual supplies for the perfecting of that salvation that God hath designed for us.

This was that which comforted Paul, when the messenger of Satan was sent to buffet him: it was said unto him by Christ, "My grace is sufficient for thee." As if he should say, 'Paul, be not utterly cast down, I have wherewithal to make thee stand, and overcome; and that is my grace, by which thou shalt be supported, strengthened, comforted, and made to live a triumphant life, notwithstanding all that oppress thee." But this came to him upon his praying "For this I prayed to God thrice," saith he. So again, "God is able to make all grace abound toward you, that ye, always having all sufficiency in all things, may abound to every good work." Thus you see, that by grace, in these places in meant that Spirit and those principles of grace, by the increase and continual supply of which, we are inwardly strengthened, and made to abound to every good work.

This, then, is the conclusion: That as there is mercy to be obtained by us at the throne of grace, for the pardon of all our weaknesses; so there is also grace there to be found that will yet strengthen us more, to all good walking and living before him. He giveth more grace; and thus they receive, one time or another, abundance of grace that shall reign in life by one Jesus Christ.

This then teaches us several things, some of which I will mention: as,

1. That nature, as nature, is not capable of serving God; no, not nature where grace dwells, as considered abstract from that grace that dwells in it. Nothing can be done aright without grace; I mean, not a part or piece of gospel duty. "Let us have grace, whereby we may serve God acceptably." Nature, managed by grace, seasoned with grace, and held up with grace, can serve God acceptably. "Let us have grace" —that is, seek for, and find grace to do so; for we cannot do so but by grace. "By the grace of God, (says Paul,) I am what I am: and his grace, which was bestowed on me, was not in vain; but I labored more abundantly than they all: yet not I, but the grace of God which was with me."

What can be more plain than this beautiful text? For the Apostle doth here quite shut out nature—sanctified nature, (for he indeed was a sanctified man,) and concludes that even he, as of himself, did nothing of all the works that he did; but they were done, he did them, by the grace of God that was in him. Wherefore, nature—sanctified nature, as nature, can of itself do nothing to the pleasing of God the Father.

Is not this the experience of all the godly? Can they do that at all times which they can do at some times? Can they pray, believe, love, fear, repent, and bow before God always alike? No. Why so? they are the same men, the same human nature, the same saints. Aye, but the samo grace, in the same degree, operation, and life of grace, doth not so now work on that man, that nature, that saint; therefore, notwithstanding he is what he is, he cannot do at all times alike.

Thus, therefore, it is manifest, that nature, simply as such, is a great way off doing that which is acceptable with God. Refined, purified, sanctified nature, cannot do but by the immediate supplies, lifts, and helps of that Spirit and principle of grace by the which it is so sanctified.

2. As nature, even where grace is, cannot, without the assistance of that grace, do any thing acceptably before God; so grace received, if it be not also supplied with more grace, cannot cause that we continue to do acceptable service to God. This also is clear by the text. For he speaketh here to them that have received grace; yea, puts himself into the number, saying, Let us come boldly to the throne of grace, that we may find grace to help in time of need. If grace received would do, what need of more? What need we pray for more? What need we go to the throne of grace for more? This very exhortation saith it will not. Present supplies of grace are proportioned to our present need, and to help us to do a present work or duty. But is our present need all the need that we are like to have, and the present work all the work that we have to do in the world? Even so the grace that we have received at present, though it can help us to do a present work, cannot, without a further supply, help us

to do what is to be done hereafter. Wherefore, the Apostle saith, that this continuing to do, was through his obtaining help, continued help, of God. "Having, therefore," saith he, "obtained help of God, I continue unto this day, witnessing both to small and great," &c. There must be a daily imploring of God for daily supplies from him, if we will do our daily business as we should.

A present dispensation of grace, is like a good meal, a seasonable shower, or a penny in one's pocket, all which will serve for the present necessity. But will that good meal that I ate last week, enable me, without supply, to do a good day's work in this? Or will that seasonable shower which fell last year, be, without supplies, a seasonable help to the grain and grass that are growing now? Or will that penny that supplied my want the other day, I say, will the same penny also, without a supply, supply my wants to-day?

The same, I say, may be said of grace received. It is like the oil in the lamp, it must be fed, it must be added to, and there shall be a supply. "Wherefore he giveth more grace." Grace is the sap, which from the root maintaineth the branches: stop the sap, and the branch will wither. Not that the sap shall be stopped where there is union, not stopped altogether; for, as from the root the branch is supplied, so from Christ is every member furnished with a continual supply of grace, if it doth as it should. "Of his fulness have all we received, and grace for grace."

The day of grace is the day of expense: this is our spending time. Hence we are called pilgrims and strangers in the earth; that is, travellers from place to place, from state to state, from trial to trial. Now, as the traveller at a fresh inn is made to spend fresh money; so Christians, at a fresh temptation, at a new temptation, are made to spend afresh, and need a new supply of grace. Great men, when, and while, their sons are travellers, appoint that their bags of money be lodged ready, or conveniently paid in at such and such a place, for the suitable relief of them; and so they meet with supplies. Why, so are the sons of the Great One, and he has allotted that we should travel beyond sea, or at a great distance from our Father's house: wherefore, he has appointed, that grace shall be provided for us, to supply, at such a place, such a state, or temptation, as need requires. But, withal, as my lord expecteth his son should acquaint him with the present emptiness of his purse, and with the difficulty he hath now to grapple with; so God our Father expects that we should plead by Christ, our need at the throne of grace, in order to a supply of grace. "Let us, therefore, come boldly to the throne of grace, that we may obtain mercy, and find grace to help in time of need."

Now, then, this shows the reason why many Christians, that are indeed possessed of the grace of God, do yet walk so oddly, act so poorly, and live such disorderly lives in the world. They are like to those gentlemen's sons that are of the more extravagant sort, that walk in their lousy hue, when they might be maintained better. Such young men care not, perhaps, scorn to acquaint their fathers with their wants, and therefore, walk in their threadbare jackets, with hose and shoes out at heels; a right emblem of the uncircumspect child of God.

This also shows the reason of all those dreadful falls and miscarriages that many of the saints sustain. They make it not their business to watch to see what is coming, and to pray for a supply of grace to uphold them. They, with Da vid, are too careless, or with Peter, too confident, or with the disciples, too sleepy, and so the temptation comes upon them, and their want like an armed man.

This also shows the reason why some that, to one's thinking, would fall every day, for that their want of parts, their small experience, their little knowledge of God's matters, do seem to bespeak it; yet stand, walk better, and keep their garments more white, than those that have, when compared with them, twice as much as they. They are praying saints, they are often at the throne of grace, they are sensible of their weakness, keep a sight of their danger before their faces, and will not be contented without more grace.

3. And this leads me, in the third place, to show you, that were we wise, and did we ply it at the throne of grace, for grace, as we should, O, what spotless lives might we live! We should then have always help in time of need; for so the text insinuates. "That we may obtain mercy, and find grace to help in (every) time of need."

That is that which Peter means, when he says, "And besides all this," that is, besides your faith in Christ, and besides your happy state of justification, "giving all diligence, add to your faith, virtue; and to virtue, knowledge; and to knowledge, temperance; and to temperance, patience; and to patience, godliness; and to godliness, brotherly kindness; and to brotherly kindness, charity. For if these things be in you and abound," that is, be continually supplied with a supply from the throne of grace, "they make you that ye shall neither be barren nor unfruitful in the knowledge of our Lord Jesus Christ. But he that lacketh these things is blind, and cannot see afar off, and hath forgotten that he was purged from his old sins. Wherefore, the rather, brethren, give diligence to make your calling and election sure: for if you do these things, ye shall never fall; for so an entrance shall be ministered unto you abundantly into the everlasting kingdom of our Lord and Saviour Jesus Christ."

The greatest part of professors now a-days take up their time in contracting guilt, and asking for pardon, and yet are not much the better. Whereas, if they had but the grace to add to their faith, virtue &c. they might have more peace, live better lives, and not have their heads so often in a bag as they have. "To him that ordereth his conversation aright, will I show the salvation of God:" to him that disposeth his way aright. Now this cannot be done without a constant supplicating at the throne of grace, for more grace. This then is the reason why every new temptation that comes upon thee, so foils, so overcomes thee, that thou wilt need a new conversion to be recovered from under its power, and the guilt that cleaves to thee, by its overshadowing of thee.

A new temptation, a sudden temptation, an unexpected temptation, usually foils those that are not upon their watch, and that have not been before with God to be inlaid with grace proportionable to what may come upon them.

"That ye may find grace to help in time of need." There is grace to be found at the throne of grace, that will help us under the greatest straits. "Seek and ye shall find." It is there, and it is to be found there; it is to be found there of the seeking soul, of the soul that seeketh him. Wherefore I will conclude as I did begin; "Let us therefore come boldly unto the throne of grace, that we may obtain mercy, and find grace to help in time of need."

CHAPTER X.

APPLICATION OF THE SUBJECT.

WE will now speak something by way of conclusion, and and so wind up the whole.

1. You must remember that we have been hitherto speaking of the throne of grace, and showing what it is; that we have also been speaking of Christ's sacrifice, and how he manages his high priest's office before the throne of grace. We have also here, as you see, been speaking of the mercy that is to be obtained and grace found at this throne of grace; and of what advantage it is to us in this our pilgrimage. Now, from all this it follows, that sin is a fearful thing; for all this ado is, that men might be saved from sin. What a devil then is sin! It is the worst of devils; it is worse than all devils: those that are devils, sin has made them so; nor could any thing else have made them devils but sin. Now, I pray, what is it to be a devil, but to be under, for ever, the power and dominion of sin, an implacable spirit against God? such a one, from whose implacableness all the power in heaven and earth cannot release them, because God of his justice has bound them over to judgment. These spirits are by sin carried quite away from themselves as well as from God that made them; they cannot design their own good; they cannot leave that which yet they know will be everlastingly mischievous to themselves. Sin has bound them to itself so fast, that there can be no deliverance for them, but by the Son of God; who also has refused them, and left them to themselves, and to the judgment which they have deserved. Sin also has got a victory over man; has made him an enemy to God, and to his own

salvation; has caught him, captivated him, carried away his mind, and will, and heart, from God; and made him choose to be vain, and to run the hazard of eternal damnation, with rejoicing and delight. But God left not man where he left those wicked spirits, namely, under the everlasting chains of darkness, reserved unto judgment; but devised means for their ransom, and reconciliation to himself; which is the thing that has been discoursed of in the foregoing part of this book. But, I say, what a thing is sin! what a devil, and master of devils is it, that it should, where it takes hold, so hang, that nothing can unclench its hold, but the mercy of God and the heart-blood of his dear Son! Oh, the fretting, eating, infecting, defiling, and poisonous nature of sin, that it should so eat into our flesh and spirit, body and soul, and so stain us with its vile and stinking nature; yea it has almost turned man into the nature of itself; insomuch that sometimes, when nature is mentioned, sin is meant; and when sin is mentioned, nature is meant.

Wherefore, sin is a fearful thing; a thing to be lamented, a thing to be abhorred, a thing to be fled from with more astonishment and trembling, than one would fly from any devil; because it is the worst of things, and that without which nothing can be bad; and because where it takes hold, it so fasteneth, that nothing, as I have said, can release whom it has made a captive, but the mercy of God, and the heart-blood of his dear Son. Oh, what a thing is sin!

2. As by what hath been said, sin appears to be exceeding sinful; so, from hence it also follows, that the soul is a precious thing: for you must know all this is for the redemption of the soul. "The redemption of the soul is precious." I say it is for the redemption of the soul: it was for this that Christ was made a priest, a sacrifice an altar, a throne of grace; yea, sin, a curse, and what not, that was necessary for our deliverance from sin, and death, and everlasting damnation.

He that would know what a soul is, let him read in letters of blood the price and purchase of the soul. It was not for a light, a little, an inconsiderate thing, that Christ Jesus underwent what he suffered, when he was in the world, and gave himself a ransom for souls. No, no : the soul is a great, a vastly great thing, notwithstanding it is so little set by of some. Some prefer any thing that they fancy, above the soul; a slut, a lie, a pot of liquor, an act of fradulency, the swing of a prevailing passion; any thing shall be preferred when the occassion offereth itself. If Christ had set as little by souls, as some men do, he had never left his Father's bosom, and the glory that he had with him; he had never so humbled himself, so given himself to punishment, affliction, and sorrow, and made himself so an object of scorn, and contempt, and reproach as he did, and all that the souls of sinners might live a life in glory with him.

But methinks this is the mystery of all as to this, that the soul should take that pains, contrive such ways, and take such advantages against itself; for it is the soul that sins, that the soul might die. Oh! sin, what art thou! What hast thou done! and what still wilt thou further do, if mercy, and blood, and grace do not prevent thee! Oh, silly soul! what a fool has sin made of thee! what an ass art thou become to sin! that ever an immortal soul, at first made in the image of God, for God, and for his delight, should so degenerate from its first station, and so abase itself that it might serve sin, as to become the devil's ape, and to play like a Jack Pudding for him upon any stage or theatre in the world!

But I recall myself; for, if sin make one who was some time a glorious angel in heaven, now so to abuse himself as to become, to appearance, as a filthy frog, a toad, a rat, a cat, a fly, a mouse, a dog, or bitch's whelp, to serve its ends upon poor mortals, that it might gull them of everlasting life; no marvel if the soul is so beguiled as to sell itself from God and all good, for so poor a nothing, as a momentary pleasure is. But,

3. If sin and the soul are such great things, then behold the love and care of God—the love to souls, the care he hath taken to deliver them from sin. Sin, as I have said, is such a thing as from which no man can deliver himself. The soul is such a thing, so rich and valuable in the nature of it, that scarce one in twenty thousand counts of it as they should. But God, the lover of mankind, and the greatest enemy to sin, has provided means effectually to overthrow the one, and to save and secure the other. Behold, therefore, the love of God, the care of God for us; for when we neither loved nor cared for ourselves, God both loved us and cared for us. God commended his love toward us, in sending his Son to be the propitiation for our sins.

Let it be then concluded, that God is love, and that the love that God hath to us is such as we never had for ourselves. We have been often tried about our own love to ourselves; and it has been proved over and over, that sometimes even we that are Christians could, and would, if it had been possible, have pawned ourselves, our souls, and our interest in Christ, for a foul and beastly lust. But God, who is rich in mercy, for his great love, wherewith he loved us, would not suffer it so to be. Now, if we are so fickle and uncertain in our love to ourselves, as to value our salvation at so low and so base a rate, can it be imagined that ever we should, had it been left to our choice, have given the best of what we have for the salvation of our souls?

Yet God gave his Son to be the Saviour of the world. I say again, if our love is so slender to our own souls, can any think that it should be more full to the souls of others? And yet God had such love to us, as to give his only begotten Son for our sins. Yet again, how should it be, that we, who are usually so affected with the conceit of our own happiness, since we care no more for our own souls, should do our best to secure the souls of others? And yet God, who is infinitely above all creatures, has so condescended, as to concern himself, and to give the best of his flock, even his only beloved Son, for very dust and ashes. Wherefore, herein is love, not that we loved God, or our neighbor, but that God loved us, and gave his Son to be a propitiation for our sins.

4. Is sin so vile a thing? is the soul so precious a thing? and is God's love and care of the salvation of the souls of sinners, infinitely greater than is their own care for their own souls? Then this should teach those concerned to blush, to blush, I say, and to cover their faces with shame. There is nothing, that I know of, that more becomes a sinner, than blushing and shame doth; for he is the harborer, the nurse, and the nourisher of that vile thing called *sin;* that so great an enemy of God, and that so great an enemy to the soul. It becomes him, also, if he consider what a creature God has made him, and how little he hath set by his own creation, and by the matter of which God hath made his soul. Let him also consider unto what base things he has stooped and prostrated himself, while things infinitely better have stood by and offered themselves unto him freely; yea, how he has cast that God that made him, and his Son that came to redeem him, quite behind his back, and before their faces embraced, loved, and devoted himself unto him that seeks nothing but the damnation of his soul.

Ah, Lord! when will foolish man be wise, and come to God with his hands upon his head, and with his face covered with shame, to ask of him forgiveness for that wickedness which he has committed? which is wickedness committed not only against holiness and justice, against which also men by nature have an antipathy, but against mercy and love, without which man cannot tell what to do.

Blush, sinner, blush! Ah, that thou hadst grace to blush! But this is God's complaint, "Were they ashamed when they had committed abomination? Nay, they were not at all ashamed, neither could they blush." It is a sad thing that men should be thus void of consideration; and yet they are so. They are at a continual jest with God and his word, with the devil and sin, with hell and judgment. Ah, they will be in earnest one day; but that one day will be too late!

5. Is it so, that God, though sin is so fearful a thing, has prepared an effectual remedy against it, and purposed to save us from the evil and damning effects thereof? Then this should beget thankfulness in the hearts of the godly, for they are made partakers of this grace. I say, it should beget thankfulness in thy heart. "Thanks be to God for his unspeakable gift," said the Apostle, when he seriously thought of that which was much inferior to what we have been discoursing of. That was about men's willingness to do good; this is about God's. That was about men's willingness to give money to poor saints; this about God's willingness to give Christ Jesus his Son to the world. It was the thought of this redemption and salvation that made David say, "Bless the Lord, O my soul: and all that is within me, bless his holy name."

Oh! they that are partakers of redeeming grace, and that have a throne of grace, (a covenant of grace,) and a Christ that is the Son of God's love, to come to, and to live by, should be a thankful people. "By him, therefore, let us offer the sacrifice of praise to God continually—giving thanks to his name."

How many obligations has God laid upon his people, to give thanks to him at every remembrance of his holiness!

And to help you do this, study the priesthood, the high priesthood of Jesus Christ, both the first and second part thereof. The first part was that, when he offered up himself without the gate, when he bare our sins in his own body on the tree. The second part is that which he executeth there whither he is now gone, even in heaven itself, where the throne of grace is. I say, study what Christ has done, and is doing. Oh! what is he doing now? He is sprinkling his blood, with his priestly robes on, before the throne of grace. That is too little thought on by the saints of God. "We have such an High Priest, who is set down on the right hand of the throne of the Majesty in the heavens, a minister of the sanctuary, and of the true tabernacle, which the Lord pitched, and not man." Busy thyself, fellow Christian, about this blessed office of Christ. It is full of good, it is full of sweet, it is full of heaven, it is full of relief and succor for the tempted and dejected; wherefore, I say again, study these things, give thyself wholly to them.

6. Since God has prepared himself a lamb, a sacrifice, a priest, a throne of grace, and has bid thee come to him; come to him as there sitting—come, come boldly, as he bids thee. What better warrant canst thou have to come, than to be bid to come of God? When the good man himself bids the beggar come to his house, then he may come boldly; the consideration of the invitation doth encourage. That we have a friend at court, should also make us come boldly. Jesus, as has been showed, as sacrifice and High Priest, is there, in whom we may "have boldness and access with confidence, by the faith of him." Again, "By him also we have access by faith unto this grace wherein we stand, and rejoice in hope of the glory of God." Again, "We have boldness, brethren, to enter into the holiest by the blood of Jesus."

What can be more plain, more encouraging, more comfortable to them that would obtain mercy, and find grace to help in time of need?

It is a dishonor to God, disadvantage to thee, and an encouragement to Satan, when thou hangest back and seemest afraid to come boldly to the throne of grace. "Let us, therefore, draw near with a true heart, in full assurance of faith, having our hearts sprinkled from an evil conscience, and our bodies washed with pure water. Let us hold fast the profession of our faith without wavering, (for he is faithful that promised;) and let us consider one another, to provoke unto love and to good works."

THE

DESIRE OF THE RIGHTEOUS GRANTED:

OR,

A DISCOURSE OF THE RIGHTEOUS MAN'S DESIRES

THE

DESIRE OF THE RIGHTEOUS GRANTED.

THE DESIRE OF THE RIGHTEOUS IS ONLY GOOD.—Prov. xi. 23.

CHAPTER I.

GENERAL COMMENTS ON THE TEXT.

THE FEAR OF THE WICKED, IT SHALL COME UPON HIM: BUT THE DESIRE OF THE RIGHTEOUS SHALL BE GRANTED.—Prov. x. 24.

THIS book of the Proverbs is so called, because it containeth hard, dark, and pithy sentences of wisdom, by which is taught unto young men knowledge and discretion. Wherefore this book is not such as discloseth truths by words antecedent or subsequent to the text, so as other Scriptures generally do, but has its texts, or sentences more independent. For usually each verse standeth upon its own bottom, and presenteth by itself some singular thing to the consideration of the reader; so that I shall not need to bid my reader look back to what went before, nor yet to that which follows, for the better opening of the text; and shall therefore come immediately to the words, and search into them for what hidden treasures are contained therein.

The words, then, in the first place, present us with the *general condition of the whole world;* for all men are ranked under one of these conditions, the wicked or the righteous:

for he that is not wicked is righteous; and he that is not righteous is wicked. "The thoughts of the righteous are right; but the councils of the wicked are deceit." So again, "Lay not wait, O wicked man, against the dwelling of the righteous; spoil not his resting place." I might give you out of this book many such instances, for it flows with such, but the truth hereof is plain enough.

The world is also divided by other general terms; as by these: believers, unbelievers; saints, sinners; good, bad; children of God, and children of the wicked one, &c. These, I say, are general terms, and comprehend not this or that sect, or order of each, but the whole. The believer, saint, good, and child of God is one, namely, the righteous. The unbeliever, the sinner, the bad, and the child of the devil is one, namely, the wicked; as also the text expresses it. So that I say, the text, or these two terms in it comprehend all men; the one, all that shall be saved; the other, all that shall be damned for ever in hell fire.

The wicked, who is he, but the man that loves not God, nor to do his will? The righteous, who is he, but the man that loveth God, and his holy will, to do it?

Of the wicked there are several sorts: some more ignorant, some more knowing. The more ignorant of them are such as go to be executed, as the ox goes to the slaughter, or as a fool to the correction of the stocks; that is, as creatures whose ignorance makes them as unconcerned, while they are going down the stairs to hell. But, alas! their ignorance will be no plea for them before the bar of God. For it is written, "It is a people of no understanding: therefore he that made them will not have mercy on them, and he that formed them will show them no favour."

Though I must confess, the more knowing the wicked is, or the more light and goodness such a one sins against, the greater will his judgment be. "These shall have greater damnation." "It shall be more tolerable at the judgment for Sodom than for them."

There is a wicked man that goes blinded, and a wicked man that goes with his eyes open, to hell. There is a wicked man that cannot see, and a wicked man that will not see, the danger he is in; but hell fire will open both their eyes.

There are that are wicked, and cover all with a cloak of religion, and there are that proclaim their profaneness; but they will both meet in the lake that burns with fire and brimstone. "The wicked shall be turned into hell, and all the nations that forget God."

There are also several sorts (if I may so express myself) of those that are truly righteous, as children, young men, fathers; or saints that fear God, both small and great. Some have more grace than some, and some do better improve the grace they have than others of their brethren do; some also are more valiant for the truth upon the earth than others of their brethren are; yea, some are so swallowed up with God, and love to his word and ways, that they are fit to be a pattern or example in holiness to all that are about them; and some again have their light shining so dim, that they render themselves suspicious to their brethren, whether they are of the number of those that have grace or no. But being gracious they shall not be lost, although such will at the day of reward suffer loss; for this is the will of the Father that sent the Son to be the Saviour of the world, that of all that he had given him he should lose nothing, but should raise it up at the last day.

In the next place, we are here presented with *some of the qualities of the wicked and the righteous.* The wicked has his fears; the righteous has his desires.

The wicked has his fears. "The fear of the wicked, it shall come upon him; but the desire of the righteous shall be granted."

Indeed it seems to the godly, that the wicked feareth not,

—nor doth he after a godly sort; for he that feareth God aright, must not be reputed a wicked man. The wicked, through the pride of his countenance, declareth that he feareth not God aright, because he doth not graciously call upon him; but yet for all that, the wicked at times are haunted, sorely haunted, and that with the worst of fears. "Terrors," says Bildad, "shall make them afraid on every side." And again, "His confidence shall be rooted out of his tabernacle, and it shall bring him to the king of terrors."

A wicked man though he may hector it at times with his proud heart, as though he feared neither God nor hell, yet again at times, his soul is even drowned with terrors. "The morning is to them even as the shadow of death; if one knew them, they are in the terrors of the shadow of death." At times, I say, it is thus with them, especially when they are under warm convictions that the day of judgment is at hand, or when they feel in themselves as if death was coming as a tempest, to steal them away from their enjoyments, and lusts, and delights. Then the bed shakes on which they lie; then the proud tongue doth falter in their mouth, and their knees knock one against another; then their conscience stares, and roars, and tears, and arraigns before God's judgment seat or threatens to follow them down to hell, and there to wreak its fury on them, for all the abuses and affronts this wicked wretch offered to it in the day in which it controlled his unlawful deeds.

Oh! none can imagine what fearful plights a wicked man is in sometimes; though God in his just judgment towards them suffers them again and again to stifle and choke such awakenings, from a purpose, to reserve them unto the day of judgment to be punished.

In the third place, as the wicked has his fears, so the *righteous has his desires.* "The desire of the righteous shall be granted." But this must not be taken exclusively, as if the wicked had nothing but fears, and the righteous nothing but desires. For, both by Scripture and experience also, we find the wicked has his desires, and the righteous man his fears.

1. For the wicked; they are not without their desires. "Let me die the death of the righteous, and let my last end be like his," was the desire of wicked Balaam: and another place saith, "The wicked boasteth of his heart's desire"—that he is for heaven as well as the best of you all; but yet, even then, "he blesseth the covetous, whom the Lord abhorreth."

Wicked men have their desires and their hopes too, but the hope and desire of unjust men perisheth; yea, and though they look and long too, all the day long, with desires of life and glory, yet their fears, and them only, shall come upon them; for they are the desires of the righteous that shall be granted.

The desires of the wicked want a good bottom. They flow not from a sanctified mind, nor from love to the God, or the heaven now desired; but only from such a sense as devils have of torments, and so, as they, they cry out, "I beseech thee, torment me not."

But their fears have a substantial foundation; for they are grounded upon the view of an ill-spent life, the due reward of which is hell fire. "The unrighteous shall not inherit the kingdom of God." Their place is without. "For without are dogs, and sorcerers, and whoremongers, and murderers, and idolators, and whosoever loveth and maketh a lie."

Their fears, therefore, have a strong foundation; they have also matter to work upon, which is guilt and justice, the which they shall never be able to escape, without a miracle of grace and mercy.

Therefore it saith, and that with emphasis, "The fear of the wicked, it shall come upon him;" wherefore, his desire shall die with him: for the promise of a grant of that which is desired, is only entailed to righteousness. "The desire of the righteous shall be granted; but, "Grant not, O Lord, the desires of the wicked," saith David.

2. Nor are the righteous without their fears, and that even all their life long. "Through fear of death, they (some of them) are all their lifetime subject to bondage."

But, as the desires of the wicked shall be frustrate, so shall also the fears of the godly. Hence you have them admonished, yea, commanded, not to be afraid, neither of devils, death, nor hell; for the fear of the righteous shall not come upon them to eternal damnation. "The desire of the righteous shall be granted."

No, they are not to fear what sin can do unto them, nor what all their sins can do unto them. I do not say they should not be afraid of sinning, nor of those temporal judgments that sin shall bring upon them; for of such things they ought to be afraid; as saith the Psalmist, "My flesh trembleth for fear of thee, and I am afraid of thy judgments."

But of eternal ruin, of that they ought not to be afraid with slavish fear. "Wherefore should I fear," said the prophet, "in the days of evil, when the iniquity of my heels shall compass me about?" And again, "Ye have done all this wickedness: yet turn not aside from following the Lord; for the Lord will not forsake his people, for his great name's sake."

The reason is, because the righteous are secured by their faith in Christ Jesus; also, their fears stand upon a mistake of the nature of the covenant, in which they are wrapped up, which is ordered for them in all things, and sure. Besides, God is purposed to magnify the riches of his grace in their salvation; therefore, goodness and mercy shall, to that end, follow them all the days of their life, that they may dwell in the house of the Lord forever. They have also their Intercessor and Advocate ready with God, to take up matters for them, in such a way as may maintain true peace betwixt their God and them; and as may encourage them to be sober, and hope to the end, for the grace that is to be brought unto them at the revelation of Jesus Christ.

Wherefore, though the godly have their fears, yea, sometimes dreadful fears, and that of perishing forever and ever; yet the day is coming, when their fears and tears shall be done away, and when their desires only shall be granted. "The fear of the wicked, it shall come upon him: but the desire of the righteous shall be granted."

The words, then, are a prediction or prophecy, and that both concerning the wicked and the righteous, with reference to time and things to come, and both shall certainly be fulfilled in their season.

Hence it is said concerning the wicked, that their triumphing is short, and that the joy of the hypocrite is but for a moment. Oh, their end will be bitter as wormwood, and will cut like a two-edged sword! Of this, Solomon admonishes youth, when he saith, "Rejoice, O young man, in thy youth, and let thy heart cheer thee in the days of thy youth, and walk in the ways of thine heart, and in the sight of thine eyes: but know thou, that for all these things God will bring thee into judgment."

These Scriptures show the desperate spirit that possesses the children of men, who, though they hear and read all this, yet cannot be reclaimed from such courses as are wicked, and that lead to such a condition. I say they will not be reclaimed from such courses as lead to ways that go down to hell, where their soul must mourn, even then when their flesh and body are consumed. Oh! how dear-bought are their pleasures, and how will their laughter be turned into tears and anguish unutterable! and that presently, for it is coming. "Their judgment now of a long time lingereth not, and their damnation slumbereth not." But what good will their covenant of death now do them? And will their agreement with hell yield them comfort? Is not God as well mighty to punish as to save? Or can these sinners believe God out of the world? or cause that he should not pay them home for their sins, and recompense them for all the evil they have loved, and continued in the commission of? "Can thy heart endure, or can thy hands be strong, in the day that God shall deal with thee?"

Thou art bold now, I mean, bold in a wicked way; thou sayest now, thou wilt keep thy sweet morsels of sin under thy tongue, thou wilt keep them still within thy mouth. Poor wretch! read Job xx. 11. Thy sins shall lie down in the dust with thee. Thou hast sucked the poison of asps, and the viper's tongue shall slay thee. Thou shalt not see the rivers, the streaming floods, the brooks of butter and honey. All darkness shall be hid in thy secret places, a fire not blown shall consume thee, &c. "This is the portion of a wicked man from God, and the heritage appointed to him by God." Ver. 16–29.

And as they predict or prophesy what shall become of the wicked; so also they plentifully foretell what shall happen to the righteous, when he saith, their desire shall be granted: of which more anon.

Only here I will drop this short hint, That the righteous have great cause to rejoice. For what more pleasing, what more comfortable to a man, than to be assured, and that from the Spirit of truth, that what he desireth shall be granted? And this the righteous are assured of here; for he saith it in words at length, "The desire of the righteous shall be granted."

This then should comfort them against their fears, and the sense of their unworthiness; it should also make them hold up their heads under all their temptations, and the affronts that is usual for them to meet with in the world. The righteous! who so vilified as the righteous? He by the wise men of the world is counted a very Abraham, a fool; like to him who is the father of us all. But as he left all for the desire that he had of a better country, and at last obtained his desire; (for after he had patiently endured, he obtained the promise;) so those that walk in the steps of that faith which our father Abraham had, even those also in the end shall find place in Abraham's bosom. Wherefore it is meet that we should cheer up and be glad, because what we desire shall be granted unto us.

CHAPTER II.

WHO ARE THE RIGHTEOUS.

But I shall here leave off this short way of paraphrasing upon the text, and shall come more distinctly to inquire into the nature of the words: but my subject matter shall be the last part of the verse, "The desire of the righteous shall be granted." From which words there are these things to be inquired into. 1. What, or who is the righteous man? 2. What are the desires of a righteous man? 3. What is meant or to be understood by the granting of the desires of the righteous: "The desire of the righteous shall be granted."

I. For the first of these, namely, What, or who is the righteous man?

My way of prosecuting this head shall be to show you, First, that I intend a righteous man, not in every sense, but in that which is the best; otherwise I shall miscarry as to the intendment of the Holy Ghost. For it may not be supposed, that these words reach to them that are righteous in general, but in a special sense; such I mean as are so in the judgment of God. For, as I hinted, there are several sorts of righteous men, that yet have nothing to do with this blessed promise, or that shall never, as such, have their desires granted.

There is one that is *righteous in his own eyes*, and is yet far enough off from the blessing of the text: "There is a generation that are pure (or righteous) in their own sight, yet are not purged from their filthiness." These are they that you also read of in the Evangelist Luke, that are said to trust in themselves that they were righteous, and despised others. These are set so low, by this their foolish confidence, in the eyes of Jesus Christ, that he even preferred a praying publican before them. Wherefore, these cannot be the men, I mean those righteous men, to whom this promise is made.

There are those that *by others are counted righteous.* I mean they are so accounted by their neighbours. Thus Korah and his company are called the people of the Lord, and all the congregation by them also called holy, every one of them. Num. xvi. 3, 41. But as he who commends himself is not approved, so it is no great matter if all the world should count us righteous, if God esteemeth us not for such. "For not he that commendeth himself is approved, but whom the Lord commendeth."

There are those that indeed are *righteous when compared with others:* "I came not to call the righteous." "For scarcely for a righteous man will one die," and the like, are texts thus to be understood. For such as these are, as to life mortal, better than others. But these, if they are none otherwise righteous, than by acts and works of righteousness of their own, are not the persons contained in the text, that are to have their desires granted.

The righteous man, therefore, in the text is, and ought to be thus described. 1. He is one whom God makes righteous, by reckoning him so in Christ. 2. He is one that God makes righteous by possessing him with a principle of righteousness. 3. He is one that is practically righteous.

1. He is one that God makes righteous by reckoning him so in Christ. Now, if God makes him righteous, his righteousness is not his own, I mean this sort of righteousness. "Their rigthcousness is of me, saith the Lord."

God then makes a man righteous by putting righteousness upon him; by putting the righteousness of God upon him. Hence we are said to be made the righteousness of God in Christ. "For God hath made him to be sin for us, who knew no sin; that we might be made the righteousness of God in him."

Thus God, therefore, reckoneth us righteous, even by imputing that unto us which is able to make us so. "He is made unto us of God righteousness." Wherefore, he saith again, "In the Lord shall all the seed of Israel be justified, and shall glory."

The righteousness then by which a man is made righteous, with righteousness to justification of life before God, (for that is it we are speaking of now,) is the righteousness of another than he who is justified thereby. Hence it is said again, by the soul thus justified and made righteous. "The Lord hath clothed me with the garments of salvation, he hath covered me with the robe of righteousness." As he also saith in another place, "I spread my skirt over thee, and covered thy nakedness."

This we call a being made righteous by reckoning, by the reckoning of God; for none is of power to reckon one righteous but God, because none can make one so to be but him.

He that can make me rich, though I am, in myself, the poorest of men, may reckon me rich, if together with his so reckoning, he indeed doth make me rich. This is the case: God makes a man righteous by bestowing righteousness upon him, by counting the righteousness of his Son for his. He gives him righteousness, a righteousness already performed, and completed by the obedience of his Son.

Not that this righteousness, by being bestowed upon us, is severed from Jesus Christ; for it is still his and in him. How then, may some say, doth it become ours?

I answer, by our being put into him. "For of God are we in Christ Jesus, who is made unto us, of him, righteousness." And again, "We are made the righteousness of God in him." So then the righteousness of Christ covereth his, as a man's garments cover the members of his body; "For we are the body of Christ, and members in particular." The righteousness therefore is Christ's; resideth still in him, and covereth us, as the child is lapped up in its father's skirts, or as the chicken is covered with the feathers of the hen. I make use of all these similitudes, thereby to inform you of my meaning; for by all these things are set forth the way of our being made righteous to justification of law.

Now thus a man is made righteous, without any regard to what he has, or to what is of him; for as to him it is utterly another's. Just as if I should with the skirts of my garment take up and clothe some poor and naked infant, that I find cast out into the open field. Now, if I cover the person, I cover scabs, and sores, and ulcers, and all blemishes. Hence God, by putting this righteousness upon us, is said to hide and cover our sins. "Blessed is the man whose transgressions are forgiven, and whose sin is covered. Blessed is the man to whom the Lord will not impute sin."

For since this righteousness is Christ's, and counted or reckoned ours by the grace of God, it is therefore bestowed upon us, not because we are, but to make us righteous before the face of God. Hence, as I said, it is said to make us righteous, even as gay clothes do make a naked body fine. "He hath made him to be sin for us, who knew no sin, that we might be made the righteousness of God in him."

This is of absolute necessity to be known, and to be believed. For without this no man can be counted righteous before God; and if we stand not righteous before God, it will benefit us nothing as to life eternal, though we should be counted righteous by all the men on earth. Besides, if God counts me righteous, I am safe, though in and of myself I am nothing but a sinner, and ungodly. The reason is, because God has a right to bestow righteousness upon me, for he has righteousness to spare; he has also a right to forgive, because sin is the transgression of the law. Yea, he has therefore sent his Son into the world to accomplish righteousness for sinners, and God of his mercy bestows it upon those that shall receive it by faith. Now, if God shall count me righteous, who will be so hardy as to conclude I yet shall perish? "It is God that justifieth; who is he that condemneth? It is Christ that died, yea, rather that is risen again, who is even at the right hand of God, who also maketh intercession for us. Who shall separate us from the love of Christ?"

Thus, therefore, is a man made righteous, even of God by Christ, or through his righteousness. Now, if, as we said, a man is thus made righteous, then, in this sense he is good before God, before he has done any thing of that which the law calls good before men; for God maketh not men righteous with this righteousness, because they have been or have done good, but before they are capable of doing good at all. Hence we are said to be justified while ungodly, even as an infant is clothed with the skirt of another, while naked, as touching itself.

Works, therefore, do not precede, but follow after, this righteousness; and even thus it is in nature: the tree must be good before it bear good fruit, and so also must a man. It is as impossible to make a man bring forth good fruit to God, before he is of God made good, as it is for a thorn or bramble bush to bring forth figs or grapes.

But again, a man must be righteous before he can be good; righteous by imputation, before his person, his intellectuals, can be qualified with good, as to the principle of good. For neither the Spirit, nor any grace is given unto the sinner, before God has made him righteous with this righteousness of Christ by faith. Wherefore, it is said, that after he had spread his skirt over us, he washed us with water; that is, with the washing of sanctification.

And to conclude otherwise, is as much as to say, that an unjustified man has faith, the Spirit, and the graces thereof; which to say, is to overthrow the gospel. For what need of Christ's righteousness, if a man may have faith and the Spirit of Christ without it; since the Spirit is said to be the earnest of our inheritance, and that by which we are sealed unto the day of redemption.

But the truth is, the Spirit which makes our person good, I mean that which sanctifies our natures, is the fruit of the righteousness which is by Jesus Christ. For as Christ died and rose again, before he sent the Holy Ghost from heaven to his; so the benefit of his death and resurrection is by God bestowed upon us, in order to the Spirit's possessing our souls.

2. And this leads me to the second thing, namely, That God makes a man righteous by possessing him with a principle of righteousness, even with the Spirit of rightousness. For though, as to justification before God from the curse of the law, we are made righteous while we are ungodly, and yet sinners; yet being made free from sin thus, we forthwith become, through a change which the Holy Ghost works in our minds, the servants of God. Hence it is said, "There is therefore, now no condemnation to them which are in Christ Jesus, who walk not after the flesh, but after the Spirit." For though, as the Apostle also insinuates here, that being in Christ Jesus is antecedent to our walking after the Spirit; yet a man can make no demonstration of his being in Christ Jesus, but by his walking in the Spirit; because the Spirit is an inseparable companion of imputed righteousness, and immediately follows it, to dwell with whomsoever it is bestowed upon.

Now, it dwelling in us, principles us in all the powers of our souls, with that which is righteousness in the habit and nature of it. Hence the fruits of the Spirit are called the fruits of goodness and righteousness, as the fruits of a tree are called the fruit of that tree.

And again, "He that doeth righteousness is righteous," not only in our first sense, but even in this also. For who can do righteousness without he be principled so to do? Who can act reason, that hath not reason? So none can bring forth righteousness that hath not in him the root of righteousness, which is the Spirit of God, which comes to us by virtue of our being made sons of God. Hence the fruits of the Spirit are called "The fruits of righteousness, which are by Jesus Christ to the praise and glory of God."

This, then, is the thing we say, namely, That he that is made righteous unto justification of life before God, is also habituated with a principle of righteousness, as that which follows that righteousness by which he stands just before; I say, as that which follows it; for it comes by Jesus Christ, and by our being justified before God, and made righteous through him.

This second gift, then, also comes to us before we do any act spiritually good. For how can a man act righteousness but from a principle of righteousness? And seeing this principle is not of, or by, nature, but of, and by, grace, through Christ, it follows, that as no man is just before God, that is not covered with the righteousness of Christ, so no man can do righteousness but by the power of the Spirit of God which must dwell in him. Hence we are said, by the Spirit to mortify the deeds of the body, which work is preparatory to fruitful actions. The husbandman that laboreth, says Paul, must first be partaker of the fruit; so he that worketh righteousness, must first be blessed with a principle of righteousness.

Men must have eyes before they see, tongues before they speak, and legs before they go; even so must a man be made inwardly good and righteous, before he can work righteousness. This, then, is the second thing: God makes a man righteous by possessing him with a principle of righteousness; which principle is not of nature, but of grace; not of man, but God.

3. The man in the text is practically righteous, or one that declareth himself by works that are good, a virtuous, a righteous man, even as the tree declares by the apple or plum it beareth, what manner of tree it is. "Ye shall know them by their fruits."

Fruits show outwardly what the heart is principled with. Show me then thy faith, which abideth in the heart, by thy works in a well spent life.

Mark how the apostle words it. "We being," saith he, "made free from sin, and become servants to God, have our fruit unto holiness, and the end everlasting life." Mark his order: First we are made free from sin. Now that is by "being justified freely by the grace of God, through the redemption which is in Jesus Christ, whom God has set forth to be a propitiation through faith in his blood." Now this is God's act, without any regard at all to any good that the sinner has, or can accomplish; "not by works of righteousness which we have done, but according to his mercy," thus he saveth us. Now, "being made free from sin," what follows? "We become the servants of God," that is, by that turn which the Holy Ghost makes upon our heart, when it reconciles it to the word of God's grace; for that, as was said afore, is the effect of the indwelling and operation of the Holy Ghost. Now, having our hearts thus changed by God and his word, the fruits of righteousness put forth themselves by us. For as "when we were in the flesh, the motions of sin, which is in our members, did bring forth fruit unto death;" so now, if we are in the Spirit, (and we are not in the flesh, but in the Spirit if so be the Spirit of Christ dwells in us,) by the motions and workings of that, "we have our fruit unto holiness, and the end everlasting life."

But now by these fruits we are neither made righteous nor good; for the apple maketh not the tree good, it only declares it so to be. Here, therefore, all those are mistaken, that think to be righteous by doing righteous actions, or good by doing good. A man must first be righteous, or he cannot do righteousness, I mean, that which is evangelically such. Now, if a man is, and must be righteous, before he acts righteousness, then all his works are born too late to make him just before God; for his works, if they be right, flow from the heart of a righteous man, of a man that had, before he had any good work, a two-fold righteousness bestowed on him; one to make him righteous in the sight of God, the other to principle him to be righteous before the world, that he might be called "a tree of righteousness, the planting of the Lord, that he might be glorified."

The want of understanding of this, is that which keeps so many in a mist of darkness about the way of salvation; for they, poor hearts, when they hear of the need that they have of a righteousuess to commend them to God, "being ignorant of the righteousness of God," that is, of that which God imputeth to a man, and that by which he counteth him righteous, have it not in their thoughts to accept of that unto justification of life; but presently betake themselves to the law of works, and fall to work there for the performing of a righteousness, that they may be accepted of God for the same, and so "submit not themselves to the righteousness of God," by which, and by which only, the soul stands just before God.

Wherefore, I say, it is necessary that this be distinctly laid down: That a man must be righteous first, even before he doeth righteousness. The argument is plain from the order of nature. "For a corrupt tree cannot bring forth good fruit. Wherefore make the tree good, and so his fruit good; or the tree corrupt, and his fruit corrupt." Reason also says the same; for how can blacks beget white children, when both father and mother are blacks? How can a man without grace, and the Spirit of grace, do good? Nature is defiled, even to the mind and conscience; how then can good fruit come from snch a stock?

Besides, God accepteth not any work, of a person who is not first accepted of him. "The Lord had respect to Abel and to his offering:" to Abel first, that is, before that Abel offered. But how could God have respect to Abel, if Abel was not pleasing in his sight? and how could Abel be yet pleasing in his sight for the sake of his own righteousness, when it is in plain that Abel had not yet done good works? He was therefore first made acceptable in the sight of God, by and for the sake of that righteousness which God of his grace had put upon him to justification of life; through and by which also the Holy Ghost, in the graces of it, dwelt in Abel's soul. Now Abel being justified, and also possessed with this holy principle, he offers his sacrifice to God. Hence it is said, that he "offered by faith," by the faith which he had precedent to his offering; for if through faith he offered, he had that faith before he offered,—that is plain. Now this faith looked not for acceptance for the sake of what he offered, but for the sake of that righteousness which it did apprehend God had already put upon him, and by which he was made righteous. Wherefore his offering was the offering of a righteous man, of a man made righteous first; and so the text saith, "By faith Abel offered unto God a more excellent sacrifice than Cain, by which he obtained witness that he was righteous," that is, antecedent to his offering. For he had faith in Christ to come, by which he was made righteous; he also had the Spirit of faith, by which he was possessed with a righteous principle: and so being in this manner made righteous, righteous before God, and also principled to work, he comes and offereth his more acceptable sacrifice to God. For this all will grant, namely, that the works of a righteous man are more excellent than are even the best works of the wicked. Hence Cain's works came behind; for God had not made him righteous, had not respect unto his person, had not given him the Spirit and faith, whereby alone men are made capable of offering acceptably. "But to Cain and to his offering, the Lord had not respect."

From all which it is manifest, that the person must be accepted, before the duty performed can be pleasing unto God; and if the person must first be accepted, it is evident that the person must first be righteous; but if the person be righteous; before he doeth good, then it follows that he is made righteous by righteousness that is none of his own, that he hath had no hand in, further than to receive it as the gracious gift of God. Deny this, and it follows that God accepteth men without respect to righteousness; and then what follows that, but that "Christ is dead in vain?'

We must not, therefore, be deceived: "He that doeth righteousness is righteous, even as the Lord is righteous." He doth not say, He that doeth righteousness shall be righteous; as if his doing works would make him so before God; but He that doeth righteousness is righteous, antecedent to his doing righteousness. And it must be thus understood, else that which follows signifies nothing; for he saith, "He that doeth righteousness is righteous, even as he (the Lord his God) is righteous." But how is the Lord righteous? Even antecedent to his works. The Lord was righteous before he wrought righteousness in the world; and even so are we, that is, every child of God. "As he is, so are we, in this world."

But we must, in this admit of this difference: the Lord was eternally and essentially righteous before he did any work: but we are imputatively righteous, and also made so by a second work of creation, before we do good works. It holds, therefore, only as to order; God was righteous before he made the world, and we are righteous before we do good works.

Thus, therefore, we have described the righteous man. 1. He is one whom God makes righteous by reckoning, or imputation. 2. He is one that God makes righteous by possessing him with a principle of righteousness. 3. He is one that is practically righteous.

Nor dare I give a narrower description of a righteous man than this; nor otherwise than thus.

I dare not give a narrower description of a righteous man

than this, because whoever pretends to justification, if he be not sanctified, pretends to what he is not; and whoever pretends to sanctification, if he shows not the fruit thereof by a holy life, he deceiveth his own heart, and professeth but in vain.

Nor dare I give this description otherwise than thus, because there is a real distinction to be put between that righteousness by which we should be just before God, and that which is in us a principle of sanctification; the first being the obedience of the Son of God without us, the second being the work of the Spirit in our hearts.

There is also a difference to be put betwixt the principle by which we work righteousness, and the works themselves; as a difference is to be put betwixt the cause and the effect, the tree and the apple.

CHAPTER III.

WHAT ARE THE DESIRES OF THE RIGHTEOUS.

I COME now to the second thing into which we are to inquire, and that is, WHAT ARE THE DESIRES OF A RIGHTEOUS MAN?

My way of handling this question shall be, 1. To speak of the nature of Desire in the general. 2. And then to show you, more particularly, what are the desires of the righteous.

For the first. Desires in general may be thus described: they are the workings of the heart or mind after that, of which the soul is persuaded that it is good to be enjoyed. This, I say, is so without respect to regulation; for we speak not now of good desires, but of desires themselves, even as they flow from the heart of a human creature; I say, desires are, or may be called, the workings of the heart after this or that; the strong motions of the mind unto it. Hence the love of women to their husbands is called "their desire;" and the wife also is called "the desire of the husband's eyes." Also love to a woman, to make her one's wife, is called by the name of "desire." Now, how strong the motions or passions of love are, who is there that is an utter stranger thereto? Hunger is also a most vehement thing; and that which is called "hunger" in one place, is called "desire" in another. "And he desired to be fed with the crumbs which fell from the rich man's table." Exceeding desires are called "lustings," to show the vehemency of desires. Longings, pantings, thirstings, prayers, &c., if there be any life in them, are all fruits of a desirous soul.

Desires, therefore, flow from the consideration of the goodness or profitableness, or pleasureableness of a thing, yea, all desires flow from thence; for a man desires not that about which he has had no consideration, nor that neither on which he has thought, if he doth not judge it will yield him something worth desiring.

When Eve saw the forbidden fruit was a beautiful tree, (though her sight deceived her,) then she desired it, and took thereof herself, and gave to her husband, and he did eat; yea, saith the text, "when she saw that it was a tree to be desired, to make one wise, she took."

Hence that which is called "coveting" in one place, is called "desiring" in another; for desires are craving; and by desires a man seeks to enjoy what is not his.

From all these things, therefore, we see what desire is. It is the working of the heart after that which the soul is persuaded is good to be enjoyed. And of desires there are these two effects: One is, (on a supposition that the soul is not satisfied with what it has,) to cause the soul to range and hunt through the world, for something that may fill up that vacancy that yet the soul finds in itself, and would have supplied. Hence desires are said to be wandering, and the soul said to walk by them. "Better is the sight of the eyes, than the wandering of the desire;" or, than the walking of the soul. Desires are hunting things, and how many things do some empty souls seek after, both as to the world, and also as to religion, who have desirous minds! The second effect is this. If desires be strong, they carry all away with them. They are like Samson, they will pull down the gates of a city, but they will go out abroad. Nothing can stop the current of desires, but the enjoyment of the thing desired, or a change of opinion as to the worth, or want of worth, of the thing desired.

But we will now come to the thing more particularly intended, which is, to show, what are the desires of the righteous. This is that which the text calls us to the consideration of, because it saith, "The desire of the righteous shall be granted."

We have hitherto spoken of desires, as to the nature of them, without respect to them as good or bad; but now we shall speak of them, as they are the effects of a sanctified mind, as they are the breathings, pantings, lustings, hungerings, and thirstings of a righteous man.

The text says, "The desire of the righteous shall be granted." What, then, are the desires of the righteous? Now, I will, 1. Speak of their desires in the general, or with reference to them as to their bulk. 2. I will speak of them more particularly as they work this way, and that.

1. For their desires in the general. The same Solomon that saith, "The desire of the righteous shall be granted," saith also, "The desire of the righteous is only good."

This text giveth us, in the general, a description of the desires of a righteous man; and a sharp and smart description it is. For, where, may some say, is then the righteous man, or the man that hath none but good desires? And if it be answered, They are good in the main, or good in the general; yet that will seem to come short of an answer: for in that he saith, "The desire of the righteous is only good," it is as much as to say, that a righteous man has none but good desires, or desireth nothing but things that are good.

Wherefore, before we go any further, I must labor to reconcile the experience of good men with this text, which thus gives us a description of the desires of the righteous.

A righteous man, then, is to be considered more generally, or more strictly. More generally, as he consisteth of the whole man, of flesh and spirit, of body and soul, of grace and nature; now consider him thus, and you can by no means reconcile the text with his experience, nor his experience with the text. For, as he is body, flesh, and nature, (for all these are with him, though he be a righteous man,) so he has desires vastly different from those described in this text, vastly differing from what is good; yea, what is it not, that is naught, that the flesh and nature, even of a righteous man, will not desire? Do you think that the Scripture speaketh in vain, "The spirit that dwelleth in us lusteth to envy?" And again, "In me, that is, in my flesh, dwelleth no good thing." And again, "The flesh lusteth against the Spirit." And again, the lusts thereof "war against the soul."

From all these texts we find, that a righteous man has other workings, lusts, and desires, than such only as are good. Here, then, if we consider a righteous man thus generally, is no place of agreement betwixt him and this text.

We must then consider him, in the next place, more strictly, as he may, and is to be distinguished from his flesh, his carnal lusts, and sinful nature. Then, a righteous man is taken sometimes as to his prevailing principle, his best part, or as he is a second creation; and so, or as so considered, his desires are only good.

He is taken, sometimes, I say, as to, or for, his best part, or as he is a second creation; as these Scriptures declare:—"If any man be in Christ, he is a new creature; all things are become new; created in Christ Jesus; born of God; believing heavenly things; renewed after the image of him that created them;" and the like. By all which places, the sinful flesh, the old man, the law of sin, the outward man, all which are corrupt according to the deceitful lusts, are excluded, and so pared off from the man, as he is righteous; for his delight in the law of God is after the inward man.

And Paul himself was forced thus to distinguish of himself, before he could come to make a right judgment in this matter. Saith he, "That which I do I allow not: for what I would, I do not; but what I hate, that do I." See you not here how he cleaves himself in twain, severing himself as he is spiritual, from himself as he is carnal; and ascribeth his motions to what is good, to himself only as he is spiritual, or the new man. "If then I do that which I would not, I consent unto the law that it is good." But I trow, sir, your consenting to what is good, is not by that part which doth do what you would not. 'No, no, saith he, that which doth do what I would not, I disown, and count it no part of sanctified Paul.' "Now then it is no more I that do it, but sin that dwelleth in me. For in me, (that is, in my flesh,) dwelleth no good thing: for to will is present with me; but how to perform that which is good I find not. For the good that I would, I do not: but the evil which I would not, that I do. Now, if I do that I would not, it is no more I that do it, but sin that dwelleth in me." Thus, you see, Paul is forced to make two men of himself, saying, I and I: I do not—I do —I would not do: "what I hate, that I do." Now it cannot be the same I, unto whom these contraries are applied; but his sinful flesh is one I, and his godly mind the other; and, indeed, so he concludes it in this chapter, saying, "So, then, with the mind I myself serve the law of God, but with the flesh the law of sin."

Thus, therefore, the Christian man must distinguish concerning himself; and doing so, he shall find, though he has flesh, and as he is such, he hath lusts contrary to God; yet as he is a new creature, he allows not, but hates the motions and desires of the flesh; consents to, and wills and delights in the law of God. Yea, as a new creature, he can do nothing else: for the new man, inward man, or hidden man of the heart, being the immediate work of the Holy Ghost, and consisting only of that which is divine and heavenly, cannot breathe, or act, or desire to act, in ways and courses that are carnal. Wherefore, in this sense, or as the righteous man is thus considered, his desires are only good.

As the righteous man, now, must here be taken for the best part, for the I that would do good, for the I that hates the evil; so again we must consider the desires of this righteous man, as they flow from that fountain of grace, which is the Holy Ghost within him; and as they are immediately mixed with those foul channels, in and through which they must pass, before they can be put forth into acts.

For though the desire as to its birth and first being, is only good; yet, before it comes into much motion, it gathers that from the defilements of the passages through which it comes, which makes it to bear a tang of flesh, and weakness in the skirts of it; and the evil that dwells in us is so universal, and also always so ready, that as sure as there is any motion to what is good, so sure evil is present with it. For when, or whenever I would do good, says Paul, evil is present with me.

Hence it follows, that all our graces, and so our desires, receive disadvantage by our flesh; *that* mixing itself with what is good, and so abating the excellency of the good.

There is a spring that yieldeth water good and clear, but the channels through which this water comes to us are muddy, foul, or dirty. Now, of the channels the waters receive a disadvantage, and so come to us savoring of what came not with them from the fountain, but from the channels.

This is the cause of the coolness, and of the weakness, of the flatness, and of the many extravagancies that attend some of our desires. They come warm from the Spirit and grace of God in us; but as hot water running through cold pipes, or as clear water running through dirty conveyances, so our desires gather soil.

You read, in Solomon's Ecclesiastes, of a time when desires fail, for that man goeth to his long home. And as to good desires, there is not one of them, when we are in our prime, but they fail also as to the perfecting of that which a man desires to do. "To will is present with me," says Paul, "but how to perform that which is good I find not." To will or to desire, that is present with me; but when I have willed or desired to do, to perform is what I cannot attain to. But why not attain to a performance? Why, says he, "I find a law in my members warring against the law of my mind;"

and this law takes me prisoner, and "brings me into captivity to the law of sin, which is in my members." Now, where things willed and desired meet with such obstructions, no marvel if our willing and desiring, though they set out lustily at the beginning, come yet lame home in conclusion.

There is a man, who, when he first prostrates himself before God, doth it with desires as warm as fire-coals; but erewhile he finds, for all that, that the mettle of those desires, were it not revived with fresh supplies, would be quickly spent and grow cold. But yet the desire is good, and only good, as it comes from the breathing of the Spirit of God within us.

We must, therefore, as I said, distinguish betwixt what is good and that which doth alloy it, as gold is to be distinguished from the earth and dross that doth attend it.

The man that believed, desired to believe better, and so cries out, "Lord, help my unbelief." The man that feared God, desired to fear him better, saying, "I desire to fear thy name." But these desires failed, as to the performance of what was begun, so that they were forced to come off but lamely, as to their faith and fear they had; yet the desires were true, good, and such as were accepted of God by Christ; not according to what they had not, but as to those good motions which they had. Distinguish, then, the desires of the righteous in the nature of them, from that corruption and weakness of ours that cleave to them, and then again, they are only good.

There is another thing to be considered, and that is, the different frames that our inward man is in, while we live as pilgrims in the world. A man, as he is not always well without, so neither is he always well within. Our inward man is subject to transient, though not utter decays. And as it is when the outward man is sick, strength and stomach, lust and desire fail, so it is, when our inward man has caught a cold likewise.

The inward man I call the new creature, of which the

Spirit of God is the support, as my soul supports my body. But, I say, this new man is not always well. He knows nothing, that knows not this. Now being sick, things fail. As when a man is not in health of body, his pulse beats so as to declare that he is sick; so when a man is not well within, his inward pulses, which are his desires—for I count the desires for the pulses of the inward man—they also declare that the man is not well within. They beat too little after God; weak and faintly after grace. They also have their halts; they beat not evenly as when the soul is well, but so as to manifest all is not well there.

We read that the church of Sardis was under sore sickness insomuch that some of her things were quite dead, and they that were not so, were yet ready to die. Yet life is life, we say; and as long as there is a pulse, or breath, though breath scarce able to shake a feather, we cast not away all hope of life. Desires, then, though they be weak, are notwithstanding true desires, if they be the desires of the righteous thus described, and therefore are truly good, according to our text.

David says he opened his mouth and panted, for he longed for God's commandments. This was a sickness, but not such a one as we have been speaking of. The spouse also cried out that she was sick of love. Such sickness would do us good, for in it the pulse beat, strongly and well.

Objection. But it may be objected, 'I am yet in doubt of the goodness of my desires, both because my desires run both ways, and because those that run towards sin and the world, seem more and stronger than those that run after God, and Christ, and grace.'

Answer. There is not a Christian under heaven but has desires that run both ways, as is manifest from what hath been said already. Flesh will be flesh: grace shall not make it otherwise. By flesh I mean that body of sin and death that dwelleth in the godly. As grace will act according to its nature, so sin will act according to the nature of sin. Now, the flesh has desires, and the desires of the flesh and of the mind are both one in the ungodly. Thank God it is not so in thee.

The flesh, I say, hath its desires in the godly. Hence, it is said to lust enviously; to lust against the Spirit: "The flesh lusteth against the Spirit." And if it be so audacious as to fly in the face of the Holy Ghost, wonder that thou art not wholly carried away with it.

Objection. 'But those desires that run to the world and sin, seem most and strongest in me.'

Answer. "The works of the flesh are manifest;" that is, more plainly discovered even in the godly, than are the works of the Holy Ghost.

And this their manifestation ariseth from these following particulars:

1. We know the least appearance of a sin better by its native hue, than we know a grace of the Spirit.

2. Sin is sooner felt in its bitterness to, and upon, a sanctified soul, than is the grace of God. A little aloes will be sooner tasted, than will much sweet, though mixed therewith.

3. Sin is dreadful and murderous in the sight of a sanctified soul. Wherefore the apprehending of that makes us often forget, and often question whether we have any grace or no.

4. Grace lies deep in the hidden part, but sin lies high, and floats above in the flesh; wherefore, it is easier, oftener seen, than is the grace of God. The little fishes swim on the top of the water, but the biggest and best keep down below, and so are seldomer seen.

5. Grace, as to quantity, seems less than sin. What is a little leaven, or a grain of mustard seed, to the bulky lump of a body of death?

6. Sin is seen by its own darkness, and also in the light

of the Spirit; but the Spirit itself neither discovers itself, nor yet its graces, by every glance of its own light.

7. A man may have the Spirit busily at work in him; he may also have many of his graces in their vigorous acts, and yet may be greatly ignorant of either; wherefore we are not competent judges in this case. There may a thousand acts of grace pass through thy soul, and thou be sensible of few, if any of them.

8. Do you think that he that repents, believes, loves, fears, or humbles himself before God, and acts in other graces too, does always know what he doeth? No, no: Grace many times, even in a man, is acted by him, unawares unto him? Did Gideon, think you, believe that he was so strong in grace as he was? Nay, was he not ready to give the lie to the angel, when he told him, God was with him? Or, what do you think of David, when he said he was cast off from God's eyes? Or of Heman, when he said he was free among them whom God remembered no more? Did these then see their graces so clearly, as they saw themselves by their sins to be unworthy ones?

9. I tell you it is a rare thing for some Christians to see their graces; but a thing very common for such to see their sins; yea, and to feel them too in their lusts and desires, to the shaking of their souls.

Question. 'But since I have lusts and desires both ways, how shall I know to which my soul adheres?'

Answer. This may be known thus:

1. Which wouldst thou have to prevail—the desires of the flesh, or those of the Spirit? whose side art thou of? Doth thy soul now inwardly say, and that with a strong indignation, 'O let God, let grace, let my desires that are good, prevail against my flesh, for Jesus Christ's sake?'

2. What kind of secret wishes hast thou in thy soul, when thou feelest the lusts of thy flesh to rage? Dost thou not inwardly, and with indignation against sin, say, 'O that

I might never, never, feel one such motion more! O that my soul were so full of grace, that there might be no longer room for even the least lust to come into my thoughts?'

3. What kind of thoughts hast thou of thyself now thou seest these desires of thine that are good, so briskly opposed by those that are bad? Dost thou not say, 'Oh! I am the basest of creatures; I could even spew at myself! There is no man in all the world in my eyes, so loathsome as myself. I abhor myself: a toad is not so vile as I am. O Lord, let me be any thing but a sinner! any thing, so thou subduest mine inquities for me?'

4. How dost thou like the discovery of that which thou thinkest is grace in other men? Dost thou not cry out, 'O I bless them in my heart! O methinks grace is the greatest beauty in the world! Yea, I could be content to live and die with those people that have the grace of God in their souls.' A hundred times, and a hundred, when I have been upon my knees before God, I have desired, were it the will of God, that I might be in their condition.

5. How art thou, when thou thinkest that thou thyself hast grace? 'O then,' says the soul, 'I am as if I could leap out of myself; joy, joy, joy, then is with my heart! It is, methinks, the greatest mercy under heaven to be made a gracious man.'

And is it thus with thy soul, indeed? Happy man! It is grace that has thy soul, though sin at present works in thy flesh. Yea, all these breathings are thy very actings of grace, even of the grace of desire, of love, of humility, and of the fear of God within thee. Be of good courage, thou art on the right side. Thy desires are only good, for thou hast desire against thy sin, thy sinful self; which indeed, is not thyself, but sin that dwelleth in thee.

CHAPTER IV.

DESIRES OF THE RIGHTEOUS FOR THIS WORLD.

I COME next to speak of desires more distinctly, or particularly, as they work this way and that.

The desires of the righteous are either such as they would have accomplished here, or else such as they know they can not come at the enjoyment of, till after death.

For the *first* of these. The desires of the righteous are for such good things as they would have accomplished *here;* that is, in this world, while they are on this side glory. And they, in general, are comprised under these two general heads: 1. Communion with their God in spirit, or spiritual communion with him. 2. The liberty of the enjoyment of his holy ordinances. And, indeed, this second is, that they may both attain to, and have the first maintained with them. But for the first,

1. They desire now communion with God. "With my soul," said the Church, "have I desired thee in the night; yea, with my spirit within me will I seek thee early." The reason of this she renders in the verse foregoing, saying, "The desire of our soul is to thy name, and to the remembrance of thee.'

Now thus to desire, declares one already made righteous. For herein there appears a mind reconciled to God. Wherefore the wicked are set on the other side, even in flat opposition to these: they say unto God, "Depart from us, for we desire not the knowledge of thy ways." They neither love his presence, nor to be frequenters of his ordinances. "What is the Almighty, that we should serve him? and what profit shall we have if we pray unto him?" So, again, speaking of the wicked, he saith, "Ye have said, It is in vain to serve God; and what profit is it that we have kept his ordinance?"

This, then, to desire truly to have communion with God, is the property of a righteous man, of a righteous man only; for this desire ariseth from a suitableness which there is in the righteous unto God: "Whom," said the Psalmist, "have I in heaven but thee? and there is none upon earth that I desire besides thee." This could never be the desire of a man, were he not a righteous man, a man with a truly sanctified mind. "The carnal mind is enmity against God; for it is not subject to the law of God, neither, indeed, can be."

When Moses, the man of God, was with the children of Israel in the wilderness, he prays that God would give them his presence unto Canaan, or else to let them die in that place. It was death to him to think of being in the wilderness without God. And he said unto God, "If thy presence go not with me, carry us not hence."

Here, then, are the desires of a righteous man, namely, after communion with God. He chooses rather to be a stranger with God in the world, than to be a citizen of the world, and a stranger to God. "For I am," said David, "a stranger with thee, and a sojourner, as all my fathers were." Indeed, he that walketh with God, is but a stranger to this world. And the righteous man's desires are after communion with God, though he be so.

The reasons of these desires are many.

In communion with God is *life and favor*; yea, the very presence of God with a man is a token of it. For by his presence he helps, succors, relieves, and supports the hearts of his people, and therefore, is communion with him desired. "I will," said David, "behave myself wisely in a perfect way. O when wilt thou come unto me?"

The *pleasures* that such a soul finds in God, that has communion with him, are surpassing all pleasure and delights, yea, infinitely surpassing them. "In thy presence is fulness of joy; at thy right hand there are pleasures for evermore." Upon this account he is called "The desire of all nations" —of all in all nations that know him.

Job desired God's presence, that he might *reason with God.* "Surely," said he, "I would speak to the Almighty, and I desire to reason with God:" And again, "O that he would hear me! Behold, my desire is that the Almighty would answer me." But why doth Job thus desire to be in the presence of God? Oh! he knew that God was good, and that he would speak to him that which would do him good. "Will he plead against me with his great power? No; but he would put strength in me. There the righteous might dispute with him; so should I be delivered forever from my judge."

God's presence is the *safety* of man. "If God be for us, who can be against us?" As if he had said, If God be with one, who can hurt one? Now, if so much safety flows from God's being for one, how safe are we when God is with us? "The beloved of the Lord," said Moses, "shall dwell in safety by him: and the Lord shall cover him all the day long, and he shall dwell between his shoulders."

God's presence *keeps the heart awake to joy,* and will make a man sing in the night. "Can the children of the bride-chamber mourn while the bridegroom is with them?" God's presence is feasting, and feasting is made for mirth.

God's presence *keeps the heart tender,* and makes it ready to fall in with what is made known as duty or privilege. "I will run the way of thy commandments," said the Psalmist, "when thou shalt enlarge my heart."

The presence of God *makes a man affectionately and sincerely good;* yea, makes him willing to be searched and stripped from all the remains of iniquity.

What shall I say? God's presence is renewing, transforming, seasoning, sanctifying, commanding, sweetening, and enlightening the soul. Nothing like it in all the world: his presence supplies all wants, heals all maladies, saves from all dangers; is life in death, heaven in hell, all in all. No marvel then if the presence of, and communion with God, is become the desire of a righteous man.

To conclude this. By the presence of God being with us, *it is known to ourselves, and to others what we are.* "If thy presence." said Moses, "go not with me, carry us not hence. For wherein shall it be known here, that I and thy people have found grace in thy sight? is it not in that thou goest with us? So shall we be separated, I and thy people, from all the people, that are upon the face of the earth."

They are then best known to themselves. They know they are his people, because God's presence is with them. Therefore, he saith, "My presence shall go with thee, and I will give thee rest;" that is, let thee know that thou hast found grace in my sight, and art accepted of me. For if God withdraws himself, or hides his presence from his people, it is hard for them to bear up in the steadfast belief that they belong to him. "Be not silent unto me, O Lord," said David, "lest I be like unto them that go down into the pit." "Be not silent unto me;" that is, as he has it in another place, "Hide not thy face from me." "Hear me speedily, O Lord," saith he; "my spirit faileth: hide not thy face from me, lest I be like unto them that go down into the pit." So that God's presence is the desire of the righteous for this cause also, even that by it they gather that God delighteth in them. "By this I know that thou favorest me, because mine enemy doth not triumph over me." And is this all? No: "And as for me, thou upholdest me in mine integrity, and settest me before thy face forever."

As by the presence of God being with us we know ourselves to be the people of God: so by this presence of God, the world themselves are sometimes convinced who we are also. Thus Abimelech saw that God was with Abraham.

Thus Abimelech saw that God was with Isaac. Pharaoh knew that God was with Joseph. Saul saw and knew that the Lord was with David. Saul's servant knew that the Lord was with Samuel. Belshazzar's queen knew that the Lord was with Daniel. Darius knew also that God was with Daniel. And when their enemies saw the boldness of Peter and John, they took knowledge of them that they had been with Jesus. The very girl that was a witch, knew that Paul was a servant of the Most High God.

There is a glory upon them that have God with them; a glory that sometimes glances and flashes out into the faces of those that behold the people of God. "And all they that sat in the council, looking steadfastly on him, saw Stephen's face, as if it had been the face of an angel:" such rays of divine Majesty did show themselves therein.

The reason is, that, such have with them the wisdom of God. Such also have special bowels and compassions of God for others. Such also have more of his majesty upon them than others. Such, their words and ways, their carriages and doings are attended with that of God that others are destitute of. Such are holier, and of more convincing lives in general, than other people are. Now there is both comfort and honor in this; for what comfort like that of being a holy man of God? And what honor like that of being a holy man of God?

This, therefore, is the desire of the righteous, namely, to have communion with God. Indeed, none like God, and to be desired as he, in the thoughts of a righteous man.

2. And this leads me to the second thing, namely, The liberty of the enjoyment of his holy ordinances. For next to God himself, nothing is so dear to a righteous man, as the enjoyment of his holy ordinances.

"One thing, said David, "have I desired of the Lord; that I will seek after, namely, that I may dwell in the house of the Lord all the days of my life, to behold the beauty of the Lord, and to inquire in his temple." The Temple of the Lord was the dwelling house of God; there he recorded his name, and there he made known himself unto his people. Wherefore this was the cause why David so earnestly desired to dwell there too: "To behold," saith he, "the beauty of the Lord, and to inquire in his temple. There he had promised his presence to his people, yea, and to bring thither a blessing for them. "In all places where I record my name, I will come unto thee, and I will bless thee."

For this cause, therefore, as I said, it is why the righteous do so desire that they may enjoy the liberty of the ordinances and appointments of their God; namely, that they may attain to, and have communion maintained with God in them.

Alas! the righteous are as it were undone, if God's ordinances be taken from them. "How amiable are thy tabernacles, O Lord of hosts! My soul longeth, yea, even fainteth for the courts of the Lord; my heart and my flesh crieth out for the living God." Behold, what a taking the good man was in, because at this time he could not attain to so frequent a being in the temple of God as his soul desired. He even longed and fainted, yea, and his heart and his flesh cried out for the God that dwelt in the temple of Jerusalem. Yea, he seems in the next words to envy the very birds that could more commonly frequent the temple than he: "The sparrow," saith he, "hath found an house, and the swallow a nest for herself, where she may lay her young—even thine altars, O Lord of hosts, my King, and my God."

And then he blesseth all them that had the liberty of temple worship, saying, "Blessed are they that dwell in thy house; they will be still praising thee." Then he cries up the happiness of those that in Zion do appear before God. After this he cries out unto God, that he would grant him to be partaker of this high favor, saying, "O Lord God of hosts, hear my prayer, &c. For a day in thy courts is better than a thousand. I had rather be a door keeper in the house of my God, than to dwell in the tents of wickedness."

But why is all this? What aileth the man thus to express himself? Why, as I said, the temple was the great ordinance of God. There was his true worship performed; there God appeared, and there his people were to find him. This was, I say, the reason why the Psalmist chose out, and desired this one thing, above all the things that were under heaven, even to behold there the beauty of the Lord, and to inquire in his temple. There were to be seen the shadows of things in the heavens; the candlestick, the table of shew bread, the holiest of all, where was the golden censer, the ark of the covenant overlaid round about with gold, the golden pot that had manna, Aaron's rod that budded, the tables of the covenant, and the cherubims of glory overshadowing the mercy-seat, which were all of them then things by which God showed himself merciful to them.

Do you think that love letters are not desired between lovers? Why these, God's ordinances, they are his love letters, and his love tokens too. No marvel, then, if the righteous do so desire them; "More to be desired are they than gold, yea, than much fine gold; sweeter also than honey and the honeycomb." Yea, this judgment Wisdom itself passes upon this thing. "Receive," saith she, "my instruction, and not silver; and knowledge rather than choice gold. For wisdom is better than rubies; and all the things that may be desired are not to be compared to it."

For this cause, therefore, are the ordinances of God so much desired by the righteous. In them they meet with God; and by them they are builded, and nourished up to eternal life.

"As new born babes," says Peter, "desire the sincere milk of the word, that ye may grow thereby." As milk is nourishing to children, so is the word heard, read, and meditated on, to the righteous. Therefore it is their desire.

He has made himself known to them in breaking of bread:

who would not, then, that loves to know him, be present at such an ordinance? Ofttimes the Holy Ghost, in the comfortable influence of it, has accompanied the baptized in the very act of administering it. "Therefore, in the way of thy judgments, (or appointments,) O Lord, thy people have waited for thee: the desire of their soul is to thy name, and to the remembrance of thee."

Church fellowship, or the communion of saints, is the place where the Son of God loveth to walk. His first walking was in Eden; there he converted our first parents: and, "Come, my beloved, says he, let us go early to the vineyards; let us see if the vine flourish, whether the tender grapes appear, and the pomegranates bud forth: there will I give thee my loves."

Church fellowship rightly managed is the glory of all the world. No place, no community, no fellowship, is adorned and bespangled with those beauties, as is a church rightly knit together to their head, and lovingly serving one another. In his temple every one speaks of his glory. Hence the church is called the place of God's desire on earth. "This is my rest; here I will dwell forever, for I have desired it." And again, thus the church confesseth when she saith, "I am my beloved's, and his desire is towards me."

No marvel, then, if this be the one thing that David desired, and that which he would seek after, namely, to dwell in the house of the Lord all the days of his life.

And this also shows you the reason why God's people of old used to venture so hardly for ordinances, and to get to them with the peril of their lives, because of the sword of the wilderness. They were their bread, they were their water, they were their milk, they were their honey. Hence the sanctuary was called the desire of their eyes, and that which their soul pitied, or the pity of their soul. They had rather have died than lost it, or than that it should have been burned down as it was.

When the children of Israel had lost the ark, they counted the glory was departed from Israel. But when they had lost all, what a complaint made they then! "He hath violently taken away his tabernacle, as if it were of a garden; he hath destroyed his places of the assembly. The Lord hath caused the solemn feasts and Sabbaths to be forgotten in Zion, and hath despised, in the indignation of his anger, the king and the priest." Wherefore, upon this account it was, that the church in those days counted the punishment of her iniquity greater than the punishment of Sodom.

By these few hints you may perceive what is the desire of the righteous. But this is spoken of in reference to things present; to things that the righteous desire to enjoy while they are here: communion with God while here; and his ordinances in their purity while here. I come, therefore, in the second place, to show you, that the righteous have desires that reach further, desires that have so long a neck as to look into the world to come.

CHAPTER V.

DESIRES OF THE RIGHTEOUS FOR THE WORLD TO COME.

SECONDLY, then, The desires of the righteous are after that which yet they know cannot be enjoyed till AFTER DEATH. And those are comprehended under these two heads: 1. They desire that presence of their Lord which is personal. 2. They desire to be in that country where their Lord personally is; that heavenly country.

1. For the first of these, says Paul, "I have a desire to depart and to be with Christ." Thus you have it in Philippians i. 23. I have a desire to be with Christ.

In our first sort of desires, I told you, that the righteous desired spiritual communion with God; and now I tell you they desire to be with Christ's person. "I have a desire to be with Christ;" that is, with his person, that I may enjoy his personal presence, such a presence of his as we are not able to enjoy while here. Hence he says, I have a desire to depart, that I might be with him; "knowing," as he says in another place, "that while we are at home in the body, we are" (and cannot but be) "absent from the Lord."

Now this desire, as I said, is a desire that hath a long neck; for it can look over the brazen wall of this, quite into another world; and as it hath a long neck, so it is very forcible and mighty in its operations.

This desire breeds a divorce, a complete divorce, betwixt the soul and all inordinate love and affections to relations and worldly enjoyments. This desire makes a married man live as if he had no wife, a rich man live as if he possessed not what he has, &c. This is a soul-sequestering desire. This desire makes a man willing rather to be absent from all enjoyments, that he may be present with the Lord. This is a famous desire: none hath this desire but a righteous man.

There are that profess much love to Christ, that yet never had such a desire in them, all their life long. No; the relation that they stand in to the world, together with those many flesh-pleasing accommodations with which they are surrounded, would never yet suffer such a desire to enter into their hearts.

The strength of this desire is such, that it is ready, so far forth as it can, to dissolve that sweet knot of union that is betwixt body and soul, a knot more dear to a reasonable creature than that can be which is betwixt wife and husband, parent and child, or a man and his estate; for even all that a man has will he give for his life, and to keep body and soul firmly knit together. But now, when this desire comes, this silver cord is loosed, is loosed by consent. This desire grants to him that comes to dissolve this union leave to do it delightfully. "We are confident, and willing rather to be absent from the body, and to be present with the Lord."

Yea, this desire makes this flesh, this mortal life, a burden. The man that has this desire, exercises self-denial, while he waits till his desired change comes. For were it not that the will of God is that he should live; and did he not hope that his life might be serviceable to the truth and church of God; he would not have wherewith to cool the heat of this desire, but would rather in a holy passion with holy Job cry out, "I loathe, (or I abhor) it; I would not live alway: let me alone, (that I may die,) for my days are vanity."

The strength of this desire shows itself in this also, namely, in that it is willing to grapple with the king of terrors, rather than to be detained from that sweet communion that the soul looks for, when it comes into the place where its Lord is. Death is not to be desired for itself. The apostle chose rather to be clothed upon with his house which is from heaven, that "mortality might be swallowed up of life."

But yet rather than he would be absent from the Lord, he was willing to be absent from the body. Death, in the very thoughts of it, is grievous to flesh and blood; and nothing can so master it in our apprehensions, as that by which we attain to these desires. These desires do deal with death as Jacob's love to Rachel did deal with the seven long years which he was to serve for her. It made them seem few, or but a little time; now so, I say, doth these desires deal with death itself. They make it seem little, nay, a servant, nay a privilege; for only by that a man may come to enjoy the presence of his beloved Lord. 'I have a desire to depart, to go from the world and relations, to go from my body thac great piece of myself; I have a desire to venture the tugs and pains, and the harsh handling of the king of terrors, so I may be with Jesus Christ.' These are desires of the righteous.

Are not these, therefore, strong desires? Is there not life and mettle in them? Have they not in them power to loose the bands of nature, and to harden the soul against sorrow? flow they not, think you, from faith of the finest sort? and are they not bred in the body of a truly mortified soul? Are these the effects of a purblind spirit? are they not rather the fruits of an eagle-eyed confidence? Oh these desires! they are peculiar to the righteous; they are none others but the desires of the righteous.

Question. 'But why do the righteous desire to be with Christ?'

Answer. And, first, I ask, Why does the wife, that is as the loving hind, love to be in the presence of her husband?

Christ in glory is worth the being with. If the man out of whom the Lord Jesus did cast a legion, prayed that he might be with him, notwithstanding all the trials that attended him in this life; how can it be but that a righteous man must desire to be with him now he is in glory?

What we have heard concerning the excellency of his

person, the unspeakableness of his love, the greatness of his sufferings, and the things that he still is doing for us, must needs command our souls into a desire to be with him. When we have heard of a man among us that has done for us some excellent thing, the next thing that our heart doth pitch upon is, 'I would I could set mine eyes upon him.' But was ever heard the like to what Jesus Christ has done for sinners? Who then that hath the faith of him, can do otherwise, but desire to be with him? It was that which some time comforted John, that the time was coming that he should see him. But that consideration made him pray and pant like a hart, to hasten the time, that he might set his eyes upon him quickly.

To see Jesus Christ then, to see him as he is, to see him as he is in glory, is a sight that is worth going from relations, and out of the body, and through the jaws of death, to see; for this is to see him "head over all," to see him possessed of heaven for his church, to see him preparing mansion houses for those his poor ones that are now by his enemies kicked to and fro, like foot balls in the world; and is not this a blessed sight?

Secondly, I have a desire to be with him, to see myself with him. This is more blessed still. For a man to see himself in glory, this is a sight worth seeing. Sometimes I look upon myself, and say, Where am I now? and do quickly return answer to myself again, Why, I am in an evil world, a great way from heaven, in a sinful body, among devils and wicked men; sometimes benighted, sometimes beguiled, sometimes fearing, sometimes hoping, sometimes breathing, sometimes dying, and the like. But then I turn the tables, and say, But where shall I be shortly? where shall I see myself anon, after a few times more have passed over me? And when I can but answer this question thus; 'I shall see myself with Jesus Christ;' this yields glory, even glory to one's spirit now. No more marvel, then, if the righteous desire to be with Christ.

Thirdly, I have a desire to be with Christ. There the spirits of the just are prefected; there the spirits of the righteous are as full as they can hold. A sight of Jesus in the word, some know how it will change them from glory to glory; but how then shall we be changed and filled, when we shall see him as he is? "When he shall appear, we shall be like him, for we shall see him as he is."

Moses and Elias appeared to Peter, and James, and John, at the transfiguration of Christ, "in glory." How so? Why, they had been in the heavens, and came thence with some of the glories of heaven upon them. Gild a bit of wood, yea, gild it seven times over, and it must not compare in its difference from wood not gilt, to the soul that but a little while has been dipt in glory.

Glory is a strange thing to men that are on this side of the heavens; it is that which eye hath not seen, nor ear heard, nor entered hath it into the heart of man to conceive of; only the Christian has a word and Spirit, that at times do give a little of the glimmering thereof unto him.

But, Oh! when he is in the Spirit, and sees in the Spirit, do you think his tongue can tell? But, I say, if the sight of heaven, at so vast a distance, is so excellent a prospect, what will it look like when one is in it?

No marvel then, if the desires of the righteous are to be with Christ.

Objection. 'But if this be the character of a righteous man, the desire to depart and to be with Christ, I am none of them; for I never had such a desire in my heart; no, my fears of perishing will not suffer me either to desire to die to be with Christ, nor that Christ should come to judge the world.'

Answer. Though thine is a sad case that must be excepted, for that thy desires may not as yet be grown so high, yet if thou art a righteous man, thy heart has in it the very seeds thereof.

There are therefore desires, and *desires* to desire, as one child can reach so high, and the other can but desire to do so. Thou, if thou art a righteous man, hast desires, these desires, ready to put forth into act, when they are grown a little stronger, or when their impediment is removed.

Many times it is with our desire as it is with saffron: it will bloom, and blossom, and be ripe, and all in a night. Tell me, dost thou not *desire* to desire? Yea, dost thou not vehemently *desire*, to desire to depart and to be with Christ? I know if thou art a righteous man thou dost. There is a man sows his field with wheat; but as he sows, soon it is covered with great clods: now, that grows as well as the rest, though it runs not upright as yet; it grows, and yet is kept down. So do thy desires; and when one shall remove the clod, the blade will soon point upwards.

I know thy mind. That which keeps thee that thou canst not yet arrive to this, to desire to depart and to be with Christ, is, because some strong doubt or clod of unbelief, as to thy eternal welfare, lies hard upon thy desiring spirit. Now let but Jesus remove this clod, and thy desires will quickly start up to be gone. I say, let but Jesus Christ give thee one kiss, and with his lips, as he kisses thee, whisper to thee the forgiveness of thy sins, and thou wilt quickly break out, and say, Nay, then, Lord, let me die in peace, since my soul is persuaded of thy salvation.

There is a man upon the bed of languishing; but, Oh! he dares not die, for all is not as he would have it betwixt God and his poor soul; and many a night he lies thus in great horror of mind. But do you think that he doth not *desire*, to desire to depart? Yes, yes; he also waits and cries to God to set his desires at liberty. At last, the visiter comes and sets his soul at ease, by persuading him that he belongs to God. And what then? 'Oh! now let me die! welcome death!'

Now he is like the man in Essex, who, when his neighbour at his bedside prayed for him, that God would restore him to health, started up in his bed, and pulled him by the arm, and cried out, 'No, no; pray that God will take me away; for to me it is best to go to Christ.'

The desires of some good Christians are pinioned, and cannot stir, especially this sort of desires. But Christ can and will cut the cord some time or other; and then thou that wouldst, shalt be able to say, "I have a desire to depart, and to be with Jesus Christ."

Meantime be thou earnest to desire to know thy interest in the grace of God; for there is nothing short of the knowledge of that can make thee desire to depart, that thou mayst be with Christ. This is that, that Paul laid as the ground of his desires to be gone. "We know," says he, "that if our earthly house of this tabernacle were dissolved, we have a building of God, an house not made with hands, eternal in the heavens. For in this we groan, earnestly desiring to be clothed upon with our house which is from heaven."

And know, that if thy desires be right, they will grow as other graces do, from strength to strength; only in this they can grow no faster than faith grows as to justification, and than hope grows as to glory.

But we will leave this and come to the second thing.

2. As the righteous men desire to be present with Jesus Christ, so they desire to be with him in that country where he is. "But now they desire a better country, that is, an heavenly: wherefore God is not ashamed to be called their God; for he hath prepared for them a city." But now they desire a better country. Here is a comparison. There was

another country, namely, their native country, the country from whence they came out, that in which they left their friends and their pleasures. That they left for the sake of another world, which, indeed, is a better country, as is manifest from its character. It is an heavenly. As high as heaven is above the earth, so much better is that country which is an heavenly, than is this in which now we are.

A heavenly country, where there is a heavenly Father, a heavenly host, heavenly things, heavenly visions, heavenly places, a heavenly kingdom, and the heavenly Jerusalem, for them that are partakers of the heavenly calling, and that are thus part of the heavenly things themselves.

This is a country to be desired; and therefore it is a marvel if any, except those that have lost their wits and senses, refuse to choose themselves an habitation here. Here is the mount Zion, the city of the living God, the heavenly Jerusalem, and an innumerable company of angels: here is the general assembly and church of the first born, and God the Judge of all, and Jesus, and the spirits of just men made perfect. Who would not be here?

This is the country that the righteous desire for a habitation. "But now they desire a better country, that is, an heavenly: wherefore God is not ashamed to be called their God; for he hath prepared for them a city."

Mark, they desire a country, and God prepareth for them a city: he goes beyond their desires, beyond their apprehensions, beyond what their hearts could conceive to ask for.

There are none that are weary of this world, from a gracious disposition that they have to an heavenly, but God will take notice of them, will own them, and not be ashamed to own them; yea, such shall not lose their longing. They desire an handful, God gives them a seaful; they desire a country, God prepares for them a city; a city that is an heavenly, a city that hath foundations, a city whose builder and maker is God. And all this is, that the promise to them might be fullfilled, "The desire of the righteous shall be granted." And this is the last thing propounded to be spoken to from the text.

CHAPTER VI.

HOW RIGHTEOUS DESIRES ARE GRANTED.

WE then, in conclusion, come to inquire into WHAT IS MEANT, OR TO BE UNDERSTOOD BY THE GRANTING OF THE RIGHTEOUS THEIR DESIRES: "The desire of the righteous shall be granted."

To grant, is *to yield to what is desired*, to consent that it shall be even so as is requested. "The Lord hear thee in the time of trouble; the name of the God of Jacob defend thee. Send thee help from his sanctuary, and strengthen thee out of Zion. Remember all thy sacrifices. Grant thee according to thine own heart and fulfil all thy counsel."

To grant, is also *to accomplish what is promised*. Thus, God granted to the Gentiles repentance unto life, namely, because he had promised it by the prophets from the days of old.

To grant, therefore, *is an act of grace* and condescending favor; for if God is said to humble himself when he beholds things in heaven, what condescension is it for him to hearken to a sinful wretch on earth, and to tell him, Have the thing that thou desirest? A wretch I call him, if compared to him that hears him, though he is a righteous man, when considered as the new creation of God.

To grant, then, is not to part with the thing desired, as if a desire merited, purchased, earned, or deserved it; but, of bounty and good will, *to bestow* the thing desired upon the humble. Hence God's grants are said to be gracious ones.

I will add, that to grant is sometimes taken for giving one authority or power to do, or possess, or enjoy such and such privileges: and so it may by taken here: for the righteous has a right or a power, to enjoy the things bestowed on them by their God.

So, then, to grant is to give, to accomplish, even of free grace, the desires of the righteous.

This is acknowledged by David, where he saith to God, "Thou hast given him his heart's desire, and hast not withholden the request of his lips."

And this is promised to all that delight themselves in God: "Delight thyself in the Lord; and he shall give thee the desires of thy heart." And again, "He will fulfil the desire of them that fear him: he also will hear their cry, and will save them." By all these places it is plain, that the promise of granting desire is entailed to the righteous, and also the grant to them is an act of grace and mercy.

But it also follows, that though the desires of the righteous are not meritorious, yet they are pleasing in his sight; and this is manifest several ways, besides the promise of a grant of them.

First, In that the desires of God, and the desires of the righteous, jump or agree in one: they are of one mind in their desires. God's desire is to the work of his hands, and the righteous are for surrendering that up to him.

1. In giving up *the heart* unto him: "My son," says God, "Give me thy heart." "I lift my heart to thee," says the righteous man. Here, therefore, there is an agreement between God and the righteous. It is, I say, agreed on both sides that God should have the heart. God desires it; the righteous man desires it, yea, he desires it with earnest prayer, saying, "Incline my heart unto thy testimonies; let my heart be sound in thy statutes."

2. They are also agreed about the disposing of *the whole man.* God is for having body, and soul, and spirit; and the righteous desire that God should have all. Hence, they are said to give *themselves* to the Lord, and to addict themselves to his service.

3. God desireth *truth in the inward parts*, that is, that truth may be at the bottom of all; and this is the desire of the righteous man likewise: "I have hid thy word in my heart," said David, "that I might not sin against thee."

4. They agree, moreover, in the way of justification, in the way of sanctification, in the way of preservation, and in the way of glorification, namely, which way to come at and enjoy all; wherefore, who should hinder the righteous man, or keep him back from enjoying the desire of his heart?

5. They also agree about the sanctifying of God's name in the world, saying, "Thy will be done on earth as it is in heaven." There is a great agreement between God and the righteous: "he that is joined to the Lord is one spirit." No marvel, then, if their desires in the general, so far as the righteous man doth know the mind of his God, are one; consequently their desires must be granted, or God must deny himself.

Secondly, The desires of the righteous are the life of all their prayers; and it is said, "the prayer of the upright is God's delight."

Jesus Christ put a difference betwixt the form and the spirit that is in prayer, and intimates that the soul of prayer is in the desires of a man. "Therefore," saith he, "I say unto you, what things soever ye desire, when ye pray, believe that ye receive them, and ye shall have them."

If a man prays ever so long, and has ever so many brave expressions in prayer, yet God counts it prayer no further than there are warm and fervent desires in it, after those things the mouth maketh mention of. In Psalm xxxviii. 9, saith David, "Lord, all my desire is before thee; and my groanings are not hid from thee."

Can you say you desire when you pray? or that your prayers come from the crying, panting, and longing of your hearts? If not, they shall not be granted; for God looks when men are at prayer, to see if their hearts and spirits are in their prayers; for he counts all other but vain speaking. "Ye shall seek me, and find me," says he, "when ye shall search for me with all your heart." The people that you read of in 2 Chron. xv. 11—15, are there said to do what they did, with all their heart, and with all their soul; for they sought God with their whole desire.

When a man's desires put him upon prayer, run along with him in his prayer, break out of his heart and ascend up to heaven with his prayers, it is a good sign that he is a righteous man, and that his desires shall be granted.

Thirdly, By his desires a righteous man shows more of his mind for God, than he can by any manner of ways besides. Hence, it is said, "The desire of a man is his kindness;" and that a poor man, that is sincere in his desires, is better than he that with his mouth shows much love, if he be a liar.

Desires are copious things. You read that a man may enlarge his desires as hell, that is, if they be wicked; yea, and a righteous man may enlarge his desires as heaven.

No grace is so extensive as desires. Desires outgo all. Who believes as he desires to believe, and loves as he desires to love? and fears as he desires to fear God's name? Might it be as a righteous man doth sometimes desire it should be, both with God's church, and also with his own soul, stranger things would be than there are; faith, and love, and holiness, would flourish more than they do. Oh, what does a righteous man desire! What do you think the prophet desired, when he said, "O that thou wouldst rend the heavens and come down?" And Paul, when he said he could wish that himself were accursed from Christ, for the vehement desire that he had that the Jews might be saved? Yea, what do you think John desired, when he cried out to Christ to come quickly?

Love to God, as I said, is more seen in desires than in any Christian act. Do you think that the woman with her two mites cast in all that she desired to cast into the treasury of God? Or do you think, when David said that he had prepared for the house of God with all his might, that his desires stinted when his ability was at its utmost? No, no; desires go beyond all actions; therefore I said it is the desires of a man that are reckoned for his kindness.

Kindness is that which God will not forget: I mean the kindness which his people show to him; specially in their desires to serve him in the world. When Israel was come out of Egypt, you know how many stumbles they had before they got to Canaan. But forasmuch as they were willing or desirous to follow God, he passes by all their failures, saying, "I remember thee," (and that almost a thousand years after,) "the kindness of thy youth, the love of thine espousals, when thou wentest after me in the wilderness, in a land that was not sown. Israel was holiness to the Lord, and the first fruits of his increase."

There is nothing that God likes of ours better than he likes our true desires. For, indeed, true desires, they are the smoke of our incense, the flower of our graces, and the very vital part of our new man. They are our desires that ascend, and them that are the sweet of all the sacrifices that we offer to God. The man of desires is the man of kindness.

Fourthly, Desires, true and right desires, they are they by which a man is taken up from the ground, and brought away to God in spite of all opposers. A desire will take a man upon its back, and carry him away to God, if ten thousand men stand by and oppose it. Hence it is said, that "through desire a man separates himself," namely, from what is contrary to the mind of God, and so "seeketh and intermeddleth with all wisdom."

All convictions conversions, illuminations, savors, tastes, revelations, knowledge, and mercies, will do nothing, if the soul abide without desires: all I say are but like rain upon stones, or favors bestowed upon a dead dog. Oh! but a poor man with desires, a man that sees but little, that finds in himself but little, if he has but strong desires, they will supply all. His desires take him up from his sins from his companions, from his pleasures, and carry him away to God.

Suppose thou wast a minister, and wast sent from God with a whip, whose cords were made of the flames of hell, thou mightest lash long enough before thou couldst so much as drive one man that abides without desires, to God or to his kingdom, by that thy so sore a whip.

Suppose again that thou wast a minister, and wast sent from God to sinners with a crown of glory in thy hand, to offer to him that first comes to thee for it: yet none can come without desires; but desire takes the man upon its back, and so brings him to thee.

What is the reason that men will with their mouth commend God, and commend Christ, and commend and praise both heaven and glory, and yet all the while fly from him, and from his mercy, as from the worst of enemies? Why, they want good desires; their desires being mischievous, carry them another way. Thou entreatest thy wife, thy husband, and the son of thy womb, to fall in with thy Lord and thy Christ, but they will not. Ask them the reason why they will not, and they know none, only they have no desires. "When we shall see him," says the prophet, "there is no beauty in him that we should desire him." And I am sure if they do not desire him, they can by no means be made to come to him.

But now, desires, desires that are right, will carry a man quite away to God, and to do his will, let the work be ever so hard. Take an instance or two for this.

1. You may see it in Abraham, Isaac, and Jacob. The second text says plainly, they were not mindful of that country from whence they came out, through their desires of a better. God gave them intimation of a better country, and their minds did cleave to it with desires of it; and what

then? Why, they went forth, and desired to go, though they did not know whither they went. Yea, they all sojourned in the land of promise, because it was but a shadow of what was designed for them by God and looked to by their faith, as in a strange country; wherefore they also cast that behind their back, looking for that city that has foundations, of which mention was made before.

Had not now these men desires that were mighty? They were their desires that thus separated them from their dearest and choice relations and enjoyments. Their desires were pitched upon the heavenly country, and so they broke through all difficulties for that.

2. You may see it in Moses, who had a kingdom at his foot, and was the alone visible heir thereof; but the desire of a better inheritance made him refuse it, and choose rather to take part with the people of God in their afflicted condition, than to enjoy the pleasures of sin for a season.

You may say, The Scripture attributes this to his faith. I answer, So it attributes to Abraham's faith, his leaving his country. But his faith begat in him these desires after the country that is above. So, indeed, Moses saw these things by faith; and therefore his faith begat in him these desires. For it was because of his desires that he did refuse, and did choose, as you read. And here we may opportunely take an opportunity to touch upon the vanity of that faith that is not breeding, and that knows not how to bring forth strong desires of enjoying what is pretended to be believed: all such faith is false. Abraham's, Isaac's, Jacob's and Moses' faith, bred in them desires, strong desires; yea, desires so strong as to take them up, and to carry them after what by their faith was made known unto them. Yea, their desires were so mightily set upon the things made known to them by their faith, that neither difficulties nor dangers, nor yet frowns nor flatteries, could stop them from the use of all lawful attempts of enjoying what they believed was to be had, and what they desired to be possessed of.

3. The women also that you read of, and others that would not upon unworthy terms, accept of deliverance from torments and sundry trials, chose death itself, that they might (or because they had a desire to) be made partakers of a "better resurrection." "And others," saith he, "had trial of cruel mockings and scourgings, yea, moreover, of bonds and imprisonment; they were stoned, they were sawn asunder, were tempted, were slain with the sword: they wandered about in sheep-skins and goat-skins; being destitute, afflicted, tormented: of whom the world was not worthy: they wandered in deserts, in mountains, and in dens and caves of the earth."

4. But we will come to the Lord Jesus himself. Whither did his desires bring him? Whither did they carry him? and to what did they make him stoop? for they were his desires after us, and after our good, that made him humble himself to do as he did.

What was it, think you, that made him cry out, "I have a baptism to be baptized with; and how am I straitened till it is accomplished?" What was that baptism but his death? and why did he so long for it, but of desire to do us good? Yea, the passover being to be eaten on the eve of his sufferings, with what desires did he desire to eat it with his disciples?

Yea, his desires to suffer for his people, made him go with more strength to lay down his life for them, than they for want of them, had to go to see him suffer. "And they were in the way going up to Jerusalem;" he to suffer, and they to look on; "and Jesus went before them: and they were amazed: and as they followed, they were afraid."

I tell you, desires are strange things, if they be right; they jump with God's mind; they are the life of prayer;

they are a man's kindness to God; and they which will take him up from the ground, and carry him away after God to do his will, let the work be ever so hard. Is it any marvel, then, if the desires of the righteous are so pleasing to God as they are? and that God has so graciously promised that the desires of the righteous shall be granted?

CHAPTER VII.

USE OF INFORMATION, EXAMINATION AND CAUTION.

WE come now to the use and application.

The first use shall be a use of INFORMATION. You have heard what hath been said of desires, and what pleasing things right desires are unto God. But you must know that they are the desires of his people, of the righteous, that are so. No wicked man's desires are regarded.

This men must be informed of, lest their desires become a snare to their souls. You read of a man whose desire kills him. And why, but because he rests in desiring, without considering what he is, whether he is such a one as they unto whom the promise of granting desires is made? He coveteth greedily all the day long, but to little purpose. The grant of desires, of the fulfilling of desires, is entailed to the righteous man.

There are four sorts of people that desire, that desire the kingdom of heaven; consequently, desires have a fourfold root from whence they flow.

First, The *natural man* desires to be saved, and to go to heaven when he dies. Ask any natural man, and he will tell you so. Besides, we see it is so with them, especially at certain seasons. As when some guilt or conviction for sin takes hold upon them; or when some sudden fear terrifies them; when they are afraid that the plague or pestilence will come upon them, and break up housekeeping for them; or when death has taken them by the throat, and is hauling them down stairs to the grave Then, O then! 'Lord save me! Lord have mercy upon me! Good people pray for me! Oh! whither shall I go when I die, if sweet Christ has not pity for my soul?' And now the bed shakes and the poor soul is as loath to go out of the body for fear the devil should catch it, as the poor bird is to go out of the bush, while it sees the hawk waits there to receive her. But the fears of the wicked, they must come upon the wicked: they are the desires of the righteous that must be granted. Pray take good notice of this.

And to back this with the authority of God, consider, first, that scripture, "The wicked man travaileth with pain all his days, and the number of years is hidden to the oppressor. A dreadful sound is in his ears: in prosperity the destroyer shall come upon him. Trouble and anguish shall make him afraid; they shall prevail against him, as a king ready to the battle."

Can it be imagined, that when the wicked are in this distress, but that they will desire to be saved? Therefore he saith again, "Terrors take hold of him as waters, a tempest stealeth him away in the night. The east wind, (that blasting wind,) carrieth him away, and he departeth, and as a storm hurleth him out of (the world) his place. For God shall cast upon him, and not spare; (in flying) he would fain flee out of his hand."

Their terrors and their fears must come upon them; their desires and wishes for salvation must not be granted. "They shall call upon me," says God, but I will not answer; they shall seek me early, but they shall not find me."

Secondly, There is the *hypocrite's* desire. Now his desire seems to have life and spirit in it. Also he desires in his youth, his health, and the like; yet it comes to nought. You shall see him drawn to the life in Mark x. 17. He comes running, and kneeling, and asking, and that, as I said, in youth and health; and that is more than men merely natural do. But all to no purpose: he went as he came, without the thing desired. The conditions propounded were too hard for this hypocrite to comply withal.

Some, indeed, make a great noise with their desires over some others, but in conclusion all comes to one: they meet together there, where they go whose desires are not granted.

For what is the hope of the hypocrite, though he has gained to a higher strain of desires, when God taketh away his soul? Will God hear his cry when trouble cometh upon him? Did he not, even when he desired life, yet break with God in the day when conditions of life were propounded to him? Did he not, even when he asked what good things were to be done that he might have eternal life, refuse to hear, or comply, with what was propounded to him? How then can his desires be granted, who himself refused to have them answered?

No marvel, then, if he perishes like his own dung—if they that have seen him shall say they miss him among those that are to have their desires granted.

Thirdly, There are the desires of the *cold formal professor;* the desires, I say, of him whose religion lies in a few of the shells of religion; even as the foolish virgins who were content with their lamps, but gave not heed to take oil in their vessels. These I take to be those whom the wise man calls the slothful. "The soul of the sluggard desireth, and hath nothing: but the soul of the diligent shall be made fat." The sluggard is one that comes to poverty through idleness, that contents himself with forms, that will not plough in winter by reason of the cold; therefore, shall he beg in harvest, or at the day of judgment, and have nothing.

Thus you see, that there are many that desire. The natural man, the hypocrite, the formalist, all desire. For heaven is a brave place, and nobody would go to hell. "Lord, Lord, open to us!" is the cry of many in this world, and will be the cry of more in the day of judgment.

Of this, therefore, thou shouldst be informed; and that for these reasons. 1. Because ignorance of this may keep thee asleep in security, and cause thee to fall under such disappointments as are the worst, and the worst to be borne. For, for a man to think to go to heaven because he desires it, and when all is done, to fall into hell, is a frustration of the most dismal complexion. And yet thus it will be when desires shall fail, when man goes to his long home, and when the mourners go about the city. 2. Because, as was said before, else thy desires and that which should be for thy good, will kill thee. They will kill thee at death, when thou shalt find them every one empty; and at judgment, when thou shalt be convinced that thou oughtest to go without what thou desirest, because thou wast not the man to whose desires the promise was made, nor the man that didst desire aright. 3. Because, to be informed of this is the way to put thee upon such sense and sight of thy case, as will make thee in earnest betake thyself in that way that is acceptable to him, who grants the desires of the righteous.

And then shalt thou be happy when thou shunnest to desire as the natural man desireth, as the hypocrite desireth, or as the formalist desireth: when thou desirest as the righteous do, thy desires shall be granted.

The second use is of EXAMINATION. If this be so, then what cause hast thou, that art conscious to thyself that thou art a desiring man, to examine thyself, whether thou art one whose desires shall be granted! For to what purpose would a man desire, and what fruits will desires bring him whose desires shall not be granted? Such a man is but like to her that longs, but loses her longings; or like to him that looks for peace, while evil overtakes him.

Thou hast heard it over and over, that the grant of desires belongs to the righteous. Shouldst thou then not inquire into thy condition, and examine thyself whether thou art a righteous man or no? The apostle saith to the Corinthians, "Examine yourselves, whether ye be in the faith; prove your own selves; know ye not how that Jesus Christ is in you, except ye be reprobates?" You may be reprobates and not be aware of it, if you do not examine and prove your own selves.

It is, therefore, for thy life; wherefore do not deceive thyself.

I have given you before a description of a righteous man, namely, that he is one made so of God by imputation, by an inward principle, and one that brings forth fruit to God. Now this last thou mayst think thou hast. For it is easy and common for men to think, when they bring forth fruit to themselves, that they bring it forth to God. Wherefore examine thyself:

1. Art thou righteous? If thou sayst, Yea, I ask, How camest thou righteous? If thou thinkest that obedience to the law of righteousness has made thee so, thou art utterly deceived. For he that thus seeks righteousness, yet is not righteous, because he cannot by so doing attain that thing he seeketh for.

Did not I tell thee before, that a man must be righteous before he doeth one good work, or he never can be righteous? The tree must be good first, even before it brings forth one good apple.

2. Art thou righteous? In whose judgment art thou righteous? Is it in the judgment of God, or of man? If not of God, it is no matter though all the men on earth should justify thee; thou for that art no whit the more righteous.

3. Art thou righteous in the judgment of God? Who told thee so? or dost thou but dream thereof? Indeed, to be righteous in God's sight, is that, and only that, which can secure a man from wrath to come: for if God justifies, who is he that condemns? And this only is the man whose desires shall be granted.

But still I say, is the question, How comest thou to know that thou art righteous in the judgment of God? Dost thou know by what it is that God makes a man righteous? Dost thou know where that is, by or with which God makes a man righteous? and also how God doth make a man righteous with it? These are questions, in the answer of which thou must have some heavenly skill, or else all that thou sayest about thy being righteous will seem without a bottom.

Now, if thou answerest, that 'that which makes me righteous is the obedience of Christ to his Father's will; that this righteousness is before the throne of God, and that it is made mine by an act of God's free grace;' I shall ask thee yet again,

How camest thou to see thy need of this righteousness? And by what is this righteousness by thee applied to thyself? For this righteousness is bestowed upon those that see their need thereof. This righteousness is the refuge whereto the guilty fly for succor, that they may be sheltered from the wrath to come. Hast thou then fled, or dost thou indeed fly to it?

None fly to this righteousness for life, but those who feel the sentence of condemnation by God's law upon their conscience, and that in that extremity have sought for righteousness first elsewhere, but cannot find it in all the world. For man, when he findeth himself at first a sinner, doth not straightway betake himself for righteousness to God by Christ; but in the first place, seeks it in the law on earth, by laboring to yield obedience thereto, to the end he may, when he stands before God at death and judgment, have something to commend him to him, and for the sake of which he may at least help forward his acceptance with him. But being wearied out of this, (and if God loves him he will weary him out of it,) then he looks unto heaven, and cries to God for righteousness; the which God shows him in his own good time, he hath reckoned to him for the sake of Jesus Christ.

Now by this very discovery the heart is also principled

with the spirit of the gospel; for the Spirit comes with the gospel down from heaven to such a one, and fills his soul with good; by which he is capacitated to bring forth fruit, true fruit, which are the fruits of righteousness imputed, and of righteousness infused, to the glory and praise of God.

Nor can any thing but faith make a man see himself thus made righteous; for this righteousness is revealed from faith to faith; from the object of faith to the grace of faith, by the Spirit of faith. A faithless man then can see this no more than a blind man can see colors; nor relish this, more than a dead man tasteth victuals. As, therefore, blind men talk of colors, and as dead men relish food, so do carnal men talk of Jesus Christ; namely, without sense or savor; without sense of the want, or savor of the worth and goodness of him to the soul.

Wherefore, I say, it is of absolute necessity, that with thy heart thou deal in this point, and beware of self-deceiving; for if thou fail here, thy desires will fail thee forever: for "the desire of the righteous," and that only, "shall be granted."

The third use is CAUTIONARY.

Let me here, therefore, caution thee to beware of some things, by which else, perhaps, thou mayst deceive thyself.

1. Take heed of taking such things for grants of desires, as accidentally fall out; accidentally, I mean, as to thy desires; for it is possible, that that very thing that thou desirest, may come to pass in the current of providence, not as an answer of thy desires. Now if thou takest such things for a grant of thy desires, and consequently concludest thyself a righteous man, how mayst thou be deceived!

The ark of God was delivered into the hand of the Philistines, which they desired; but not for the sake of their desire, but for the sins of the children of Israel.

The land of Canaan was given unto Israel, not for the sake

of their desires, but for the sins of those whom God cast out before them, and to fulfil the promise that God, before they were born, had made unto their fathers.

Israel was carried away captive out of their own land, not to fulfil the desires of their enemies, but to punish them for their transgressions.

These, with many of smaller importance, or more personal, might be mentioned, to show that many things happen to us, some to our pleasing, and some to the pleasing of our enemies; which, if either we or they should count the returns of our prayer, or the fruits of our desires, and so draw conclusions of our estate to be for the future happy, because in such things we seemed to be answered of God, we might greatly swerve in our judgments and become the greatest at self-deceiving.

2. Or shouldst thou take it for granted, that what thou enjoyest thou hast as the fruit of they desires. Yet if the things thou boast of are things pertaining to this life, such may be granted thee, as thou art considered of God as his creature, though thyself art far enough off from being a righteous man. "Thou openest thy hand," says the Psalmist, "and satisfiest the desires of every living thing." Again, "He feeds the young ravens that cry unto him; and, the young lions seek their meat from God." Cain, Ishmael, Ahab, too, had in some things their desires granted them of God.

For if God will hear the desire of the beasts of the field, the fishes of the sea, and of the fowls of heaven; no marvel if the wicked also may boast him of his heart's desire, into whose hand, as he saith in another place, God bringeth abundantly.

Take heed therefore: neither these things, nor the grant of them, are any signs that thou art a righteous man, or that the promise made to the righteous in granting their desires, is accomplished upon thee. I think a man may say, that the men that know not God, have a fuller grant, I mean generally, of their desires to temporal things, than has the child of God himself; for his portion lying in better things, his desires are answered another way.

3. Take heed again: God grants to some men their desires in anger, and to their destruction.

He gave to some their own desires, but sent leanness into their souls. All that God gives to the sons of men, he gives not in mercy. He gives to some an inferior, and to some a superior portion; and yet so also he answereth them in the joy of their heart.

Some men's desires are narrow upwards, and wide downwards; narrow as to God, but wide for the world; they gape for the one, but shut themselves up against the other; so as they desire, they have of what they desire. "Thou fillest their belly with thy hid treasures," for that they do desire; "But as for me," said David, (these things will not satisfy,) "I shall be satisfied when I awake, with thy likeness."

I told you before, that the heart of a wicked man was widest downwards. But it is not so with the righteous: therefore, "the portion of Jacob is not like them;" to him God has given himself. The temple that Ezekiel saw in the vision, was still widest upward; it spread itself toward heaven. So is the church, and so is the righteous, and so are their desires.

Thy great concern, therefore, is to consider, since thou art confident that God also heareth thy desires, I say, to consider whether he answereth thee in his anger; for if he doth so, thy desires come with a woe; therefore, I say, Look to thyself.

A full purse and a lean soul, is a sign of a great curse. "He gave them their desires; but sent leanness into their soul." Take heed of that. Many men crave by their desires, as the dropsical man craves drink. His drinking makes his belly swell big, but consumes other parts of his body. Oh! it is a sad grant, when the desire is granted, only to make the belly big, the estate big, the name big; when even by this bigness the soul pines, is made to dwindle, to grow lean and to look like an anatomy.

I am persuaded that it is thus with many, who, while they were lean in estates, had fat souls; but the fattening of their estates has made their souls as to good, as lean as a rake. They cannot now breathe after God; they cannot now look to their hearts; they cannot now set watch and ward over their ways; they cannot now spare time to examine who goes out, or who comes in. They have so much their desires in things below, that they have no leisure to concern themselves with, or to look after things above; their hearts are now as fat as grease; their eyes do now too much start out, to be turned and made to look inward. They are now become as to their best part, like the garden of the slothful, all grown over with nettles and briars, that cover the face thereof; or, like Saul, when removed from a little estate and low condition, to much, even worse and worse.

Men do not know what they do in desiring things of this life, things over and above what is necessary: they desire them, and they have them with a woe. "Surely he shall not feel quietness in his belly." (His belly is here taken for his conscience.) "He shall not save of that which he desired," to help him in an evil day.

I shall not here give my caution to the righteous, but shall reserve that for the next use. But, O that men were as wise in judging of the answering of their desires, as they are in judging of the extravagances of their appetites! You shall have a man even from experience reclaim himself from such an excess of eating, drinking, smoking, sleeping, talking, or pleasurable actions, as by his experience he finds is hurtful to him, (and yet all this may but hurt the body, at least the body directly;) but how blind, how unskilled are they in the evils that attend desires! For like the man in the dropsy, made mention of before, they desire this world, as he doth drink, till they desire themselves quite down to hell. Look to it, therefore, and take heed; God's granting the things pertaining to this life unto thee, doth neither prove that thou art righteous, nor that he acts in mercy toward thee, by giving thee thy desires.

CHAPTER VIII.

FINAL USE OF ENCOURAGEMENT.

THE last use is for ENCOURAGEMENT. Is it so? Shall the desire of the righteous be granted? Then this should encourage them that in the first place have sought the kingdom of God and his Son's righteousness, to go on in their desires.

God has given thee his Son's righteousness, to justify thee; he has also, because thou art a son, sent forth the Spirit of his Son into thy heart to sanctify thee, and to help thee to cry unto him, Father, Father. Wilt thou not cry? Wilt thou not desire? Thy God has bidden thee open thy mouth; he has bid thee open it wide, and promised saying, "And I will fill it;" and wilt thou not desire?

Oh! thou hast a license, a leave, a grant to desire; wherefore be not afraid to desire great mercies of the God of heaven; this was Daniel's way, and he set others to do it too.

Objection. 'But I am an unworthy creature.'

Answer. That is true; but God gives to no man for his worthiness, nor rejects any for their sinfulness, that come to him sensible of the want and worth of mercy. Besides, I told thee before, that the desires of a righteous man, and the desires of his God, do jump or agree. God has a desire to thee, thou hast a desire to him; God desires truth in the inward parts, and so dost thou with all thy heart; God desires mercy, and to show it to the needy; that is what thou also wantest, and that which thy soul craves at his hand.

Seek, man! ask, knock; and do not be discouraged. The Lord grant all thy desires! Thou sayest thou art unworthy to ask the biggest things, things spiritual and heavenly.

Well, will carnal things serve thee, and answer the desires of thy heart? Canst thou be content to be put off with a belly well filled, and a back well clothed?

'Oh! better I had never been born.'

See, thou wilt not ask the best, and yet canst not make shift without them.

'Shift, no! no shift without them; I am undone without them; undone forever and ever,' sayst thou.

Well, then desire.

'So I do,' sayst thou.

Ah! but desire with more strong desires, desire with more large desires, desire spiritual gifts, covet them earnestly; thou hast a license too to do so. God bids thee do so. And "I," says the apostle, "desire that ye faint not;" that is, in the prosecution of your desires, what discouragements soever you may meet with in the way: for he hath said, "The desire of the righteous shall be granted."

Objection. 'But I find it not so,' says one: 'for though I have desired and desired, a thousand times upon my knees for something that I want, yet I have not my desires; and indeed, the consideration of this hath made me question whether I am one of those to whom the promise of granting desires is made.'

Answer. To this objection many things must be replied: 1. By way of question; 2. Then by way of answer.

1. By way of question. What are the things thou desirest? are they *lawful* or *unlawful*? For a Christian may desire unlawful things; as the mother of Zebedee's children did when she came to Christ, (nay, her sons themselves had their heart therein,) saying, "Master, we would that thou shouldst do for us whatsoever we shall desire." They came with a wide mouth; but their desire was unlawful, as is evident, for Christ would not grant it. James also himself caught those unto whom he wrote in such a fault as this,

where he says, "Ye kill, and desire to have, and cannot obtain."

There are four things that are unlawful to be desired: 1. To desire the life of thine enemy is unlawful. 2. To desire any thing that is thy neighbor's is unlawful. 3. To desire to share in the prosperity of the wicked is unlawful. 4. To desire spiritual things for evil ends is unlawful.

2. Are they lawful things which thou desirest? Yet the question is, Are they *absolutely* or *conditionally* promised? If absolutely promised, hold on in desiring; if conditionally promised, then thou must consider, (1.) Whether they are such as are essential to the well being of thy soul in thy Christian course in this life. (2.) Or whether they are things that are of a more inferior sort.

If they are such as are essential to the well being of thy soul in thy Christian course in this world; then hold on in thy desires; and look also for the conditions that that word calls for, that proffereth them to thee; and if it be not possible to find them in thyself, look for them in Christ, and cry to God for them, for the Lord's sake.

But if they be of an inferior sort, and thou canst be a good Christian without them; desire them, and yet be content without them; for who knows but it may be better that thou shouldst be denied, than that thou shouldst have now a grant of some things thou desirest? And herein thou hast thy Lord for thy pattern; who, though he desired that his life might be prolonged, yet wound up that prayer with a "Nevertheless, not my will, but thine be done."

But we will suppose, that the thing thou desirest is good; and that thy heart may be right in asking; as suppose thou desirest more grace; or as David has it, more truth in the inward and hidden part; yet there are several things for thy instruction, may be replied to thy objection: as,

1. Though, thou desirest more of this, thou mayst not yet be so *sensible of the worth of what thou askest*, as per-

haps God will have thee be, before he granteth thy desire. Sometimes Christians ask for good things without having in themselves an estimate proportionable to the worth of what they desire; and God may hold it therefore back, to learn them to know better the worth and greatness of that thing they asked for. The good disciples asked they knew not what. I know they asked what was unlawful, but they were ignorant of the value of that thing, and the same may be thy fault when thou askest for the things most lawful and necessary.

2. Hast thou *well improved what thou hast received* already? Fathers will hold back more money, when the sons have spent that profusely which they had received before? He that is faithful in that which is least, says Christ, is faithful also in much: and he that is unjust in that which is least, is unjust also in much. And if you have not been faithful in that which is another man's, who shall give you that which is your own?" See here an objection made against a further supply, or rather against such a supply as some would have, because they have misspent, or been unfaithful in, what they have already had.

If thou, therefore, hast been faulty here, go, humble thyself to thy friend, and beg pardon for thy faults that are past, when thou art desiring of him more grace.

3. When God gives to his the grant of their desires, *he doth it so as may be best for their advantage.* Now there are times wherein the giving of grace may be best to our advantage: as (1.) Just *before a temptation* comes; then, if it rains grace on thee from heaven, it may be most for thy advantage. This is like God's sending plenty in Egypt just before the years of famine came. (2.) For God to restrain that which thou desirest, *even till the spirit of prayer is in a manner spent,* may be further to inform thee, that though prayer and desires are a duty, and that also to which the promise is made; yet God sees those imperfections in

both thy prayers and desires, as would utterly bind his hands, did he not act towards thee merely from motives drawn from his own bowels and compassion, rather than from any deserving that he sees in thy prayers.

Christians, even righteous men, are apt to lean too much to their own doings; and God, to wean them from them, ofttimes defers to do what they by doing expect, even until in doing their spirits are spent, and they as to doing can do no longer. When they that cried for water had cried till their spirits failed, and their tongue cleaved to the roof of their mouth for thirst; then the Lord did hear, and then the God of Israel did give them their desire. Also when Jonah's soul was fainting under the consideration of all the evils that he had brought upon himself; then his prayer came unto God into his holy temple.

The righteous would be too light in asking, and would too much overprize their works, if their God should not sometimes deal in this manner with them.

It is also to the advantage of the righteous, that they be kept, and led in that way which will *best improve grace already received:* and that is, when they spin it out and use it to the utmost; when they do with it as the prophet did with that meal's meat that he ate under the juniper tree,—go in the strength of it forty days and forty nights, even to the mount of God; or when they do as the widow did, spend upon their handful of flour in the barrel, and upon that little oil in the cruise, until God shall send more plenty.

The righteous are apt to be, like well fed children, too wanton, if God should not appoint them some fasting days. Or they would be apt to cast away fragments, if God should give them every day a new dish. So, then, God will grant the desires of the righteous in that way which will be most for their advantage. And that is, when they have made the best of the old store.

If God should give us two or three harvests in a year, we

should incline to feed our horses and hogs with wheat; but being as it is, we learn better to husband the matter.

By this means also we are made to see, that there is virtue sufficient in our old store of grace to keep us with God in the way of our duty, longer than we could imagine it would.

I myself have cried out, 'I can stand no longer, hold out no longer, without a further supply of grace;' and yet I have by my old grace been kept even after this, days, and weeks, and months, in a way of waiting on God. A little true grace will go a great way, yea, and do more wonders than we are aware of. If we have but grace enough to keep us groaning after God, it is not all the world that can destroy us.

4. Perhaps, here thou mayst be mistaken. The grace thou prayest for, *may in a great measure be come* unto thee. Thou hast been desiring of God, thou sayest, more grace, but hast it not.

But how, if whilst thou lookest for it to come to thee at one door, it should come to thee in at another? And that we may a little inquire into the truth of this, let us a little consider what are the effects of grace in its coming to the soul, and then see if it has not been coming unto thee almost ever since thou hast set upon this fresh desire after it.

Grace, in the general effect of it, is to *mend the soul,* and to make it better disposed. Hence, when it comes, it brings convincing light along with it, by which a man sees more of his baseness than at other times; more, I say of his inward baseness. It is through the shinings of the Spirit of grace that those cobwebs and dirt spots that yet remained in thee are discovered. "In thy light we shall see light." And again, "Whatsoever doth make manifest is light." If then thou seest thyself more vile than formerly, grace by its coming to thee has done this for thee.

Grace, when it comes, *breaks and crumbles the heart,* in the sense and sight of its vileness. A man stands amazed and confounded in himself; breaks and falls down on his face before God; is ashamed to lift up so much as his face to God, at the sight and apprehension of how wicked he is.

Grace, when it comes, *shows to a man more of the holiness and patience of God;* his holiness to make us wonder at his patience, and his patience to make us wonder at his mercy, that yet, even yet, such a vile one as I am, should be admitted to breathe in the land of the living, yea more, suffered to come to the throne of grace.

Grace is of a *heart-humbling nature:* it will make a man count himself the most unworthy of any thing—of all saints. It will make a man put all others afore him, and be glad too, if he may be one beloved, though least beloved because most unworthy. It will make him with gladness accept of the lowest room, as counting all saints more worthy of exaltation than himself.

Grace will make a man *prize other men's graces* and gracious actions *above his own;* as he thinks every man's candle burns brighter than his; every man improves grace better than he; every good man does more sincerely his duty than he. And if these be not some of the effects of the renewings of grace, I will confess I have taken my mark amiss.

Renewings of grace beget renewed self-bemoanings, self-condemnation, self-abhorrence.

And say thou prayest for communion with, and the presence of God. God can have communion with thee, and grant thee his presence, and all this shall, instead of comforting thee at present, more confound thee, and make thee see thy wickedness.

Some people think they never have the presence and renewings of God's grace upon them, but when they are comforted, and when they are cheered up; when, alas! God may be richly with them, while they cry out by these visions,

'My sorrows are multiplied;' or, 'Because I have seen God, I shall die.'

And tell me now, all these things considered, has not grace, even the grace of God, which thou hast so much desired, been coming to thee, and working in thee, in all these hidden methods? And so doing, has it not also accommodated thee with all the aforenamed conveniences? The which when thou considerest, I know thou wouldst not be without, for all the good of the world. Thus, therefore, thy desire is accomplishing and when it is accomplished, will be sweet to thy soul.

5. But we will follow thee a little in the way of thy heart. Thou sayest thou desirest, and desirest grace, yea, hast been a thousand times upon thy knees before God for more grace, and yet thou canst not attain.

I answer, it may be the grace which thou prayest for, is worth thy being upon thy knees yet a thousand times more. We find, that usually they that go to kings' courts for preferment, are there at great expenses; yea, and wait a great while, even perhaps until they have spent their whole estates, and worn out their patience too. Yet they at last prevail, and the thing desired comes. Yea, and when it is come, it sets them up anew, and makes them better off, though they did spend all that they had to obtain it, than ever they were before. Wait, therefore; wait, I say, on the Lord.

Wait, therefore, with David; wait patiently; bid thy soul cheer up, and wait. "Blessed are all they that wait for him."

Thou must consider, again, that great grace is reserved for great service. Thou desirest abundance of grace: thou dost well; and thou shalt have what shall qualify and fit thee for the service that God has for thee to do for him, and for his name in the world. The apostles themselves were to stay for great grace until the time their work was come.

I will not allot thy service; but assure thyself, when thy desire cometh, thou wilt have occassion for it: new work, new trials, new sufferings, or something that will call for the power and virtue of all the grace thou shalt have, to keep thy spirit even, and thy feet from slipping, while thou art exercised in new engagements.

Assure thyself, thy God will not give thee straw but he will expect brick. "For unto whomsoever much is given, of him shall be much required; and to whom men have committed much, of him they will ask the more." Wherefore, as thou art busy in desiring more grace, be also desirous that wisdom to manage it with faithfulness, may also be granted unto thee. Thou wilt say, 'Grace, if I had it, will do all this for me.' It will, and will not. It will, if thou watch and be sober; it will not, if thou be foolish and remiss. Men of great grace may grow consumptive in grace; and idleness may turn him that wears a plush jacket into rags. David was once a man of great grace; but his sin made the grace which he had, so to shrink up, and dwindle away, as to make him cry out, "O take not thy Spirit utterly from me."

Or, perhaps God withholds what thou wouldst have, that it may be the more prized by thee when it comes. "Hope deferred makes the heart sick: but when the desire cometh, it is a tree of life."

Lastly, But dost thou think that thy having more grace will exempt thee from temptations? Alas! the more grace, as was hinted, the greater trials. Thou must be for all that, like the ship of which thou readest, sometimes high, sometimes low; sometimes steady, sometimes staggering; sometimes in, and sometimes even at the end of thy very wits: for so he brings us to our desired haven.

Yet grace is the gold and preciousness of the righteous man: yea, and herein appears the uprightness of his soul, in that though all these things attend the grace of God in him, yet he chooseth grace here above all, for it makes him the more like God and his Christ, and seasons his heart best to his own content; and also capacitates him to glorify God in the world. But I must come to

The conclusion.—Is it so? Is this the sum of all, namely, That the fears of the wicked shall come upon him, and that the desire of the righteous shall be granted? *Then this shows us what is determined concerning both:* Concerning the wicked, that all his hopes shall not bring him to heaven; and concerning the righteous, that all his fears shall not bring him to hell.

But *what a sad thing it is for one to be a wicked man!* Nothing can help him! his wickedness is too strong for him: "His own iniquities shall take the wicked himself, and he shall be holden with the cords of his sins." He may twist and twine, and seek to work himself from under the sentence passed upon him; but all will do him no pleasure. "The wicked is driven away in his wickedness: but the righteous hath hope in his death."

And yet for all this the wicked will not hear. When I read God's word, and see how the wicked follow their sins, yea, dance in the ways of their own destruction, it is astonishing to me. Their actions declare them, though not Atheists in principle, yet such in practice. What do all their acts declare but this, that they either know not God, or fear not what he can do unto them?

But, Oh! how will they change their note, when they see what will become of them! How wan will they look! Yea, the hair of their heads will stand on end for fear—for their fear is their portion; nor can their fears, nor their prayers, nor their entreaties, nor their wishes, nor their repentings, help them in that day.

And thus have I showed you what are the desires of the righteous; and that "the fear of the wicked shall come upon him, but the desire of the righteous shall be granted."

THE

UNSEARCHABLE RICHES OF CHRIST:

OR,

THE SAINT'S KNOWLEDGE

OF

CHRIST'S INCOMPREHENSIBLE LOVE.

A FULL ANSWER TO ALL TEMPTATIONS AND OBJECTIONS, AND AN UNFAILING ENCOURAGEMENT TO PRAYER.

THE

UNSEARCHABLE RICHES OF CHRIST.

CHAPTER I.

BREADTH AND LENGTH OF MERCY IN CHRIST.

THAT YE MAY BE ABLE TO COMPREHEND WITH ALL SAINTS WHAT IS THE BREADTH, AND LENGTH AND DEPTH, AND HEIGHT; AND TO KNOW THE LOVE OF CHRIST, WHICH PASSETH KNOWLEDGE.—Ephesians iii. 18, 19.

THE apostle, having in the first chapter of this epistle treated of the doctrine of election, and in the second, of the reconciling of the Gentiles with the Jews to the Father, by his Son, through the preaching of the gospel, comes in the third chapter to show that this also was, as that of election, determined before the world began.

Now, lest the afflictions that attend the gospel should, by their raging among these Ephesians, darken the glory of these things unto them; therefore, he makes here a brief repetition and explanation, to the end they might be supported and made to live above them. He also joins thereto a fervent prayer for them, that God would let them see in the Spirit of faith, how they, by God and by Christ, are secured from the evil of the worst that might come upon them: "For this cause I bow my knees to the Father of our Lord Jesus Christ, of whom the whole family in heaven and earth is named; that he would grant you according to the riches of his glory, to be strengthened with might by his Spirit in the inner man; that Christ may dwell in your hearts by faith, that ye being rooted and grounded in love, may be able to comprehend with all saints, what is the breadth and length, and depth, and height, and to know the love of Christ, which passeth knowledge," &c.; knowing, that from their deep understanding, what good by these is reserved for them, they would never be discouraged, whatever troubles should attend their profession.

Breadth, and length, and depth, and height, are words that in themselves are both ambiguous, and to wonderment; ambiguous, because unexplained, and to wonderment, because they carry in them an unexpressible something; and something that far outgoes all things that can be found in this world. The apostle here was under a surprise; for, while meditating and writing, he was caught: the strength and glory of the truths that he was endeavoring to fasten upon the people to whom he wrote, took him away into their glory, beyond what could to the full be uttered. Besides, many times things are thus expressed, on purpose to command attention, a stop and pause in the mind about them; and by their greatness, to divert the heart from the world, unto which they naturally are so inclined. Also, truths are often delivered to us like wheat in full ears, to the end we should rub them out before we eat them, and take pains about them, before we have the comfort of them.

"Breadth, length, depth, and height." In attempting to open these words, I will first give you some that are of the same kind; and then show you the reasons of them; and also something of their fullness.

Firstly, Those of the same kind, are used sometimes to show us the power, force, and subtility of the enemies of God's church, Dan. iv. 11; Rom. viii. 38, 39. But,

Secondly, Most properly to show us the infinite and unsearchable greatness of God. Job xi. 7, 8, 9; Rom. xi. 33.

They are here to be taken in this second sense, that is, to suggest unto us the unsearchable and infinite greatness of God; who is a breadth beyond all breadths, a length beyond all lengths, a depth beyond all depths, and a height beyond all heights, and that in all his attributes. He is an eternal being, an everlasting being, and in that respect he is beyond all measures, whether they be of breadth, or length, or depth, or height. In all his attributes he is beyond all measure; whether you measure by words, by thoughts, or by the most enlarged and exquisite apprehension. His greatness is unsearchable; his judgments are unsearchable; he is infinite in wisdom. "O! the depth of the riches both of the wisdom and knowledge of God!—If I speak of strength, lo, he is strong; yea, the thunder of his power who can understand?—There is none holy as the Lord; and his mercy is from everlasting to everlasting, on them that fear him." The greatness of God, of the God and Father of our Lord Jesus Christ, is that, if rightly considered, which will support the spirits of those of his people that are frighted with the greatness of their adversaries. For here is a greatness against a greatness. Pharaoh was great, but God more great; more great in power, more great in wisdom, more great every way for the help of his people; wherein they dealt proudly, he was above them. These words, therefore, take in for this people, the great God who in his immensity, and infinite greatness, is beyond all beings.

But, to come to the reason of the words.

First, They are made use of to show to the Ephesians, that God, with what he is in himself, and with what he hath in his power, is all for the use and profit of believers in Christ. Else, no great matter is held out to them thereby. But this God is our God! there is the comfort. For this cause, therefore, he presented them with this description of him. namely, by breadth, and length, and depth, and height; as if he should say, 'The most high God is yours; the God that fills heaven and earth is yours; the God whom the heaven of heavens cannot contain, is yours; yea, the God whose works are wonderful, and whose ways are past finding out, is yours. Consider, therefore, the greatness that is for you, that taketh part with you, and that will always come in for your help against them that contend with you. It is my support, it is my relief; it is my comfort in all my tribulations, and I would have it yours; and so it will be when we live in the lively faith thereof.'

Nor should we admit of distrust in this matter from the consideration of our own unworthiness, either taken from the finiteness of our state, or the foulness of our ways. For now, though God's attributes, several of them in their own nature, are set against sin and sinners; yea, were we righteous, are so high that they must needs look over us; (for it is in him a condescension to behold things in heaven, how much more then to open his eyes upon such as we!) yet by the passion of Jesus Christ, they harmoniously agree in the salvation of our souls. Hence God is said to be love. God is love, might some say, and justice too. But his justice is turned with wisdom, power, holiness, and truth, to love, yea, to love those that be found in his Son; forasmuch, as there is nothing fault-worthy in his righteousness which is put upon us. So, then, as there is in God's nature a length, and breadth, and depth, and height, that is beyond all that we can think, so we should conclude that all this is love to us, for Christ's sake: and then dilate with it thus in our minds, and enlarge it thus in our meditations, saying still to our low and trembling spirits, "It is high as heaven, what canst thou do? deeper than hell, what canst thou know? the measure thereof is longer than the earth, and broader than the sea."

But we will pass generals, and more particularly speak

something of their fulness, as they are fitted to suit and answer to the whole state and condition of a Christian in this life. The words are boundless: we have here a breadth, a length, a depth, and height, made mention of: but what breadth, what length, what depth, what height, is not so much as hinted. It is, therefore, infiniteness suggested to us, and that has engaged for us. For the apostle conjoins therewith. "And to know the love of Christ which passeth knowledge." Thus, therefore, it suits and answers a Christian's condition while in this world, let that be what it will. If his afflictions be broad, here is a breadth; if they be long, here is a length; if they be deep, here is a depth; and if they be high, here is a height. And I will say, there is nothing that is more helpful, succoring, or comfortable to a Christian while in a state of trial and temptation, than to know that there is a breadth to answer a breadth, a length to answer a length, a depth to answer a depth, and a height to answer a height. Wherefore, this is that the apostle prayeth for, namely, that the Ephesians might have understanding in these things, "That ye may know what is the breadth, and length, and depth, and height."

Of the largeness of the apostle's heart in praying for his people, namely, that they might "be able to comprehend with all saints, what" these great things are, of that we shall speak afterwards.

But, first, to speak of these four expressions, breadth, length, depth, and height.

1. "What is the *breadth.*" This word is to show, that God is over all, every where, spreading of his wings, stretching out his goodness to the utmost bounds, for the good of those that are his people.

In the sin of his people there is a breadth; a breadth that spreadeth over all, wheresoever a man shall look. The sin even of saints is a spreading leprosy. Sin is a scab that spreadeth; in sinners it is a spreading plague; it knows no bounds: or, as David saith, "I have seen the wicked spreading himself." Hence it is compared to a cloud, to a thick cloud, that covereth or spreadeth over the face of all the sky. Wherefore, here is a breadth called for, a breadth that can cover all, or else what is done is to no purpose. Therefore, to answer this, here we have a breadth, a spreading breadth. "I spread my skirt over thee." But how far? Even so far as to cover all. "I spread my skirt over thee, and covered thy nakedness." Here now is a breadth, according to the spreading nature of the sin of this wretched one; yea, a super-abounding spreading, a spreading beyond, a spreading to cover. "Blessed is he whose sin is covered," whose spreading sin is covered by the mercy of God through Christ. This is the spreading cloud, whose spreadings none can understand. "He spread a cloud for a covering, and fire to give light in the night."

This breadth that is in God, also overmatcheth that spreading and overspreading rage of men, that is sometimes as if it would swallow up the whole church of God. You read of the rage of the king of Assyria, that there was a breadth in it, an overflowing breadth, "to the filling of the breadth of thy land, O Immanuel." But what follows? "Associate yourselves, O ye people," (ye Assyrians,) "and ye shall be broken to pieces; and give ear, all ye of far countries; gird yourselves, and ye shall be broken to pieces. Take counsel together, and it shall come to nought; speak the word, and it shall not stand, for God is with us;" that is, God will overmatch and go beyond you.

Wherefore, this word, "breadth," and "what is the breath," is here expressed on purpose to succor and relieve, or to show what advantage, for support, the knowledge of the overspreading grace of God by Christ yieldeth unto those that have it, let their trials be what they will. Alas! the sin of God's children seemeth sometimes to overspread, not only their flesh, and the face of their souls, but the whole face of heaven. And what shall he have to do now, that is a stranger to this breadth, made mention of in the text? Why he must despair, lie down and die, and shut up his heart against all comfort unless he, with his fellow-Christians, can, at least, apprehend what is this breadth, or the breadth of mercy intended in this place. Therefore Paul, for the support of the Ephesians, prays, that they "may know what is the breadth."

This largeness of the heart and mercy of God towards his people, is also signified by the spreading out of his hands to us in the invitations of the gospel. "I said," (saith he,) "Behold me, behold me! I have spread out my hands all the day to a rebellious people, to a people that provoke me continually. "I have spread out my hands," that is, opened my arms as a mother affectionately doth, when she stoopeth to her child in the warm workings of her bowels, and claspeth it up in them, and kisseth, and putteth it into her bosom. For, by spreading out the hands or arms to embrace, is showed the breadth and largeness of God's affections; as by our spreading out our hands in prayer, is signified the great sense that we have of the spreading nature of our sins, and of the great desires that are in us, that God would be merciful to us.

This word also answereth to, or may fitly be set against, the wiles and temptations of the devil, who is like that great and dogged leviathan, that "spreadeth his sharp pointed things upon the mire;" for be the spreading nature of our corruptions ever so broad, he will find sharp pointed things enough to stick in the mire of them, for our affliction. These sharp pointed things are those that in another place are called "fiery darts," and he has abundance of them, with which he can, and will sorely prick and wound our spirits; yea, so sharp some have found these things to their souls, that they have pierced beyond expression. "When" (said Job) "I say, my bed shall comfort me, my couch shall ease my complaint, then thou scarest me with dreams, and terrifiest me through visions, so that my soul chooseth strangling and death, rather than life." But now, answerable to the spreading of these sharp pointed things, there is a super-abounding breadth in the sovereign grace of God, the which whoso seeth and understandeth, as the apostle doth pray we should, is presently helped: for he seeth that his grace spreadeth itself, and is broader than can be either our mire, or the sharp pointed things that Satan spreadeth thereupon for our vexation and affliction: "it is broader than the sea."

This, therefore, should be that upon which those that see the spreading nature of sin, and the leprosy and contagion thereof, should meditate, namely, the broadness of the grace and mercy of God in Christ. This will poise and stay the soul; this will relieve and support the soul in and under those many misgiving and desponding thoughts unto which we are subject, when afflicted with the apprehensions of sin, and the abounding nature of it.

Shall another man pray for this, one that knew the goodness and benefit of it, and shall not I meditate upon it? and shall not I exercise my mind about it? Yes, surely, for it is my duty, it is my privilege and mercy so to do. Let this, therefore, when thou seest the spreading nature of sin, be a *memento* to thee, to the end thou mayest not sink and and die in thy soul.

2. "What is the breadth and *length.*" As there is a breadth in this mercy and grace of God by Christ, so there is a length therein, and this length is as large as the breadth, and as much suiting the condition of the child of God, as the other is. For, though sin sometimes is most afflicting to the conscience, while the soul beholdeth the overspreading nature of it, yet here it stoppeth not, but ofttimes through the power and prevalency of it, the soul is driven with it, as a ship by a mighty tempest, or as a rolling thing before the wirlwind; driven, I say, from God and from all hopes of

his mercy, as far as the east is from the west, or as the ends of the world are asunder. Hence it is supposed by the prophet, that for and by sin they may be driven from God to the utmost part of heaven; and that is a sad thing, a sad thing, I say, to a gracious man. "Why," (saith the prophet to God) "art thou so far from helping me, and from the words of my roaring?"

Sometimes a man, yea, a man of God, is, as he apprehends, so far off from God, that he can neither help him, nor hear him; and this is a dismal state. "And thou hast removed my soul," saith the church "far off from peace; I forgot prosperity." This is the state sometimes of the godly, and that not only with reference to their being removed by persecutors from the appointments and gospel seasons, which are their delight and the desire of their eyes; but also with reference to their faith and hope in their God. They think themselves beyond the reach of his mercy.

Therefore, in answer to this sad conceit it is, that the Lord asketh, saying, "Is my hand shortened at all that I cannot redeem?" And again, "Behold the Lord's hand is not shortened, that it cannot save; neither his ear heavy that he cannot hear." Wherefore, he saith again, "If any of thine be driven out unto the uttermost parts of heaven, from thence will the Lord thy God gather thee, and from thence will be fetch thee." God has a long arm, and he can reach a great way further than we can conceive he can. When we think his mercy is clean gone, and that ourselves are "free among the dead," and of the number that he remembereth no more, then he can reach us, and cause that again we stand before him. He could reach Jonah, though he seemed "in the belly of hell;" and reach thee, even then when thou thinkest thy way is hid from the Lord, and thy judgment passed over from thy God. There is a length to admiration, beyond apprehension or belief, in the arm of the strength of the Lord: and this is that which the apostle intendeth by this word "length," namely, to insinuate what a reach there is in the mercy of God, how far it can extend itself. "If I take the wings of the morning," said David, "and dwell in the uttermost parts of the sea, even there shall thy hand lead me, and thy right hand shall hold me." "I will gather them from the east, and from the west, and from the north, and from the south," saith he, that is from the utmost corners.

This, therefore, should encourage them that for the present cannot stand, but that do fly before their guilt: them that feel no help nor stay, but that go, as to their thinking, every day by the power of temptation driven yet farther off from God, and from the hope of obtaining his mercy to their salvation. Poor creature! I will not now ask thee how thou camest into this condition, or how long this has been thy state; but I will say before thee, and I prithee hear me, O the length of the saving arm of God! As yet thou art within the reach thereof; do not thou go about to measure arms with God, as some good men are apt to do; I mean, do not thou conclude, that because thou canst not reach God by thy short stump, therefore, he cannot reach thee with his long arm. Look again, hast thou an arm like God, an arm like his for length and strength? It becomes thee, when thou canst not perceive that God is within the reach of thy arm, then to believe that thou art within the reach of his; for it is long, and none knows how long.

Again, Is there such a length? such a length in the arm of the Lord, that he can reach those that are gone away, as far as they could? Then this should encourage us to pray, and hope for the salvation of any one of our backsliding relations, that God would reach out his arm after them, saying, "Awake, O arm of the Lord! Art not thou it that hast cut Rahab, and wounded the dragon? Art not thou it which hast dried the sea, the waters of the great deep, and hast made the depths of the sea a way for the ransomed to pass over?" 'Awake, O arm of the Lord! and be stretched out as far as to where my poor husband is, where my poor child, or where my poor backslidden wife or dear relation is, and lay hold, fast hold! They are gone from thee, but, O, thou! the hope of Israel, fetch them again, and let them stand before thee.' I say, here is in this word "length" matter of encouragement for us thus to pray; for if the length of the reach of mercy is so great, and if also this length is for the benefit of those that may be gone off far from God, (for they at present have no need thereof that are near,) then improve this advantage at the throne of grace for such, that they may come to God again.

CHAPTER II.

DEPTH AND HEIGHT OF MERCY IN CHRIST.

As there is a breadth and length here, so there is also a depth. "What is the breadth and length, and *depth*." And this depth is also put in here, on purpose to help us under a trial that is diverse from the two former. I told you, that by the breadth, the apostle insinuates a remedy and succor to us, when we see our corruptions spread like a leprosy; and by length he would show us, that when sin has driven God's elect to the furthest distance from him, yet his arm is not long enough to reach them, and fetch them back again

But, I say, as we have here a breadth, and a length, so we have also a depth. "That ye may know what is the depth." Christians have sometimes their sinking fits, and are as if they were always descending; or, as Heman says, "counted with them that go down into the pit.' Now guilt is not to such so much a wind and a tempest, as a load and burden. The devil, and sin, and the curse of the law, and death, are gotten upon the shoulders of this poor man, and are treading him down, that he may sink into, and be swallowed up of his miry place.

"I sink," says David, "in deep mire, where there is no standing; I am come into deep waters, where the floods overflow me." Yea, there is nothing more common among the saints of old, than this complaint. "Let not the water flood overflow me, neither let the deep swallow me up, neither let the pit shut her mouth upon me." Heman also saith, "Thou hast laid me in the lowest pit, in darkness in the deeps. Thy wrath lieth hard upon me, and thou hast afflicted me with all thy waves." Hence it is again that the Psalmist says, "Deep calleth unto deep, at the noise of thy water spouts; all thy waves and thy billows are gone over me." Deep calleth unto deep: what is that? why, it is expressed in the verse before: "O God," says he, "my soul is cast down within me." "Down;" that is, deep into the jaws of distrust and fear. 'And, Lord, my soul in this depth of sorrow calls for help to thy depth of mercy; for though I am sinking and going down, yet not so low, but that thy mercy is yet underneath me. Do of thy compassions open those everlasting arms, and catch him that has no help or stay in himself;' for so it is with one that is falling into a well or a dungeon.

Now mark, as there is in these texts the sinking condition of the godly man set forth, of a man whom sin and Satan are treading down into the deep; so in our text which I am speaking of at this time, we have a depth that can more than counterpoise these deeps, set forth with a hearty prayer, that we may know it. And although the deeps, or depths of calamity, into which the godly may fall, may be as deep as hell, and methinks they should be no deeper, yet this is the comfort, and for the comfort of them of the godly that are thus sinking, the mercy of God for them lies deeper. "It is deeper than hell, what canst thou know?" And this is that which made Paul say that he was not afraid of this depth. "I am persuaded," saith he, "that neither height nor depth shall separate us from the love of God, which is in Christ Jesus our Lord." But of this he could by no means have been persuaded, had he not believed that mercy lieth deeper for the godly to help them, than can all other depths be to destroy them. This is it at which he stands and wonders, saying, "O the depth of the riches, both of the wisdom and knowledge of God:" that is, to find out a way to save his people, notwithstanding all the deep contrivances that the enemy hath invented and may invent, to make us come short of home.

This is also that, as I take it, which is wrapped up in the blessing wherewith Jacob blessed his son Joseph. "God shall bless thee," saith he, "with the blessings of heaven above, and with the blessings of the deep that lieth under:" a blessing which he had ground to pronounce, as well from his observation of God's good dealing with Joseph, as in a spirit of prophecy. For he saw that he lived and was become a flourishing bough, by a well, after that the archers had done their worst to him. Moses also blesseth God for blessing Joseph thus, and blesseth his portion to him, as counting it sufficient for his help in all afflictions: "Blessed," saith he, "of the Lord, be his land, for the precious things of heaven, for the dew, and for the deep that coucheth beneath."

I am not of belief that these blessings are confined to things temporal or carnal, but that they take in things spiritual and divine; and that they have most respect to the soul and eternal good. Now mark, he tells us here, that the blessings of the deep do couch beneath; *couch*, that is, lie close, so as hardly to be discerned by him that willingly would see that himself is not below these arms that are beneath him. But that, as I said, is hard to be discerned by him that thus is sinking, and that has, as he now smartingly feels, all God's waves, and his billows rolling over him. However, whether he sees or not, (for this blessing lieth couched,) yet there it is, and there will be, though one should sink as deep as hell; and hence they are said to be "everlasting arms" that are "underneath:" that is, arms that are long and strong, and that can reach to the bottom, and also beyond, all the misery and distress that Christians are subject to in this life. Indeed Mercy seems to be asleep when we are sinking; (for then we are as if all things were careless of us,) but it is but as a lion couchant, it will awake in time for our help. And forasmuch as this term is it which is applicable to the lion in his den, it may be to show, that as a lion, so will God at the fittest season, arise for the help and deliverance of a sinking people. Hence, when he is said to address himself to the delivering of his people, it is, that he comes as a roaring lion. "The Lord shall go forth as a mighty man, he shall stir up jealousy like a man of war: he shall cry, yea roar, he shall prevail against his enemies." However, here is a depth against the depth that is against us, let that depth be what it will. Let it be the depth of misery, the depth of mercy is sufficient. If it be the depth of hellish policy, the depth both of the wisdom and knowledge of God shall go beyond it, and prevail.

This, therefore, is worthy of the consideration of all sinking souls; of the souls that feel themselves descending into the pit. There is such a thing as this experienced among the godly. Some, (when tempted) come to them when you will, they will tell you, they have no ground to stand on, their feet have slipped, their foundation is removed, and they feel themselves sinking, as into a pit that has no bottom. They inwardly sink, not for want of something to relieve the body, but for want of some spiritual cordial to support the mind. "I went down to the bottoms of the mountains," (said Jonah) "the earth with her bars was about me forever: my soul fainted within me."

Now for such to consider, that underneath them even at the bottom, there lieth a blessing, or that in this deep whereinto they are descending, there lieth a delivering mercy couching to catch them, and to save them, from sinking forever, this would be a relief unto them, and help them to hope for good.

Again as this, were it well considered by the sinking ones, would yield them stay and relief, so this is it by the virtue whereof they that have been sinking heretofore have been lifted up, and above their castings down again. There are of those that have been withal in the pit, now upon Mount Sion, with the harps of God in their hands, and with the song, of the Lamb in their mouths. But how is it that they are there? Why David by his own deliverance shows you the reason. "For great is thy mercy towards me," (saith he,) "and thou hast delivered my soul from the lowest hell." And again, "He brought me up also out of an horrible pit," (a pit of noise, a pit wherein was the noise of devils, and of my heart answering them with distrust and fear,) "out of the miry clay," (into which I did not only sink, but was by it held from getting up: but he brought me up,) "and set my feet upon a rock, and established my goings. And he hath put a new song in my mouth, even praises to our God."

But let me here give, if it may be, a timely caution to them that think they stand upon their feet. Give not way to falling, because everlasting arms are underneath. Take heed of that. God can let thee fall into mishief; he can let thee fall, and not help thee up. Tempt not God, lest he cast thee away. Indeed, I doubt there are many that have presumed upon this mercy, that thus doth couch beneath, and have cast themselves down from their pinnacles into vanity, of a vain conceit that they shall be lifted up again: whom yet God will leave to die there, because their fall was rather of wilfulness than weakness, and of stubbornness and desperate resolutions, than for want of means and helps to preserve them from it.

4. As there is a breadth, and length, and depth, in this mercy and grace of God through Christ towards his people, so there is also a *height*. "That ye may comprehend with all saints, what is the breadth and length, and depth, and height." There are things that are high, as well as things that are low; things that are above us, as well as things that are under, that are distressing to God's people. It is said when Noah was a preacher of righteousness, "there were

giants in the earth in those days:" and these, as I conceive, were some of the heights that were set against Noah; yea, they were the very fathers of all that monstrous brood that followed in the world in that day. Of this sort were they who so frighted and terrified Israel, when they were to go to inherit the land of promise. Then men that were tall as the cedars and strong as the oaks, frighted them: they were in their own sight, when compared with these high ones but as grasshoppers. This, therefore, was their discouragement.

Besides, together with these, they had high walls, walls as high as heaven; and these walls were of purpose to keep Israel out of his possession. See how it is expressed, "The people is greater and taller than we, the cities are great, and walled up to heaven: and moreover, we have seen the sons of the Anakims there." One of those, that is, Goliah by name, how did he fright the children of Israel in the days of Saul! How did the appearance of him make them scuttle together on heaps before him! By these giants, and by these high walls, God's children to this day are sorely distressed, because they stand in the crossways to cut off Israel from his possesion.

But now to support us against all these, and to encourage us to take heart notwithstanding all these things; there is for us a height in God. He hath made his Son "higher than the kings of the earth." His word also "is settled forever in heaven," and therefore must needs be higher than their walls. He also saith in another place, "If thou seest the oppression of the poor, and violent perverting of judgment and justice in a province, marvel not at the matter; for he that is higher than the highest, regardeth, and there be higher than they." It was this that made Paul say, that he feared not the height; nor of things present, nor things to come.

But again, as there are these things standing or lying in our way; so there is another sort of heights that are more mischievous than these; and they are the fallen angels. These are called spiritual wickedness, or wicked spirits, in "high places." For God has suffered them for a time, to take to themselves principality and power, and so they are become "the rulers of the darkness of this world." By these we are tempted, sifted, threatened, opposed, undermined: also by these there are snares, pits, holes, and what not made, and laid for us, if peradventure by something we may be destroyed. Yea, and we should most certainly be so, were it not for the Rock that is higher than they. "But he that cometh from heaven is above all." These are they that our King has taken captive, and hath rode (in his chariot of salvation) in triumph over their necks. These are they, together with all others, whose most devilish designs he can wield, and turn, and make work together for his ransomed's advantage. There is a height, and an infinitely overtopping height in the mercy and goodness of God for us, against them.

There are heights also that build up themselves *in* us, which are not but to be taken notice of; yea, there are many of them, and they place themselves directly so, that if possible they may keep the saving knowledge of God out of our hearts. These high things, therefore, are said to "exalt themselves against the knowledge of God;" and do ofttimes more plague, afflict, and frighten Christian men and women, than any thing besides. It is from these that our faith and spiritual understanding of God and his Christ is opposed and contradicted; and from these also that we are so inclinable to swerve from right doctrine into destructive opinions. It is from these that we are so easily persuaded to call in question our former experience of the goodness of God towards us, and from these that our minds are so often clouded and darkened, that we cannot see afar off. These would betray us into the hands of fallen angels and men; nor should we by any means help or deliver ourselves, were it not for one that is higher. These are the dark mountains at which our feet would certainly stumble, and upon which we should fall, were it not for one who can leap and skip over these mountains of division, and come unto us.

Further, there is a height also that is obvious to our senses, the which, when it is dealt withal by our corrupted reason, proves a great shaking to our mind, and that is the height, and exceeding distance, that heaven is off from us, and we off from it. "Is not God in the height of heaven? and behold the height of the stars, how high are they?" Hence heaven is called the place for height. Also when Ahaz is bid to ask with reference to heaven, he is bid to ask it, in the height, in the height above. Now, saith reason, how shall I come thither? especially when a good man is at his furthest distance therefrom; which is, when he is in the grave. Now I say, every height is a difficulty to him that is loaden with a burden, especially the heaven of heavens, where God is, and where is the resting place of his, to them that are oppressed with the guilt of sin. And besides, the dispensation which happeneth to us last, namely, death, as I said before, makes this heaven in my thoughts, while I live, so much the more inaccessible. 'Christ, indeed, could mount up: but me, poor me, how shall I get thither? Elias, indeed, had a chariot sent him to ride in thither, and went up by it into that holy place, but I, poor I, how shall I get thither? Enoch is there because God took him; but as for me, how shall I get thither?' Thus some have mourningly said. And although distrust of the power of God, as to the accomplishing of this thing, is by no means to be smiled upon, yet methinks the unconcernedness of professors thereabout, doth argue, that considering thoughts about that, are wanting.

I know the answer is ready. Get Christ and go to heaven. But methinks the height of the place, and the glory of the state that we are to enjoy therein, should a little concern us, at least so as to make us wonder in our thinking, that the time is coming that we must mount up thither. And since there are so many heights between this place, between us and that, it should make us admire the heights of the grace and mercy of God, by which means are provided to bring us thither. And I believe that this thing, this very thing, is included here by the apostle, when he prays for the Ephesians, that they might know the height.

Methinks, how shall we get thither, will still stick in my mind. "I will ascend," says one, "above the height of the clouds, and I will be like the Most High." "And I," says another, "will set my nest among the stars of heaven." Well, but what of all this? If heaven has gates, and they shall be shut, how wilt thou go in thither? Though such should climb up to heaven, from thence will God bring them down. Still, I say, therefore, how shall we get in thither? Why, for them that are godly, there is the power of God, the merits of Christ, the help of angels, and the testimony of a good conscience, to bring them thither; and he that has not the help of all these, let him do what he can, shall never come thither. Not that all these go to the making up of the height that is intended in the text; for the height there, is what is in God through Christ to us, alone. But the angels are the servants of God for that end; and none with ill consciences enter in thither. "What, know you not that the unrighteous shall not inherit the kingdom of God? Be not deceived, such have no inheritance in the kingdom of Christ and of God.

This, then, should teach us, that in God is a power that is able to subdue all things to himself. In the completing of many things, there seems to man to be an utter impossibility, as that a virgin should conceive in her womb, as a virgin, and bring a Son into the world; and that the body that is turned into dust, should arise and ascend into the highest heaven. These things, with many more, seem to be utterly impossible: but there is that which is called the power of God, by the which he is able to make all things bend to his will, and to make all obstructions give place to what he pleases. God is high above all things, and can do whatever it pleaseth him.

But since he can do so, why doth he suffer this and that thing, to appear, to act, and do, so horribly repugnant to his word? I answer, he admits of many things, to the end that he may show his wrath, and make his power known; and that all the world may see how he checks and overrules the most vile and unruly things, and can make them subservient to his holy will. And how would the breadth and the length, and the depth, and the height of the love and mercy of God in Christ to us-ward, be made to appear, so as in all things it doth, were it not admitted that there should be breadths, lengths, and depths, and heights, to oppose? Wherefore, these opposites are, therefore, suffered, that the greatness of the wisdom, the power, the mercy, and grace of God to us in Christ, might appear and be made manifest unto us.

This calls, therefore, upon Christians wisely to consider the doings of their God. How many opposing breadths, and lengths, and depths, and heights, did Israel meet with in their journey from Egypt to Canaan, and all to convince them of their weakness, and also of the power of their God! And they that did wisely consider his doings there, did reap the advantage thereof. 'Come, behold the works of the Lord towards me,' may every Christian say. 'He hath set a Saviour against sin; a heaven against a hell; light against darkness; good against evil; and the breadth, and length, and depth, and height of the grace that is in himself, for my good, against all the power, and strength, and force, and subtilty of every enemy.

This also, as I hinted but just before, shows both the power of them that hate us, and the inability in us to resist. The power that is set against us none can crush and break but God: for it is the power of the devils, of sin, of death, and hell. But we, for our parts, are crushed before the moth, being a shadow, a vapor, and a wind that passes away. O how should we, and how would we, were but our eyes awake, stand and wonder at the preservations, the deliverances, the salvations and benefits with which we are surrounded daily; while so many mighty evils seek daily to swallow us up, as the grave! See how the golden Psalm of David reads it: "Be merciful unto me, O God, for man would swallow me up: he fighting daily oppresseth me. Mine enemies would swallow me up: for they be many that fight against me, O most High." This is at the beginning of it. And he concludes it thus; "Thou has delivered my soul from death; wilt not thou deliver my feet from falling, that I may walk before God in the light of the living."

By this also we see the reason why it is so impossible for man or angel to persuade unbelievers to come in to, and close with Christ. Why, there is a breadth that they cannot get over, a length that they cannot get beyond, a depth that they cannot pass, and heights that so hinder them of the prospect of glory and the way thereto, that they cannot be allured thither. And that nothing can remove these, but those infinite attributes that are in God, and that are opposite thereto; even the breadth and length, and depth and height that are in the text expressed, is to all awakened men an undoubted truth.

One item I would here give to him that loveth his own soul, and then we will pass on in pursuance of what is to come. Since there is a height obvious to sense, and that height must be overcome ere a man can enter into life eternal; let thy heart be careful that thou go the right way to overpass this height, that thou mayest not miss of the delectable plains, and the pleasures that are above. Now there is nothing so high as to overtop this height, but Jacob's ladder, and that can do it: that ladder, when the foot thereof doth stand upon the earth, reacheth with its top to the gate of heaven. This is the ladder by which angels ascend thither: and this is the ladder by which thou mayest ascend thither. "And he dreamed a dream, and behold a ladder set upon the earth, and the top of it reached to heaven: and behold the angels of God ascending and descending on it."

This ladder is Jesus Christ the Son of man, as is clear by the Evangelist John. And in that it is said to stand upon the earth, that is to show that he took hold of man who is of the earth, and therein laid a foundation for his salvation: in that it is said the top reached up to heaven, that is to show, that the divine nature was joined to the human, and by that means he was every way made a Saviour complete. Now, concerning this ladder, it is said, Heaven was open where it stood, to show, that by him there is entrance into life. It is said also concerning this ladder that the Lord stood there, at the top above it; saying, "I am the God of Abraham," to show his hearty and willing reception of those that ascend the height of his sanctuary this way. All which Christ further explains by saying, "I am the way, the truth, and the life; no man cometh to the Father but by me." Look to thyself, then, that thou do truly, and after the right manner, embrace this ladder; so will he draw thee up thither after him. All the rounds of this ladder are sound, and fitly placed, not one of them is set further than that by faith thou mayest ascend step by step, even until thou shalt come to the highest step thereof, from whence or by which thou mayst step in at the celestial gate, where thy soul desireth to dwell.

Take my caution, then, and be wary; no man can come thither but by him. Thither, I say to be accepted; thither, there to dwell, and there to abide with joy forever. "That you may be able to comprehend with all saints, what is the breadth, and length, and depth, and height; and to know the love of Christ which passeth knowledge."

CHAPTER III.

THE ABILITY AND ADVANTAGE OF COMPREHENDING THIS MERCY.

HAVING thus spoken of the breadth, and length, and depth, and height that are in God's mercy by Christ to usward; we will now come more directly to the prayer of the Apostle for these Ephesians, with reference thereunto; namely, that they might be able to comprehend with all saints what they are.

And first, as to the ability that he prays for, to the end that they might be able to do this thing.

"That ye may be *able.*" The weakness that is here supposed to hinder their thus comprehending, &c., did, doubtless, lie in their grace, as well as their nature; for in both, with reference to them that are Christians, there is a great disability, unless they be strengthened mightily by tbe Holy Ghost. Nature's ability depends upon grace, and the ability of grace depends upon the mighty help of the Spirit of God Hence, as nature itself, where grace is not, sees nothing; so nature by grace sees but weakly, if that grace is not "strengthened with all might by the Spirit of grace." The breadths, lengths, depths, and heights, here made mention of, are mysteries, and in all their operations do work wonderfully mysteriously: insomuch that many times, though they are all of them busily engaged for this and the other child of God, yet they themselves see nothing of them. As Christ said to Peter, "What I do, thou knowest not now;" so may it be said to many where the grace and mercy of God in Christ is working; they do not know, they understand not what it is, nor what will be the end of such dispensations of God towards them. Wherefore they also say as Peter to Christ, "Dost thou wash my feet? thou shalt never wash my feet:" yea, and when some light to convince of this folly breaks in upon them; yet if it be not very distinct and clear, causing the person to know the true cause, nature and end of God's doing this or that, they swerve with Peter, as much on the other side. 'They have not known my ways and my methods with them in this world,' was that which caused Israel 'always to err in their hearts,' and lie cross to all and each of these breadths, lengths, depths, and heights, whenever they were under the exercise of any of them in the wilderness.

And the reason is, as I said before, that they are very mysterious in their workings; for they work by, upon, and against oppositions; in order to the help and salvation of his people. Also, (as was hinted a while since) that the power and glory of this breadth, and length, &c., of the mercy and grace of God may the more show its excellency and sufficiency as to our deliverance; we by him seen quite to be delivered up to the breadths, lengths, and depths, and heights, that oppose, and that utterly seek our ruin: wherefore at such times nothing of the breadths, lengths, depths, or heights of mercy can be seen, save by those that are very well skilled in those mysterious methods of God, in his gracious actings towards his people. "Who will bring me into the strong city? Wilt not thou, O God, which hast cast us off? and thou, O God, which didst not go forth with our armies?" is a lesson too hard for every Christian man to say over, believingly. And what was it that made Jonah say, when he was in the belly of hell, "yet will I look again towards thy holy temple," but the good skill that he had in understanding the mystery of these breadths, and lengths, and depths, and heights of God, and of the way of his working by them. Read the text at large: "Thou hast cast me into the deep, in the midst of the sea, and the floods compassed me about. All thy billows and thy waves passed over me. Then I said, I am cast out of thy sight; yet will I look again toward thy holy temple."

These, and such like sentences, are easily played with by a preacher, when in the pulpit, especially if he has a little of the notion of things; but of the difficulty and strait that those are brought into, out of whose mouth such things, or words, are extorted by reason of the force of the labyrinths they are fallen into, of those they experience nothing; wherefore to those they are utterly strangers.

He then that is *able* to comprehend with all saints what is the breadth, and length, and depth, and height, must be a good expositor of providences, and must see the way, and the workings of God by them. Now there are providences of two sorts, seemingly good and seemingly bad, and those do usually as Jacob did, when he blessed the sons of Joseph, cross hands, lay the blessing where he would not. "And when Joseph saw that his father laid his right hand upon the head of Ephraim, it displeased him." I say there are providences unto which we would have the blessings entailed, but they are not. And they are providences that smile upon the flesh, namely, such as cast into the lap, health, wealth, plenty, ease, friends, and abundance of this world's good: because these *Manassehs*, (as the name doth signify,) have in them an aptness to make us *forget* our toil, our low estate, and from whence we were: but the great blessing is not in them. There are providences, again, that take away from us whatever is desirable to the flesh: such are sickness, losses, crosses, persecution, and affliction; and usually in these, though they make us feel a shock whenever they come upon us, the blessing coucheth, and is ready to help us. For God, (as the name of *Ephraim* signifies,) makes us *fruitful* in the land of our affliction. He, therefore, in blessing his people, lays his hands across, guiding them wittingly, and laying the chiefest blessing on the head of Ephraim, or in that providence that sanctifies affliction.

Abel! what to the reason of Eve was he, in comparison of Cain?* Rachel called Benjamin the son of her sorrow: but Jacob knew how to give him a better name. Jabez also, though his mother so called him, because, as it seems, she brought him forth with more than ordinary sorrow, was yet more honorable, more godly, than his brethren.

He that has skill to judge of providences aright, has a great ability in him to comprehend with other saints, what is the breadth, and length, and depth, and height; but he that has no skill as to discerning them, is but a child in his judgment in those high and mysterious things. And hence it is that some shall suck honey out of that, at the which others tremble for fear it should poison them. I have often been made to say, 'sorrow is better than laughter, and the house of morning better than the house of mirth." And I have more often seen, that the afflicted are always the best sort of Christians. There is a man, never well, never prospering, never but under afflictions, disappointments, and sorrows: why, this man, if he be a Christian, is one of the best of men. "They that go down to the sea, that do business in great waters, they see the works of the Lord, and his wonders in the deep." And it is from hence, for aught I know, that James admonishes the brother of high degree to rejoice in that he is made low; and he renders the reason of it, namely, that the fashion of the world perisheth; the rich man fadeth away in his ways; but the tempted, and he that endureth temptation is blest. Now, I know these things are not excellent in themselves, nor yet to be desired for any profit that they can yield; but God doth use by these, as by a tutor or instructor, to make known to them that are exercised with them, so much of himself, as to make them understand that riches of his goodness that is seldom by other means broken up to the sons of men. And

*Cain signifies *possession*, and implies the gladness of gratified hope; Abel, on the contrary, signifies *vanity*, or the grief of disappointment. J. N. B.

hence it is said, that the "afterwards" of affliction doth yield the peaceable fruits of righteousness to them that are exercised thereby.

The sum is, these breadths, and lengths, and depths, and heights of God, are to be discerned; and some that are good do more, and some do less discern them, and how they are working, and putting forth themselves in every providence, in every change, in every turn of the wheel that passeth by us in this world. I do not question but that there are some that are alive, that have been able to say, the days of affliction have been the best unto them, and that could, if it were lawful, pray that they might always be in affliction, if God would always do to them as he did when his hand was last upon them. For by them he caused his light to shine; or, as Job has it, "Thou huntest me as a fierce lion," and again, "thou showest thyself marvellously unto me." See also the writing of Hezekiah, and read what profit he found in afflictions.

But again, these breadths, lengths, depths, and heights, have in themselves naturally that glory that cannot be so well discerned, or kept in view by weak eyes. He had need have an eye like an eagle, that can look upon the sun, that can look upon these great things, and not be stricken blind therewith. You see how Saul was served when he was going to Damascus; but Stephen could stand and look up steadfastly into heaven: and that, too, when with Jonah he he was going into the deep. But I have done with this, and proceed.

"That ye may be able to *comprehend*." Although apprehending is included in comprehending, yet to comprehend is more. To comprehend is to know a thing fully; or, to reach it all. But here we must distinguish, and say, that there is a comprehending that is absolute, and a comprehending that is comparative. Of comprehending absolutely or perfectly, we are not here to speak; for that the apostle could not, in this place, as to the thing prayed for, desire; for it is utterly impossible perfectly to know whatsoever is in the breadths, lengths, depths, and heights, here spoken of; whether you call them mercies, judgments, or the ways of God with men. "How unsearchable are his judgments, and his ways past finding out." Or, if you take them to signify his love, unto which you see I am inclined,* why, that you read of in the same place, to be it which passes knowledge. Wherefore, should the apostle, by this term, conclude, or insinuate, that what he calls here breadths, lengths, depths, or heights, might be fully or perfectly understood and known, he would not only contradict other Scriptures, but himself, in one and the self-same breath. Wherefore, it must be understood *comparatively:* that is, (and that he says,) with, or as much as others, as any, even with all saints. "That ye may be able to comprehend, with all saints, what is the breadth, and length, and depth, and height." 'I would ye were as able to understand, to know, and to find out these things, as ever any were; and to know with the very best of saints, "the love of Christ, which passeth knowledge."' There are, as has before been hinted, degrees of knowledge of these things; some know more, some less; but the apostle prays that these Ephesians might see, know, and understand as much thereof as the best, or as any under heaven.

And this, in the first place, shows us the love of a minister of Jesus Christ. A minister's love to his flock is seen in his praying for them; wherefore Paul commonly, by his epistles, either first or last, or both, gives the churches to understand, that he did often heartily pray to God for them: and not only so, but also specifies the mercies, and

---

* The context seems to *settle* this as the true meaning. "That ye being rooted and grounded *in love*, may be able to comprehend, &c., and to know the *love of Christ*, which passeth knowledge, that ye might be filled with *all the fulness of God*." So John says, "He *that dwelleth in love*, dwelleth in God," J. N. B.

blessings, and benefits, which he earnestly begged for them of God

But, secondly, This implies that there are great benefits accrue to Christians by the comprehending of these things: yea, it implies that something very special is ministered to us by this knowledge of these. And here to touch upon a few of them.

1. He that shall arrive to some competent knowledge of these things, shall understand more thoroughly *the greatness*, (the wisdom, the power, &c.) *of the God that is above.* For by these expressions are the attributes of God set forth unto us. And although I have discoursed of them hitherto under the notion of grace and mercy, yet it was not that I judged they excluded the expressing of his other attributes, but because they all, as it were, turn into loving methods in the wheel of their heavenly motion towards the children of God. Hence it is said, "God is light," "God is love." God is what he is for his own glory, and the good of them that fear him. God! why, God, in the breadth, length, depth, height, that is here intended, comprehends the whole world. The whole world is in him; for he is before, above, beyond, and round about all things. Hence it is said, the heavens for breadth are but his span, that he gathereth the wind in his fists, measureth the waters in the hollow of his hand, weigheth the mountains in scales, and the hills in a balance. Yea, that all nations before him are as nothing, and they are counted to him less than nothing, and vanity. Hence we are said to "live and move in him," and he is beyond all search.

I will add one word more. Notwithstanding there is such a revelation of him in his word, in the book of creatures, and in the book of providences, yet the Scripture says, "Lo, these are parts of his ways; but how little a portion is heard of him!" So great is God above all that we have read, heard, or seen of him, either in the Bible, in heaven, or earth, the sea, or what else is to be understood. But now, that a poor mortal, a lump of sinful flesh, or, as the Scrip. ture phrase is, poor dust and ashes, should be in the favor, in the heart, and wrapped up in the compassions of such a God! O amazing! O astonishing consideration! And yet, "this God is our God forever and ever; and he will be our guide even unto death."

It is said of our God that "he humbleth himself when he beholds things in heaven." How much more when he openeth his eyes upon man; but most of all when he makes it, as one may say, his business to visit him every morning, and to try him every moment, having set his heart upon him, being determined to set him also among his princes! "The Lord is high above all nations, and his glory above the heavens. Who is like to the Lord our God, who dwelleth on high; who humbleth himself to behold the things that are in heaven, and in the earth? He raiseth up the poor out of the dust and lifteth the needy out of the dunghill; that he may set him with princes, even with the princes of his people."

2. If this God be our God; or if our God be such a God, and could we but attain to that knowledge of the breadth, and length, and depth, and height, that is in him, as the Apostle here prays, and desires we may, we should *never be afraid of any thing we shall meet with*, or that shall assault us in this world. The great God, the former of all things, taketh part with them that fear him, and that engage themselves to walk in his ways, of love and respect they bear unto him; so that such may boldly say, "The Lord is my helper, and I will not fear what man shall do unto me." Would it not be amazing, should you see a man encompassed with chariots and horses, and weapons for his defence, yet afraid of being sparrow-blasted, or overrun by a grasshopper? Why "it is he that sitteth upon the circle of the easth, and to whom the inhabitants thereof be as grasshoppers," that is the God of the people that are lovers of Jesus

Christ; therefore we should not fear them. To fear man, is to forget God; and to be careless in a time of danger, is to forget God's ordinance. What is it then? Why, let us fear God, and diligently keep his way, with what prudence and regard to our preservation, and also the preservation of what we have, we may: and if, we doing this, our God shall deliver us and what we have, into the hands of them that hate us, let us laugh, be fearless and careless, not minding now to do any thing else but to stand up for him against the workers of iniquity; fully concluding, that both we and our enemies are in the hand of him that loveth his people, and that will certainly render a reward to the wicked, after that he has sufficiently tried us by their means. "The great God that formed all things, both rewardeth the fool, and plentifully rewardeth the transgressors."

3. Another thing that the knowledge of what is prayed for of the Apostle, if we attain it, will minister to us, is a *holy fear* and reverence of this great God in our souls; both because he is great, and because he is wise and good. "Who would not fear thee, O Lord, and glorify thy name?"

Greatness should beget fear, greatness should beget reverence: now who is so great as our God? and so, who to be feared like him? He also is wise, and will not be deceived by any. "He will bring evil, and not call back his words; but will rise against the house of evil doers, and against the help of them that work iniquity." Most men deal with God as if he were not wise; as if he either knew not the wickedness of their hearts and ways, or else knew not how to be even with them for it: when alas! "he is wise in heart, and mighty in power;" and although he will not without cause afflict, yet he will not let wickedness go unpunished. This, therefore, should make us fear He also is good, and this should make us serve him with fear. Oh! that a great God should be a good God; a good God to an unworthy, to an undeserving people, and to a people that continually do what they can to provoke the eyes of his glory; this should make us tremble. He is fearful in service, fearful in praises.

The breadth, and length, and depth, and height, of his outgoing towards the children of men, should also beget in us a very great fear and dread of his Majesty. When the prophet saw the height of the wheels, he said they were dreadful, and cried out unto them, "O wheel!" His judgments also are a great deep; nor is there any searching of his understanding. He can tell how to bring his wheel upon us, and to make our table a snare, a trap, and a stumbling-block unto us. He can tell how to make his Son to us a rock of offence, and his gospel a savor of death unto death unto us. He can tell how to choose delusions for us, and to lead us forth with the workers of iniquity. He can out-wit, and out-do us, and prevail against us forever; and therefore we should be afraid and fear before him, for our good, and the good of ours forever; yea, it is for these purposes, with others, that the apostle prayeth thus for this people: for the comprehending of these things will poise and keep the heart in an even course. This yields comfort, this gives encouragement, this begets fear and reverence in our hearts of God.

4. This knowledge will make us *willing that he should be our God;* yea, will also make us abide by that willingness. Jacob said with a vow, "If God will be with me, and will keep me in this way that I go, and will give me bread to eat and rainment to put on; so that I come again to my father's house in peace; then shall the Lord be my God. And this stone which I have set for a pillar, shall be God's house: and of all that thou shalt give me, I will surely give the tenth unto thee." Thus he considered the greatness of God, and from a supposition that he was what of his father, he had heard him, to be: he concluded to choose him for his God and that he would worship him, and give him that honor that was due to him as God. How did the king of

Babylon set him above all gods, when but some sparkling rays from him did light upon him! He calls him a God of gods, prefers him above all gods, charges all people and nations that they do nothing amiss against him. He calls the Most High God, the God that liveth forever; and confesses, that he doeth whatsoever he will in heaven and earth; and concludes with praising and extolling him. We naturally love greatness; and when the glorious beauty of the King of glory shall be manifest to us, and we shall behold it, we shall say as Joshua did, "Let all men do as seems them good; but I, and my house, will serve the Lord."

When the Apostle Paul sought to win the Athenians to God, he sets him forth before them with such terms as bespeak his greatness; calling him, (and that rightly,) "God that made the world, and all things; the Lord of heaven and earth; one that giveth to all life and breath, and all things; one that is nigh to every one of us; he in whom we live, and move, and have our being: God that hath made of one blood all nations of men, and that hath determined the times before appointed, and the bounds of their habitation, &c." These things bespeak the greatness of God and are taking to considering men. Yea, these very Athenians, while ignorant of him, from those dark hints that they had by natural light concerning him, erected an altar to him, and put this singular inscription upon it, "To the unknown God;" to show, that according to their mode, they had some kind of reverence for him. But how much more when they came to know him, and to believe that God in all his greatness, had engaged himself to be theirs, and to bring them to himself, that they might in time be partakers of his glory!*

5. The more a man knows or understands of the great-

* As was the case with some of them.—Dionysius the venerable judge of Areopagus, Damaris a lady of distinction, and others who constituted the first Christian church in Athens. Noble first fruits of Attica to God and to the Lamb! J. N. B.

ness of God towards him, expressed here by the terms of unsearchable breadth, length, depth, and height, the better will he be able in his heart to conceive of *the excellent glory and greatness of the things that are laid up in the heavens* for them that fear him. They that know nothing of this greatness, know nothing of them; they that think amiss of this greatness, think amiss of them; they that know but little of this greatness, know but little of them; but he that is able to comprehend with all saints what is the breadth, and length, and depth, and height, he is best able to conceive of, and consequently to make a judgment concerning the due worth, and blessed glory of them.

This is evident to reason; also experience confirmeth the same. For as for those dark souls that know nothing of his greatness, they have in derision those who are through the splendor of the glory, captivated and carried away after God. Also, those whose judgments are corrupted, and themselves thereby made as drunkards, to judge of things foolishly, they, as it were, step in the same steps with the other, and vainly imagine thereabout. Moreover, we shall see those little-spirited Christians, though Christians indeed, that are but in a small measure acquainted with this God, with the breadths, and lengths, and depths, and heights, that are in him, taken but little with the glory and blessedness that they are to go to when they die; wherefore, they are neither so mortified to this world, so dead to sin, so self-denying, so delighted in the book of God, nor so earnest in desires to be acquainted with the heights and depths that are therein. No, this is reserved only for those who are devoted thereto; who have been acquainted with God in a measure beyond that which your narrow-spirited Christians understand. There doth want as to these things, enlargings in the hearts of the most of saints, as there did in those of Corinth, and also in those at Ephesus. Wherefore, as Paul bids the one, and prays that the other may be enlarged, and have great knowledge thereabout; so we should, to answer such love, through desire, separate ourselves from terrene things, that we may seek and intermeddle with all wisdom. Christ says, if any man will do his will, he shall know of the doctrine. Oh! that we were indeed enlarged as to these breadths, and lengths, and depths, and heights, of God, as the apostle desired the Ephesians might be.

6. Then those great truths, the coming of Christ, the resurrectiou of the dead, and eternal judgment, would *neither seem so like fables, nor be so much off our hearts* as they do, and are. For the thorough belief of them depends upon the knowledge of the abilities that are in God to perform what he has said thereabout. And hence it is that your inferior sort of Christians live so like as if none of these things were at hand; and hence it is again, that they so soon are shaken in mind about them, when tempted of the devil, or briskly assaulted by deceivers. But this cometh to pass, that there may be fulfilled what is written, "And while the bridegroom tarried, they all slumbered and slept." Surely, the meaning is, they were asleep about his coming, the resurrection, and the judgment, and consequently had lost much of that knowledge of God, the which if they had retained these truths with power, would have been upon their hearts. The Corinthians were horribly decaying here, though some more than others: hence Paul, when he treats of this doctrine, bids them awake to righteousness, and not sin, telling them, that some among them had not the knowledge of God. To be sure, they had not such a knowledge of God as would keep them steady in the faith of these things.

Now, the knowledge of the things above mentioned, that is, this comprehending knowledge, will greaten these things, bring them near, and make them to be credited, as are the greatest of God's truths, and the virtue of the faith of them is, to make one die daily. Therefore,

7. Another advantage that floweth from this knowledge, is, that *it makes the next world desirable.* Not simply as it is with those lean souls, that desire it only as the thief desireth the judge's favor, that he may be saved from the halter; but out of love such have to God and to the beauties of the house he dwells in, and that they may be rid of this world, which is to such as a dark dungeon. The knowledge of God that men pretend they have, may easily be judged of, by the answerableness or unanswerableness of their hearts and lives thereto. Where is the man that groans earnestly to be gone to God, that counts this life a strait unto him; that saith as a sick man of my acquaintance did, when his friend at his bed side prayed to God to spare his life; "no, no," said he, "pray not so; for it is better to be dissolved and be gone?" Christians should show the world how they believe; not by words or on paper, not by gay and flourishing notions, but by those desires they have to be gone; and the proof that these desires are true, is a life in heaven while we are on earth. I know words are cheap, but a drachm of grace is worth all the world. But where, as I said, shall it be found? Not among carnal men, not among weak Christians, but among those, and those only, that enjoy a great measure of Paul's wish here

CHAPTER IV.

THE NATURE AND MANIFESTATION OF CHRIST'S LOVE.

BUT to come to the second part of the text.

"And to know the love of Christ, which passeth knowledge." These words are the second part of the text, and they deal mainly about the love of Christ, who is the Son of God. We have spoken already briefly of God, and therefore, now we shall speak also particularly of his Son. These words are a part of the prayer aforementioned, and have something of the same strain in them. In the first part, he prays that they might comprehend that which cannot, absolutely, by any means be comprehended; and here he prays that that might be known, which yet in the same breath he saith "passeth knowledge," that is, the love of Christ. "And to know the love of Christ, which passeth knowledge."

In the words we are to take notice of three things:

I. Of the love of Christ.

II. Of the exceeding greatness of it.

III. Of the knowledge of it.

I. We will begin with the first of these, namely, of the love of Christ. Now for the explication of this we must inquire into three things. 1. Who Christ is. 2. What love is. 3. What the love of Christ is.

1. Christ is a person of no less quality than is he of whom we treated before, that is, very God; so I say, not titularly, not nominally, not so counterfeitly, but the self-same in nature with the Father. Wherefore, what we have under consideration, is so much the more to be taken notice of;

namely, that a person so great, so high, so glorious, as this Jesus Christ is, should have love for us, that passes knowledge. It is common for equals to love, and for superiors to be beloved; but for the King of princes, for the Son of God, for Jesus Christ to love man thus; this is amazing, and that so much the more, that man, the object of this love, is so low, so mean, so vile, so undeserving, and so inconsiderable, as he is described by the Scriptures every where to be.

But to speak a little more particularly of this person. 1. He is called God. 2. The King of glory, and the Lord of glory. 3. The Brightness of the glory of his Father. 4. The Head over all things. 5. The Prince of life. 6. The Creator of all things. 7. The Upholder of all things. 8. The Disposer of all things. 9. The Only Beloved of the Father.

But the persons beloved of him are called transgressors, sinners, enemies, dust and ashes, worms, fleas, shadows, vapors, vile, sinful, filthy, unclean, ungodly, fools, madmen. And now is it not to be wondered at? And are we not to be affected herewith, saying, "and wilt thou set thine eye upon such a one?" But how much more when he will "set his heart" upon us? And yet this great, this high, this glorious person, verily, verily, loveth such!

2. We now come to the second thing, namely, to show what is love; not in a way of nice distinction of words, but in a plain and familiar discourse, yet respecting the love of the person under consideration.

Love ought to be considered with reference to the subject, as well as to the object of it.

The subject of love in the text is Christ; but forasmuch as love in him is diverse from the love that is in us; therefore it will not be amiss, if a little of the difference be made to appear.

Love in us is a passion of the soul, and being such, is

subject to ebb and flow, and to be extreme both ways. For whatever is a passion of the soul, whether love or hatred, joy or fear, is more apt to exceed or come short, than to keep within its due bounds. Hence, ofttimes that which is loved to-day is hated to-morrow; yea, and that which should be loved within bounds of moderation, is loved to the drowning of both soul and body in perdition and destruction.

Besides, love in us is apt to choose to itself undue and unlawful objects, and to reject those that, with leave of God, we may embrace and enjoy; so unruly, as to the laws and rules of divine government, ofttimes is this passion of love in us.

Love in us requires that something pleasing and delightful be in the object loved, at least so it must appear to the lust and fancy of the person loving, or else love cannot act; for the love that is in us, is not of power to set itself on work, where no allurement is in the thing to be beloved.

Love in us decays, though once ever so warm and strongly fixed, if the object falls off, as to its first alluring provocation; or disappointeth our expectation with some unexpected reluctancy to our fancy or our mind.

All this we know to be true from nature, for every one of us are thus; nor can we refuse, or choose to love, but upon, and after the rate, and the working thus of our passions Wherefore our love, as we are natural, is weak, unorderly; it fails, and miscarries, either by being too much or too little; yea, though the thing which is beloved be allowed for an object of love, both by the law of nature and grace. We, therefore, must put a vast difference betwixt love as found in us, and love as found in Christ, and that both as to the nature, principle, or object of love.

Love in Christ is not love of the same nature, as is love in us. Love in him is essential to his being; but in us it is not so, as has been already showed. God is love, Christ is

God; therefore Christ is love, love naturally. Love, therefore, is essential to his being. He may as well cease to be, as cease to love. Hence, therefore, it follows, that love in Christ floweth not from so low and beggarly a principle as doth love in man; and consequently is not, nor can be attended with those infirmities or defects that the love of man is attended with.

It is not attended with those unruly or uncertain motions that ours is attended with; here is no ebbing, no flowing, no going beyond, no coming short, and so nothing of uncertainty. "Having loved his own which were in the world, he loved them to the end."

True, there is a way of manifesting this love, which is suited to our capacities as men, and by that we see it sometimes more, sometimes less: also, it is manifested to us as we do, or do not walk with God in this world. I speak now of saints.

Love in Christ pitcheth not itself upon undue, or unlawful objects; nor refuseth to embrace what by the eternal covenant is made capable thereof. It always acteth according to God; nor is there at any time the least shadow of swerving as to this.

Love in Christ requireth no taking beauteousness in the object to be beloved, as not being able to put forth itself without such attracting allurements. It can act of and from itself, without all such kind of dependencies. This is manifest to all who have the least true knowledge of what that object is in itself, on which the Lord Jesus has set his heart to love them.

Love in Christ decays not, nor can be tempted to do so by any thing that happens, or that shall happen hereafter in the object so beloved. But as this love at first acts by and from itself, so it continues to do until all things that are imperfections are completely and everlastingly subdued. The reason is, because Christ loves to make us comely; not because we are so.

Objection. 'But all along Christ compareth his love to ours; now, why doth he so, if they be so much unlike?'

Answer. Because we know not love but by the passions of love that work in our hearts; wherefore, he condescends to our capacities, and speaketh of his love to us, according as we find love to work in ourselves to others. Hence he sets forth his love to us, by borrowing from us instances of our love to wife and children. Yea, he sometimes sets forth his love to us, by calling to mind how sometimes a man loves a woman that yet is an adulteress. "Go," (saith God to the prophet,) "love a woman beloved of her friend, yet an adulteress, according to the love of the Lord toward the children of Israel, who look to other gods, and love flagons of wine." But then, these things must not be understood with respect to the nature, but the dispensations and manifestations of love; no, nor with reference to these neither, any further than by making use of such similitudes, thereby to commend his love to us, and thereby to beget in us affections to him for the love bestowed upon us.

Wherefore Christ's love must be considered both with respect to the essence, and also as to the diverse workings of it. For the essence thereof, it is, as I said, natural with himself, and as such, it is the root and ground of all those actions of his, whereby he hath showed that himself is loving to sinful man. But now, though the love that is in him is essential to his nature, and can vary no more than God himself: yet we see not this love but by the fruits of it, nor can it otherwise be discerned. "Hereby *perceive* we the love of God, because he laid down his life for us." We must then betake ourselves to the discoveries of this love, of which there are two sorts: 1. Such as are the foundations. 2. Such as are the consequences of those fundamental acts.

Those which I call the foundations, are they upon which all other discoveries of his goodness depend, and they are two: 1. His dying for us. 2. His improving of his death for us at the right hand of God.

3. And this leads me to the third particular, I had proposed to show you, what the love of Christ is, that is, in the discovery of it. "And to know the love of Christ."

The love of Christ is made known unto us, as I said, 1. By his dying for us. 2. By his improving of his dying for us.

His dying for us appears, to be wonderful in itself, and also in his preparations for that work.

First, it appears to be wonderful *in itself*, and that both with respect to the nature of that death, as also with respect to the persons for whom he so died.

The love of Christ appears to be wonderful, by the death he died, in that he died such a death. It was strange love in Christ, that moved him to die for us: strange, because not according to the custom of the world. Men do not use in cool blood, deliberately, to come upon the stage or ladder, to lay down their lives for others; but this did Jesus Christ, and that too for such, whose qualification, if it be duly considered, will make this act of his far more amazing. He laid down his life for his enemies, and for those that could not abide him; yea, for those, even for those that brought him to the cross! not accidentally, or because it happened so, but knowingly, designedly! he knew it was for those he died, and yet his love led him to lay down his life for them. I will add, that though those very people for whom he laid down his life, by all sorts of carriages did what they could to provoke him to pray to God his Father, that he would send and cut them off by the flaming sword of angels, yet he would not be provoked, but would lay down his life for them. Nor must I leave off here. We never read that Jesus Christ was more cheerful in all his life on earth, than when he was going to lay down his life for them; now he thanked God, now he sang!

But this is not all. He did not only die, but died such a death, as indeed cannot be expressed. He was content to be counted the sinner; yea, to be counted the sin of the sinner; nor could this but be odious to so holy a Lamb as he was, yet he was willing to be this and thus, for that love that he bare to men.

This being thus, it follows, that his sufferings must be unconceivable. For what in justice was the proper wages of sin and sinners, he must undergo; and what that was can no man so well know as he himself, and damned spirits; for the proper wages of sin, and of sinners for their sin, is that death which layeth pains, such pains as it deserveth, upon the man that dieth so. But Christ died so, and consequently was seized by those pains, not only in body but in soul. His tears, his cries, his bloody sweat, the hiding of his Father's face; yea, God's forsaking him in his extremity, plainly enough declares the nature of the death he died. For my part, I stand amazed at those that would not have the world believe, that the death of Jesus Christ was, in itself, so terrible as it was.

I will not stand here to discourse of the place called "hell," where the spirits of the damned are; we are discoursing of the nature of Christ's sufferings. And I say, if Christ was put into the very capacity of one that must suffer what in justice ought to be inflicted for sin; then, how we can so diminish the greatness of his sufferings, as some do, without undervaluing the greatness of his love, I know not; and how they will answer it, I know not. And on the contrary, what if I should say, that the soul of Christ suffered as long as his body lay in the grave, and that God's "loosing the pains of death" at Christ's resurrection, must not so much be made mention of with reference to his body, as to his soul, if to his body at all? For what pain of death was his body capable of, when his soul was separate from it? and yet God's loosing the pains of death, seems to be but an immediate antecedent to his rising from the dead. And this sense Peter doth indeed seem to pursue, saying, "For David speaketh concerning him; I foresaw the Lord always before my face, for he is on my right hand, that I should not be moved. Therefore did my heart rejoice, and my tongue was glad; moreover, also, my flesh shall rest in hope; because thou wilt not leave my soul in hell, neither wilt thou suffer thine Holy One to see corruption." "This," saith Peter, "was not spoken of David, but he being a prophet, and knowing that God had sworn with an oath that of the fruit of his loins, according to the flesh, he would raise up Christ to sit on his throne; he seeing this before, spake of the resurrection of Christ, that his soul was not left in hell, neither did his flesh see corruption." "Thou wilt not leave my soul in hell." "His soul was not left in hell." Of what use are these expressions, if the soul of Christ suffered not, if it suffered not when separated from the body? for of that time the Apostle Peter seems to treat. Besides, if it be not improper to say, that a soul was not left there that never was there, I am at a loss. "Thou wilt not leave;" his soul was not left there: *ergo*, it was there, seems to be the natural conclusion. If it be objected, that by hell is meant the grave, it is foolish to think that the soul of Christ lay there, while his body lay dead therein. But again, the Apostle seems clearly to distinguish between the places where the soul and the body of Christ were, counting his body to be in the grave, and his soul, for the time, in hell. If there be objected what was said by him to the thief upon the cross, I can answer, Christ might speak that with reference to his Godhead, and if so, that lies as no objection to what hath been insinuated. And why may not that be so understood, as well as where he said, when on earth, "The Son of man which is in heaven?" meaning himself. For the personality of the Son of God, call him Son of man, or what other term is fitting, resideth not in the human, but divine nature of Jesus

Christ.* However, since hell is sometimes taken for the grave, sometimes for the state, sometimes for the place, and sometimes for a figure of the place where the damned are tormented, I will not strictly assign to Christ the place, the prison where the damned spirits are; but will say, as I said before, that he was put into the place of sinners, into the sins of sinners, and received what by justice was the proper wages of sin both in body and soul; as is evident from the 53d of Isaiah. This soul of his I take to be that, of which the inwards and the fat of the burnt sacrifices was a figure or shadow. And the fat and the inwards were burnt upon the altar, whilst the body was burned for sin without the camp.

And now having said thus much, wherein have I derogated from the glory and holiness of Christ? Yea, I have endeavored to set forth something of the greatness of his sorrows, the odiousness of sin, the nature of justice, and the love of Christ. And be sure, by how much the sufferings of the Son of God abounded for us, by so much was this unsearchable love of Christ made manifest. Nor can they that would, before the people, pare away, and make but little these infinite sufferings of our Lord, make his love to be so great as they ought, let them use what rhetoric they can.

Having thus spoken of the death and sufferings of Christ, I shall in the next place, speak of his preparations for his so suffering for us; and by so doing, show you yet something more of the greatness of his love.

Christ, as I have told you, was even before his sufferings, a person of no mean generation, being the Son of the eternal

---

* This argument is very ingenious, pious, and modest, and the supposition it supports not unnatural. Some of the Greek Fathers held a kindred opinion. Yet the objections here mentioned, seem stronger than the evidence in its favor, even in the view of Bunyan himself, as appears from what follows. And it seems impossible to reconcile it with the declared fact, that Christ triumphed over principalities and powers "by his cross," or with the Saviour's expiring words, "It is finished!"
J. N. B.

God. Neither had his Father any more such sons but he; consequently he of right was Heir of all things, and so to have dominion over all worlds. For, "for him were all things created." And hence all creatures are subject to him; yea, the angels of God worship him. Wherefore, as so considered, he augmented not his state by becoming lower than the angels for us; for what can be added to him who is naturally God? Indeed, he did take for our sakes, the human nature into union with himself, and so began to manifest his glory; and the kindness that he had for us before all worlds, began now eminently to show itself. Had this Christ of God, our friend, given all he had to save us, had not his love been wonderful? But when he shall give for us *himself*, this is more wonderful.

But this is not all; the case was so betwixt God and man, that this Son of God could not, as he was before the world was, give himself a ransom for us, he being altogether incapable so to do; being such a one as could not be subject to death, the condition that we by sin had put ourselves into. Wherefore, that which would have been a death to some, namely, the laying aside of glory, and of the King of princes becoming a servant of the meanest form; this he of his own good will was heartily content to do. Wherefore, he that once was the object of the fear of angels, is now become a little creature, a worm, an inferior one, born of a woman, brought forth in a stable, laid in a manger, scorned of men, tempted of devils, beholden to his creatures for food, for raiment, for harbor, and a place wherein to lay his head when dead. In a word, "he made himself of no reputation, took upon him the form of a servant, and was made in the likeness of men," that he might become capable of doing this kindness for us.

And it is worth your noting, that all the while that he was in the world, putting himself upon those other preparations, which were to be antecedent to his being made a sacrifice for us, no man, though he told what he came about to many, had, as we read of, a heart once to thank him for what he came about. No, they railed on him, they degraded him, they called him devil, they said he was mad, and a deceiver, a blasphemer of God, and a rebel against the state. They accused him to the governor; yea, one of his disciples sold him, another denied him, and they all forsook him, and left him to shift for himself in the hands of his horrible enemies; who beat him with their fists, spit upon him, mocked him, crowned him with thorns, scourged him, made a gazing stock of him, and finally, hanged him up by the hands and the feet alive, and gave him vinegar to increase his affliction, when he complained that his anguish had made him thirsty. And yet all this could not take his heart off the work of our redemption. To die he came, die he would, and die he did, for our sins, before he made his return to the Father, that we might live through him.

Now, may what we read of in the word concerning those temporal sufferings that he underwent be overlooked, and passed by without serious consideration, they being a part of the curse that our sin had deserved? For all temporal plagues are due to our sin while we live, as well as the curse of God to everlasting perdition, when we die. Wherefore this is the reason why the whole life of the Lord Jesus was such a life of affliction and sorrow, he therein bare our sicknesses, and took upon him our deserts: so that now the curse in temporals, as well as the curse in spirituals and of everlasting malediction, is removed by him away from God's people: and since he overcame them, and got to the cross, it was by reason of the worthiness of the humble obedience that he yielded to his Father's law in our flesh; for his whole life (as well as his death) was a life of merit and purchase and desert. Hence it is said, he "increased in favor with God:" for his works made him still more acceptable to him; for he, standing in the room of man, and becoming our Reconciler to God, he was by the heavenly Majesty counted as such, and so got for us what he earned by his mediatory works; and also partook thereof as he was our Head himself. And was there not in all these things love, and love that was infinite? Love which was not essential to his divine nature, could never have carried him through so great a work as this: passions here would have failed, would have retreated, and have given the recoil: yea, his very humanity would have flagged and fainted, had it not been managed, governed, and strengthened by his eternal Spirit. Wherefore, it is said, that "through the eternal Spirit, he offered himself without spot to God;" and that he was declared to be the Son of God with so doing, and by the resurrection from the dead.

We come now to the second thing propounded, and by which his love is discovered, and that is, his improving of his dying for us. But I must crave pardon of my reader, if he thinks that I can discover the ten hundred thousandth part thereof, for it is impossible; but my meaning is, to give a few hints what beginnings of improvement he made thereof, in order to his further progress therein.

1. Therefore, this his death for us was so virtuous, that in the space of three days and nights it reconciled to God in the body of his flesh, as a common person, all and every one of God's elect. Christ, when he addressed himself to die, presented himself to the justice of the law, as a common person; standing in the stead, place, and room of all that he undertook for; he gave his life a ransom for many; he came into the world to save sinners. And as he thus presented himself, so God, his Father, admitted him to this work; and therefore, it is said, "The Lord laid upon him the iniquity of us all:" and again, "surely he hath borne our griefs, and carried our sorrows." Hence it unavoidably follows, that whatever he felt, and underwent, in the manner or nature, or horribleness of the death he died, he felt and

underwent as a common person; that is, as he stood in the stead of others: therefore, it is said, "He was wounded for our transgressions, and bruised for our iniquities;" and that "the chatisement of our peace was upon him." And that "he suffered for our sins, the just for the unjust."

Now then if he presented himself as a common person to justice, if God so admitted and accounted him, if also God laid the sins of the people, whose persons he represented, upon him, and under that consideration punished him with those punishments and deaths, that he died; then Christ in life and death, is concluded by the Father to live and die as a common or public person, representing all in this life and death, for whom he undertook thus to live, and thus to die. So then it must needs be, that what next befalls this common person, it befalls him with respect to them in whose room and place he stood and suffered. Now the next that follows is, that he is justified of God; that is, acquitted and discharged from this punishment, for the sake of the worthiness of his death and merits; for that must be before he could be raised from the dead. God raised him not up as guilty, to justify him afterwards: his resurrection was the declaration of his precedent justification. He was raised from the dead, because it was neither in equity or justice possible that he should be holden longer there; his merits procured the contrary.

Now, he was condemned of God's law, and died by the hand of justice; he was acquitted by God's law, and justified of justice; and all as a common person; so then in his acquittal, we are acquitted, in his justification we are justified; and therefore the Apostle applieth God's justifying of Christ to himself, and that rightly. For if Christ be my undertaker, will stand in my place, and do for me, it is but reasonable that I should be a partaker. Wherefore we are also said to be "quickened together with him," that is, when he was quickened in the grave, "raised up together, and made to sit together in heavenly places in Christ Jesus." Therefore, another Scripture saith, "He hath quickened us together with him, having forgiven us all trespasses." This quickening must not be understood merely of the renovation of our hearts, but of the restoring of Jesus Christ to life after he was crucified; and we are said to be quickened together with him, because we were reckoned in him at his death, and were to fall or stand by him quite through the three days and nights' work: and were to take, therefore, our lot with him. Wherefore, it is said again, that his resurrection is for our justification; that by one offering he has purged our sins forever; and that by his death he hath delivered us from the wrath to come. But I say, I would be understood aright; this life resideth yet in the Son, and is communicated from him to us, as we are called to believe his word: meanwhile we are secured from wrath and hell, being justified in his justification, quickened in his quickening, raised up in his resurrection, and made to sit already together in heavenly places in Christ Jesus.

And is not this a glorious improvement of his death, that after two days the whole body of the elect, in him, should be revived, and that in the third day we should live in the sight of God, in and by him?

2. Another improvement of his death for us was this: by that he slew for us our infernal foes; by it he abolished death; "by death he destroyed him that had the power of death;" by death he took away the sting of death; by death he made death a pleasant sleep to saints, and the grave for a while an easy house and home for the body.

By death he made death such an advantage to us, that it is become a means of translating the souls of them that believe in him to life. And all this is manifest, for death is ours, a blessing to us, as well as Paul and Apollos, the world, and life itself. And that all this is done for us by his death, is apparent, for that his person is where it is, and that by himself as a common person he has got the victory for us. For though as yet all things are not put under our feet, yet we see Jesus crowned with honor and glory, who by the grace of God tasted death for every man. "For it became God, for whom are all things, and by whom are all things, to make the Captain of our salvation perfect through sufferings." It became him; that is, it was but just and right he should do so, if there was enough in the virtuousness of his death and blood to require such a thing. But there was so. Wherefore God has exalted him, and us in him, above these infernal foes. Let us, therefore, first, see ourselves delivered from death by the exaltation of our Jesus; let us behold him, I say, as crowned with glory and honor, because he tasted death for us; and then we shall see ourselves already in heaven by our Head, our Undertaker, our Jesus, our Saviour.

3. Another improvement that has already been made of his death for us, is this: he hath at his entrance into the presence of God, for his worthiness' sake obtained that the Holy Ghost should be given unto him for us, that we by that might in all things yet to be done, be made meet to be partakers personally in ourselves, as well as virtually by our Head and Forerunner, of the inheritance of the saints in light. Wherefore, the abundant pouring out of that was forborne until the resurrection and glorification of our Lord Jesus. "For the Holy Ghost was not yet given, because that Jesus was not yet glorified." Nor was it given so soon as received. For he received it upon his entering into the holy place, when he had sprinkled the mercy-seat with the blood of sprinkling: but it was not given out to us till some time after. However, it was obtained before. And it was meet that it should in that infinite immeasurableness in which he received it, first abide upon him, that his human nature, which was the first fruits of the election of God, might re-

ceive by its abidings upon him, that glory for which it was ordained; and that we might receive, as we receive all other things, first by our Head and Undertaker, sanctification in the fulness of it. Hence it is written, that as he is "made unto us of God, wisdom and righteousness, and redemption," so "sanctification" too. For, first, we are sanctified in his flesh, as we are justified by his righteousness. Wherefore he is that Holy One, that setteth us, in himself, a holy lump before God, not only with reference to justification and life, but with reference to sanctification and holiness. For we that are elect are all considered in him, as he has received that, as well as in that he has taken possession of heaven for us. I count not this all the benefit that accrueth to us, by Jesus receiving the Holy Ghost, at his entrance into the presence of God for us. For we also are to receive it ourselves from him, according as by God we are placed in the body at the times appointed of the Father; that we, as was said, may receive personal quickening, personal renovation, personal sanctification, and in conclusion, glory. But I say, for that he hath received this Holy Spirit to himself, he received it as the effect of his ascension, which was the effect of his resurrection, and of the merit of his death and passion. And he received it as a common person, as a head and undertaker for the people.

4. Another improvement that has been made of his death, and of the merits thereof for us, is, that he has obtained to be made of God, the chief and high Lord of heaven and earth for us. All this while we speak of the exaltation of the human nature, in, by, and with which, the Son of God became capable of being our Reconciler unto God. "All things," saith he "are delivered unto me of my Father," and "all power in heaven and earth is given unto me;" and all this because he died. "He humbled himself, and became obedient unto death, even the death of the cross; wherefore God hath highly exalted him, and given him a name above

every name, that at the name of Jesus every knee should bow, of things in heaven, of things in earth, or things under the earth: and that every tongue should confess that Jesus Christ is Lord, to the glory of God the Father." And all this is, as was said afore, for our sakes. He has given him to be "head over all things to the church."

Wherefore, whoever are set up on earth, they are set up by our Lord. "By me," saith he, "kings reign, and princes decree justice. By me princes rule, and nobles even all the judges of the earth." Nor are they when set up, left to do, though they should desire it, their own will and pleasure. The *Metheg Ammah,* the bridle is in his own hand, and he giveth reins, or check, even as it pleaseth him. He hath this power for the well being of his people. Nor are the fallen angels exempted from being put under his rebuke. He is the "only potentate," and in his times will show it. Peter tells us, "he is gone into heaven, and is on the right hand of God; angels, and authorities, and powers, being made subject unto him."

This power, as I said, he has received for the sake of his church on earth, and for her conduct and well being among the sons of men. Hence, as he is called the King of nations, in general: so the King of saints, in special. And as he is said to be Head over all things, in general; so to his church, in special.

5. Another improvement that he hath made of his death for us, is, he hath obtained, and received into his own hand, sufficiency of gifts to make ministers for his church withal; I say, to make and maintain, in opposition to all that would hinder, a sufficient ministry. Wherefore he saith. "When he ascended on high, he led captivity captive, and gave gifts unto men: and he gave some apostles, some prophets, some evangelists, some pastors and teachers; for the perfecting of the saints for the work of the ministry, for the edifying of the body of Christ: until we all come in the unity of the

faith, and knowledge of the Son of God, unto a perfect man, unto the measure of the stature of the fulness of Christ." Many ways has Satan devised to bring into contempt this blessed advantage that Christ has received of God for the benefit of his church; partly while he stirs up persons to revile the sufficiency of the Holy Ghost, as to this thing; partly while he stirs up his own limbs and members to broach his delusions in the world, in the name of Christ, and as they blasphemously call it, by the assistance of the Holy Ghost; partly while he tempteth novices in the faith, to study and labor in nice distinctions, and the affecting of uncouth expressions, that vary from the form of sound words, thereby to get applause, and a name, a forerunner of their own destruction.

But notwithstanding all this, "Wisdom is justified of her children:" and at the last day, when the outside and inside of all things shall be seen and compared, it will appear that the Son of God has so managed his own servants in the ministry of his word, and so managed his word while they have been laboring in it, as to put in his blessing, by that, upon the souls of sinners, and has blown away all other things as chaff.

6. Another improvement that the Lord Christ has made of his death for his, is the obtaining, and taking possession of heaven for them. "By his own blood he has entered into the holy place, having obtained eternal redemption for us." This heaven! who knows what it is? This glory! who knows what it is? It is called God's throne, God's house, God's habitation, paradise, the kingdom of God, the high and holy place, Abraham's bosom, and the place of heavenly pleasures. In this heaven is to be found the face of God forever, immortality, the person of Christ, the prophets, the angels, the revelation of all mysteries, the knowledge of all the elect, eternity!

Of this heaven, as was said before, we are possessed

already, we are in it, we are set down in it, and partake already of the benefits thereof, but all by our Head and Undertaker; and it is fit that we should believe this, rejoice in this, talk of this, tell one another of this, and live in the expectation of our own personal enjoyment of it. And as we should do all this, so we should bless and praise the name of God, who has put over his house, this kingdom and inheritance, the hand of so faithful a friend: yea, a brother, a Saviour, and blessed undertaker for us. And lastly, since all these things already mentioned are the fruit of the sufferings of our Jesus, and his sufferings the fruit of that love of his that passeth knowledge; how should we bow the knee before him, and call him tender Father! yea, how should we love and obey him, and devote ourselves unto his service, and be willing to be also sufferers for his sake, to whom be honor and glory forever! And thus much of the love of Christ, in general.

CHAPTER V.

EXCEEDING GREATNESS OF CHRIST'S LOVE.

I MIGHT here add many other things, but, as I told you before, we would under the head but now touched upon, treat about the fundamentals, or great and chief parts thereof, and then the exceeding greatness of it more particularly: wherefore of that we must say something now.

"And to know the love of Christ which passeth knowledge." In that it is said to pass knowledge, it is manifest it is exceeding great, or going greatly beyond what can be known: for to exceed, is to go beyond, be above, or to be out of the reach of what would comprehend that which is so. And since the expression is absolutely indefinite, and respecteth not the knowledge of this or the other creature only: it is manifest, that Paul, by his thus saying, challengeth all creatures in heaven and earth to find out the bottom of this love, if they can. "The love of Christ which passeth knowledge." I will add, that forasmuch as he is indefinite also about the knowledge, as well as the persons knowing, it is out of doubt, that he here engageth all knowledge, in what enlargements, attainments, improvements, and heights soever it hath, or may forever attain unto. It "passeth knowledge."

Of the same import also is that other passage of the apostle, a little above, in the self-same chapter. I preach (saith he) among the Gentiles, "the unsearchable riches of Christ;" or those riches of Christ that cannot by searching be found out in all of them: the riches, the riches of his love and grace; the riches of his love and grace towards us.

"For ye know the grace of our Lord Jesus Christ, that though he was rich, yet for our sakes he became poor, that ye through his poverty might be made rich." Ye "know the grace," that is, so far; and so far every believer knows it: for his leaving heaven, and taking upon him flesh, that he might bring us thither, is manifest to all. But yet, all the grace that was wrapped up in that amazing condescension, knoweth none, nor can know: for if that might be, that possibility would be a flat contradiction to the text: "the love of Christ which passeth knowledge." Wherefore the riches of this love in the utmost of it, is not, cannot be known by any: let their understanding and knowledge be heightened and improved what it may: yea, and being heightened and improved, let what search there can, by it be made into this love and grace. That which is afar off, and exceeding deep, who can find out?" And that this love of Christ is so, shall anon be made more apparent.

But at present we will proceed to particular challenges for the making out of this, and then we will urge those reasons that will be for the further confirmation of the whole.

1. This love passes the knowledge of *the wisest saint.* We now single out the greatest proficient in this knowledge. And to confirm this, I need go no further than to the man that spake these words, namely, Paul, for in his conclusion he includes himself: "the love of Christ which passeth knowledge," even my knowledge. As if he should say, 'though I have waded a great way in the grace of Christ, and have as much experience of his love as any one in all the world, yet I confess myself short, as to the fulness that is therein, nor will I stick to conclude of any other, that he knows nothing yet as he ought to know.'

2. This love passeth the knowledge of *all the saints,* were it all put together. We, we all, and every one, did we each of us contribute for the manifesting of this love, what it is, the whole of what we know, it would amount but to a broken

knowledge; "we know but in part; we see darkly; we walk not by sight, but faith." True, now we speak of saints on earth.

3. But we will speak of *saints in heaven;* they cannot to the utmost know this love of Christ. For though they know more thereof than saints on earth, because they are more in the open visions of it, and also are more enlarged, being spirits perfect, than we on earth; yet, to say no more now, they do not see the rich and unsearchable runnings out thereof unto sinners here on earth. Nor may they there measure that to others, by what they themselves knew of it here. For sins, and times, and persons and other circumstances, may much alter the case. But were all the saints on earth, and all the saints in heaven, to contribute all that they know of this love of Christ, and to put it into one sum of knowledge, they would greatly come short of knowing the utmost of this love, for that there is an infinite deal of this love yet unknown by them. It is said plainly, that they on earth do not yet know what they shall be. And as for them in heaven, they are not yet made perfect as they shall be. Besides, we find the souls under the altar, how perfect now soever, when compared with that state they were in when with the body, yet are not able in all points, though in glory, to know, and so to govern themselves there without directions; I say, they are not able, without directions and instructions, to know the kinds and manner of the workings of the love of Christ towards us that dwell on earth.

4. We will join with these, *the angels;* and when all of them, with men, have put all and every whit of what they know of this love of Christ together, they must come far short of reaching to, or of understanding the utmost bound thereof. I grant, that angels do know, in some certain parts of knowledge of the love of Christ, more than saints on earth can know while here; but then again, I know that even they do also learn many things of saints on earth; which shows that themselves know also but in part. So then,

all, as yet, as to this love of Christ, and the utmost knowledge of it, are but as so many imperfects; nor can they all, put all their imperfects together, make up a perfect knowledge of this love of Christ; for the texts do yet stand where they did, and say, his riches are "unsearchable," and his love that which "passeth knowledge."

We will come now to show you, besides what has been already touched on, THE REASONS WHY this riches is unsearchable, and this love such as passeth knowledge; and,

The first is, because it is eternal. All that is eternal, has attending on it, as to the utmost knowledge of it, a fourfold impossibility: 1. It is without beginning. 2. It is without end. 3. It is infinite. 4. It is incomprehensible.

It is *without beginning*. That which was before the world was, is without a beginning; but the love of Christ was before the world. This is evident from Prov. viii. His delights, before God had made the world, are there said to be with the sons of men; not that we then had being, for we were as yet uncreated: but though we had not being as created, we had being in the love and affections of Jesus Christ. Now, this love of Christ must needs, as to the fulness of it, as to the utmost of it, be absolutely unknown to man. Who can tell how many heart-pleasing thoughts Christ had of us before the world began? Who can tell how much he then was delighted in that being we had in his affections, as also in the consideration of our beings, believings, and being with him afterwards?

In general, we may conclude it was great: for there seems to be a parallel betwixt his Father's delights in him and his delights in us. "I was daily his delight, and my delights were with the sons of men." But I say, who can tell, who can tell altogether, what and how much the Father delighted in his Son before the world began? Who can tell what kind of delight the Father had in the Son before the world began? Why, there seems to be a paralled betwixt the Father's love to Christ, and Christ's love to us: the Father's delight in Christ, and his delight in us. Yea, Christ confirms it, saying, "as my Father hath loved me, so have I loved you; continue ye in my love." I know that I am not upon the nature of the word "eternal;" yet since, by "eternal," we understand before the world began, as well as forward to an endless forever, we may a little inquire of folks as they may read, if they can tell the kind or measure of the love wherewith Christ then loved us. I remember the question that God asked Job. "Where," saith he, "wast thou when I laid the foundations of the earth? declare if thou hast understanding:" thereby insinuating, that because it was done before he had his being, therefore he could not tell how it was done. Now, if a work so visible, as the creation is, is yet as to the manner of the workmanship thereof, wholly unknown to them that commenced their being afterwards, how shall that which has, in all the circumstances of it, been more hidden and inward, be found out by them that have intelligence by the ear, and but in part, and that in mystery, and long afterwards. But to conclude this, that which is eternal is without all beginning; (this was presented to consideration before,) and therefore, it cannot to perfection be known.

That which is eternal is *without end*, and how can an endless thing be known? That which has no end has no middle, wherefore it is impossible that the one half of the love that Christ has for his church should ever by them be known.

I know that those visions that the saved shall have in heaven of this love, will far transcend our utmost knowledge here, even as far as the light of the sun at noon goes beyond the light of a blinking candle at midnight. And hence it is, that when the days of these visions are come, the knowledge that we now have shall be swallowed up. "When that which is perfect is come, then that which is in part shall be done away." And although he speaks here of perfection "when that which is perfect is come," &c., yet even that perfection must not be thought to be such as is the perfection of God; for then should all that are saved be so many eternals, and so many infinites, as he is infinite. But the meaning is, we shall then be with the Eternal, shall immediately enjoy him with all the perfection of knowledge, as far as is possible for a creature, when he is brought up to the utmost height that his created substance will bear, to be capable of. But for all that, this perfection will yet come short of the perfection of him that made him, and consequently short of knowing the utmost of his love; since that in the root is his very essence and nature.

I know it says, also, that we shall "know, even as we are known." But yet this must not be understood, as if we should know God as fully as he knows us. It would be folly and madness so to conclude. But the meaning is,—we are known for happiness; we are known of God, for heaven and felicity; and when that which is perfect is come, then shall we perfectly know, and enjoy that for which we are now known of God. And this is that which the Apostle longed for, namely, if by any means he might approach that for which he was also apprehended of Christ Jesus: that is, know, and see that, unto the which he was appointed of God, and apprehended of Christ Jesus.

It is said again, "We shall be like him, for we shall see him as he is." This text has respect to the Son, as to his humanity, and not as to his divinity; certainly not as to his divinity simply, or distinctly considered; for as to that, it is as possible for a spirit to drink up the sea, as for the most enlarged saint that is, or ever shall be in glory so to see God as to know him altogether, to the utmost, or throughout. But the humanity of the Son of God, we shall see throughout, in all the beauty and glory that is upon him, and that was prepared for him before the foundation of the world. And

Christ wills that we see this glory, when he takes us up in glory to himself; but the utmost boundlessness of the divine Majesty, the eternal deity of the Son of God, cannot be known to the utmost, or altogether, I do not doubt that there will then in him, (I mean in Christ,) and in us also, break forth those glorious rays and beams of eternal Majesty, which will make him in each of us admirable one to another; and that then, that of God shall be known of us, that now never entered into our hearts to think of. But the whole is not, cannot, shall never be, fully known of any. And therefore, the love of Christ, it being essential to himself, cannot be known, because of the endlessness that is in it. I said before, that which has no end has no middle. How then shall those that shall be in heaven eternally, ever pass over half the breadth of eternity?

True, I know that all enjoyments there will be enjoyments eternal: yea, that whatever we shall there embrace, or what embraces we shall be embraced with, shall be eternal; but I put a difference betwixt that which is eternal, as to the nature, and that which is so as to the durableness thereof. The nature of eternal things we shall enjoy, so soon as ever we come to heaven, but the duration of eternal things, this we shall never be able to pass through, for it is endless. So then the eternal love of Christ, as to the nature of it, will be perfectly known to saints, when they shall dwell in heaven; but the endlessness thereof they shall never attain unto. And this will be their happiness. For could it be, that we should in heaven ever reach the end of our blessedness; (as we should, could we reach to the end of this love of Christ) why, then, as the saying is, we should be at the land's end, and feel the bottom of all our enjoyments. Besides, whatsoever has an end, has a time to decay, and to cease to be, as well as to have a time to show forth its highest excellencies. Wherefore, from all these considerations it is most manifest, that the love of Christ is unsearchable, and that it passes knowledge.

Now the other two things follow of course, namely, that this love is *infinite* and *incomprehensible.* Wherefore here is that, that still is above and beyond even those that are arrived at the uttermost of their perfections. And this, if I may so say, will keep them in an employ, even when they are in heaven; though not an employ that is laborsome, tiresome, burdensome, yet an employ that is dutiful, delightful, and profitable. For though the work and worship of saints in heaven is not particularly revealed as yet, and so "it doth not yet appear what we shall be," yet in the general, we may say, there will be that for them to do, that has not yet by them been done; and by that work which they shall do there, their delight will be delight unto them. The law was "the shadow, and not the very image of heavenly things." The image is an image, and not the heavenly things themselves, (the heavenly things that are for saints;) but there shall be service in the heavens. Nor will this at all derogate from their glory. The angels now wait upon God, and serve him; the Son of God is now a minister, and waiteth upon his service in heaven; some saints have been employed about service for God, after they have been in heaven; and why we should be idle spectators, when we come thither, I see not reason to believe. It may be said, 'They there rest from their labors.' True, but not from their delights. All things then that once were burdensome, whether in suffering or service, shall be done away, and that which is delightful and pleasurable shall remain. 'But then will be a time to receive, and not to work.' True, if by work you mean such as we now count work: but what if our work be there, to receive and bless? The fishes in the sea do drink, swim and drink. But for a further discourse of this, let that alone till we come thither. But to come down again into the world, (for now we are talking of things aloft.)—

Secondly, This love of Christ must needs be beyond our knowledge because we cannot possibly know the utmost of our sin. Sin is that which sets out, and sets off, the knowledge of the love of Christ. There are four things that must be spoken for the clearing of this. 1. The nature of sin. 2. The aggravations of sin. 3. The utmost tendencies of sin. 4. And the perfect knowledge of all this.

1. Before we know this love of Christ, as afore, we must necessarily know the *nature* of sin, that is, what sin is in itself. But no man knows the nature of sin to the full; not what sin in itself is to the full. The Apostle saith, that sin, (that is, in itself) is "exceeding sinful." That is, exceeding as to its filthiness,—it goes beyond our knowledge. But this is seen by the commandment. Now the reason why none can, to the full, know the horrible nature of sin, is because none, to the full, can know the blessed nature of the blessed God. For sin is the opposite to God. There is nothing that seeketh absolutely, and in its own nature to overcome, and to annihilate God but sin; and sin doth so. Sin is worse than the devil; he, therefore, that is more afraid of the devil than of sin, knows not the badness of sin as he ought, nor but little of the love of Jesus Christ. He that knows not what sin would have done to the world, had not Christ stepped betwixt those harms and it, how can he know so much as the extent of the love of Christ in common? And he that knows not what sin would have done to him in particular, had not Christ the Lord stepped in and saved, cannot know the utmost of the love of Christ to him in particular. Sin, therefore, in the utmost evil of it, cannot be known by us: so, consequently, the love of Christ, in the utmost goodness of it, cannot be known of us.

Besides, there are many sins committed by us, dropping from us, and that pollute us, that we are not at all aware of.

How then should we know that love of Christ by which we are delivered from them? "Lord, who can understand his errors?" said David. Consequently, who can understand the love that saves him from them? Moreover, he that knows the love of Christ to the full, must also know to the full that wrath and anger of God, that like hell itself, burneth against sinners for the sake of sin: but this knows none. "Lord, who knows the power of thine anger?" said Moses. Therefore, none knows this love of Christ to the full. The nature of sin is to get into our good, to mix itself with our good, to lie lurking many times under the formality and show of good; and that so close, so cunningly, and invisibly, that the party concerned embraces it for virtue, and knows not otherwise to do; and yet from this he is saved by the love of Christ. And therefore, as was hinted but now, if a man doth not know the nature of his wound, how should he know the nature and excellency of the balsam that hath cured him of his wound?

2. There are the due *aggravations* that belong to sin, which men are unacquainted with. It was one of the great things that the prophets were concerned with, from God towards the people, as to show them their sins, so to show them what aggravations did belong thereto.

There are sins against light; sins against knowledge; sins against love; sins against learning; sins against threatenings; sins against promises, vows, and resolutions; sins against experience; sins against examples of anger; and sins that have great, and high, and strange aggravations attending them; the which we are ignorant of, though not altogether, yet in too great a measure. Now, if these things be so, how can the love that saveth us from them be known or understood to the full?

Alas! our ignorance of these things is manifest by our unwillingness to abide affliction; by our secret murmuring under the hand of God; by our wondering why we are so chastised as we are; by our thinking it long that the affliction is not sooner removed.

Or, if our ignorance of the vileness of our actions is not manifest this way, yet it is in our lightness under our guilt; our slight thoughts of our doings; our slovenly doing of duties, and asking of forgiveness after some evil or unbecoming actions. It is to no boot to be particular, the whole course of our lives doth too fully make it manifest, that we are wonderful short in knowing both the nature, and also the aggravations of our sins; and how then should we know that love of Christ in its full dimensions, by which we are saved and delivered therefrom?

3. Who knows the *utmost tendencies* of sin? I mean, what the least sin driveth at, and what it would unavoidably run the sinner into? There is not a plague, a judgment, an affliction, an evil under heaven, that the least of our transgressions has not called for at the hands of the great God: nay, the least sin calleth for all the distresses that are under heaven, to fall upon the soul and body of the sinner at once. This is plain, for that the least sin deserveth hell; which is worse than all the plagues that are on earth. But I say, Who understandeth this? And I say again, if one sin, the least sin, deserveth all these things, what thinkest thou do all thy sins deserve? how many judgments? how many plagues? how many lashes with God's iron whip dost thou deserve? Besides there is hell itself, the place itself, the fire itself, the nature of the torments, and the durableness of them, who can understand?

But this is not all, the tendencies of thy sins are to kill others. Men, good men, little think how many of their neighbours one of their sins may kill. As, how many good men and good women do unawares, through their uncircumspectness, drive their own children down into the deep? We will easily count them very hard hearted sinners, that used to offer their children in sacrifice to devils; when it is easy to do worse ourselves; they did but kill the body, but we body and soul in hell, if we have not a care!

Do we know how our sins provoke God? how they grieve the Holy Ghost? how they weaken our graces? how they spoil our prayers? how they weaken faith? how they tempt Christ to be ashamed of us? and how they hold back good from us? and if we know not every one of all these things to the full, how then shall we know to the full the love of Christ which saveth us from them all?

4. Again, let me ask, Who has the *perfect knowledge* of all these things? I will grant that some good souls may have waded a great way in some one or more of them; but I know that there is not any that thoroughly knows them all. And yet the love of Christ doth save us from all, notwithstanding all the vileness and soul-damning virtue that is in them. Alas! how short are we of the knowledge of ourselves, of what is in us! How many are there that do not know that man consisteth of a body made of dust, and of an immortal soul! yea, and how many be there of those that confess it, that know not the constitution of either! I will add, how many are there that profess themselves to be students of these two parts of man, that have oftentimes proved themselves to be but fools as to both! And I will conclude, that there is not a man under heaven that knoweth it altogether. For man is fearfully and wonderfully made: nor can the manner of the union of these two parts be perfectly found out. How much more then must we needs be at loss to the fulness of the knowledge of the love of Christ!

But, thirdly, He that altogether knoweth the love of Christ, must, precedent to that, know not only all the wiles of the devil, but also all the plottings, contrivings, and designs and attempts of that wicked one; yea, he must know all the times that he hath been with God, together with all the motions that he has made that he might have leave to fall upon us, as upon Job and Peter, to try if he might swallow us up. But who knows all this? No man, no angel. For if the heart of man be so deep, that save God, none by all his actions, can tell the utmost secrets therein; how should the heart of angels, which in all likelihood are deeper, be found out by any mortal man! And yet this must be found out, before we can find out the utmost of the love of Christ to us. I conclude, therefore, from all these things, that the love of Christ passeth knowledge; or, that by no means the bottom, the utmost bound thereof, can be understood.

Fourthly, He that will presume to say, this love of Christ can be to the utmost known by us, must presume to say that he knoweth the utmost of the merits of his blood, the utmost exercise of his patience, the utmost of his intercession, the utmost of the glory that he has prepared and taken possession of us for us. But I presume that there is none that can know all this; therefore, I may without any fear assert, there is none that knows, that is, that knows to the full, the other.

CHAPTER VI.

WHAT KNOWLEDGE OF CHRIST'S LOVE IS ATTAINABLE.

We come now more particularly to speak of the knowledge of the love of Christ. We have spoken of the love of Christ, that is, of the exceeding greatness of it. And now we come to speak of the knowledge of it; that is to say, we will show WHAT KNOWLEDGE OF IT IS ATTAINABLE IN THIS WORLD, under these three heads. As to this,

1. It may be known as to the nature of it. 2. It may be known in many of the degrees of it. 3. But, the greatest knowledge that we can have of it here, is to know that it passes knowledge.

1. We may know it in the NATURE of it; that is, that it is love, free, divine, heavenly, everlasting, incorruptible. And this no love is but the love of Christ; all other love is either love corruptible, transient, mixed, or earthly. It is divine, for it is the love of the holy nature of God. It is heavenly, for it is from above. It is everlasting, for it has no end. It is immortal, for there is not the appearance of corruptibleness in it, or likelihood of decay.

This is general knowledge, and this is common among the saints, at least in the notion of it; though I confess, it is hard in time of temptation, practically to hold fast the soul to all these things. But as I have said already, this love of Christ must be such, because love in the root of it is essential to his nature; as also I have proved now. As is the root, such are the branches; and as is the spring, such are the streams, unless the channels in which those streams do run, should be corrupted, and so defile it. But

I know no channels through which this love of Christ is conveyed unto us, but those made in his side, his hands, and his feet, &c., or those gracious promises that dropped like honey from his holy lips, in the day of his love in which he spake them; and seeing his love is conveyed to us, as through those channels, and so by the conduit of the holy and blessed Spirit of God, to our hearts, it cannot be that it should hitherto be corrupted. I know the cisterns, that is, our hearts, into which it is conveyed, are unclean, and may take away much, through the damp that they may put upon it, of the native savor and sweetness thereof. I know also that there are those that tread down and muddy those streams with their feet; but yet neither the love, nor the channels in which it runs, should bear the blame of this. And I hope those that are saints indeed, will not only be preserved to eternal life, but nourished with this that is incorruptible unto the day of Christ.

I told you before, that in the hour of temptation it will be hard for the soul to hold fast to these things, that is, to the true definition of this love; for then, or at such seasons, it will not be admitted, but that the love of Christ is either transient or mixed; but we count that we cannot be loved long, unless something better than yet we see in us, be found there, as an inducement to Christ to love, and to continue to love our poor souls. But these the Christian at length gets over; for he sees by experience he hath no such inducement; also that Christ loves freely, and not for or because of such poor, silly imaginary enticements.

Thus, therefore, the love of Christ may be known, that is, in the nature of it: it may, I say, but not easily. For this knowledge is neither easily got, though got; nor easily retained, though retained. There is nothing, that Satan setteth himself more against than the breaking forth of the love of Christ in its own proper native lustre; for he knows it destroys his kingdom, which standeth in profaneness, in errors and delusions, the only destruction of which is the knowledge of this love of Christ.

What mean those swarms of opinions that are in the world? What is the reason that some are carried about as clouds, with a tempest? What mean men's waverings, men's changings, and interchanging truth for error, and one error for another? Why, this is the thing, the devil is in it. This work is his, and he makes this ado, to make a dust, and a dust to darken the light of the gospel withal. And if he once attained to that, then farewell the true knowledge of the love of Christ. Also, he will assault the spirits of Christians with divers and sundry cogitations, such as shall have in them a tendency to darken the judgment, delude the fancy, to abuse the conscience. He has an art to metamorphose all things. He can make God seem to be to us a most fierce and terrible destroyer, and Christ a terrible exactor of obedience, and most amazingly pinching of his love. He can make supposed sins unpardonable, and unpardonable ones appear as virtues. He can make the law to be received for gospel, and cause that the gospel shall be thrown away as a fable. He can persuade that faith is fancy, and that fancy is the best faith in the world. Besides he can tickle the heart with false hope of a better life hereafter, even as if the love of Christ were there.

But, as I said before, from all these things the true love of Christ, in the right knowledge of it, delivereth those that have it shed abroad in the heart by the Holy Ghost that he hath given. Wherefore it is for this purpose that Christ biddeth us to continue in his love, because the right knowledge, and faith of that to the soul disperseth and driveth away all such fogs and mists of darkness, and makes the soul to sit fast in the promise of eternal life by him; yea, and to grow up into him who is the Head, in all things.

Before I leave this head, I will present my reader with these things, as helps to the knowledge of the love of Christ,

(I mean the knowledge of the nature of it,) and as helps to retain it.

1. Know thyself, what a vile, horrible, abominable sinner thou art; for thou canst not know the love of Christ, before thou knowest the badness of thy nature. "O wretched man that I am," must be, before a man can perceive the nature of the love of Christ. He that sees himself but little, will hardly know much of the love of Christ: he that sees of himself nothing at all, will hardly ever see any thing of the love of Christ: but he that sees most of what an abominable wretch he is, he is like to see most of what is the love of Christ. All errors in doctrine take their rise from the want of this, (I mean errors in doctrine as to justification,) all the idolizing of men's virtues, and human inventions, rise also from the want of this. So then, if a man would be kept sure and steadfast, let him labor before all things to know his own wretchedness. People naturally think that the knowledge of their sins is the way to destroy them, when, in very deed, it is the first step to salvation. Now, if thou wouldst know the badness of thyself, begin in the first place to study the law, then thy heart, and so thy life. The law thou must look into, for that is the glass; thy heart thou must look upon, for that is the face; thy life thou must look upon, for that is the body of a man, as to religion. And without the wary consideration of these three, it is not to be thought that a man can come at the knowledge of himself, and consequently, to the knowledge of the love of Christ.

2. Labor to see the emptiness, shortness, and the pollution that cleave to a man's own righterusness. This also must in some measure be known, before a man can know the nature of the love of Christ. They that see nothing of the loathsomeness of man's best things, will think, that the love of Christ is of that nature, as to be procured or won, obtained or purchased, by man's good deeds. And although

so much gospel light is broke forth, as to stop men's mouths from saying this, yet it is nothing else but sound conviction of the vileness of man's righteousness that will enable men to see that the love of Christ is of that nature, as to save a man without it: as to see that it is of that nature as to justify him without it: I say, without it, or not at all. There is shortness, there is hypocrisy, there is a desire of vain-glory, there is pride, there is presumption, in man's own righteousness; nor can it be without these wickednesses, when men know not the nature of the love of Christ. Now these defile it and make it abominable. Yea, if there were no imperfection in it, but that which I first did mention, that is, shortness, how could it cover the nakedness of him that hath it, or obtain for the man, in whole or in part, that Christ should love, and have respect unto him?

Occasions many thou hast given thee to see the emptiness of man's own righteousness, but all will not do unless thou hast help from heaven. Wherefore thy wisdom will be, if thou canst tell where to find it, to lie in the way of God; that when he comes to visit the men that wait upon him in the means of his own appointing, thou mayest be there; if, perhaps, he may cast an eye of pity upon thy desolate soul, and make thee see the things above mentioned that thou mayest know the nature of the love of Christ.

3. If thou wouldst know the nature of this love, be much in acquainting thy soul with the nature of the law, and the nature of the gospel; the which, though they are not diametrically opposite to one another, yet do propound things so differently to man, that if he knows not where, when, and how to take them, it is impossible but that he should confound them, and in confounding them, lose his own soul. The law is a servant both first and last, to the gospel: when, therefore, it is made a lord, it destroyeth; and then to be sure it is made a lord and saviour, when its dictates and commands are depended upon for life.

Thy wisdom, therefore, will be to study these things distinctly and thoroughly; for, so far as thou art ignorant of the true knowledge of the nature of these, so far thou art ignorant of the true knowledge of the nature of the love of Christ. Read Paul to the Galatians. That epistle was indited by the Holy Ghost, on purpose to direct the soul in and about this very thing.

4. The right knowledge of the nature of the love of Christ, is obtained and retained, by keeping these two doctrines at an everlasting distance as to the conscience; namely, not suffering the law to rule, but over my outward man, not suffering the gospel to be removed one hair's breadth from my conscience. When Christ dwells in my heart by faith, and the moral law dwells in my members, the one to keep up peace with God, the other to keep my conversation in good decorum, then am I right, and not till then.

But this will not be done without much experience, diligence, and delight in Christ. For there is nothing that Satan more desireth, than that the law may abide in the conscience of an awakened Christian, and there take up the place of Christ and faith; for he knows if this may be obtained, the veil is presently drawn over the face of the soul, and the heart darkened as to the knowledge of Christ; and being darkened, the man is driven into despair of mercy, or is put upon it to work for life. There is, therefore, as I say, much diligence required of him that will keep these two in their places assigned them of God. I say much diligent study of the word, diligent prayer, with diligence to walk with God in the world. But we will pass this and come to the second head.

CHAPTER VII.

HOW TO OBTAIN HIGHER DEGREES OF THIS KNOWLEDGE.

As the love of Christ may be known in the nature of it, so it may be known IN MANY DEGREES of it. That which is knowable, admits of degrees of knowledge: the love of Christ is knowable. Again, that which is not possible to be known to the utmost, is to be known, we know not how much; and therefore, they that seek to know it, should never be contented or satisfied, to what degree of the knowledge of it soever they attain; but still should be reaching forward, because there is more to be known of it before them: "Brethren," said Paul, "I count not myself to have apprehended," (that is to the utmost,) "but this one thing I do: forgetting those things which are behind, and reaching forth to those things which are before, I press towards the mark for the prize of the high calling of God in Christ Jesus."

I might here discourse of many things, since I am upon this head of reaching after the knowledge of the love of Christ in many of the degrees of it. But I shall content myself with few.

First, he that would know the love of Christ in several degrees of it, must *begin at his person.* For in him dwells all the treasures of wisdom and knowledge. Nay, more, "in him are *hid* all the treasures of wisdom and knowledge;" in him, that is, in his person: for the godhead of Christ, and our nature to be united in one person, is the highest mystery; and the first appearance of the love of Christ by himself to the world. Here, I say, lie hid the treasures of wisdom, and here, to the world, springs forth the riches of his love. That the eternal Word, for the salvation of sinners, should come down from heaven and be made flesh, is an act of such condescension, a discovery of such love, that it can never to the full be found out. Only here we may see love in him was deep, was broad, was long, and high; let us, therefore, first begin here to learn to know the love of Christ, in the high degrees thereof.

1. Here, in the first place, we perceive love, in that the human nature, the nature of man, not of angels, is taken into union with God. Whoso could consider this, as it is possible for it to be considered, would stand amazed till he died with wonder. By this very act of the heavenly wisdom, we have an inconceivable pledge of the love of Christ to man. For in that he hath taken unto union with himself our nature, what doth it signify, but that he intendeth to take into union with himself our persons? For this very purpose did he assume our nature. Wherefore, we read, that in the flesh he took upon him, in that flesh he died for us, "the just for the unjust, that he might bring us unto God."

2. As he was made flesh, so, as was said afore, he became a public or common person for us: and hereby is perceived another degree of his love; undertaking to do for his what it was not possible they should do for themselves, perfecting righteousness to the very end of the law, and doing for us to the reconciling of us unto his Father and himself.

3. Herein also we may attain to another degree of knowledge of his love, by understanding that he has conquered, and disabled our foes, so that they cannot now accomplish their designed enmity upon us; but that when Satan, death, the grave, and sin, have done to his people, whatever can by them be done, we shall be still "more than conquerors over them, (though on our side be many disadvantages,) through him that loved us."

4. By this also we may yet see more of his love, in that

as a forerunner he is gone into heaven to take possession thereof for us: there to make ready, and to prepare for us our summer houses, our mansions, our dwelling places; as if we were the lords, and he the servant! O this love!

5. Also, we may see another degree of this love, in this, that now in his absence he has sent the third person in the Trinity to supply his place as another Comforter of us; that we may not think he has forgot us, nor be left destitute of a revealer of truth unto us. Yea, he has sent him to fortify our spirits and to strengthen us under all adversity, and against our enemies of what account or degree soever.

6. In this also we may see yet more of the love of Christ, in that though he is in heaven, and we on earth, nothing can happen to his people to hurt them, but he feels it, is touched with it, and counteth it as done unto himself; yea, sympathizes with them, and is afflicted and grieved in their griefs, and their afflictions.

7. Another thing by which also yet more of the love of Christ is made manifest, and so may by us be known, is this. He is now, and has been, ever since his ascension into glory, laying out himself as high priest for us, that by the improving of his merits before the throne of grace, in the way of intercession, he might preserve us from the ruins that our daily infirmities would bring upon us: yea, and make our persons and performances acceptable in his Father's sight.

8. We also see yet more of his love by this, that he will have us where himself is, that we may behold and be partakers of his glory. And in this degree of his love, there are many loves. (1.) Then he will come for us, as a bridegroom for his bride. (2.) Then shall a public marriage be solemnized, and eternized betwixt him and his church. (3.) Then she shall be wrapped up in his mantles and robes of glory. (4.) Then they shall be purified, and separated from other sinners, and all things that offend shall be taken

away from among them. (5.) Then shall they be exalted to thrones, and power of judgment; and shall also sit in judgment on sinful men and fallen angels, acquiescing, by virtue of authority, with their king and head, upon them. (6.) Then, or from thenceforth forever, there shall be no more death, sorrow, hidings of his face, or eclipsing of their glory forever.

And thus you may see what rounds this our Jacob's ladder hath, and how by them we may climb, and climb, even until we are climbed up to heaven. But now we are set again; for all the glories, all the blessings, and all the good things that are laid up in heaven for these, who can understand?

Secondly, A second thing whereby the love of Christ in some degrees of it may be known, is this, That he should pass by angels, and take hold of us. Whoso considereth the nature of spirits, as they are God's workmanship, must needs confess, that as such they have a preeminency above that which is made of dust. This, then, was the disparity betwixt us and them, they being by birth far more noble than we. But now, when both are fallen, and by our fall both in a state of condemnation, that Jesus Christ should choose to take up us, the most inconsiderable, and pass by them, to their eternal perdition and destruction, O herein is love! love in a high degree to man! For verily he took not hold of angels, but of the seed of Abraham he took hold.

Yet this is not all: in all probability the Lord Jesus has ten times as much to do now, he has undertaken to be our Saviour, as he would have had, had he stepped over us and taken hold on them. 1. He needed not to have stooped so low as to take flesh upon him: theirs being a more noble nature. 2. Nor would he, in all likelihood, have met with those contempts, those scorns, those reproaches and undervaluings from them, that he has all along received in this his undertaking, aud met with from sinful flesh. For they were more noble than we, and would sooner have perceived the design of grace, and so, one would think, more readily have fallen in therewith, than such darkness as we were, and still by sin are. 3. They would not have had those disadvantages that we have, for they would not have had a tempter, a destroyer, so strong and mighty as ours is. Alas! had God left us, and taken them, though we should have been ever so full of envy against their salvation, yet being but flesh, what could we have done to them to have laid obstacles in the way of their faith, and hope, as they can and do in ours? 4. They, it may fairly be presumed, had they been taken, and we left, and made partakers in our stead, while we had been shut out as they are, would not have put Christ so to it, now in heaven, (pray bear with the expression, because I want a better,) as we by our imperfections have done, and do: sin, methinks, would not have so hanged in their natures as it doth in ours; their reason, and sense, and apprehensions, being more quick, and so more apt to have been taken with this love of Christ, and by it more easily have been sanctified. 5. The law which they have broken being not so intricate as that against which we have offended, (theirs being a commandment with faithfulness to abide in the place in which their Creater had set them;) methinks, considering also the aptness of their natures as angels, would not have made their complete obedience so difficult. 6. Nor can I imagine, but had they been taken, they, as creatures excelling in strength, would have been more capable of rendering praises and blessings to God for eternal mercies, than such poor sorry creatures as we are could. But, "behold what manner of love the Father hath bestowed upon us, that we should be called the children of God!" that we, not they; that we, notwithstanding all that they have, or could have done to hinder it, should be called the children of God.

This, therefore, is a high degree of the love of Jesus

Christ to us, that when we and they were fallen, he should stoop and take up us, the more ignoble, and leave so mighty an order of creatures in their sins to perish.

Thirdly, A third thing whereby the love of Christ, in some of the degrees of it, may be known, will be, to consider more particularly the way, and unwearied work, that he hath with man, to bring him to that kingdom, that by his blood he hath obtained for him.

1. Man, when the Lord Jesus takes him in hand, to make him partaker of the benefit, is found an enemy to his Redeemer; nor doth, all the intelligence that he has had of the grace and love of Christ to such, mollify him at all, that is, before the day of God's power comes. And this is a strange thing. Had man, though he could not have come to Christ, been willing that Christ should have come to him, it had been something; it would have shown that he had taken his grace to heart, and considered it; yea, and that he was willing to be a sharer in it. But verily here is no such thing: man, though he has free will, yet is willing by no means to be saved God's way, that is, by Jesus Christ, before, (as was said just now) the day of God's power comes upon him. When the good shepherd went to look for his sheep that was lost in the wilderness, and had found it, did it go one step homewards upon its own legs? Did not the shepherd take her, and lay her upon his shoulder, and bring her home rejoicing? This, then, is not love only, but love to a high degree.

2. When man is taken, and laid under the day of God's power; when Christ is opening his ear to discipline and speaking to him, that his heart may receive instruction, many times that poor man is as if the devil had found him, and not God. How frenzily he imagines! how crossly he thinks! how ungainly he carries it under convictions, counsels, and his present apprehension of things! I know some are more powerfully dealt with, and more strongly bound

at first by the word; but others more in an ordinary manner, that the flesh and reason may be seen to the glory of Christ. Yea, and where the will is made more quickly to comply with its salvation, it is no thanks to the sinner at all. It is the day of the power of the Lord that has made the work so soon to appear. Therefore, count this act of love, in the height of love; love in a great degree.

3. When Christ Jesus has made this madman to come to himself, and persuaded him to be willing to accept of his salvation, yet he may not be trusted, nor left alone; for then the corruptions that still lie scattered up and down in his flesh will tempt him to sin, and he will be gone. Yea, so desperately wicked is the flesh of saints, that should they be left to themselves but a little while, none knows what horrible transgressions would break out. Proof of this we have to amazement, plentifully scattered here and there in the word. Hence we have the patience of God, and his gentleness, so admired; for through that it is that they are preserved. "He that keepeth Israel neither slumbers nor sleeps," but watches for them, and over them every moment, for he knows else they will be hurt.

4. Yea, notwithstanding this, how often are saints found playing truant, and lurking like thieves in one hole or other; now in the guilt of backsliding by the power of this corruption, and then in filth by the power of that. Yea, and when found in such decayings, and under such revoltings from God, how commonly do they hide their sin, with Adam, and David, even until their Saviour fetcheth out of their mouth a confession of the truth of their naughtiness! "When I kept silence," said David, (and yet he chose to keep silence after he had committed his wickedness,) "my bones waxed old through my roaring all the day long. For day and night thy hand was heavy upon me; my moisture is turned into the drought of summer." But why didst thou not

confess what thou hadst done then? So I did, saith he, at last, "and thou forgavest the iniquity of my sin."

5. When the sins of saints are so visible and apparent to others, that God for the vindication of his name and honor must punish them in the sight of others; yea, must do it as he is just; yet then, for Christ's sake he waiveth such judgments, and refuseth to inflict such punishments, as naturally tend to their destruction, and chooseth to chastise them with such rods and scourges, as may do them good in the end, and that they may not be condemned with the world. Wherefore, the Lord loves them; and they are blessed, whom he chasteneth and teacheth out of his law. And these things are love to a degree.

6. That Christ should supply out of his fulness the beginnings of grace in our souls, and carry on that work of so great concern, and that which at times we have so little esteem of, is none of the least of the aggravations of the love of Christ to his people. And the work is as common as any of the works of Christ, and as necessary to our salvation, as is his righteousness and the imputation thereof to our justification. For else how could we hold out to the end? and yet none else can be saved.

7. And that the love of Christ should be such to us, that he will thus act, thus do to, and for us with gladness, (as afore is manifest by the parable of the lost sheep,) is another degree of his love towards us: and such a one too, as is none of the lowest rate. I have seen hot love soon cold; and love that has continued to act, yet act towards the end as the man, that by running, and who has run himself off his legs, pants, and can hardly run any longer; but I never saw love like the love of Christ, who as a giant, and bridegroom coming out of his chamber, and as a strong man, rejoiceth to run his race; loving higher and higher, stronger and stronger, I mean as to the lettings out of love, for he reserveth the best wine even till the last.

8. I will conclude with this, that his love may be known in many degrees of it, by that sort of sinners whose salvation he most rejoiceth in, and that is, in the salvation of the sinners that are of the biggest size: great sinners, Jerusalem sinners, Samaritan sinners, publican sinners. I might urge, moreover, how he hath proportioned invitations, promises, and examples of his love, for the encouragement and support of those whose souls would trust in him; by which also great degrees of his love may be understood.

CHAPTER VIII.

THE HIGHEST ATTAINMENT IN THIS KNOWLEDGE.

BUT we will come now to the third thing that was propounded. The greatest attainment, as to the understanding of the love of Christ, that we can arrive at here, is TO KNOW THAT IT PASSES KNOWLEDGE. "And to know the love of Christ that passeth knowledge."

This truth discovereth itself,

First, by the text itself. For the Apostle here, in this prayer of his for the Ephesians, doth not only desire that they may know, but describeth that thing which he prays they may know, by this term, it "passeth knowledge:" "and to know the love of Christ which passeth knowledge." As our reason and carnal imagination will be rudely and unduly tampering with any thing of Christ; so more especially with the love and kindness of Christ: judging and concluding that just such it is, and none other, as may be apprehended by them: yea, and will have a belief that just so, and no otherwise are the dimensions of this love; nor can it save beyond our carnal conceptions of it. This is saying to the soul, as Pharaoh once did to Israel in another case, "Let the Lord be with you as I shall" (judge it meet he should) "let you go." We think Christ loves us no more than we think he can; and so conclude that his love is such as may by us be comprehended, or known to the utmost bounds thereof. But these are false conceptions; and this love of Christ that we think is such, is indeed, none of the love of Christ, but a false image thereof, set before our eyes. I speak not now of weak knowledge, but of foolish and bold conclusions. A man, through unbelief, may think that Christ has no love for him, and yet Christ may love him with a love that passeth knowledge. But when men, in the common course of their profession, will be always terminating here that they know how, and how far Christ can love; and will thence be bold to conclude to their own safety, and of the loss and ruin of all that are not in the same notions, opinions, formalities, or judgments as they; this is the worst and greatest of all. The text, therefore, to rectify those false and erroneous conclusions, says, it is a love that passeth knowledge.

And it will be worth our observation to take notice that men, erroneous men, do not put these limits so commonly to the Father and his love, as to the Son and his. Hence you have some that boast, that God can save some who have not the knowledge of the person of the Mediator, Jesus Christ the righteous—as those among the heathen that have made, and still make great improvement of the law and light of nature; crying out with disdain against the narrowness, rigidness, censoriousness, and pride of those that think the contrary: being not ashamed all the while to eclipse, to degrade, to lessen and undervalue the love of Jesus Christ; making of him, and his undertaking to offer himself a sacrifice to appease the justice of God for our sins, but a thing indifferent, and in its own nature but as other smaller matters.

But all this while the devil knows full well at what game he plays; for he knows, that without Christ, without faith in his blood, there is no remission of sins. Wherefore, saith he, 'let these men talk what they will of the greatness of the love of God as Creator, so they slight and undervalue the love of Christ as Mediator.' And yet it is worth our consideration, that the greatness of the love of God is most expressed in his giving of Christ to be a Saviour, and in bestowing his benefits upon us, that we may be happy through him.

But to return; the love of Christ that is so indeed, is love that passeth knowledge: and the best and the highest of our knowledge of it is, that we know it to be such.

Secondly, because I find that at this point the great men of God, of old, were wont to stop, be set, and beyond which they could not pass. It was this that made Moses wonder. It was this that made David cry out, "How great and wonderful are thy works, O God! Thy thoughts to us-ward, they cannot be reckoned up in order unto thee. If I should declare and speak of them, they are more than can be numbered." And again, "How precious also are thy thoughts unto me, O God! how great is the sum of them? If I should count them, they are more in number than the sand." And a little before, "such knowledge is too wonderful for me." Isaiah saith, "there hath not entered into the heart of man what God has prepared for them that wait for him." Ezekiel says, "This is the river that cannot be passed over." And Micah hath compared to the sea, and Zechariah to a fountain, this unsearchable love. Wherefore, the apostle's position, That the love of Christ is that which "passeth knowledge," is a truth not to be doubted of: consequently, to know this, and that it is such, is the farthest that we can go. This is to justify God, who has said it, and to magnify the Son, who has loved us with such a love: and the contrary is to dishonor him, and lessen him, and to make him a deficient Saviour. For, suppose this should be true, that thou couldest to the utmost comprehend this love: yet unless, by thy knowledge, thou canst comprehend beyond all the evil of sin, or beyond what any man's sins, who shall be saved, can spread themselves or infect, thou must leave some pardonable man in an unpardonable condition; for that thou canst comprehend this love, and yet canst not comprehend that sin. This makes Christ a deficient Saviour.

Besides, if thou comprehendest truly, then the word that says it passeth knowledge, has lost its sanctity, its truth.

It must, therefore be, that this love passeth knowledge, and that the highest pitch that a man by knowledge can attain unto, as to this, is to know that it passeth knowledge. My reason is, that all degrees of love, be they ever so high, or many and high, yet, if we can comprehend them, they rest in the bowels of our knowledge; for that only which is beyond us, is that which passeth knowledge. That which we can reach, cannot be the highest; and if a man thinks there is nothing beyond what he can reach, he has no more knowledge as to that: but if he knows that together with what he hath already reached, there is that which he cannot reach before; then he has a knowledge for that also, even a knowledge that it passeth knowledge. It is true a man that thus knoweth, may have divers conjectures about that thing that is beyond his knowledge; yea, in reason it will be so, because he knows that there is something yet before him: but since the thing itself is truly beyond his knowledge, none of his conjectures about that thing may be counted knowledge. Or suppose a man that thus conjectureth should hit right as to what he now conjectures, his right hitting about that thing may not be called knowledge; it is as yet to him but as an uncertain guess, and the thing is still beyond his knowledge.

Question. But, may some say, 'What good will it do a man to know that the love of Christ passeth knowledge? One would think that it should do one more good to believe, that the knowledge of the whole love of Christ might be attainable.'

Answer. That there is an advantage in knowing that the love of Christ passeth knowledge, must not be questioned, for the apostle saith it doth. For to know what the holy word affirms, is profitable; nor would he pray that we might know that which passeth knowledge, were there not by our knowing it, some help to be administered. But to show you some of the advantages that will come to us by knowing that the love of Christ passeth knowledge.

1. By knowing this a child of God has *something in reserve for himself*, at a day, when all that he otherwise knows, may be taken from him through the power of temptation. Sometimes a good man may be so put to it, that all that he knows comprehensively may be taken from him, as the knowledge of the truth of his faith, or that he has the grace of God in him, or the like; this, I say, may be taken from him. Now, if at this time "he knows the love of Christ that passeth knowledge, he knows a way in all probability to be recovered again; 'for if Christ Jesus loves with a love that passeth knowledge, 'then' (saith the soul that is thus in the dark,) 'he may love me yet, for aught I know; for I know that he loves with a love that passeth knowledge, and therefore, I will not utterly despond.'

Yea, if Satan should attempt to question whether ever Christ Jesus will look upon me or no; if I know the love that passeth knowledge, the answer is—'But he *may* look upon me, Satan, yea, and love, and save me too, for aught I a poor sinner know; for he loves with a love that passeth knowledge.'

If I be fallen into sin that lies hard upon me, and my conscience fears that for this there is no forgiveness, the help for a stay from utter despair is at hand,—'But there may be, say I, for Christ loves with a love that passeth knowledge.'

If Satan would dissuade me from praying to God, by suggesting as if Christ would not regard the stammering and chattering prayer of mine; the answer is ready,—'But he may regard for aught I know; for he loves with a love that passeth knowledge.'

If the tempter doth suggest, that thy trials, and troubles, and afflictions, are so many that it is to be thought thou shalt never get beyond them; the answer is near,—'But for aught we know, Christ may carry me through them all; for he loves with a love that passeth knowledge.'

Thus, I say, is relief at hand, and a help in reserve for the tempted, let their temptations be what they will. This, therefore, is the weapon that will baffle the devil when all other weapons fail,—'For aught I know Christ may save me; for he loves with a love that passeth knowledge.' Yea, suppose he should drive me to the worst of fears, and that is to doubt that I neither have, nor shall have forever the grace of God in my soul; the answer is at hand—'But I have, or may have it; for Christ loves with a love that passeth knowledge.'

Thus, therefore, you may see, that in this prayer of Paul there is a great deal of good. He prays, when he prays that we might know the love of Christ that passeth knowledge, that we may have a help at hand, and relief against all the horrible temptations of the devil. For this is a help at hand, a help that is ready to fall in with us, if there be yet remaining with us but the least grain of right reasoning, according to the nature of things: for if it be objected against a man that he is poor, because he has but a groat in his pocket; yet if he has an unknown deal of money in his trunks, how easy is it for him to recover himself from that slander, by returning the knowledge of what he has upon the objector. This is the case, and thus it is, and will be with them that know the love of Christ that passeth knowledge. Wherefore,

2. By this knowledge, room is made for a Christian, and liberty is ministered unto him, *to turn himself every way* in all spiritual things. This is the Christian's Rehoboth; that Well for which the Philistines have no heart to strive, and that which will cause that we be fruitful in the land.

If Christians know not with this knowledge, they walk in the world as if they were pinioned, or as if fetters were hanged on their heels. But this enlarges their steps under them. By the knowledge of this love they may walk at liberty, and their steps shall not be straitened. This is that which Solomon intends when he saith, "Get wisdom, and get understanding.—Then, when thou goest, thy steps shall not be straitened, and when thou runnest, thou shalt not stumble." A man that has only from hand to mouth, is oft put to it to know how to use his penny, and comes off also, many times, but with an hungry belly; but he that has not only that, but always over and to spare, he is more at liberty, and can live in fulness, and far more like a gentleman. There is a man has a cistern, and that is full of water; there is another also that has his cistern full, and withal his springs in his yard; but a great drought is upon the land in which they dwell; I would now know which of these two has the most advantage to live in his own mind at liberty, without fear of wanting water? Why this is the case in hand. There is a Christian that knows Christ in all those degrees of his love that are knowable, but he knoweth nothing of Christ in his love that passeth knowledge. There is another Christian, and he knows Christ, as the first, but withal he also knows him as to his love that passeth knowledge. Pray, now, tell me, which of these two is likeliest to live most like a Christian, that is, like a spiritual prince, and like him that possesseth all things? Which has most advantage to live in godly largeness of heart, and is most at liberty in his mind? Which of these two has the greatest advantage to believe, and the greatest engagements laid upon him to love the Lord Jesus? Which of these has also most in readiness to resist the wiles of the devil, and to subdue the power and prevalency of corruptions?

It is this that makes men fathers in Christianity. "I write unto you, fathers, because ye have known." "I have written unto you, fathers, because ye have known." Why, have not others known? Not so as the fathers. The fathers have known and known. They have known the love of Christ in those degrees of love which are knowable, and have also known the love of Christ to be that which passeth knowledge.

"In my father's house is bread enough, and to spare," was that that fetched the prodigal home. And when Moses would speak an endless all to Israel for the comfort and stay of their souls, he calls their God "the fountain of Jacob upon a land of corn and wine."

3. By this knowledge, or knowledge of the love of Christ which passeth knowledge, there is begot in Christians *a greater desire to press forward* to that which is before them. What is the reason of all that sloth, carnal contentedness, and listlessness of spirit in Christians, more than the ignorance of this? For he that thinks he knows what can be known, is beyond all reason that should induce him to seek yet after more. Now the love of Christ may be said, not to be knowable, upon a threefold account. (1.) That my knowledge is weak. (2.) That my knowledge is imperfect. (3.) Or though my knowledge be ever so perfect, because the love of Christ is eternal.

There is love that is not to be apprehended by weak knowledge. Convince a man of this, and then if the knowledge of what he already has, be truly sweet to his soul, it will stir him up with great heartiness to desire to know what more of this is possible.

There is love beyond what he knows already, who is endowed with the most perfect knowledge, that man here may have. Now, if what this man knows already of this love is, indeed, sweet unto him, then it puts him upon hearty desires that his soul may yet know more. And because there is no bound set to man, how much he may know thereof, in this life, therefore his desires, notwithstanding what he has attained, are yet kept alive, and in the pursuit after the knowledge of more of the love of Christ. And God in old time has taken it so well at the hands of some of his, that their desires have been so great, that when, as I may say, they have known as much on earth as is possible for them to know, (that is by ordinary means,) he has come down to them in visions and revelations, or else taken them up to him for an hour or two into paradise, that they might know, and then let them down again.

But this is not all. There is a knowledge of the love of Christ, that we are by no means capable of until we be possessed of the heavens. And I would know, if a man, indeed, loveth Christ, whether the belief of this be not one of the highest arguments that can be urged, to make such a one weary of this world, that he may be with him. To such a one, "to live is Christ, and to die is gain." And to such a one, it is difficult to bring his mind to be content to stay here a longer time; except he be satisfied that Christ has still work for him here to do.

I will yet add, There is a love of Christ, I will not say that cannot be known, but I will say that cannot be enjoyed; no, not by them now in heaven (in soul) until the day of judgment. And the knowledge of this, when it has possessed even men on earth, has made them choose a day of judgment, before a day of death, that they might know what is beyond that state and knowledge which even the spirits of just men made perfect now do enjoy in heaven. Wherefore, as I said at first, "To know the love of Christ which passeth knowledge," is advantageous upon this account: it begetteth in Christians a great desire to reach, and press forward to that which is before.

One thing more, and then, as to this reason, I have done. Even that love of Christ that is absolutely unknowable, as to the utmost bound thereof, because it is eternal, will be yet in the nature of it sweet and desirable, because we shall enjoy or be possessed of it so. This, therefore, if there were no more, is enough, when known to draw away the heart from things that are below, to itself.

4. The love that "passeth knowledge—" the knowledge of this is *very fruitful knowledge.* It cannot be but it must be fruitful. Some knowledge is empty and alone, not attended with that good and with those blessings wherewith this knowledge is attended. Did I say it, it is fruitful? I will add, it is attended with the best fruit; it yieldeth the best wine; it fills the soul with all the fulness of God. "And to know the love of Christ which passeth knowledge, *that ye may be filled with all the fulness of God.*" God is in Christ, and makes himself known to us by the love of Christ. "Whosoever transgresseth, and abideth not in the doctrine of Christ, hath not God;" for God is not to be found nor enjoyed, but in him, consequently he that hath, and "abideth in the doctrine of Christ, hath both the Father and the Son." Now, since there are degrees of knowledge of this doctrine, and since the highest degree of the knowledge of him, is to know that he has a love "that passeth knowledge," it follows, that if he that has the least saving knowledge of this doctrine, hath God; he that hath the largest knowledge of it, has God much more, or, according to the text, is filled with all the fulness of God.

What this fulness of God should be, is best gathered from such sayings of the Holy Ghost, as come nearest to this in language, as, (1.) Full of goodness. (2.) Full of faith. (3.) Full of the Holy Ghost. (4.) Full assurance of faith. (5.) Full assurance of hope. (6.) Full of joy unspeakable. (7.) Full of glory. (8.) Full of good works. (9.) Filled with the knowledge of his will. (10.) Filled with the Spirit. (11.) Filled with the fruits of righteousness, which are by Jesus Christ to the glory and praise of God.

These things, to be sure, are included, either for the cause or effect of this fulness. The cause they cannot be; for that is God, by his Holy Spirit. The effects thereof they are; for wherever God dwells, in the degree intended in the text, there is shown, in an eminent manner by these things, what is the riches of the glory of his inheritance in the saints. But these things dwell not in that measure specified by the text, in any but those who "know the love of Christ which passeth knowledge."

But what a man is he, that is filled with all these things? or that is, as we have it in the text, "filled with all the fulness of God?" Such men are, at this day, wanting in the churches. These are the men that sweeten churches, and that bring glory to God and to religion. And knowledge will make us such, such knowledge as the apostle here speaks of.

CHAPTER IX.

THE USE OF WHAT HAS BEEN SAID.

I HAVE now done, when I have spoken something by way of use unto you, from what hath been said. And,

1. Is there such breadth, and length, and depth, and height in God, for us? And is there towards us love in Christ that passeth knowledge? Then this shows us, not only the greatness of the majesty of the Father and the Son, but the great good will that is in their hearts to them that receive their word.

God has engaged the breadth, and length, and depth, and height of the love, the wisdom, the power and truth, that is in himself for us; and Christ has loved us with a love that passeth knowledge. We may well say, "Who is like thee, O Lord, among the gods?" Or, as another prophet has it, "Who is a God like unto thee, that pardoneth iniquity, and passeth by the transgressions of the remnant of his heritage! He retaineth not his anger forever; because he delighteth in mercy." Yea, no words can sufficiently set forth the greatness of this love of God and his Son to us poor miserable sinners.

2. Is there so great a heart for love towards us, both in the Father and in the Son? Then let us be much in the study and search after the greatness of this love. This is the sweetest study that a man can devote himself unto, because it is the study of the love of God and of Christ to man. Studies that yield far less profit than this, how close are they pursued by some who have adapted themselves thereunto! Men do not use to count the telling over their money burdensome to them, nor yet the recounting of their

grounds, their herds and their flocks, when they increase. Why, the study of the unsearchable love of God in Christ to man, is better in itself, and yields more sweetness to the soul of man, than can ten thousand such things as but now are mentioned. I know the wise men of this world, of whom there are many, will say, as to what I now press you unto, "Who can show us any good in it?" But, "Lord, lift thou up the light of thy countenance upon us. Thou hast put gladness in my heart, more than in the time that their corn and their wine increaseth." David also said, that his meditation on the Lord should be sweet. Oh! there is in God and in his Son that kindness for the sons of men, that, did they know it, they would like to retain the knowledge of it in their hearts. They would cry out, as she did of old, "Set me as a seal upon thy heart, as a seal upon thine arm: for love is strong as death." Every part, crumb, grain, or scrap of this knowledge, is to a Christian as drops of honey are to sweet-palated children, worth the gathering up, worth the putting to the taste, to be relished. Yea, David says of the word, which is the ground of this knowledge, it is sweeter than honey, or the honeycomb. "More" (said he) "to be desired are they than gold; yea, than much fine gold; sweeter also than honey or the honeycomb."

Why, then, do not Christians devote themselves to the meditation of this so heavenly, so goodly, so sweet, and so comfortable a thing, that yieldeth such advantage to the soul? The reason is, these things are talked of, but not believed. Did men believe what they say, when they speak so largely of the love of God, and the love of Jesus Christ, they would, they could not but meditate upon it. There are so many wonders in it, and men love to think of wonders; there is so much profit in it, and men love to think of that which yields them profit. But, as I said, the belief of things is wanting. Belief of a thing will have strong effects, whether the ground for it be true or false. As, suppose one of you should, when you are at a neighbor's house, believe that your own house is on fire, whilst your children are fast asleep in bed, though indeed there were no such thing; I shall appeal to any of you, if this belief would not make notable work with and upon your hearts. Let a man believe he shall be damned, though afterwards it is evident he believed a lie, yet what work does that belief make in that man's heart. Even so, and much more the belief of heavenly things will work, because true and great, and most good; also, where they are, indeed, believed, their evidence is managed upon their spirit, by the power and glory of the Holy Ghost himself. Wherefore, let us study these things.

3. Let us cast ourselves upon this love. No greater encouragement can be given us, than what is in the text and about it. It is great, it is love that passeth knowledge. Men that are sensible of danger, are glad when they hear of such helps, upon which they may boldly venture for escape. Why, such a help and relief the text helpeth trembling and fearful consciences, to. Fear and trembling, as to misery hereafter, can flow but from what we know, feel, or imagine; but the text speaks of a love that is beyond all that we can know, feel, or imagine, even of a love that passeth knowledge, consequently, of a love that goes beyond all these.

Besides, the apostle's conclusion upon this subject plainly makes it manifest, that this meaning which I have put upon the text is the mind of the Holy Ghost. "Now, unto him," saith he, "that is able to do exceeding abundantly above all that we ask or think, according to the power that worketh in us, unto him be glory in the church by Christ Jesus, throughout all ages, world without end. Amen." What can be more plain? What can be more full? What can be more suitable to the most desponding spirit in any man? He can do more than thou knowest he will. He can do more than thou thinkest he can. What dost thou think? 'Why, I think,' saith the sinner, 'that I am cast away.' Well, but there are worse thoughts than these, therefore, think again. 'Why,' saith the sinner, 'I think that my sins are as many as all the sins of the world.' Indeed, this is a very black thought, but there are worse thoughts than this; therefore, prithee, think again. 'Why, I think,' saith the sinner, 'that God is not able to pardon all my sins.' Aye, now, thou hast thought, indeed; for this thought makes thee look more like a devil than a man. And yet, because thou art a man, and not a devil, see the condescension and the boundlessness of the Love of thy God. He is able to do above all that we think. Couldst thou, sinner, (if thou hadst been allowed,) thyself express what thou wouldst have expressed, the greatness of the love thou wantest, with words that could have suited thee better? For it is not said, he can do above what we think, meaning our thinking at present; but above *all* we think, meaning, above the worst and most soul dejecting thoughts that we have at any time. Sometimes the dejected have worse thoughts than they have at other times. Well, take them at their worst times, at times when they think, and think, till they think themselves down into the very pangs of hell, yet this word of the grace of God is above them, and shows that he can yet recover and save these miserable people.

And now I am upon this subject, I will a little further walk and travel with the desponding ones, and will put a few words in their mouths for their help, against temptations that may come upon them hereafter. For as Satan follows such now, with charges and applications of guilt, so he may follow them with interrogatories and appeals: for he can tell how by appeals, as well as by charging sin, to sink and drown the sinner whose soul he has leave to engage. Suppose, therefore, that some distressed man or woman should after this way be engaged, and Satan should with his interrogatories and appeals be busy with them, to drive them to desperation, the text last mentioned, to say nothing of the subject of our discourse, yields plenty of help for the relief of such a one. Says Satan, 'dost thou not know that thou hast horribly sinned?'—'Yes.' says the soul, 'I do.' Says Satan, 'dost thou not know that thou art one of the vilest in all the pack of professors.' 'Yes,' says the soul, 'I do.' Says Satan, 'does not thy conscience tell thee that thou art, and hast been, more base than any of thy fellows can imagine thee to be?' 'Yes,' says the soul, 'my conscience tells me so.' 'Well,' saith Satan, 'now will I come upon thee with my appeals. Art thou not a graceless wretch?'—'Yes.' 'Hast thou an heart to be sorry for this wickedness?'—'No, not as I should.' 'And albeit,' saith Satan, 'thou prayest sometimes, yet is not thy heart possessed with a belief that God will not regard thee?'—'Yes,' says the sinner. 'Why then, despair and go hang thyself,' saith the devil. And now we are at the end of the thing designed and driven at by Satan. 'But what shall I do now?' saith the sinner. I answer, take up the words of the text against him, Christ loves with a love that "passeth knowledge." And answer him farther, saying, 'Satan, though I cannot think that God loves me, though I cannot think that God will save me, yet I will not yield to thee; for God can do more than I think he can. And whereas, thou appealest unto me, if whether when I pray, my heart is not possessed with unbelief, that God will not regard me, that shall not sink me neither; for God can do abundantly above what I can ask, or think.' Thus this text helpeth where obstructions are put in against our believing, and thereby casting ourselves upon the love of God in Christ for salvation.

And yet this is not all; for the text is yet more full. He is able to do abundantly more, yea, 'exceeding abundantly' more, or 'above all that we ask or think.' It is a text made up of words picked and packed together by the wisdom of God; picked and packed together on purpose for the succor and relief of the tempted, that they may, when in the midst of their distresses, cast themselves upon the Lord their God. He can do abundantly more than we ask. 'Oh!' says the soul, 'that he would but do so much for me as I could ask him to do? how happy a man should I then be!' Why, what wouldst thou ask for, sinner? 'You may be sure,' says the soul, 'I would ask to be saved from my sins; I would ask for faith in, and love to Christ; I would ask to be preserved in this evil world, and ask to be glorified with Christ in heaven.' He that asketh for all this, doth, indeed, ask for much, and for more than Satan would have him believe that God is able or willing to bestow upon him: but mark, the text doth not say, that God is able to do all that we ask or think, but that he is able to do above all, yea, abundantly above all, yea, 'exceeding abundantly above all that we ask or think.' What a text is this! What a God have we! God foresaw the sins of his people, and what work the devil would make with their hearts about them; and therefore, to prevent their ruin by his temptation, he has thus largely, as you see, expressed his love by his word. Let us, therefore, as he has bidden us, make this good use of this doctrine of grace, to cast ourselves upon this love of God in the times of distress and temptation.

4. Take heed of abusing this love. This exhortation seems needless: for love is such a thing, as one would think none could find in their heart to abuse. But for all that, I am of opinion, that there is nothing that is more abused among professors this day, than is this love of God. There has of late broke out more light about the love of Christ than formerly; every boy now can talk of the love of Christ; but this love of Christ has not been rightly applied by preachers, or else not rightly received by professors. For never was this grace of Christ so turned into lasciviousness

as now. Now it is a practice among professors to learn to be vile of the profane; yea, and to plead for that vileness; nay, we will turn it the other way; now it is so that the profane do learn to be vile of those that profess, (for they teach the wicked ones their ways:) a thing that no good man should think on but with blushing cheeks.

Jude speaketh of these people, and tells us, that they, notwithstanding their profession, "deny the only Lord God, and our Saviour Jesus Christ." "They profess" (saith Paul) "that they know God, but in works they deny him, being abominable, disobedient, and to every good work reprobate."

But I say, let not this love of God and of Christ be abused. It is unnatural to abuse love; to abuse love is a villany condemned of all; yea, to abuse love is the most inexcusable sin of all. It is next the sin of devils to abuse love, the love of God and of Christ. And what says the Apostle? "Because they received not the love of the truth that they may be saved, therefore, God shall send them strong delusion, that they may believe a lie, that they all may be damned, who believed not the truth, but had pleasure in unrighteousness." And what can such a one say for himself in the judgment, that shall be charged with the abuse of love?

If you would not abuse love, Christians, deny yourselves; deny your lusts, deny the vanities of this present life, devote yourselves to God; become lovers of God, lovers of his ways, and a people zealous of good works; then shall you show one to another, and to all men, that you have not received the grace of God in vain. Renounce, therefore, the hidden things of dishonesty, walk not in craftiness, nor handle God's word deceitfully, but by manifestation of the truth, commend yourselves to every man's conscience in the sight of God. Do this, I say, yea, and so endeavor such a closure with this love of God in Christ, as may graciously constrain you to do it; because, when all proofs of the right receiving of this love of Christ shall be produced, none will be found of worth enough to justify the simplicity of our profession, but that which makes us zealous of good works. And what a thing will it be to be turned off at last, as one that abused the love of Christ! as one that presumed upon his lusts, this world, and all manner of naughtiness, because the love of Christ to pardon sins was so great! What an unthinking, what a disingenuous one, wilt thou be counted at that day! Yea, thou wilt be found to be the man that made a prey of love, that made a stalking horse of love, a slave to sin, the devil, and the world; and will not that be bad?

5. Is the love of God and of Christ so great? Let us then labor to improve it to the utmost for our advantage, against all the hindrances of faith.

To what purpose else is it revealed, made mention of, and commended to us? We are environed with many enemies, and faith in the love of God and of Christ is our only succor and shelter. Wherefore, our duty, and wisdom, and privilege are, to improve this love for our own advantage; improve it against daily infirmities; improve it against the wiles of the devil; improve it against the threats, rage, death, and destruction, that the men of this world continually with their terror set before you. But how must that be done? Why, set this love and the safety that is in it, before thine eyes; and behold it while these things make their assaults upon thee. These words, the faith of this, 'God loves me,' will support thee in the midst of what dangers may assault thee. And this is that which is meant, when we are exhorted to rejoice in the Lord to make our boast in the Lord, to triumph in the Lord, and to set the Lord always before our face. For he that can do this thing steadfastly, cannot be overcome. For 'in God there is more than can be in the world, either to help or hinder; wherefore, if God be my helper, if God loves me, if Christ be my Redeemer, and has bestowed his love that passeth knowledge upon me, who can be against me? and if they be against me, what disadvantage reap I thereby; since even all this worketh for my good?' This is improving the love of God, and of Christ, for my advantage.

The same course should Christians also take with the *degrees* of this love, even set it against all the degrees of danger; for here deep calleth unto deep. There cannot be wickedness and rage wrought up to such or such a degree, as that it may be said, there are not degrees in the love of God and of Christ to match it. Wherein Pharaoh dealt proudly against God's people, the Lord was above him, did match and overmatch him; he came up to him, and went beyond him; he collared with him, overcame him, and cast him down. "The Lord is a man of war, the Lord is his name. Pharaoh's chariots and his hosts hath he cast into the sea—they sank unto the bottom as a stone." There is no striving against the Lord that hath loved us; there are none that strive against him can prosper. If the shields of the earth be the Lord's, then he can wield them for the safeguard of his body the church; or if they are become incapable of being made use of any longer in that way, and for such a thing, can he not lay them aside, and make himself new ones? Men can do after this manner, much more God.

But again, if the miseries or afflictions which thou meetest with, seem to thee, to overflow, and to go beyond measure, above measure, and so to be above strength, and begin to drive thee to despair of life, then thou hast also, in the love of God, and of Christ, that which is above, and that goes beyond all measure also, namely, love unsearchable, unknown, and that can do exceeding abundantly above all that we ask or think. Now God hath set them one against the other, and it will be thy wisdom to do so too, for this is the way to improve this love.

CHAPTER X.

CONCLUDING COUNSELS.

But though it be easy thus to admonish you to do, yet you shall find the practical part more difficult; wherefore, here it may not be amiss, if I add to these, another head of counsel.

1. First, then, Wouldst thou improve this love of God and of Christ to thy advantage? Why then, thou must labor after the knowledge of it. This was it that the Apostle prayed for, for these Ephesians, as was said before; and this is that, that thou must labor after, or else thy reading, and my writing will, as to thee, be fruitless. Let me then say to thee, as David to his son Solomon, "And thou, Solomon, my son, know thou the God of thy father." Empty notions of this love will do nothing but harm; wherefore they are not empty notions that I press thee to rest in, but that thou labor after the knowledge of the savor of this good ointment, which the apostle calleth "the savor of the knowledge of Christ." Know it until it becometh sweet or pleasant to thy soul, and then it will preserve and keep thee. Make this love of God and of Christ thine own, and not another's. Many there are that can talk largely of the love of God to Abraham, to David, to Peter, and Paul. But that is not the thing. Give not over until this love be made thine own; until thou find and feel it to run warm in thy heart, by the shedding of it abroad there, by the Spirit that God hath given thee. Then thou wilt know it with an obliging and engaging knowledge; yea, then thou wilt know it with a soul-strengthening and soul-encouraging knowledge.

2. Wouldst thou improve this love? Then set it against the love of all other things whatsoever, even until this love shall conquer thy soul from the love of them to itself.

This is Christian. Do it, therefore, and say, 'Why should any thing have my heart but God—but Christ? he loves me with love that passeth knowledge. He loves me, and he shall have me: he loves me, and I will love him; his love stripped him of all for my sake; Lord, let my love strip me of all for thy sake. I am a son of love, an object of love, a monument of love, of free love, of distinguishing love, of peculiar love, and of love that passeth knowledge, and why should not I walk in love? in love to God, in love to men, in holy love, in love unfeigned?' This is the way to improve the love of God for thy advantage, for the subduing of thy passions, and for the sanctifying of thy nature.

It is an odious thing to hear men of base lives talking of the love of God, of the death of Christ, and of the glorious grace that is presented unto sinners by the word of the truth of the gospel. "Praise is comely for the upright;" not for the profane. Therefore, let him speak of love that is taken with love, that is captivated with love, that is carried away with love. If this man speaks of it, his speaking signifies something: the powers and bands of love are upon him, and he shows to all that he knows what he is speaking of. But the very mentioning of love is, in the mouth of the profane, like a parable in the mouth of fools—as salt unsavory. Wherefore, Christian, improve this love of God as thou shouldst, and that will improve thee as thou wouldst. Wherefore,

3. If thou wouldst improve this love, keep thyself in it. "Keep yourselves in the love of God." This text looks as if it favored the Socinians, but there is nothing of that in it. And so doth that, "If ye keep my commandments, ye shall abide in my love: even as I have kept my Father's

commandments and abide in his love." The meaning then is this, that living a holy life is the way, after a man has believed unto justification, to keep himself in the savor and comfort of the love of God. And, oh! that thou wouldst indeed so do. And that because, if thou shalt want the savor of it, thou wilt soon want tenderness to the commandment, which is the rule by which thou must walk, if thou wilt do good to thyself, or honor God in the world. "To him that ordereth his conversation aright, I will show the salvation of God." He that would live a sweet, comfortable, joyful life, must live a very holy life. This is the way to improve this love to thyself indeed.

4. To this end, you must "take root and be grounded in love;" that is, you must be well settled, and established in this love, if, indeed, you would improve it. You must not be shaken as to the doctrine, and grounds of it. These you must be well acquainted with; for he that is but a child in this doctrine, is not capable as yet of falling in with these exhortations; for such waver and fear when tempted; and he that feareth is not made perfect in love, nor can he so improve it for himself and souls' good as he should.

5. And lastly, keep, to this end, those grounds and evidences that God hath given you of your call to be partakers of this love, with all clearness upon your hearts, and in your minds. For he that wants a sight of them, or a proof that they are true and good, can take but little comfort in this love. There is a great mystery in the way of God with his people. He will justify them without their works, he will pardon them for his Son's sake. But they shall have but little comfort of what he hath done, doeth, and will do, for them, that are careless, carnal, and not holy in their lives. Nor shall they have their evidences for heaven at hand, nor out of doubt with them, yea, they shall walk without the sun, and have their comforts by bits and knocks; while others sit at their Father's table, have liberty to go into the

wine cellar, rejoice at the sweet and pleasant face of their heavenly Father towards them, and know it shall go well with them at the end.

Something now for a conclusion should be spoken to the carnal world, who have heard me tell of all this love. But what shall I say unto them, if I should speak to them, and they should not hear; or if I should testify unto them, and they should not believe; or entreat them, and they should scorn me: all will but aggravate, and greaten their sin, and tend to their further condemnation. And therefore, I shall leave the obstinate where I found them, and shall say to him that is willing to be saved, sinner, thou hast the advantage of thy neighbor, not only because thou art willing to live, but because there are those that are willing thou shouldst, namely, those unto whom the issues from death do belong, and they are the Father and the Son, to whom be glory, with the blessed Spirit of grace, world without end. Amen.

PAUL'S DEPARTURE AND CROWN:

OR,

PRACTICAL DEVOTION TO THE WORK OF LIFE

ALLOTTED TO US BY GOD,

THE WAY TO BE ALWAYS READY FOR DEATH.

PAUL'S
DEPARTURE AND CROWN.

CHAPTER I.

CONNECTION AND MEANING OF THE WORDS.

FOR I AM NOW READY TO BE OFFERED, AND THE TIME OF MY DEPARTURE IS AT HAND. I HAVE FOUGHT A GOOD FIGHT, I HAVE FINISHED MY COURSE, I HAVE KEPT THE FAITH: HENCEFORTH THERE IS LAID UP FOR ME A CROWN OF RIGHTEOUSNESS, WHICH THE LORD, THE RIGHTEOUS JUDGE, SHALL GIVE ME AT THAT DAY; AND NOT TO ME ONLY, BUT UNTO ALL THEM ALSO THAT LOVE HIS APPEARING.—2 TIMOTHY iv. 6, 7, 8.

THESE words were by the Apostle Paul written to Timothy, whom he had begotten to the faith, by the preaching of the gospel of Christ; in which are many things of great concernment both for instruction and consolation, something of which I shall open unto you for your profit and edification.

But before I come to the words themselves, as they are a relation of Paul's case, I shall take notice of something from them as they depend upon the words going before, being a vehement exhortation to Timothy to be constant and faithful in his work; which in brief may be summed up in these particulars; 1st. A solemn binding charge before God and Jesus Christ our Lord, that he be constant in preaching the word, whether in or out of season, reproving, rebuking, and exhorting with all long suffering and doctrine; and that because of that ungodly spirit that would possess professors after he was dead. "For the time will come," saith he, "when they will not endure sound doctrine, (neither sound reproof, nor sound trial of their state and condition by the word,) but after their own lusts shall they heap to themselves teachers, having itching ears, (the plague that once God threatened to rebellious Israel,) and be turned unto fables." Much like this is that prediction in the Acts of the Apostles (xx. 29—31.) "For I know this, that after my departing, shall grievous wolves enter in among you, not sparing the flock. Also of your own selves shall men arise, speaking preverse things to draw away disciples after them. Therefore, watch, and remember, that, by the space of three years I ceased not to warn every one night and day with tears."

This evil then is to be prevented; 1. By a diligent watchfulness in ministers; 2. By a diligent preaching the word of the Lord; and 3. By sound and close rebukes, reproofs, and exhortations to those in whomsoever there appears any the least swerving or turning aside from the gospel. The ministers of the gospel have each of them all that authority that belongs to their calling and office, and need not to stay for power from men, to put the laws of Christ in his church into due and full execution. This remnant of Jacob should be in the midst of many people as a dew from the Lord, that tarrieth not for man, nor waiteth for the sons of men. Therefore, he adds, "Watch, thou, in all things; endure afflictions, (if thou shouldst be opposed in thy work;) do the work of an evangelist; make full proof of thy ministry." How our time-serving and self-saving ministers will salve their conscience from the stroke that God's word will one day give them, and how they will stand before the judgment seat to render an account of these their doings, let them see to it; surely God will require it of their hand.

But, O Timothy, says the Apostle, do thou be diligent; do thou watch in all things; do thou endure affliction; do thou the work of an evangelist; make thou full proof of thy ministry; "For I am now ready to be offered, &c." The words then of my text are a reason of this exhortation, to Timothy, that he should continue watchful, and abide faithful in his calling. "For I am now ready to be offered;" that is, to be put to death for the gospel.

Hence, then, learn two things.

First, That the murders and outrage that our brethren suffer at the hands of wicked men should not discourage those that live, from a full and faithful performance of their duty to God and man, whatever may be the consequence thereof. Or thus; when we see our brethren before us fall to the earth by death, for their holy and Christian profession, through the violence of the enemies of God, we should covet to make good their ground against them, though our turn should be next. We should valiantly do in this matter, as is the custom of soldiers in war: take great care that the ground be maintained, and the front kept full and complete. "Thou, therefore," saith Paul, "endure hardness as a good soldier of Jesus Christ." And in another place, "we should not be moved by these afflictions," but endure by resisting "even unto blood." Wherefore Paul saith again, "Be not thou, therefore, ashamed of the testimony of our Lord, nor of me, his prisoner: but be thou partaker of the afflictions of the gospel, according to the power of God." Thus let the spirit of Moses rest upon Joshua, and the spirit of Elijah rest upon Elisha. Stand up, therefore, like valiant worthies, as the ministers of my God, and fly not every man to his own, while the cause, and ways, and brethren of our Lord are buffeted and condemned by the world. And remember that those that keep the charge of the Lord when most go a-whoring from under their God, when he turns the captivity of his people, shall be counted worthy to come nigh unto him, "to offer the fat and the blood, saith the Lord God." But for the rest, though they may yet stand before the people, because they stood before them in a way of idolatry, yet it shall not be to their honor, nor to their comfort but to their shame, as the same Scripture saith.

Let this, therefore, smite with conviction those that in this day of Jacob's trouble have been false with God, his cause and people; I say those first and especially as the chief ringleaders of this cowardliness, who have done it against light, profession, and resolution. Behold, thou hast sinned against the Lord, and be sure thy sins will find thee out; and though thou mayst now have as a judgment of God upon thee, thy right eye darkened that thou mayst not see, yet a wakening time will overtake thee, and that too between the straits, when he will show thee, to the great confusion of thy face, and the amazement of them that behold thee, how great an affront he counts it to be left by thee, in a day when his truth is cast down to the ground. I have often thought of that prophet that went down from Judah to Bethel, to prophesy against the idolatry that was there set up by the king; who because he kept not the commandment of God, but did eat and drink in that place, at the persuasion of a lying prophet, was met at last by a lion, who slew him there in the way, where his carcase was made a spectacle of God to passengers. If thou be spiritual, judge what I say; and think not to be one of that number that shall have the harps of God, when God appears for Zion, and that shall sing that song of Moses, and also the song of the Lamb; for that is only for those who have fought the godly fight, and gotten the victory over the beast, his image, mark, number, and name.

Let this also be an awe to thee, who hast hankerings to do as the other. Beware, and remember Judas, and the end God brought upon him; he will not always bear such things; these times have showed us already, that he beholds them with great dislike; why shouldst thou hang up in chains as a terror to all that know thee? And never object, that some have done it and yet are at peace in their souls; for peace in a sinful course, is one of the greatest of curses. "The man that wandereth out of the way of understanding shall remain in the congregation of the dead." Prov. xxi. 16.

The second thing to be learned from these words as they have relation to those going before, is encouragement to them that are yet in the storm; and that from three great arguments. 1. Paul's peace and comfort now at the time of his death, which he signifieth to Timothy by these three expressions: "I have fought a good fight, I have finished my course; I have kept the faith." 2. By the blessed reward he should have for his labor, from Christ in another world, together with all those that love the appearing of the Lord, at that great and notable day. 3. That now his last act should not be inferior to any act he did for God, while he was alive and preached in the world; for his body should now be an offering, a sacrifice well pleasing to God. To all which I shall speak something in my discourse upon these words; and therefore, to come to them:

"I am now ready to be offered."

In these words we have to inquire into two things. 1. What it is to be offered. 2. What it is to be ready to be offered.

I. For the first of these. "I am now ready to be offered."

Paul, by saying he was to be *offered*, alludeth to some of the sacrifices that of old were under the law; and thereby signifieth to Timothy, that his death and martyrdom for the gospel should be both sweet in the nostrils of God, and of great profit to his church in this world; for so were the sacrifices of old. Paul, therefore, lifts his eyes up higher than simply to look upon death, as it is the common fate of men. And he had good reason to do it, for his death was violent; it was also for Christ, for his church and truth; and it is usual with Paul thus to set out the suffering of the saints, which they undergo for the name and testimony of Jesus. Yea, he will have our prayers, a sacrifice; our praises thanksgiving, and mortification, sacrifices; alms-deeds, and the offering up of the converted Gentiles' sacrifices, being sanctified by the Holy Ghost; and here also his death must be for a sacrifice and an acceptable offering to God.

Peter also saith, we are priests "to offer up spiritual sacrifices, acceptable to God by Jesus Christ;" of which sacrifices, it seems by Paul, the death of a Christian for Jesus' sake, must needs be counted one.

Besides, Paul further insinuates this by some other sentences in his epistles: as by that in the epistle to the Colossians, where he saith, "I now rejoice in my sufferings for you, and fill up that which is behind of the afflictions of Christ in my flesh, for his body's sake, which is the church." Col. i. 24. Not by way of merit, for so Christ alone, and that by once being offered himself, hath perfected forever them that are sanctified: but his meaning is, that as Christ was offered in sacrifice for his church as a Saviour, so Paul would offer himself as a sacrifice for Christ's church, as a saint, as a minister, and one that was counted faithful. "Yea," saith he, "and if I be offered upon the sacrifice and service of your faith, I joy and rejoice with you all." This then teacheth us several things worthy our consideration.

1. That the blood of the saints that they lose for his name, is a sweet savor to God. And so saith the Holy Ghost, "Precious in the sight of the Lord is the death of his saints." Psalm cxvi. 15. And again, "He shall redeem their soul from deceit and violence, and precious shall their blood be in his sight." Psalm lxxii. 14.

Those that suffer for Christ now, are of great benefit to his church, (as the sacrifices of old were confirming and strengthening to Israel;) wherefore Paul saith his bonds encouraged his brethren, and made them much more bold in the way of God to speak his word without fear. Phil. i. 14.

The suffering, or offering of the saints in sacrifice, is of great use and advantage to the gospel; of use I say many ways: 1. The blood of the saints defends it; 2. Confirmeth it; and, 3. Recovereth that portion thereof that hath been lost in Antichristian darkness.

They do thereby *defend* the gospel from those that

would take it from us, or from those that would impose another upon us. "I am set," saith Paul, "for the defence of the gospel, and my sufferings have fallen out for the furtherance of it," (Phil. i. 17;) that is, it hath not only continued to hold its ground, but hath also got more by my contentions, sufferings, and hazards for it.

It *confirms* it; and this is part of the meaning of Paul in those large relations of his sufferings for Christ. "Are they ministers of Christ? (I speak as a fool,) I am more: in prisons more frequent," &c.; as he saith again, "And these things I do for the gospel's sake." And again, "That the truth of the gospel might be continued with you." So again, "I suffer," (saith he) in the gospel "as an evil doer, even unto bonds; but the word of God is not bound." Yea, saith he, "therefore I endure all things for the elects' sakes;" (2 Tim. ii. 9, 10;) that is, that the gospel may be preserved entire, that the souls that are yet unborn may have the benefit of it, with eternal glory.

The sufferings of the saints are of a *victorious* virtue; for by their patient enduring and losing their blood for the word, they recover the truths of God that have been buried in Antichristian rubbish, from that soil and slur that thereby hath for a long time cleaved unto them. Wherefore it is said, "They overcame (the beast) by the blood of the Lamb, and the word of their testimony; and they loved not their lives unto the death." Rev. xii. 11. They overcame him; that is, they recovered the truth from under his aspersions, and delivered it from all its enemies.

The lamps of Gideon were then discovered, when his soldiers' pitchers were broken: if our pitchers were broke for the Lord and his gospel's sake, those lamps will then be discovered that before lay hid and unseen. Much use might be made of this good doctrine. Learn thus much:

1. The judgment that is made of our sufferings by carnal men is nothing at all to be heeded; they see not the glory

that is wrapped up in our cause, nor the innocence and goodness of our conscience in our enduring of these afflictions: they judge according to the flesh, according to outward appearance. For so, indeed, we seem to lie under contempt, and to be in a disgraceful condition; but all things here are converted to another use and end. That which is contemptible when persons are guilty, is honorable when persons are clear; and that which brings shame when persons are buffeted for their faults, is thankworthy in those that endure grief, suffering wrongfully. Though to suffer for sin be the token of God's displeasure, yet to those that suffer for righteousness, it is a token of the greatest favor. Wherefore, matter not how the world doth esteem of thee and thy present distress, that thou bearest with patience for God and his word; but believe that those things that are both shame and dishonor to others, are glory and honor to thee. O for a man to be able to say, "For the hope of Israel I am bound with this chain:" it makes his face to shine like the face of an angel, and his lips to drop like the honeycomb. Acts xxviii. 20.

2. We learn also from hence, the reason why some in days before us have made light of the rage of the world. They have laughed at destruction when it cometh, and have gone forth to meet the armed men; and with Job's horse, mocked at fears, and have not been affrighted, neither turned their back from the sword. "The quiver rattleth against him, the glittering spear and the shield;" (Job xxxix. 22, 23;) but they have said among the trumpets, "Ha, ha!" It hath been their glory to suffer for Christ; as it is said of the saints of old, "they departed from the presence of the council, rejoicing that they were counted worthy to suffer shame for his name." Acts v. 41. As Paul also saith, "I will most gladly," (mark,) "most gladly, therefore, will I rather glory in my infirmities, that the power of Christ may rest upon me. Therefore, I take pleasure in infirmities,

in reproaches, in necessities, in persecutions, in distresses, for Christ's sake." Let those that suffer for theft and murder hang down their heads like a bulrush, and carry it like those that are going to hanging; but let those whose trials are for the word of God, know, by these very things they are dignified.

3. Learn also in this to be confident, that thy sufferings have their sound, and a voice before God and men. First, before God, to provoke him to vengeance, when he makes inquisition for blood. Psalm ix. 12; Gen. iv. 9—11. The blood of Abel cried until it brought down wrath upon Cain; and so did the blood of Christ and his apostles, till it had laid Jerusalem upon heaps. Secondly, thy blood will also have a voice before men, and that possibly for their good. The faithful Christian, in his patient suffering, knows not what work he may do for God. Who knows but thy blood may be so remembered by thy children, neighbors, and enemies, as to convince them thou wert for the truth? Yea, who knows, but their thoughts of thy resolution for Christ, in thy resisting unto blood, may have so good an effect upon some, as to persuade them to close with his ways? The three children in the fiery furnace made Nebuchadnezzar cry out, there was no God like theirs. Indeed this is hard labor, but be content; the dearer thou payest for it to win the souls of others, the greater will be thy crown, when the Lord the righteous Judge shall appear; and in the mean while, thy death shall be as a sacrifice pleasing to God and his saints. "I am now ready to be offered."

II. The second thing that I would inquire into is this: What it is to be *ready* to be offered? Or how we should understand this word "ready:" "I am now ready to be offered." Which I think may be understood three manners of ways. 1. With respect to that readiness that was continually in the heart of those that hated him, to destroy him with his doctrine. 2. Or it may be understood with respect to the readiness of this blessed Apostle's mind, his being ready and willing always to embrace the cross for the word's sake: or, 3. We may very well understand it that he had done his work for God in this world, and therefore was ready to be gone.

For the first of these. The enemies of God and his truth never want will and malice to oppose the word of God; they are also always so far forth in readiness to murder and slaughter the saints, as the prophet cries to Jerusalem, "Behold the princes of Israel, every one were in thee to their power to shed blood," (Ezek. xxii. 6;) that is, they had will and malice always at hand to oppose the upright in heart. And, therefore, our Lord Jesus saith, "these are they that kill the body;" he doth not say they can do it, as relating to their power merely, but that they do it, as relating to their will and their custom, if let loose: and we may understand thereby, that it is no more to them to kill the people of God, than it is to butchers to kill sheep and oxen. For though it be indeed a truth that 'God's hand is always safe upon the hilt of their sword,' yet by them, "we are killed all the day long; we are counted as sheep for the slaughter," (Psalm xliv. 22; Rom. viii. 36;) that is, in their desires always, as well as by their deeds, when they are let loose. As Paul's kinsman said to the captain, "There lie in wait for him of them more than forty men which have bound themselves with an oath, that they will neither eat nor drink until they have killed him: and now are they ready, looking for a promise from thee." Acts xxiii. 21. And hence it is that by the word they are called dragons, lions, bears, wolves, leopards, dogs, and the like: all which are beasts of prey, and delight to live by the death of others. Paul therefore seeing and knowing that this readiness was in his enemies to pour out his bowels to the earth, cried out to Timothy, saying, "Make thou full proof of thy ministry—for I am now ready to be slain; I am now ready to be offered up."

These words thus understood, may be useful many ways.

1. To show us we live, not because of any good nature or inclination that is in our enemies towards us; for they, as to their wills, are ready to destroy us; but they are in the hand of God, in whose hand are also our times. Wherefore, though by the will of our enemies we are always delivered to death, yet behold we live! 2 Cor. vi. 9. Therefore, in this sense it may be said, "Where is the fury of the oppressor?" It is not in his power to dispose of us, therefore, here it may be said again, he is not ready to destroy. Isa. li. 13. The cup that God's people in all ages have drank of, even the cup of affliction and persecution, is not in the hand of the enemy, but the hand of God; and he, not they, poureth out of the same. So that they, with all their raging waves, have banks and bounds set to them, by which they are limited with their range, as the bear is by his chain. "Surely the wrath of man shall praise thee; and the remainder of wrath thou shalt retrain." Psalm lxxvi. 10.

2. This should encourage us, not to forsake the way of our Lord Jesus, when threatened by our adversaries; because they are in his chain. Indeed, they are ready in their wills to destroy us; but as to power and liberty to do it, that is not all with them. Who would fear to go, even by the very nose of a lion, if his chain would not suffer him to hurt us. It is too much below the spirit of a Christian to fear a man that shall die; and they that have so done have forgotten the Lord their maker, who preserveth the hairs of our head. Luke xii. 7. Yea, let me tell you he that so doth, feareth to trust the Lord with his life, estate, and concernments, and chooseth rather to trust to himself, and that too out of God's way; and though such persons may lick themselves whole now, while they are fallen senseless, they must count for these things again, and then they shall see, that fear of men and to be ashamed of Christ, will load them with no light burden. Also it is an uncomely thing for any man in his

profession, to be in and out with the times: and to do this when winked at by men, that they would not do if they frowned. Do such fear God? Nay, they fear the fear of men, when they should sanctify the Lord himself, and let him be their dread, and let him be their fear.

3. Let the readiness that is in the enemies of God to destroy, provoke thee to make ready also. As I said a little before; go out to meet the armed men. David ran to meet Goliah. Rub up man; put on thy harness; "put on the whole armor of God," that thou mayst be ready, as well as thy adversaries, as blessed Paul was here. "I am now ready to be offered and the time of my departure is at hand." But because this will fall in fittest under the second head, I shall, therefore, discourse of it there.

The second thing considered in the words is this, that to be "ready," might be understood with respect to the blessed Apostle's mind, that was graciously brought over into a willingness to embrace the cross for the word's sake. And thus in other places he himself expounds it. "I am ready," saith he, "not to be bound only, but also to die at Jerusalem for the name of the Lord Jesus." Acts xxi. 13. That also implies as much, where he saith, "I count not my life dear unto myself, so that I might finish my course with joy, and the ministry which I have received of the Lord Jesus, to testify the gospel of the grace of God." Acts xx. 24. As the enemies then were ready and willing in their hearts, so he was ready and willing in his. This man was like to those mighty men of Solomon, that were ready prepared for the war, and waited on the king, fit to be sent at any time upon the most sharp and pinching service. A thing fitly becoming all the saints, but chiefly those that minister in the word and doctrine.

Understand the words thus, and they also teach us many things both for conviction and for edification.

1. Here we see that a Christian's heart should be un-

clenched from this world. For he that is ready to be made a sacrifice for Christ and his blessed word, must be one that is not entangled with the affairs of this life: how else can he please him who has chosen him to be a soldier? Thus was it with this blessed man. He was brought to God's foot with Abraham, and crucified to this world with Christ; he had passed a sentence of death upon all earthly pleasures and profits beforehand, that they might not deaden his spirit when he came to suffer for his profession.

2. This shows us the true effects of unfeigned faith and love; for they were the rise of this most blessed frame of heart. Read 2 Cor. iv. 8,—12. and compare it with chapter xii. at the 9th and 10th verses. Men may talk what they will of their faith and love to the Lord Jesus, and to his holy gospel; but if they throw up their open professing of his name for fear of those that hate him, it is evident their mouths go before their hearts, and their words are bigger than their graces. "If thou faint in the day of adversity, thy strength is small," (Prov. xxiv. 10,) and so thy faith and love. Herein is love, "that a man lay down his life for his friends." John xv. 13.

3. This shows us the true effects of a right sight and sense of the sufferings that attend the gospel; that they shall become truly profitable to those that shall bear them aright. What made he "ready" for? It was for sufferings; and why made he ready for them, but because he saw they wrought out for him "a far more exceeding and eternal weight of glory," 2 Cor. iv. 17. This made Moses also spurn at a crown and a kingdom; to look with a disdainful eye upon all the glory of Egypt. He saw the reward that was laid up in heaven for those that suffered for Christ. Therefore, "he refused to be called the son of Pharaoh's daughter; choosing rather to suffer affliction with the people of God, than to enjoy the pleasures of sin for a season; esteeming the reproach of Christ, greater riches than the

treasures in Egypt: for he had respect unto the recompense of the reward. By faith he forsook Egypt, not fearing the wrath of the king; for he endured, as seeing him who is invisible." Heb. xi. 24—27. Every one cannot thus look upon the afflictions and temptations that attend the gospel; no not every one that professeth it, as appears by their shrinking and shirking at the noise of the trumpet, and alarum to war. They can be content (as cowards in a garrison) to lie still under some smaller pieces of service, as hearing the word, entering in, to follow with loving in word and in tongue, and the like; but to "go forth unto him without the camp, hearing his reproach," (Heb. xiii. 13,) and to be "in jeopardy every hour," for the truth of the glorious gospel, that they dare not do. Nay, instead of making *ready* with Paul to engage the dragon and his angels, they study how to evade and shun the cross of Christ; secretly rejoicing if they can but delude their conscience, and make it still and quiet, while they yet do unworthily.

4. By this readiness we may discern who are unfeignedly willing to find out, (that they may do,) the whole will of God; even those that are already made willing to suffer for his sake. They are still inquiring, "Lord what wilt thou have me to do?" (Acts xx. 23, 24,) not mattering nor regarding the cross and distress that attend it. "The Holy Ghost witnesseth to me," saith Paul "that in every city, bonds and afflictions abide me; but none of these things move me, neither count I my life dear unto myself, so that I might finish my course with joy;" counting that to see and be doing heavenly things, will countervail all the trouble and sorrow that attends them. This, therefore, sharply rebuketh those that can be glad to be ignorant of the knowledge of some truths, especially of them that are persecuted; still answering those that charge them with walking irregularly, that they do but according to their light: whereas the hearts that be full of love to the name and glory of Christ,

will in quiet return and come; yea, and be glad, if they find the words of God, and will eat them with savor and sweet delight; how bitter soever they are to the belly, because of that testimony they bind us up to maintain before peoples, and nations, and kings.

"I am now ready to be offered." The third and main thing to be considered in these words is this, that the Apostle, by saying, "I am *now* ready," doth signifiy that now he had done that work that God had appointed him to do in the world. 'I am now ready, because I have done my work.' This is further manifest by the following words of the text; "I am now ready to be offered, and the *time of my departure* is at hand;" namely, my time to depart this world. The words also that follow, are much to the same purpose, "I have fought the good fight, I have *finished* my course," &c. much like those of our Lord Jesus, "I have finished the work which thou gavest me to do." John xvii. 4.

Now then put all these things together, namely, 'that I am to be offered a sacrifice; and for this my enemies are ready, my heart is also ready; and I have done my work. I am, therefore, every way ready.'

CHAPTER II.

THE DUTY AND WISDOM OF ENTIRE DEVOTEDNESS.

THIS is a frame and condition that deserveth, not only to stand in the word of God for Paul's everlasting praise, but to be a provoking argument to all that read or hear thereof, to follow the same steps. I shall, therefore, to help it forward according to grace received, draw one conclusion from the words, and speak a few words to it. The conclusion is this:

THAT IT IS THE DUTY AND WISDOM OF THOSE THAT FEAR GOD, SO TO MANAGE THE TIME AND WORK THAT HE HATH ALLOTTED UNTO THEM, THAT THEY MAY NOT HAVE PART OF THE WORK TO DO WHEN THEY SHOULD BE DEPARTING THE WORLD.

This truth I might further urge from the very words of the text, they being written on purpose by Paul to stir up Timothy, and all the godly, to press hard after this very thing. But to pass that, I shall mind you of some other Scriptures that press it hard as a duty, and then proceed to some few examples of the wise and most eminent saints. Which when I have done I shall,

I. Show you REASONS for it.

II. Give you DIRECTIONS to it.

III. Press it with several MOTIVES, and so conclude.

That this is the duty and wisdom of those that fear God, you may see by Christ's exhortation to watchfulness, and to prepare for his second coming. "Therefore, be ye also ready: for in an hour when ye think not, the Son of Man cometh." Matt. xxiv. 44. These words, as they are spoken to stir up the godly to be ready to meet their Lord at his coming, so because the godly must meet him in his judgment and providences here, as at his personal appearing at the last day; therefore, they should be diligent to be fitting themselves to meet him in all such dispensations. "And because," saith God, "I will do this unto thee, prepare to meet thy God, O Israel." Amos iv. 12. Now, death is one of the most certain of these dispensations; yea, and such, that it leaveth to those no help at all, or means to perform forever, that which, shouldst thou want it, is lacking to thy work. Wherefore, Solomon also doth press us to this very work, and that from this consideration, "Whatsoever thy hand findeth to do, do it with thy might; for there is no work, nor device, nor knowledge, nor wisdom, in the grave, whither thou goest." Eccl. ix. 10. Baulk nothing of thy duty, neither defer to do it: for thou art in thy way to thy grave, and there thou canst not finish aught that by neglect thou leavest undone; therefore, be diligent while life lasts.

Another Scripture is, that in Peter's epistle to those that were scattered abroad. "Seeing," saith he, "that you look for such things, be diligent, that you may be found of him in peace," &c. 2 Pet. iii. 14. He is there discoursing of the coming of Christ to judgment, as Christ also was in the other; and from the certainty and dread of that day he doth press them on to a continual diligence. And this is to be understood as that of Paul to Timothy, of a diligent watching in all things; that, as he saith again, they may stand complete in all the will of God; not lacking this or that of the work which was given them to do of God in this world. Much might be said for the further proof of this duty; but to give you some examples of the godly men of old, whereby it will appear, that as it is our duty to do it, so it is also our wisdom: and hence,

It is said of Enoch, that "he walked with God," Gen. v. 22; and of Noah, that he "was faithful in his generation," and also that he "walketh with God." Gen. vi 9. That is, they kept touch with him, still keeping up to the work and duty that every day required; not doing their duty by fits and starts, but in a fervent spirit they served the Lord. So again it is said of Abraham, that his work was to walk before God in a way of faith and self-denial, which he with diligence performed. And, therefore, the Holy Ghost saith he "died in a good old age;" thereby insinuating, that he made both ends meet together, the end of his work with the end of his days; and so came to his grave, in a full age, as a shock of corn coming in his season. Jacob also, when he blessed his sons, as he lay upon his death bed before them, doth sweetly comfort himself with this, after all his toil and travel, saying, "I have waited for thy salvation, O Lord." As if he had said, 'Lord I have faithfully walked before thee in the days of my pilgrimage, through the help and power of thy grace; and now having nothing to do but to die, I lie waiting for thy coming to gather me up to thyself and my fathers.' "So when he had made an end of commanding his sons," (now his bottom was wound,) "he gathered up his feet in the bed, and yielded up the ghost, and was gathered unto his people." Gen. xlix. 18, 33. Caleb and Joshua also are said to be men of excellent spirit, because they were faithful in this their work.

David was eminent this way, and had done his work before his death day came. "*After* he had served his own generation by the will of God," then "he fell on sleep." Acts xiii. 36. In the Old Testament his preparation is signified by three passages: 1. By his losing his heat before his death, thereby showing his work for God was done: he now only waited to die. 2. By that passage, "these are the last words of David," even the winding up of all the doctrines of that sweet Psalmist of Israel. 3. That in the Psalms is very significant, "The prayers of David, the son of Jesse, are ended." Psalm lxxii. 20. In the whole, they all do doubtless speak forth this in the main, that David made great conscience of walking with God, by laboring to drive his work before him, that his work and life might meet together: for that indeed is a good man's wisdom. Job had great conscience also as to this very thing, as witness both God's testimony and his own conscience for him. Elijah had brought his work to that issue, that he had but to anoint Hazael to be king of Syria, Jehu to be king of Israel, and Elisha prophet in his room, and then to be caught up into heaven. What shall I say? I might come to Hezekiah, Jehoshaphat, Josiah; with old Simeon also, whose days were lengthened chiefly, not because he was behind with God and his conscience as to his work for God in the world, but to see with his eyes now at last the Lord's Christ: a sweet fore fitting for death! Zacharias, with Elizabeth his wife, (that good old couple also,) how tender and faithful were they in this matter, to walk in all the commandments and ordinances of the Lord, in a blessed, blameless way! Their son also is not to be left out, who rather than he would be put out of his way, and hindered from fulfilling his course, would venture the loss of the love of a king, and the loss of his head for a word. All these, with many more, are as so many mighty arguments for the praise of that I asserted before, namely, that it is the duty and wisdom of those that fear God, so to manage the time and work that he here allotteth unto them, that they may not have part of their work to do when they should be departing this world.

I might urge also many REASONS to enforce this truth upon you, as,

1. Otherwise the great and chief design of God in sending us into the world, especially in converting us and possessing our souls with gifts and graces, and many other benefits, that we might here be to the glory of his grace, is as much as in us lies, frustrate and disappointed. "This people have I formed for myself (saith he;) they shall show forth my praise:" and so again, "Ye have not chosen me, but I have

chosen you, and ordained you that ye should go and bring forth fruit, and that your fruit should remain." John xv. 16. God never intended, when he covered thy nakedness with the righteousness of his dear Son, and delivered thee from the condemning power of sin and the law, that thou shouldst still live as do those who know not God. "This I say, therefore," saith Paul, "and testify in the Lord; that ye henceforth walk not as other Gentiles walk, in the vanity of their mind." Eph. iv. 17.

What! a Christian, and live as does the world? a Christian, and spend thy time, thy strength, and parts, for things that perish in the using? Remember, man, if the grace of God hath taken hold of thy soul, thou art a man of another world, and indeed a subject of another more noble kingdom, the kingdom of God, which is the kingdom of the gospel, of grace, of faith, and righteousness, and the kingdom of heaven hereafter. In these things thou shouldst exercise thyself; not making heavenly things, which God hath bestowed upon thee, to stoop to things that are of the world; but rather here beat down thy body, to mortify thy members; hoist up thy mind to the things that are above, and practically hold forth before all the world that blessed word of life. This, I say, is God's design; this is the tendency, the natural tendency of every grace of God bestowed upon thee; and herein is our Father glorified, that we bring forth much fruit.

2. A second reason why Christians should so manage their time, and the work that God hath appointed them to do for his name in this world, that they may not have part thereof to do when they should be departing this world, is, because if they do not, dying will be a hard work with them, especially if God awakeneth them about their neglect of their duty. The way of God with his people is to visit their sins in this life; and the worst time for thee to be visited for them, is when thy life is smitten down, as it were to the dust of death, even when all natural infirmities break in

like a flood upon thee, sickness, fainting, pains, wearisomeness, and the like. Now I say, to be charged also with the neglect of duty, when in no capacity to do it; yea, perhaps, so feeble, as scarce able to abide to hear thy dearest friend in this life speak to thee; will not this make dying hard? Yea, when thou shalt seem both in thine own eyes, as also in the eyes of others, to fall short of the kingdom of heaven for this and the other transgression; will not this make dying hard? David found it hard, when he cried, "O spare me, that I may recover strength, before I go hence, and be no more." Psalm xxxix. 13. David at this time was chastened for some iniquity; yea, brought for his folly to the doors of the shadow of death. But here he could not enter without great distress of mind; wherefore, he cries out for respite and time to do the will of God, and the work allotted to him. So again, "The pains of hell gat hold upon me—the sorrows of death compassed me about—and I found trouble and sorrow: then called I upon the name of the Lord." Aye, this will make thee cry, though thou be as good as David. Wherefore learn by his sorrow, as he himself also learned at last, to serve his own generation by the will of God, before he fell asleep.

God can tell how to pardon thy sins, and yet make them such a bitter thing, and so heavy a burden to thee, that thou wouldst not, if thou wast but once distressed with it, come there again for all this world. Ah! it is easy with him to have this pardon in his bosom, when yet he is breaking all thy bones, and pouring out thy gall upon the ground; yea, to show himself then unto thee in so dreadful a majesty, that heaven and earth shall seem to thee to tremble at his presence. Let then the thoughts of this prevail with thee, as a reason of great weight to provoke thee to study to manage thy time and work in wisdom while thou art well.

Another reason why those that fear God should so manage their time and work for God in this world, that they may not have part to do when they should be departing this life, is, because loitering in thy work doth as much as in it lieth, defer and hold back the second coming of our Lord and Saviour Jesus Christ. One thing amongst many, that delayeth the appearing of Christ in the clouds of heaven, is, that his body, with the several members thereof, is not yet complete and full; they are not all yet come to the knowledge of the Son of God, to the measure of the stature of the fulness of Christ; that is, to the complete making up of his body. For as Peter saith, "The Lord is not slack concerning his promise, as some men count slackness; but is long suffering to us-ward, not willing that any should perish, but that all should come to repentance," 2 Peter iii. 9; and so also to the complete performance of all their duty and work they have for God in this world. And I say, the faster the work of conversion, repentance, faith, self-denial, and the rest of the Christian duties are performed by the saints in their day, the more they make way for the coming of the Lord from heaven. Wherefore Peter saith again, "Seeing then that we look for such things, what manner of persons ought we to be in all holy conversation and godliness, looking for, and hastening unto," (or, as it is in the margin, "hastening") "the coming of the day of God, wherein the heavens, being on fire, shall be dissolved, and the elements shall melt with fervent heat?" 2 Peter iii. 11, 12. When "the bride hath made herself ready," the marriage of the Lamb is come, Rev. xix. 7; that is, the Lord will then wait upon the world no longer, when his saints are fit to receive him. As he said to Lot when he came to burn down Sodom, "Haste thee to Zoar, for I can do nothing till thou be come thither," (Gen. xix. 22;) so concerning the great day of judgment to the world, which shall be also the day of blessedness and rest to the people of God, it cannot come until the Lamb's wife hath made herself ready; until all the saints that belong to glory are ready.

And before I go further, what might I yet say to fasten this reason upon the truly gracious soul? What! wilt thou yet loiter in the work of thy day? wilt thou still be unwilling to hasten righteousness? dost thou not know that thou by so doing deferrest the coming of thy dearest Lord? Besides, that is the day of his glory, the day when he shall come in the glory of his Father and of the holy angels; and wilt not thou by thy diligence help it forwards? Must also the general assembly and church of the first-born wait upon thee, for their full portions of glory? Wilt thou by thus doing endeavor to keep them wrapt up still in the dust of the earth, there to dwell with the worm and corruption? The Lord awaken thee, that thou mayst see thy loitering doth do this, and doth also hinder thine own soul of the inheritance prepared for thee.

4. Another reason why saints should press hard after a complete performing their work that God hath allotted unto them, is, because, so far forth as they fall short, in that they impair their own glory. For as the Lord hath commanded his people to work for him in this world, so also he of grace hath promised to reward whatever they christianly do. "For whatsoever good thing any man doth, the same shall he receive of the Lord, whether he be bond or free:" yea, he counts it unrighteousness to forget their work of faith and labor of love, but a righteous thing to recompense them for it in the day of our Lord Jesus. This well considered, is of great force to prevail with those that are covetous of glory, such as Moses and Paul, with the rest of that spirit. As the Apostle saith also to the saints at Corinth, "Be ye steadfast, unmoveable, always abounding in the work of the Lord, forasmuch as ye know that your labor is not in vain in the Lord." 1 Cor. xv. 58.

CHAPTER III.

DIRECTIONS TO HELP CHRISTIAN DEVOTEDNESS.

HAVING thus given you the reasons, why God's people should be diligent in that work which God hath allotted for them to be doing for him in this world, I shall in the next place give you some directions, as helps to further you in this work. And they are such as tend to take away those hindrances that come upon thee either by discouragement, or by reason of hardness and benumbedness of spirit; for great hindrances overtake God's people from both these impediments.

1. First, then, If thou wouldst be faithful to do that work that God hath allotted thee to do in this world for his name; *labor to live in the savor and sense of thy freedom and liberty by Jesus Christ.* That is, keep this if possible, ever before thee, that thou art a redeemed one, taken out of this world, and from under the curse of the law, out of the power of the devil; and placed in a kingdom of grace, and forgiveness of sins for Christ's sake. This is of absolute use in this matter; yea, so absolute, that it is impossible for any Christian to do his work christianly without some enjoyment of it. For this in the 1st of Luke is made the very ground of all good works, both as to their nature and our continuance in them; and is also reckoned there an essential part of that covenant that God made with our fathers; even "that he would grant unto us, that we, being delivered out of the hand of our enemies, might serve him without fear, in holiness and righteousness before him, all the days of our life." Luke i. 74, 75. And indeed, take this away, and what ground can there be laid for any man to persevere

in good works? None at all. For take away grace and remission of sins for Christ's sake, and you leave men nothing to help them but the terrors of the law, and judgment of God, which at best can beget but a servile and slavish spirit in that man in whom it dwells; which spirit is so far off from being a help to us in our pursuit of good works, that it makes us so we cannot endure that which is commanded. Israel-like, it flieth from God even as from the face of a serpent. As Solomon saith, "A servant will not be corrected by words; for though he understand, he will not answer." Prov. xxix. 19.

Get then thy soul possessed with the spirit of the Son of God, and believe thou art set perfectly free by him from whatsoever thou by sin hast deserved at the hand of revenging justice. This doctrine unlooseth thy bands, takes off thy yoke, and lets thee go upright. This doctrine puts spiritual and heavenly inclinations into thy soul; and the faith of this truth doth show thee, that God hath so surprised thee, and gone beyond thee, with his blessed and everlasting love, that thou canst not but reckon thyself his debtor forever. "Therefore, brethren, we are debtors, not to the flesh, to live after the flesh." Rom. viii. 12. That argument of Paul to Philemon is here true in the highest degree; Thou owest to God for his grace to thee, even thy whole self besides. Philemon 19. This Paul further testifies, both in the 6th and 7th of the Romans. In the one he saith we are free from sin; (Rom. vi. 22;) in the other he saith we are dead to the law that our fruit might be unto holiness; that we might bring forth fruit unto God. Rom. vii. 4. For, as I said, if either thy ungodly lusts, or the power and force of the law, have dominion over thy spirit, thou art not in a condition now to be performing thy work to God in this world. I have heretofore marvelled at the quarrelsome spirit that possessed the people that Malachi speaketh of, how they in a manner found fault with all things that were commanded them to do; but I have since observed their ungodly disposition was grounded upon this, their doubting the love of God. "Yet ye say, Wherein hast thou loved us?" Mal. i. 2. And indeed if people once say to God by way of doubt, "Wherein hast thou loved us?" no marvel though that people be like those in Malachi's time, a discontented, murmuring, backward people, about every thing that is good. Read that whole book of Malachi.

2. If thou wouldst be faithful to do that work that God hath allotted thee to do in this world for his name; then *labor to see a beauty and glory in holiness, and in every good work.* This tends much to the engaging of thy heart. "O worship the Lord in the beauty of holiness: fear before him, all the earth." And for thy help in this, think much on this in general, that, "Thus saith the Lord," is the wind up of every command; for, indeed, much of the glory and beauty of duties doth lie in the glory and excellency of the person that doth command them. And hence it is, that, "Be it enacted by the King's most excellent Majesty," is in the head of every law because that law, should therefore be reverenced by, and be made glorious and beautiful to all. And we see upon this very account, what power and place the precepts of kings do take in the hearts of their subjects, every one loving and reverencing the statute, because there is the name of their king. "Will you rebel against the king?" is a word that shakes the world. Well, then, turn these things about for an argument to the matter in hand; and let the name of God, seeing he is wiser and better, and of more glory and beauty than kings, beget in thy heart a beauty in all things that are commanded thee of God.

And indeed, if thou do not in this act thus, thou wilt stumble at some of thy duties and work thou hast to do; for some of the commands of God are in themselves so mean and low, that take away the name of God from them, and thou wilt do as Naaman the Syrian, despise, instead of obeying. What is there in the Lord's supper, in baptism, yea, in preaching the word, and prayer, were they not the appointments of God? His name being entailed to them, makes them every one glorious and beautiful. Wherefore, no marvel if he that looks upon them without their title-page, goeth away in a rage, like Naaman, preferring others before them. "What is Jordan? Are not Abana and Pharpar, rivers of Damascus, better than all the waters in Israel? May I not wash in them and be clean?" saith he. 2 Kings v. 10, 11, 12. This was because he remembered not that the name of God was in the command. Israel's trumpets of ram's horns, and Isaiah's walking naked, and Ezekiel's wars against a tile, would doubtless have been ignoble acts, but that the name of God was that which gave them reverence, power, glory, and beauty. Set, therefore, the name of God, and "Thus saith the Lord," against all reasonings, defamings, and reproaches, that either by the world, or thy own heart, thou findest to arise against thy duty; and let his name and authority alone be a sufficient argument with thee, to behold the beauty that he hath put upon all his ways, and to inquire in his temple.

3. Wouldst thou be faithful to do that work that God hath appointed thee to do in this world for his name; then *make much of a trembling heart and tender conscience.* For though the word be the line and rule whereby we must order and govern all our actions, yet a trembling heart and tender couscience are of absolute necessity for our so doing. A hard heart can do nothing with the word of Jesus Christ. "Hear the word of the Lord, ye that tremble at his word." Isa. lxvi. 5. "Serve the Lord with fear, and rejoice with trembling," Psalm ii. 11.

I spake before against a servile and slavish frame of spirit, therefore, you must not understand me here, as if I meant now to cherish such a one; no, it is a heart that trembleth for, or at, *the grace of God;* and a conscience made tender by the sprinkling of *the blood of Christ;* such a conscience as is awakened both by wrath and grace, by the terror and the mercy of God; for it stands with the spirit of a son to fear before his father; yea, to fear chastisings though not to fear damnation. Let, therefore, destruction from God be a terror to thy heart, though not that destruction that attends them that perish by sin forever. Though this I might add further; it may do thee no harm, but good, to cast an eye over thy shoulder, at those that now lie roaring under the vengeance of eternal fire; it may put thee in mind of what thou wast once, and of what thou must yet assuredly be, if grace by Christ preventeth not. Keep then thy conscience awake with wrath and grace, with heaven and hell; but let grace and heaven bear sway.

Paul made much of a tender conscience, else he had never done as he did, nor suffered what we read of. "But herein," saith he, "do I exercise myself, to have always a conscience void of offence toward God, and towards men. Acts xxiv. 16. But this could not a stony, benumbed, bribed, deluded, or a muzzled conscience do. Paul was like the nightingale with his breast against the thorn. That his heart might still keep waking, he would accustom himself to the meditation of those things that should beget both love and fear; and would always be very chary, lest he offended his conscience. "Herein do I exercise myself," &c.

Be diligent, then, in this matter, if thou wouldst be faithful with God. A tender conscience, to some people is like Solomon's brawling woman, a burden to those that have it: but let it be to thee like those that invited David to go up to the house of the Lord. Hear it, and cherish it with pleasure and delight.

4. If thou wouldst be faithful to do that work that God hath appointed thee to do in this world for his name; then *let religion be the only business to take up thy thoughts and time.* "Whatsoever thy hand findeth to do, do it with thy

might," (Eccles. ix. 10,) with all thy heart, with all thy mind, and with all thy strength. Religion, to most men, is but a by-business, with which they use to fill up spare hours; or as a stalking horse, which is used to catch the game. How few are there in the world, that have their conversation only as becomes the gospel! Phil. i. 27. A heart sound in God's statutes, a heart united to the fear of God, a heart moulded and fashioned by the word of God, is a rare thing! rare, because it is hard to be found, and rare because it is indeed the fruit of an excellent spirit, and a token of one saved by the Lord. But this indifferency in religion, this fashioning ourselves in our language, gesture, behavior, and carriage, to the fancies and fopperies of this world, as it is in itself much unbecoming a people that should bear the name of their God in their foreheads; so it cannot but be a very great and sore obstruction to thy faithful walking with God in this world.

Gird up then thy loins like a man. Let God and his Christ, and his word, and his people, and cause, be the chief in thy soul; and, as heretofore, thou hast afforded this world the most of thy time, and travail, and study, so now convert all these to the use of religion. "As ye have yielded your members servants to uncleanness, and to iniquity unto iniquity, even so now yield your members servants to righteousness unto holiness." Rom. vi. 19.

Holy things must be in every heart where this advice is faithfully put in practice: (1.) *Daily bring thy heart and the word of God together, that thy heart may be levelled by it, and also filled with it.* Ps. cxix. 133. The want of performing this sincerely, is a great cause of that unfaithfulness that is in us to God. Bring then thy heart to the word daily, to try how thou believest the word to-day, to try how it agrees with the word to-day. This is the way to make clean work daily, to keep thy soul warm and living daily. "Wherewithal shall a young man cleanse his way?"

saith David, "By taking heed thereto, according to thy word." Psalm cxix. 9. So again, "Concerning the works of men, by the word of thy lips I have kept me from the paths of the destroyer." Psalm xvii. 4. And again, "Thy word have I hid in my heart, that I might not sin against thee." Psalm cxix. 11. He that delighteth in the law of the Lord, and in his law doth meditate day and night, "he shall be like a tree planted by the rivers of water, that bringeth forth his fruit in his season: his leaf also shall not wither; and whatsoever he doeth shall prosper." Psalm i. 2, 3. (2.) *Keep up a continual remembrance that to every day thou hast thy work allotted thee; and that sufficient for that day are the evils that attend thee.* Matth. vi. 34. This remembrance set Paul upon his watch daily; made him die to himself and this world daily, and provoked himself also daily to wind up the spirit of his mind; transforming himself by the power of the word, from that proneness that was in his flesh to carnal things. This will make thee keep the knife at thy throat in all places, and business, and company. (3.) *Let thy heart be more affected with what concerns the honor of God, and the profit and glory of the gospel, than with what are thy concernments as a man, with all earthly advantages.* Matt. vi. 33. This will make thee refuse things that are lawful, if they appear to be inexpedient. Yea, this will make thee, like the Apostle of old, prefer another man's peace and edification before thine own profit, and to take more pleasure in the increase of the power of godliness in any, than in the increase of thy corn and wine. (4.) *Reckon with thine own heart every day, before thou lie down to sleep; and cast up both what thou hast received from God, done for him, and where thou hast also been wanting.* This will beget praise and humility, and put thee upon redeeming the day that is past; whereby thou wilt be able through the continual supplies of grace, in some good measure, to drive thy work before thee, and to shorten it as thy life doth shorten; and in this way thou mayst comfortably live in the hope of bringing both ends sweetly together.

5. If thou wouldst be faithful to do that work that God hath appointed thee to do in this world for his name; then *beware thou do not stop and stick when hard work comes before thee.* It is with Christians as it is with other scholars, they sometimes meet with hard lessons; but these thou must also learn, or thou canst not do thy work. The word and Spirit of God come sometimes like chain shot to us, as if they would cut down all; as when Abraham was to offer up Isaac, and the Levites to slay their brethren. Paul also must go from place to place to preach, though he knew beforehand he was to be afflicted there. God may sometimes say to thee, as he said to his servant Moses, "Take the serpent by the tail;" or as the Lord Jesus said to Peter, "Walk upon the sea." These are hard things, but have not been rejected when God hath called his people to do them.

O how willingly would our flesh and blood escape the cross for Christ! The comforts of the gospel, the sweetness of the promise, how pleasing to us! Like Ephraim, here we love to tread out the corn, and to hear those pleasant songs and music that gospel sermons make, where only grace is preached, and nothing of our duty as to works of self-denial; but as for such God will tread upon their fair neck, and yoke them with Christ's yoke; for there they have a work to do, even a work of self-denial.

Now this work sometimes lieth in *acts that seem to be desperate;* as when a man must both leave and hate his life, yea, all he hath for Christ, or else he cannot serve him nor be counted his disciple. Thus it seemed with Christ himself when he went his fatal journey up to Jerusalem; he went thither, as he knew, to die; and therefore trod every step as it were in his own bowels, but yet no doubt, with great temptation to shun and avoid that voyage; and therefore, it is said he set his face steadfastly to go up, (Luke ix. 51,) scorning to be invited to the contrary. And to prevent the noise of his weak disciples, "Master save thyself," it is said, he ascended before them, (Mark x. 32—34,) insomuch that they were amazed to see his resolution, while they themselves were afraid of that dreadful effect that might follow. Also when he came there, and was to be apprehended, he went to the garden that Judas knew, his old accustomed place: and so when they asked him the killing question, he answered, "I am he!"

Sometimes our work lies in *acts that seem to be foolish;* as when men deny themselves of those comforts, and pleasures, and friendships, and honors, of the world that formerly they used to have, and choose rather to associate themselves with the very abjects of this world, (I mean such as carnal men count so,) counting their ways and manner of life, though attended with a thousand calamities, more profitable, and pleasing, and delightful, than all former glory. Thus Elisha left his father's house, though to pour water upon the hands of Elijah; and thus the disciples left their father's ships and nets, to live a beggarly life with Jesus Christ; as Paul did leave the feet of Gamaliel for the whip, and the stocks, and the deaths, that attended the blessed gospel. One would have thought that had been a simple way of Peter, to leave all for Christ, before he knew what Christ would give him, (Matt. xix. 27;) but Christ will have it so: he that will save his life must lose it, and he that will lose his life in this world for Christ, shall keep it to life eternal. John xii. 25.

I might add many things of this nature, to show you what hard chapters God sometimes sets his best people: but thy work is, if thou wouldst be faithful, not to stop nor stick at any thing. Some when they come at the cross, will either there make a stop and go no further, or else, if they can, step over it; if not, they will go round about. Do not thou do this; but take it up and kiss it, and bear it after

Jesus. "God forbid, (saith Paul,) that I should glory, save in the cross of our Lord Jesus Christ, by whom the world is crucified unto me, and I unto the world." Gal. vi. 14.

O it is hard work to pocket up the reproaches of all foolish people, as if we had found great spoil; and to suffer all their revilings, lies, and slanders, without cursing them, as Elisha did the children; to answer them with prayers and blessings for their cursings. It is far more easy to give them taunt for taunt, and reviling for reviling; to give them blow for blow; yea, to call for fire from heaven against them. But to bless them that curse us, and to pray for them that despitefully use and presecute us, even of malice, of old grudge, and on purpose to vex and afflict our mind, and to make us break out into a rage, this is work above us. Now our patience should look up to unseen things; now remember Christ's carriage to them that spilt his blood; or all is in danger of bursting, and thou of miscarrying.

I might here also dilate upon Job's case and the lesson God set him; when at one stroke he did beat down all, only sparing his life, but made that also so bitter to him, that his soul chose strangling rather than it. O when every providence of God unto thee is like the messengers of Job, and the last brings more heavy tidings than all that went before him; when life, estate, wife, children, body and soul, and all at once, seem to be struck at by heaven and earth; here are hard lessons. Now, behave myself even as a weaned child; now say, "The Lord giveth, and the Lord hath taken away; and blessed be the name of the Lord." Thus with few words Job ascribed righteousness to his Maker; but though they were but few, they proceeded from so blessed a frame of heart, as caused the penman of the word to stay himself and wonder, saying, "In all this Job sinned not with his lips, nor charged God foolishly." What a great deal will the Holy Ghost make of that which seems but little, when it flows from an upright heart! And it indeed may well be so accounted of all that know what is in man, and what he is prone unto.

Now, for thy better performing this piece of service for our Lord and Saviour Jesus Christ, take these directions.

(1.) Labor to believe that all these things are tokens of the love of God. (2.) Remember often that thou art not the first that hath met with these things in the world. "It hated me, saith Christ, "before it hated you." (3.) Arm thyself with a patient and quiet mind to bear and suffer for his sake. (4.) Look back upon thy provocations wherewith thou mayst have provoked God; then wilt thou accept of the punishment for thy sins, and confess it was less than thine iniquities deserve. (5.) Pray thou mayst "hear the voice of the rod," and have a heart to answer the end of God therein. (6.) Remember the promise; "All things shall work together for good to them that love God, to them who are the called according to his purpose."

6. If thou wouldst be faithful to do that work that God hath appointed thee to do in this world for his name; then *labor always to possess thy heart with a right understanding, both of the things that this world yieldeth, and of the things that shall be hereafter.* I am confident that most, if not all the miscariages of the saints and people of God, have their rise from deceivable thoughts here. The things of this world appear to us more, and those that are to come, less than they are; and hence it is that many are so hot and eager for things that be in the world, and so cold and heartless for those that be in heaven. Satan is here a mighty artist, and can show us all earthly things in a multiplying glass; but when we look up to things above, we see them as through sackcloth of hair. But take thou heed; be not ruled by thy sensual appetite that can only savor fleshly things, neither be thou ruled by carnal reason, which always darkeneth the things of heaven. But go to the word, and as that says, so judge thou. That tells thee all things under the sun are

vanity, nay, worse, vexation of spirit; that tells thee the world is not, even then when it doth most appear to be. "Wilt thou set thine heart upon that which is not? for riches certainly make themselves wings, and fly away as an eagle towards heaven." The same may be said of honors, pleasures, and the like; they are poor, low, base things to be entertained by a Christian's heart. The man that hath most of them may in the fulness of his sufficiency be in straits; yea, when he is about to fill his belly with them, God may cast the fury of his wrath upon him: "so is every one that layeth up treasure for himself and is not rich toward God." A horse that is loaden with gold and pearls all day, may have a foul stable and galled back at night.

And woe be to him that increases that which is not his, that ladeth himself with thick clay! O man of God! throw this bone to the dogs; suck not at it, there is no marrow there. Set thine affection on things that are above, where Christ sitteth on the right hand of God. Col. iii. 1,—4. Behold what God hath prepared for them that love him. And if God hath blessed thee with aught, set not thine heart upon it. Honor the Lord with thy substance; labor to be diligent in good works, ready to distribute, willing to communicate, laying up in store a good foundation for the time to come, that thou mayst lay hold on eternal life. See 1 Tim. vi. 17—19. Further, to lighten thine eyes a little:

First, "concerning *the glory of the world.* (1.) It is that which God doth mostly give to those that are not his; for, the poor receive the gospel. "Not many rich, not many mighty, not many noble are called." (2.) Much of this world and its glory is permitted of God to be disposed of by the devil, and he is called both the prince and god thereof; yea, when Satan told Christ, he could give it to whom he would, Christ did not say 'Thou liest;' but answered, by the word, "It is written, Thou shalt worship the Lord thy God, and him only shalt thou serve." Implying also, that commonly when men get much of the honors and glory of this world, it is by bending the knee too low to the prince and god thereof. (3.) The nature of the best of worldly things, if hankered after, is to deaden the spirit, to estrange the heart from God, to pierce thee through with many sorrows, and to drown thee in destruction and perdition. "O man of God, flee these things; and follow after righteousness, godliness, faith, love, patience, meekness. Fight the good fight of faith, lay hold on eternal life, whereunto thou art also called, and has made a good profession," &c.

Secondly, As to *the things of God,* what shall I say? The great things of his word, and Spirit, and kingdom, so far go beyond the conceivings of the heart of man, that none can utter them but the Holy Spirit. There is no deceit in them. "No lie is of the truth," 1 John ii. 21. What they promise they will perform, with additions of amazing glory. Taste them first, and then thou shalt see them. "O taste and see that the Lord is good: blessed is the man that trusteth in him." Psalm xxxiv. 8.

To stoop low in a good work, (which is an act of thine,) if it be done in faith and love, though but by a cup of cold water; is really more worth in itself, and is of higher esteem with God, than all worldly and perishing glory. There is no comparison; the one perisheth with the using, and for the other is laid up "a far more exceeding and eternal weight of glory." 2 Cor. iv. 17.

7. But again, as thou shouldst labor to possess thy heart with a right understanding of the perishing nature of the riches and pleasures of this world, and of the durable riches and righteousness hid in Christ, and in all heavenly things; so thou shouldst *labor to keep always in the eye what sin is, what hell is, what the wrath of God is, and everlasting burnings are.* Transfer them to thyself, as it were on a finger, that thou mayst learn to think of nothing more highly than is meet, but to give to what thou beholdest their own due

weight; then thou wilt fear where thou should fear, love what is worth thy love, and slight what is of no worth. These are just weights, and even balances; now thou dealest not with deceitful weights; and this is the way to be rich in good works, and to bring thy work, that God hath appointed, to a good issue against thy dying day.

8. But again, if thou wouldst be faithful to do that work that God hath appointed thee to do in this world, for his name; then *beware that thou slip not, or let pass by, the present opportunity that providence layeth before thee.* Work while it is called to-day. "The night cometh when no man can work." John ix. 4. In that parable of the man that took a far journey, it is said, as he gave to every servant his work, (Mark xiii. 34, 35,) so he commanded the porter to watch, that is, for his Lord's coming back; and in the mean time, for all opportunities to perform the work he left in their hands, and committed unto their trust.

Seest thou the poor? seest thou the fatherless? seest thou thy foe in distress? Draw out thy breast, shut not up thy bowels of compassion, deal thy bread to the hungry, bring the poor that are cast out into thine house, hide not thyself from thine own flesh; take the opportunity that presents itself to thee, either by the eye, or the hearing of the ear, or by some godly motion that passeth over thy heart. Say not to such messengers, Go, and come again to-morrow, if thou hast it by thee; now the opportunity is put into thy hand, delay not to do it, and the Lord be with thee.

Good opportunities are God's seasons for the doing of thy work; wherefore, watch for them, and take them as they come. Paul tells us, "he was in watchings often," 2 Cor. xi. 27; surely it was, that he might take the season that God should give him to do this work for him; as he also saith to Timothy, "Watch thou in all things,—do the work," &c. Opportunities as to some things come but once in one's lifetime; as in the case of Esther, and of Nicodemus, and holy Joseph; when Esther begged the lives of the Jews, and the other, the body of Jesus; which once had they let slip or neglected, they could not have recovered it again forever. Watch then for the opportunity: (1.) Because it is God's season; which, without doubt, is the best season and time for every purpose. (2.) Because Satan watches to spoil, by mistiming as well as by corrupting, whatever thou shalt do for God. "When I would do good," saith Paul, "evil is present," (Rom. vii. 21;) that is, either to withdraw me from my purpose, or else to infect my work. (3.) This is the way to be profitable unto others. "Thy wickedness may hurt a man, as thou art, and thy righteousness may profit the son of man." Job xxxv. 8. (4.) This is also the way to be doing good to thyself. "He that watereth shall be watered also himself." Prov. xi. 25. "Cast thy bread upon the waters: for thou shalt find it after many days." Eccles. xi. 1. As God said to Jehoiakim, the son of Josiah, "Did not thy father eat and drink, and do judgment and justice, and then it was well with him? He judged the cause of the poor and needy, then it was well with him." Jer. xxii. 15, 16.

And I say, that the opportunity may not slip thee, either for want of care or provision: (1.) Sit always loose from an overmuch affecting thine own concernments, and believe that thou wast not born for thyself. "A brother is born for adversity." (2.) Get thy heart tenderly affected with the welfare and prosperity of all things that bear the stamp and image of God. (3.) Study thy own place and capacity that God hath put thee in, in this world; for suitable to thy place thy work and opportunities are. (4.) Make provision beforehand, that when things present themselves, thou mayst come up to a good performance; be "prepared to every good work." (5.) Take heed of carnal reasonings; keep thy heart tender, but set thy face as a flint for God. (6.) And, lastly, look well to the *manner* of every duty.

CHAPTER IV.

MOTIVES TO CHRISTIAN DEVOTEDNESS.

FIRST. Wouldst thou be faithful to do that work that God hath appointed thee to do in this world, for his name; believe then, that *whatever good thing thou doest for him, if done according to the word, is not only accepted by him now, but recorded, to be remembered for thee against the time to come;* yea, laid up for thee as treasures in chests and coffers, to be brought out to be rewarded before both men and angels, to thy eternal comfort, by Jesus Christ our Lord. "Lay not up, (saith Christ,) treasures upon earth, where moth and rust doth corrupt, and where thieves break through and steal; but lay up for yourselves treasures in heaven, where neither moth nor rust doth corrupt, and where thieves do not break through nor steal." Matt. vi. 19, 20.

The treasure that here our Lord commands we should with diligence lay up in heaven, is found both in Luke, and Paul, and Peter, to be meant by doing good works.

Luke renders it thus: "SELL THAT YOU HAVE, AND GIVE ALMS; provide yourselves bags that wax not old, a treasure in the heavens that faileth not, where no thief approacheth, neither moth corrupteth," (Luke xii. 33;) the latter part of the verse expounding the former.

Paul saith thus: "Charge them that are rich in this world, that they be not high-minded, nor trust in uncertain riches, but in the living God, who giveth us richly all things to enjoy; that they do good, that they be RICH IN GOOD WORKS, ready to distribute, willing to communicate: laying up in store for themselves a good foundation against the time to come, that they may lay hold on eternal life;" 1 Tim. vi. 17, 18, 19.

Peter also acknowledgeth and asserteth this, where, in his exhortation, to elders to do their duty faithfully, and with cheerfulness, he affirms, if they do so, they "shall receive a CROWN OF GLORY that fadeth not away;" 1. Pet. v. 2—4. This Paul also calleth a reward for cheerful work, (1 Cor. ix. 17;) and *that* as an act of justice, by the hand of a righteous judge, in the day when the Lord shall come to give reward to his servants the prophets, and to his saints, and to all that fear his name, small and great. For "every man shall receive his own reward, according to his own labor." 1 Cor. iii. 8.

But before I go any further, I must answer three objections that may be made by those that read this.

Objection 1. The first is this. Some godly heart may say, 'I dare not own that what I do shall ever be regarded, much less rewarded, by God in another world, because of the unworthiness of my person, and because of the many infirmities and sinful weaknesses that attend me in every duty.'

Answer. This objection is built partly upon a bashful modesty, partly upon ignorance, and partly upon unbelief. My answer to it is as followeth.

You must look back to what but now hath been proved, namely, that both Christ and his apostles do all agree in this, that "there is a reward for the righteous," and that their good deeds are laid up as treasures for them in heaven, and are certainly to be bestowed upon them in the last day with abundance of eternal glory.

Now, then, to speak to thy case, and to remove the bottom of thy objection, that the unworthiness of thy person, and thy sinful infirmities, that attend thee in every duty, do make thee think thy works shall not be either regarded or rewarded in another world; consider, first, as to the unworthiness of thy person. They that are in Christ Jesus are always complete before God, in the righteousness that Christ hath obtained, how infirm, and weak, and wicked soever they appear to themselves. Before God, therefore, in this righteousness thou standest all the day long, and that upon a double account; first, by the act of faith, because thou hast believed in him that thou mightst be justified by the righteousness of Christ; but if this fail, (I mean the act of believing,) still thou standest justified by God's imputing this righteousness to thee, which imputation standeth purely upon the grace and good pleasure of God to thee, that holds thee still as just before God, though thou wantest at present the comfort thereof. Thus, therefore, thy person stands always accepted; and indeed no man's work can at all be regarded, if his person in the first place be not respected. The Lord had respect first to Abel, and after to his offering; but he can have respect to no man before works done, unless he find them in the righteousness of Christ. For they must be accepted through a righteousness; which, because they have none of their own, therefore, they have one of God's imputing, even that of his Son which he wrought for us when he was born of the Virgin, &c.

Secondly, As to thy sinful infirmities that attend thee in every work, they cannot hinder thee from laying up treasure in heaven, thy heart being upright in the way with God. Nor will he be unrighteous at all to forget thy good deeds in the day when Christ shall come from heaven. 1. Because by the same reason then he must disown all the good works of all his prophets and apostles; for they have all been attended with weaknessess and sinful infirmities. From the beginning hitherto there is not a man, "not a just man upon earth, that doeth good, and sinneth not," Eccles. vii. 20; the best of our works are accompanied with sin. "When I would do good," saith Paul, "evil is present with me." Rom. vii. 21. This, therefore, must not hinder. And for thy further satisfaction in this, consider, that as

Christ presents thy person before God, acceptable without thy works, freely and alone by his righteousness, so his office is to take away the iniquity of thy holy things that they also by him may be accepted of God. Wherefore it is further said, for the encouragement of the weak and feeble, that he shall not break a bruised reed, nor quench the smoking flax, but shall bring forth judgment unto victory." Isa. xiii. 3. The bruised reed you know is weak; and by bruises we should understand sinful infirmities. And so also concerning the smoking flax; by smoking you must understand sinful weakness. But none of these shall either hinder the justification of thy person, or the acceptation of thy performance, they being done in faith and love, let thy temptations be ever so many, because of Jesus Christ's priestly office now, at the right hand of God. By him, therefore, let us offer spiritual sacrifices; for they shall be acceptable to God and our Father. 2. Because otherwise God and Christ would prove false to their own word—which is horrible blasphemy once to imagine—who have promised, that when the Son of God shall come to judgment, he "shall render to every man according to his works;" (Matt. v. 12; Luke vi. 23, 35; Matt. vi. 1; x. 41, 42;) and upon this very account encourage his servants to a patient enduring of the hottest persecutions: "For great is your reward in heaven." From this also he bindeth his saints and servants to be sincerely liberal, and good and kind to all: first, because otherwise they have no reward of their Father which is in heaven, that is, for what they do not; but if they do it then, though it be but a cup of cold water given to a prophet or righteous man, they shall receive a prophet's reward, a righteous man's reward; yea, they shall receive it in any wise; "they shall in no wise lose their reward." 3. It must be so, otherwise he would deny a reward to the work and operations of his own good,that grace he hath freely bestowed upon us. But that he will not do. He is not unfaithful to forget your work of faith and labor of love, Heb. vi. 10. And so of all other graces, our work "shall not be in vain in the Lord." 1 Cor. xv. 58. And as I said before, temptations, weaknesses, and sins, shall not hinder the truly gracious, of this their reward, Nay, they shall further it; "you are in heaviness if need be, through manifold temptations; that the trial of your faith being much more precious than of gold that perisheth, might be found unto praise, and honor, and glory, at the appearing of Jesus Christ." 1 Pet. i. 6, 7. And the reason is, because the truth and sincerity of God's grace in us doth so much the more discover itself, by how much it is opposed and resisted by weakness and sin. It is recorded to the everlasting renown of three of David's mighties, that they did break through an host of giant-like enemies, to fetch water for their longing king; for it bespoke their valor, their love, and good will to him. The same also is true concerning thy graces and every act of them when assaulted with an host of weaknesses.

Objection 2. And now I come to the second objection, and that ariseth from our being completely justified, freely, by the grace of God through Christ; and by the same means alone brought to glory; and may be framed thus: 'But seeing we are freely justified, and brought to glory by free grace, through the redemption that is in Jesus Christ; and seeing the glory that we shall be possessed of upon the account of the Lord Jesus, is both full and complete, both for happiness and continuing therein, what need will there be that our work should be rewarded? Nay, may not the doctrine of reward for good works be here not only needless, but, indeed, an impairing and lessening the completeness of that glory, to which we are brought (and in which we shall live inconceivably happy forever,) by free grace?'

Answer. That we are justified in the sight of the Divine Majesty, from the whole lump of our sins, both past, present, and to come, by free grace, though that one offering of the body of Jesus Christ, once for all, I bless God I believe it; and that we shall be brought to glory by the same grace, through the same most blessed Jesus, I thank God by his grace I believe that also. Again, that the glory to which we shall be brought by free grace, through the only merits of Jesus, is unspeakably glorious and complete, I question no more than I question the blessed truths but now confessed. But yet, notwithstanding all this, "there is a reward for the righteous," a reward for their works of faith and love, whether in a doing or a suffering way; and that not principally to be enjoyed here, but hereafter; for "great is your reward in heaven," as I proved in the answer to the first objection. And now I shall answer further: 1. If this reward had been an impairing or derogation to the free grace of God that saveth us, he would never have mentioned it for our encouragement unto good works, nor have added a promise of reward for them that do them, nor have counted himself unfaithful if he should not do it. 2. The same may be said concerning Jesus Christ, who doubtless loveth and tendereth the honor of his own merits, as much as any who are saved by him can do, whether they be in heaven or earth; yet he hath promised a reward to a cup of cold water, or giving of any other alms; and hath further told us, they that do these things, do lay up treasure in heaven, namely, a reward when their Lord doth come, then to be received by them to their eternal comfort. 3. Paul was as great a maintainer of the doctrine of God's free grace, and of justification from sin, by the righteousness of Christ imputed by grace, as any man that ever lived in Christ's service, from the world's beginning till now; and yet he was for this doctrine. He expected himself, and encouraged others also to look for such a reward, for doing and suffering for Christ, which he calls, "a far more exceeding and eternal weight of glory." 2 Cor. iv. 17. Surely, as Christ saith, in a case not far distant from this in hand, "if it were not so, he would have told us." John xiv. 1—3.

Now, could I tell what those rewards are that Christ hath prepared, and will one day bestow upon those that do for him in faith and love in this world, I should therein also say more than now I dare say in general, they are such as should make us leap to think on, and that we should remember with exceeding joy, and never think that it is contrary to the Christian faith, to rejoice and be glad for that which yet we understand not. "Beloved, now we are the sons of God; and it doth not yet appear what we shall be," &c. But "every one that hath this hope in Him,"—namely, that he shall be more than here he can imagine,—"purifieth himself even as he is pure." 1 John iii. 2, 3. Things promised, when not revealed to be known by us while here, are therefore, not made known, because too big and wonderful. When Paul was up in paradise, he heard unspeakable words, not possible for man to utter. Wherefore, a reward I find, and that laid up in heaven; but what it is I know not; neither is it possible for any here to know it any further, than by certain general words of God, such as these, "praise," "honor," "glory," "a crown of righteousness," "a crown of glory," "thrones," "judging of angels," "a kingdom," with "a far more exceeding and eternal weight of glory," &c.

Wherefore, to both these objections, let me yet answer thus in a few words: Though thy modesty or thy opinion will not suffer thee to look for a reward for what thou dost here for thy Lord, by the faith and love of the gospel; yea, though in the day of judgment thou shouldst there slight all thou didst on earth, for thy Lord, saying, "When, Lord, when did we do it?" he will answer, "Then, even then when ye did it to the least of these my brethren, ye did it unto me."

Objection 3. But is not the reward that God hath promised to his saints for their good works, to be enjoyed only here?

Answer. Not here only, though here abundantly. For, concerning holy walking, according to God's commands, it yieldeth even here abundance of blessed fruits, as he saith, "In keeping them there is a great reward." And again, "This man shall be blessed in his deed," that is, now, even in this time, as he saith in another place. For, indeed, there is so much goodness and blessedness to be found in a holy and godly life, that were a man to have nothing hereafter, the present comfort and glory that lieth (as the juice in the grape,) in all things rightly done for God, it were sufficient to answer all our travail and self-denial in our work of faith and labor of love, to do the will of God.

Secondly, *Dost thou love thy friends, dost thou love thine enemies, dost thou love thy family or relations, or the church of God;* then cry for strength from heaven, and for wisdom, and a heart from heaven to walk wisely before them. For if a man be remiss, negligent, and careless in his conversation, not much mattering, whom he offends, displeases, or discourages, by doing this or that, so he may save himself, please his foolish heart, and get this world, or the like, this man hath lost a good report of them that are without, and is fallen into reproach and the snare of the devil. He is fallen into reproach, and is slighted, disdained, both he, his profession, and all he says, either by way of reproof, rebuke, or exhortation. "Physician, cure thyself," say all to such a one. 'This man is a sayer, but not a doer,' say they; 'he believeth not what he says;' yea, religion itself is made tc stink by this man's ungodly life. This is he that hardens his children, that stumbleth the world, that grieveth the tender and godly Christian. But I say, he that walketh uprightly, that tenders the name of God, the credit of the gospel, and the welfare of others, seeking with Paul, not his own profit, but the profit of others, that they may be saved; this man holds forth the word of life, this man is a good savor of Christ among them that are saved: yea, may prove by so doing, the instrument in God's hand of the salvation of many souls.

Thirdly, *This is the way to be clear from the blood of all men,* the way not to be charged with the ruin and everlasting misery of poor immortal souls. Great is the danger that attends an ungodly life, or an ungodly action, by them that profess the gospel. When wicked men learn to be wicked of professors, when professors cause the enemies of God to blaspheme; doubtless, sad and woful effects must needs be the fruit of so doing. How many in Israel were destroyed for that which Aaron, Gideon, and Manasseh unworthily did in their day? A godly man, if he take not heed to himself, may do that in his life that may send many to everlasting burnings, when he himself is in everlasting bliss. But on the contrary, let men walk with God, and there they shall be excused; the blood of them that perish shall lie at their own door, and thou shalt be clear. "I am pure from the blood of all men," saith Paul, Acts xx. 26; and again, "Your blood be upon your own heads; I am clean;" Acts. xviii. 6. Yea, he that doth thus, shall leave in them that perish an accusing conscience, even begotten by his good conversation, and by that they shall be forced to justify God, his people, and way, in the day of their visitation; in the day when they are descending into the pit to be damned.

Fourthly, *This is the way to maintain always the answer, the echoing answer of a good conscience in thine own soul* Godliness is of great use this way; for the man that hath a good conscience to God-ward, hath a continual feast in his own soul. While others say there is casting down, he shall say there is lifting up: for God shall save the humble person. Some, indeed, in the midst of their profession, are reproached, smitten, and condemned of their own heart, their conscience still biting and stinging them, because of the uncleanness of their hands; and they cannot lift up their face unto God, they have not the answer of a good conscience toward him, but must walk as persons false to their God, and as traitors to their own eternal welfare; but the godly, upright man shall have the light shine upon his ways, and he shall take his steps in butter and honey. "The work of righteousness shall be peace, and the effect of righteousness, quietness and assurance forever." "If our heart condemn us, God is greater than our heart, and knoweth all things. Beloved, if our hearts condemn us not, then we have confidence towards God."

Fifthly, The godly man that walketh with God, that chiefly careth to do the work that God hath allotted him to do for his name in this world, hath not only these advantages, but *further, he hath as it were a privilege of power with God.* He can sway much with him; as it is said of Jacob, "as a prince he had power with God" to prevail in times of difficulty. Gen. xxxii. 28. And so again, it is said of Judah, being faithful with the saints, they ruled with God. How many times did that good man, Moses, turn away the wrath of God from the many thousands of Israel; yea, as it were, he held the hands of God, and staved off the judgments not once nor twice. "The effectual fervent prayer of a righteous man availeth much." One man that walketh much with God, may work wonders in this very thing; he may be a means of saving whole countries and kingdoms from those judgments their sins deserve. How many times, when Israel provoked the Lord to anger, did he yet defer to destroy them? and the reason of that forbearance, he tells them; it was for David's sake; "For my servant David's sake I will not do it." As the Lord said also concerning Paul, "Lo, God hath given thee all them that sail with thee," (Acts xxvii. 23, 24,) that is to save their lives from the rage of the sea. Yea, when a judgment is not only threatened, but the decree gone forth for its execution, then godly upright men may sometimes cause the very decree itself to cease without bringing forth; or else may so time the judgment that is decreed, that the church shall best be able to bear it.

Sixthly, The man that is tender of God's glory in this world, still ruling and governing his affairs by the word, and desirous to be faithful to the work and employment that God hath appointed him to do for his name; *that man shall still be let into the secrets of God;* he shall know that which God will reserve and hide from many. "Shall I hide from Abraham the thing that I do?" said the Lord: "For I know him that he will command his children and his household after him, and they shall keep the way of the Lord," &c., Gen. xviii. 17, 19. So again, "The secret of the Lord is with them that fear him; and he will show them his covenant." Psalm xxv. 14. "And to him that ordereth his conversation aright will I show the salvation of God." Psalm l. 23. Such a man shall have things new as well as old. His converse with the Father, and the Son, and the Spirit, shall be turned into a kind of familiarity; he shall be led into the word, and shall still increase in knowledge. When others shall be stinted and look with old faces, being black and dry as a stick, he shall be like a fatted calf, like the tree that is planted by the rivers of water; his flesh shall be fresh as the flesh of a child, and God will renew the face of his soul.

Seventhly, If any shall *escape public calamities,* usually they are such as are very tender of the name of God, and that make it their business to walk before him. They either escape by being mercifully taken away before it, or by being safely preserved in the midst of the judgment, until the indignation be overpast. Therefore, God says in one place, "The righteous is taken away from the evil to come," (Isa. lvii. 1;) but if not so, as all be not, then they shall have their life for a prey. Caleb and Joshua escaped all the plagues that befel Israel in the wilderness, for they followed God fully. Somewhat of this you have also in that

Scripture, "Seek the Lord, all ye meek of the earth, which have wrought his judgment; seek righteousness, seek meekness: it may be ye shall be hid in the day of the Lord's anger." Zeph. ii. 3. According to this is that in Luke, "Watch ye, therefore, and pray always, that ye may be accounted worthy to escape all these things that shall come to pass, and to stand before the Son of Man." Luke xxi. 36. "When a man's ways please the Lord, he will make his enemies to be at peace with him." Marvellous is the work of God, in the preservation of his saints (that are faithful with him) when dangers and calamities come; as Joseph, David, Jeremiah, and Paul, with many others, make appear. "He shall deliver thee in six troubles; yea, in seven there shall no evil touch thee." "In famine he shall redeem thee from death: and in war from the power of the sword. Thou shalt be hid from the scourge of the tongue; neither shalt thou be afraid of destruction when it cometh."

Eighthly, If afflictions do overtake thee; (for whom the Lord loveth he chasteneth, and scourgeth every son whom he receiveth;) yet *those afflictions shall not befall thee for those causes for which they befall the slothful and backsliding Christian; neither shall they have that pinching and galling operation* upon thee, as on those who have left their first love and tenderness for God's glory in the world.

1. Upon the faithful upright man (though he also may be corrected and chatised for sin, yet I say, he abiding close with God) afflictions come rather for trial and for the exercise of grace received, than as rebukes for this or that wickedness; when upon the backsliding, heartless Christian these things shall come from fatherly anger and displeasure, and that for their sins against him. Job did acknowledge himself a sinner, and that God, therefore, might chatise him; but yet he rather believed it was chiefly for the trial of his grace, as indeed, and in truth, it was. 'He is a perfect man," saith God to Satan, "and one that feareth God, and escheweth

evil, and still he holdeth fast his integrity, although thou movedst me against him, to destroy him without cause." Job ii. 3. God will not say thus of every one when affliction is laid upon them, though they yet may be his children; but rather declareth and pronounceth, that it is for their transgressions, because they have wickedly departed from him.

2. Now, affliction arising from these two causes, their effects in the manner of their working (though grace turns them both for good) is very different one from the other. He who hath been helped to walk with God is not assaulted with those turnings and returnings of guilt when he is afflicted, as he who hath basely departed from God: the one can plead his integrity, when the other blusheth for shame. See both these cases in one person, even that godly, beloved David. When the Lord did rebuke him for sin, then he cries, "O blood-guiltiness! O cast me not away from thy presence;" Psalm li. 11. But when he at another time knew himself guiltless, (though then also sorely afflicted,) behold with what boldness he turns his face unto God: "O Lord my God," saith he, "if I have done this; if there be iniquity in my hands; if I have rewarded evil unto him that was at peace with me; (yea, I delivered him that without cause was mine enemy;) let the enemy persecute my soul, and take it; yea, let him tread down my life upon the earth, and lay mine honor in the dust. Selah." &c. Psalm vii. 1—5.

This, therefore, must needs be a blessed help in distress, for a man to have a good conscience when affliction hath taken hold on him; for a man then in his looking behind and before, to return with peace to his own soul, that man must needs find honey in this lion, that can plead his innocency and uprightness. "All the people curse me," (saith Jeremiah,) "but that without a cause; for I have neither lent nor taken on usury," (Jer. xv. 10,) which by the law of Moses it seems was a sin at that day.

Ninthly, When men are faithful with God in this world, to do the work he hath appointed for them, by this means *a dying bed is made easier*, and that upon a double account. 1. By reason of that present peace such shall have, even in their time of languishing. 2. By reason of the good company such shall have at their departure.

1. Such souls usually abound in present peace. They look not back upon the years they have spent, with that shame that the idle and slothful Christian does. "Remember now, Lord, how I have walked before thee in truth and with a perfect heart."

"Blessed is the man that considereth the poor: the Lord will deliver him in the time of trouble. The Lord will preserve him and keep him alive, and he shall be blessed upon the earth; and thou wilt not deliver him unto the will of his enemies. The Lord will strengthen him upon the bed of languishing: thou wilt make all his bed in his sickness." Psalm xli. 1—3. Ah! when God makes the bed, he must needs lie easy that weakness hath cast thereon: a blessed pillow hath that man for his head, though to all beholders it is hard as a stone. Jacob on his death bed, had two things that made it easy. (1.) The faith of his going to rest, "I am to be gathered unto my people," Gen. xlix. 29; that is, to the blessed that have yielded up the ghost before me. (2.) The remembrance of the sealings of the countenance of God upon him, when he walked before him in the days of his pilgrimage. When Joseph came to see him before he left this world, "Israel," (saith the word,) "strengthened himself upon his bed;" and the first word that dropped out of this good man's mouth, O how full of glory was it! "God Almighty appeared unto me," saith he, "at Luz, in the land of Canaan, and blessed me," &c. Gen. xlviii. 1—3. O blessed discourse for a sick bed, when those can talk thus that lie thereon, from as true a ground as Jacob. But thus will God make the bed of those who walk close with him in this world.

2. The dying bed of such a man is made easy by reason also of the good company such shall have at their departure; and that is, 1. The angels; 2. The good works they have done for God in the world.

(1.) The angels of heaven shall wait upon them, as they did upon the blessed Lazarus, to carry them into Abraham's bosom. I know all that go to paradise are by these holy ones conducted thither; but yet, for all that, such as die under the clouds for unchristian walking with God, may meet with darkness in that day, may go heavily hence, notwithstanding that; yea, their bed may be as uncomfortable to them as if they lay upon nothing but the cords, and their departure from it (as to appearance) more uncomfortable by far. But as for those who have been faithful to their God, they shall see before them, shall know their tabernacle shall be in peace; the everlasting gates shall be opened unto them; in all which from earth they shall see the glory.

I once was told a story of what happened at a good man's death, the which I have often remembered, with wonderment and gladness. After he had lain for some time sick, his hour came that he must depart. And behold, while he lay, drawing on, (as we call it) to the amazement of the mourners, there was heard about his bed such blessed and ravishing music as they never had heard before; which also continued till his soul departed, and then began to cease, and grow (as to its sound) as if it was departing the house, and so still seemed to go further and further off, till at last they could hear it no longer. "Eye, hath not seen, nor ear heard, neither hath it entered into the heart of man, the things that God hath prepared for them that love him." Behold, then, how God can make thy sickness easy!

(2.) A dying bed is made easy by those good works that men have done in their life for the name of God. "Blessed are the dead which die in the Lord: yea, saith the Spirit, that they may rest from their labors; and their works follow them;" yea, and go before them, too. No man need be afraid to be accompanied by good deeds to heaven. Be afraid of sins; they are like bloodhounds at the heels; "and be sure thy sins will find thee out," even thee who hast not been pardoned in the precious blood of Christ. But as for those who have submitted themselves to the righteousness of God for their justification, and who have through faith and love to his name, been frequent in deeds of righteousness, they shall not appear empty before their God; "their works," (their good works) "follow them." These shall enter into rest, and walk with Christ in white.

I observe when Israel had passed over Jordan, they were to go to possess between mount Ebal and mount Gerizim, from whence were to be pronounced the blessing and the cursing. The gospel meaning of which I take to be as followeth. I take Jordan to be a type of death; and these two mountains, with the cursing and the blessing to be a type of the judgment that comes on every man, so soon as he goes from hence; "And after death the judgment." So that he that escapes the cursing, he alone goes into blessedness; but he that mount Ebal smiteth, he falls short of heaven. O! none knows the noise that doth sound in sinners' souls from Ebal and Gerizim when they are departed hence! yet it may be they know not what will become of them till they hear these echoings from these two mountains. But here the good man is sure mount Gerizim doth pronounce him blessed. "Blessed are the dead that die in the Lord, for their works will follow them" till they are past all danger. These are the Christian's train that follow him to rest; these are a good man's company that follow him to heaven.

www.ingramcontent.com/pod-product-compliance
Lightning Source LLC
LaVergne TN
LVHW011148110826
845150LV00006B/1184
9781425547899